Freemasonry today

The Independent Voice of Freemasonry

THE
BEST OF
TEN YEARS

1997 - 2007

PUBLISHED BY

FREEMASONRY TODAY LIMITED

ABBOTSGATE HOUSE, HOLLOW ROAD, BURY ST. EDMUNDS, SUFFOLK IP32 7FA

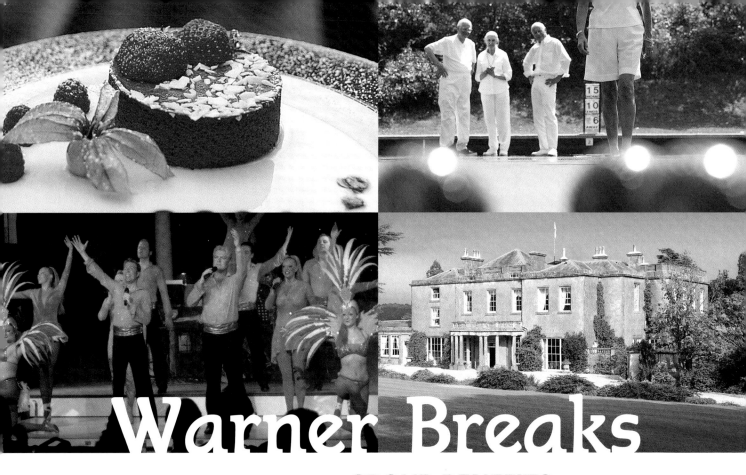

Warner Breaks

2007 Special Offers

Prices from £112* pppb

Historic Hotels
4nt Midweek from **£178*** pppb
3nt Weekend from **£162*** pppb

Character Hotels
4nt Midweek from **£172*** pppb
3nt Weekend from **£137*** pppb

Coastal Resorts
4nt Midweek from **£120*** pppb
3nt Weekend from **£112*** pppb

*All prices are from and per person per break (pppb) and applicable to groups of 10+. Prices based on 2 sharing Ambassador accommodation at Hotels/Standard Chalet accommodation at Resort. Offer prices subject to availability. Offer prices shown include discount.

GROUP BENEFITS

Book now to take advantage of these great group benefits:

- ✔ Save up to 25% discount off brochure prices†
- ✔ Dedicated Group Sales Co-ordinator to help you through the booking and admin process
- ✔ Welcome host to ensure your needs are met on arrival
- ✔ Free Group Organiser rebooking vouchers for groups of 20+
- ✔ FREE room upgrade for Group Organiser*
- ✔ FREE accommodation for coach driver†
- ✔ NEW FREE lunch & drinks vouchers for the Group Organiser
- ✔ Single rooms with no supplement†
- ✔ Complimentary ferry crossings to Isle of Wight†
- ✔ £10 to cover the cost of your telephone calls & postage costs.
- ✔ Venues/meeting rooms available for private hire

† Subject to numbers.

| JUST FOR GROWN UPS | | LIVE ENTERTAINMENT | | SPORTS & LEISURE | | DINNER, BED & BREAKFAST | |

TO BOOK OR FOR MORE INFORMATION QUOTING 28JK7
Call on **01442 236777** Click **www.warnerbreaks.co.uk/groups**
or Email **warnergroupsales@bourne-leisure.co.uk**

The 2007 Group Travel Awards *Runner-Up*

Bourne Holidays Limited trading as Warner Breaks. Registered in England No. 01854900. 1 Park Lane, Hemel Hempstead. Herts HP2 4YL. A company within Bourne Leisure Ltd.

MESSAGE FROM LORD NORTHAMPTON

When *Freemasonry Today* was launched in 1997, the move in the Craft towards more openness had begun. We have seen many changes in the past ten years as we adapt our organisation to the needs of life in the twenty-first century. Much has been written about Freemasonry based on lack of knowledge and on prejudice, and to counter that we decided to become more transparent about what we do and why we do it. Today, ten years on, we can see the fruits of that decision, and are already benefitting from the improved public perception of Freemasonry. Many influences have played their part in this. The United Grand Lodge of England has taken a more pro-active stance towards Freemasonry's relationship with society as a whole. At individual lodge level too, we have found the confidence to play a part in public events, with communities both lay and religious, and in opening dialogue where it has been necessary with local and national bodies of all kinds.

I believe that *Freemasonry Today* has played an important part in that process, not least in demonstrating the rich tapestry which is Freemasonry. When we consider its many facets, the tapestry becomes a fascinating mosaic, in which each part works with the whole in forming a harmony of ideas, aspirations and philosophies. We are a fraternity with a documented history of our Grand Lodge going back to 1717, and the three main principles on which our Order is founded are fraternal affection, charity and integrity. We are a tolerant organisation, accepting all men of good faith regardless of their status, nationality, colour, religion or politics. We ensure harmony in our meetings by banning any discussion on political or religious issues. We have three main ceremonies, of which the first deals with the importance of a moral code, the second with the importance of education and the third with trust and integrity. We have charities which look after our members and their dependants and we support non-masonic charities through our central Charity as well as through the generosity of individual lodges. We

concentrate our central giving on the vulnerable, those with disabilities, healthcare, medical research, hospices, disaster relief and religious buildings.

This book includes the best of the articles published over ten years, comprising the historical, the mystical and spiritual, the social, the symbolical, and the artistic and cultural aspects of English Freemasonry.

In shaping the character and ethos of the magazine, those producing it have drawn on the widest expertise not only in this country but from across the world. Contributors from many countries have lent their talent and knowledge of Freemasonry and related topics in order to make a magazine which is enjoyable

and informative. This in turn has meant that the appeal of the magazine goes far beyond the United Kingdom. In ten short years, we have witnessed the good effects of globalisation. The coming together of Freemasons through an international publication of this kind can only be for the good of Freemasonry worldwide.

Freemasonry Today, as part of an international growing awareness of the good that Freemasonry does, is playing a vital part, not only in the masonic movement, but in all areas where a study of moral, philosophical and spiritual pursuits is of importance. The magazine can be proud to celebrate its tenth birthday in such good heart.

Freemasonry today

Tenth Anniversary Edition   THE INDEPENDENT VOICE OF FREEMASONRY

Editor: Michael Baigent, MA

Deputy & News Editor: Julian Rees

Publisher: David Wilkinson

Board of Directors: Geoffrey Baber
Bill Hanbury-Bateman
Gavin Purser
Simon Waley
David Wilkinson

Administration, Subscriptions & Editorial
Freemasonry Today
Abbotsgate House,
Hollow Road,
Bury St. Edmunds,
Suffolk IP32 7FA
Tel/Fax: 01359 240820
Email: info@freemasonrytoday.com

Advertising: Alan Goodes
Electronic Publishing Consultancy
Holly Mount House
Southend Road
Billericay, Essex CM12 9QH
Tel: 01277 625504
Mobile: 07939 247336
Email: alan.goodes@btinternet.com

Design & Reprographics: Face Creative Services Ltd

Printed by: Woodford Litho

FREEMASONRY TODAY   **ISSN 1369-040x**

www.freemasonrytoday.com

CONTENTS

For your perfect festival weekend . . .

At the Berystede Hotel & Spa we can tailor-make your event to ensure a memorable weekend.

- Experienced in Masonic Weekends

- Idyllic location just outside Ascot, fifteen minutes from Eton town centre, close to Windsor

- Set in gardens and woodland

- 126 beautifully appointed bedrooms including 4 poster and feature rooms

- Vital Health and Beauty Spa

- Private function suites including the 300 capacity Windsor & Eton suite, serving AA Rosette cuisine

- Outdoor roof terraces offering al fresco dining during the summer months

COMPETITIVE LADIES FESTIVAL PACKAGES

Macdonald Berystede Hotel & Spa, Bagshot Road, Sunninghill, Ascot, SL5 9JH

T 0870 400 8111 **F** 01344 872 301 **E** general.berystede@macdonald-hotels.co.uk

www.macdonaldhotels.co.uk/berystede

MACDONALD
BERYSTEDE HOTEL & SPA

THE EDITOR OF FREEMASONRY TODAY MICHAEL BAIGENT

This special edition, containing the best of *Freemasonry Today*, celebrates the ten years of our existence. During that time we have put all our efforts into producing a magazine which not only entertains and informs our readers within Freemasonry and their families but which allows us to be proud of the great tradition to which we Freemasons are all heirs.

Freemasonry Today also celebrates the support of Freemasons active in many different countries of the world despite differences of language, religion, politics and culture. The wide range of subjects covered in these pages are testimony to the diverse interests and skills of those men - and women - who have chosen to become part of the international fraternity which is Freemasonry.

But this is not the limit of our vision: we also wish to introduce non-masons to the heritage of Freemasonry, to its deep wisdom, its richness, and its significant contribution to society over the last three hundred years, a contribution which has all too often been overlooked.

From the very beginning Freemasonry has concentrated on what brings men together, rather than what drives them apart. In 1723 our first printed book of *Constitutions* expressed this ambition formally as

'tis now thought more expedient only to oblige them to that Religion in which all Men agree, leaving their particular Opinions to themselves...whereby Masonry becomes the Center of Union and the Means of conciliating true Friendship among Persons that must have remain'd at a perpetual Distance.

This was, for its time, a very radical statement.

Amidst the accelerating rough and tumble of modern life we tend to forget that human nature has not changed. The world is still at the mercy of those desperate to pursue their cravings for power, control, and status.

Clearly, human nature needs tempering. While it is true that legislation can reduce the sharp edges, it cannot assure human happiness and satisfaction. These qualities, as our religions and other spiritual organisations have always known, can only come through a personal relationship with what we might term 'integrity'. And it is the journey towards a discovery of the source of that integrity which is one of the major concerns of Freemasonry and the focus of its rituals.

Within *Freemasonry Today* we have often confronted a very common question posed both inside Freemasonry and beyond: what relevance does an organisation like Freemasonry with its roots far in the past have to the world of the twenty-first century? This question is answered very easily.

Freemasonry states emphatically that it is founded upon three great principles: the brotherhood of all arising from a mutual respect between individuals; the need to give to those whom society has failed or who have been visited by disaster; and the pursuit of integrity - as expressed in the words of masonic ritual: the encouragement to 'seek eternity in all things.'

Today, as in the past, Freemasons around the world hold in common the desire to become better men, better companions to their fellows, and better citizens of their society. All hold fast to the ideal that a fairer and more just world is possible but that a positive effort is needed to achieve this. We need to remember that our civilisation is precious, and vulnerable. The constant murderous disputes - both political and religious - with which our media confront us show just how threatened its existence is when confronted by relentless greed, intolerance, and ignorance.

In the end, Freemasonry is a civilising tradition, one which praises the innate dignity of all human beings and one in which all differences are seen as potential strengths rather than sources of conflict.

Despite our scientific prowess, our world continues to be rent by political and religious disputes as if the Middle Ages were still with us. Truly, the twenty-first century, as never before, has a need for the harmonising principles of Freemasonry and the quiet contribution of Freemasons as they help nurture and protect our civilisation.

Visit De Vere Venues

For a lesuire weekend break, we can provide the perfect solution at an unparalleled choice of properties, with every detail, however small, taken care of.

• Great for Masonic Lodge weekends and Ladies festivals
• Supreme surroundings, food and beverage plus leading technology
• Fantastic selection of venues set in beautiful grounds
• Full leisure facilities at most, some with championship golf courses
• From city centres to country houses to tree houses
• Imaginative & creative banquets served by experienced and dedicated staff
• Free WiFi and internet access
• Free room upgrade for organiser

To book call **De Vere Central**
0845 136 0123
or visit www.devere.co.uk

Package prices from
£120.00
per person
2 night stay (Fri & Sat or Sat & Sun)

Central London venues offering non residential packages

DE VERE
venues

THE BROTHERHOOD

Brotherhood finds its expression in Freemasonry in many ways. The masonic pursuit is one that binds Freemasons together in a unique fashion, since it brings them closer together as a unit in their own lodge, at the same time reminding them of their global responsibility to the worldwide community, the wider 'Brotherhood of Man'.

The bonds uniting Freemasons start at the level of the individual lodge. Once initiated, by means of the first degree ceremony, the Freemason is referred to by the title 'Brother', and this is intended to give him a sense of belonging, of unity with the other members of the lodge. As an initiate, he seeks moral improvement and self-knowledge, and through this he works with his Brethren for the greater good of humanity as a whole, a group of individuals being stronger than the sum of its several parts.

In the first section, we see brotherhood at work. We learn of the development of fraternal associations in general, and the part which Freemasonry has played in that development in the past. We see Freemasonry at work in the community, on different levels. Freemasons, because of their persistence in working together to relieve distress and to counter intolerance, and because they reject totalitarian regimes, have often come under attack from those who fear the expression of liberty. We read here of the masonic brotherhood being the target of persecution by such regimes.

But since such a brotherhood is universal in its concept, in its daily practice spanning the whole globe, it also interacts with other elements in society. It interacts with different religious groups, becoming a unifying influence in areas where differences of belief or culture might cause divisions. It interacts with

communities, strengthening bonds and working to support and to enrich society.

When the brotherhood works to bring about collective giving to charitable causes of all kinds, the results can be quite amazing. The Freemasons' Grand Charity in England, in the years 1981-2006, gave over £72m. Following the Tsunami, a fund was established to receive donations from individual English Freemasons, and over £850,000 was collected. But we read also about individual Freemasons engaged in raising money, of relief for victims of natural disasters of all kinds in a way that money alone cannot achieve.

A brotherhood which practises its principles and precepts in almost all the countries of the world, acting as a source of spiritual sustenance for its members as well as a healing, binding and stabilising influence in so many communities and so many areas of life, can justly be regarded as being a force for good in the world.

STRIVING FOR CHARITY

MICHAEL BAIGENT SPEAKS TO DENNIS DAYMOND-JOHN, MBE.

Dennis Daymond-John, aged 80, during his most frightening stunt in September, 2001.   *Photo: Peter Daymond-John*

Dennis Daymond-John is now eighty-one years old. He had always suffered from poor eyesight. He managed to join the army in 1939 by memorising the eye-charts but was discharged in 1943 by a canny doctor who produced a chart Dennis had not previously seen. His sight finally failed and since 1980 he has been registered as blind. But since 1982 he has raised the extraordinary total of £150,000 for charities. He has raised it by stunts; extraordinary and often dangerous stunts.

Two years after he had gone blind, in 1982, he felt that there was more he could do with his life. He was very fit and surely, he thought, he could do something to help others who were confined to a wheel-chair or a sick-bed. He formed a committee to begin raising money for the Royal National Institute for the Blind. Every year, beginning in 1983, for the next twelve years, they ran a cycle marathon. By the end of this period they had raised £60,000.

But then the committee was dissolved and Dennis decided to pursue solo events to raise money, each dedicated to one charity – masonic or non-masonic. The events were ambitious, strenuous and increasingly quirky. In 1993, he began with a 15,000 foot parachute jump from Netheravon, Wiltshire, strapped to a Red Devil expert. Through sponsorship, he was raising money for the eye unit at St Woolos Hospital, Newport which was gathering funds for an electron microscope. Dennis knew the unit and its doctors well: he had been admitted there on seven occasions for eye operations.

In 1995 he returned to his great interest, cycling, and in May completed a tandem ride from Land's End to John O'Groats and continued riding down through Scotland to complete a total of

Dennis Daymond-John   photo*Michael Baigent*

1000 miles in ten days. He rode in tandem with cyclist Austin Heath whose wife drove the support car.

During the ride, for four days they encountered snow, sleet and hail, and

winds which became so strong that on occasion they had to pedal downhill. Dennis's spirits faltered three times in the soaking cold rain but he gathered himself together and pedalled on; his efforts raised £5000. Furthermore, en route, he celebrated his 73rd birthday. In total, since 1982, he had raised over £100,000 for charity. But he wanted to do more.

Tandem cycling adventures proved a good means of raising funds: in summer 1997 he went to Russia and rode the 436 miles from St. Petersburg to Moscow negotiating the hazards of poor tracks and roads. At the end of his first day the chain had come off seventeen times and so rough had the roads been that the seat had to be hammered back into position. Such was his enthusiasm during the trip that he "wore out" six front-riders on the bicycle. By now his total fund of money raised was approaching £120,000.

Two years later he embarked on a tandem ride across Cuba. He and his co-cyclist covered 255 miles in five days, again often over very rough roads. He recalled, "The contrast was amazing. We started off against a raging gale with waves crashing over the sea walls. Within twenty-four hours it was ninety-three degrees and I went for a swim in full cycling gear and dried off riding the bike." Then in 2001, aged 80 now, he rode a tandem across Brazil to raise money for Mencap.

Freemasonry

Freemasonry has proved the well-spring of Dennis's life. He is very active – although not to the point where his wife might get worried! He is a member of three Craft Lodges, his Mother Lodge being Tennant Lodge, No. 1992, in Cardiff and he has been Master on two occasions; he has also served as Master of Old Monktonians' Lodge, No. 8938. He has been exalted into the Royal Arch and, beyond the Craft, he is a member of Rose-Croix. When he joined Freemasonry, the process was not as simple as it is today.

He first expressed an interest in joining in 1947. His Father-in-law was in the Craft and arranged his initiation. But it took three years before he was even interviewed. And following the interview it took another two years before he was able to be initiated in the Cardiff Temple. The big night finally arrived in 1952. "Do you remember it?" I asked. "Oh yes. Not half!" he replied as though it were only yesterday. "And my Third Degree. The hall had run out of heating oil. It was freezing!"

"Is Freemasonry still a movement for a young man?" I asked.

"Oh yes!" was the emphatic reply, "It gives comradeship. My best friends are masons. You feel that if you were really in trouble you would have support."

But he did recognise certain problems which he felt needed to be addressed,

"I am in favour of opening the doors of Freemasonry. Let the public see our Temples. And one of the best kept secrets in Freemasonry is the tremendous amount of good we do for non-masonic charities. Yet our fund-raising is unique: I have many friends in the Rotary and the Lions and they raise much for charity but we are the only body which raises money from within ourselves. We need to make this known. We have allowed ourselves to be labelled an inward looking secret body."

"But today", I asked, " with so many demands on one's time, many find it difficult to attend Lodge, or to learn the rituals."

He had little sympathy for this: "Time!" he said, "We can make time!"

Dangerous stunts

While his proficiency in cycling had allowed him to raise large sums for charities, cycling was not all that Dennis had on his mind. He wanted to push the boundaries a little and see what was possible for a man of his age, with his disabilities. Sky diving had proved that such ventures were possible, and survivable. His worried wife spoke to his

eye specialist. The doctor replied, "Let him do whatever he feels he can do." Dennis decided to go flying.

An instructor from the Cardiff Wales Flying Club took Dennis up in a Piper Warrior light aircraft and then let him fly the plane himself for about thirty minutes. It was bumpy but he could feel the plane and control its flight without difficulty. A year later he went for a

Freefall parachuting above Wiltshire in 1993. Photo: Dennis Daymond-John

second flight. Then he decided to try abseiling – 210 feet down the side of Brunel House, Cardiff. This was one of the few times he found himself worried:

Once on the roof I had to climb fifteen feet up a ladder and duck through scaffolding on to a platform of planks. I was hooked up and when my instructor said, "Shuffle backwards and then step off" I wondered if this was going to be the first time ever that I would chicken out.

When he stepped out something went wrong. After he had moved down about six feet some connecting shackle had jammed and he had to be hauled back to the roof where the harness was readjusted and then start again. His nerves had become a little frayed by this point.

Six or seven times on the way down I swung around like a spider on its thread and banged my helmeted head, back and shoulders against the building. They tried to talk me down by two-way radio but something else went wrong and I could not transmit.

However, I could receive and so I knew they were ready to catch me as I neared the ground. I was very pleased to rejoin Betty (his wife) and my daughter Catherine on the ground and I confess that I was a bit wobbly for a while afterwards.

But his most frightening stunt was the last one he did: wing-walking on a vintage aeroplane. An aeroplane which itself, was doing a few stunts – just for fun. This time, he reported, he really did begin to worry:

The ground crew were so impressed with my age and track-record that they waived the fee for the aeroplane. They so impressed the pilot in the same way that he decided to give me an extra treat; instead of the ten minutes which is the normal flight you get they kept me up for twenty minutes and threw it all round the sky. A favour I could have well done without. I must confess that was frightening. I was glad to get off... The thought was in my head – when he was chucking this thing around - there is always a first time in history that the restraining harness would break.

Dennis with his wife, Betty, prior to his abseil down the side of Brunel House, Cardiff, in 2000..   Western Mail & Echo

Finally, and one assumes to the relief of his wife, Dennis reached his target of £150,000 raised. An achievement he can be very proud of.

His work did not go unnoticed in high places. In 1995, when he had reached the sum of £100,000 raised for charity, he was awarded an MBE by the Queen for Community and Charity services over fifty years. At his investiture, the Queen asked him if he was the man who had done the parachute jump. He affirmed that he was indeed the one. The Queen said that she thought him "a very brave man". "Thank you Ma'am," replied Dennis, "my wife just thinks I'm stupid." The Queen laughed.

Today, Dennis has retired from his stunts and fund-raising but he remains available to advise those who wish to benefit from his experience. He also works with those who have recently found themselves blind. Many of whom feel depressed and incapable. Dennis tells them that it is not the end of the world, that there are many activities and challenges that they can still involve themselves in: "At my age, if I can do it, you can do it."

LIGHT OF SIAM LODGE No.9791

HOWARD DIGBY-JOHNS RECALLS THE DAY THE TSUNAMI STRUCK

Aftermath: the beach at Phuket.

The appalling tsunami which struck so much of Asia one year ago, is unimaginable for those who did not experience it, unforgettable in the terror it induced for those who did. Here in Phuket, in Thailand, we have a strong expatriate British community, a core of whom have formed their own English Constitution Lodge, Light of Siam, No. 9791. In one sense, we were uniquely placed to chronicle events as they unfolded, and to offer what assistance we could.

No one needed to have died. My friends were in the sea when it receded about 1 km. They ran to their room, got clothes and valuables, and drove off in their car in time to see their chalet demolished by the water. Most people stayed to watch. One friend was on the roof of a beach cottage after the first wave. The cottages were in a row. The second wave took the people off the end cottage, and returned their bobbing bodies a little later. The third wave took those from the second cottage, and brought back the awful offering.

Another friend was awakened by the black tide of death which she saw out of the window. She rushed out to the back, only to see another tide coming from the opposite direction. Then she was felled under the weight of the house wall falling on her. The water carried her and her wall into the reservoir. Luckily on the bottom of the reservoir, under the wall she did not

The Grand Charity has now confirmed that they are giving to Light of Siam Lodge, No. 9791, £100,000 over three years to support the on-going costs of a project its members have created to help children. They are working with ChildWatch, a local Thai charity, to house fifty orphans and provide support for an additional 200 in a day care centre.

The overwhelming awfulness was that we knew nothing. You could have been 500 yards from people consumed by the water and see and hear nothing. Forget the image of a cresting wave. The tide just went out and came in. Just very far and very fast. The wave was maybe six inches high, but 100 miles long – that's a lot of water. The strange thing is the water was black with debris. Most damage was caused by the third wave, and particularly as it receded.

panic, and went down to find a way out. She found one, only to find the surface blocked by sodden mattresses. She got an arm out, and was pulled to safety – she was only at the edge of the reservoir. Another friend was in a cave and was gently pressed to its roof. Others were taken up through trees, and trapped by their clothes. Miraculous escapes.

Twelve months on, we still live with it. My friends who lost their little boy had the body identified only four weeks ago. I was with them that night. They had clung to the fantasy that he was on some remote island with fisherfolk. They took him home, and 400 attended the funeral of a little boy who was frozen in a container of corpses for all those months. They have just had a new baby.

But now Phuket's people have taken stock. Some are dead. Some are injured. Most businesses are open. But many people have lost the means to make a living. Many hotels remain open for business, but they sit empty. The beaches have been cleaned and are more beautiful than ever, but they are almost deserted. Only a few restaurants, shops, bars and attractions have been disrupted, but they lack customers. There is no shortage of drinking water, power, food or any serious threat of disease. Life in Phuket is basically normal. But the only means for the people here to recover their lives is for tourists to come back.

So now Phuket's people now face their second attack. Their recovery has been worse damaged by the second catastrophe – the tourists stayed away, and tourists are Phuket's lifeblood. Phuket's hotels are still virtually empty. For the tour guides, for those who gave massages on the beach, or took tourists on boat trips, ran stalls, or rented out deck chairs, there is still the rent and school fees and groceries to pay and

suddenly no income at all. So the need to bring the tourists back is urgent. The poorest are local, and have no skills that would allow them to go elsewhere.

LODGE INVOLVEMENT

Brethren of the Light of Siam Lodge, have collected and disbursed relief funds, cared for the injured, coordinated the medical effort, visited the injured in hospital, fed and watered those fleeing the beaches, housed the dispossessed, gathered funds for schools and nurseries, acted as chauffeurs for tourists requiring flights or medical attention, or seeking lost ones, acted as embassy officers in the relief effort, built an orphan centre, repaired fishing boats, provided both replacement boats and fishing nets and are now responding to requests by the Embassies to help with the relatives of victims who will be visiting.

We have now identified our masonic relief effort with a long term plan to help the most vulnerable – the children of the poor who have been worst affected by the tsunami and the subsequent tourist famine

We need the tourists back. But for the most vulnerable, it is already too late. They have turned to loan sharks. A £300 loan results in a daily interest

Survivors.

The Green Man Pub.

payment of £7. You may think this a stupid loan to accept, but for a new widow now homeless and destitute with two surviving children, the need for mattresses, mosquito nets, a rice cooker, and some rudimentary shelter probably seemed worth the terrible interest payments. Of course she will have to take her children out of school and finally she will probably have to give her children to the loan shark to deal with the ballooning loan. We should not dwell on what will happen to the children then. Children are amongst the worst affected of Phuket's citizens. Some are orphans, and sexual predators are already at work. We have heard terrible stories from Aceh in Indonesia.

The Thai Government has tried to help, but its facilities are in Bangkok, well away from whatever community support there is. The poorest families now have no jobs, no incomes, possibly no housing – the shanties obviously suffered worst. Even their little pre-existing possessions have gone.

Master of the Lodge, Light of Siam, No. 9791, Howard Digby-Johns, inspecting a badly damaged boat.

OUR IMMEDIATE RESPONSE

The community around The Green Man Pub in Chalong raised over £50,000, which we have disbursed to victims. The whole atmosphere of the Village Fête from Middle England sprang to life on Patak Road, including battering the landlord with his own flour, eggs and water prior to adding tasteful garnishes of mayonnaise and tomato ketchup. He looked very tasty.

There were generous donations of prizes and very spirited bidding for them. A scuba cylinder sold for £200 as a customer bid strongly against her husband, only to donate it back to be sold again at £60, only to be onsold at £30 and then passed to someone who really needed it.

Cars were washed by bikini clad sirens, raffles and stalls raised. There was a tsunami stew, and a tsunami cocktail with proceeds to charity. Many raffle prizes were re-donated to the auction. The T-shirt, printed on salvaged stock, raised over £3,000 on the day, with demand still strong.

The most vulnerable people assisted have been humbling. Three separate women were given £70 relief, which was brought back subsequently. The

Government had paid them compensation of £300, and they wanted our relief to be recycled. The manager of my business, who lost his possessions, refused our assistance because he has a job and a salary – others need it more.

We started a small relief effort for Phuket. We provided forms where they could tell us what they need: household effects, tools of trade, or a job. One reply reads 'I want the tourists to come back and for it to be like it was'. This man needs to get back to work.

The first phase was emergency aid; people needed surgery, food, clothing and medicines. This phase lasted about 2 weeks. The second phase was emergency assistance; getting people home, getting people re-housed and re-schooled, and getting people back to work. That phase is almost complete. The third phase is long term support for those who need it most.

The Light of Siam Lodge has

designed a project to house 50 orphans from the tsunami, and to support 200 additional children, largely single-parent children, and from the poorest and worst affected families, in a day care facility. We shall provide food, clothing and health care as required.

We want to give hope back to children who have lost their homes and families, have been molested by sexual predators or abused by commercial exploiters. We want to provide them with marketable skills, whatever that requires, up to and including university education for those that qualify and can benefit.

We shall deliver this through the structure of ChildWatch (www.trv.net/phuket/childwth), a charity with a 10-year record of delivering this type of programme in Phuket.

We are looking for about £300,000 in capital costs, and up to £110,000 per year in running costs. We believe we have around £100,000 in capital and around £30,000 in running costs pledged for 3 years. We think the running costs will be the hardest thing to support, and are looking for future pledges from the Craft as well as a short term response.

Given the money we wish to invest, governance is a big issue. I am looking at a Standing Committee, probably made up of (ex-officio) the Almoner, the Master, the Immediate Past Master, the Treasurer, the Senior Warden, the Junior Warden and any other Brother and wives of Brethren who wish to be involved. This Committee will have the sole signatories within it who will release funds to ChildWatch against approved expenses.

A new fishing boat about to be painted, replacing one lost in the tsunami.

DAUNTLESS, VALIANT AND HEROIC

JULIAN REES TELLS THE STORY OF THE ROYAL NATIONAL LIFEBOAT INSTITUTION

RNLB The Queen Mother lending assistance to the yacht Dasher, in difficulties at Scapa Flow, Orkney.   *photo: Frank Bradford*

In the midst of force eight winds and boiling seas with 3-metre waves, Helmswoman Aileen Jones of Porthcawl was instrumental in saving two fishermen from certain calamity. 'I had a rough idea where he fished,' she said, 'so we headed up that way, towards the top of the Nash Bank, which is where we saw him. It wasn't a nice place to be. The water was coming in at all angles, his engines had failed, none of his anchors would hold. Whatever the sea decided to do to him, he had no control over it.'

For her actions in 2004 Aileen was awarded the Royal National Lifeboat Institution bronze medal for gallantry, the first woman to be so distinguished. Conditions on that day, she recalled, were extremely difficult, to say the least. The fishing vessel Gower Pride's bow was being steadily pulled underwater. The surf was so violent, that the lifeboat was being pitched in the air. As they rounded the bank to approach the fishing vessel, they were wondering how they were going to get through the waves. All they could do was to try and hold the vessel away from the bank, otherwise it would have grounded and broken up. Several attempts were made, without success. to get a line over to the skipper of the fishing vessel. At last it seemed to hold, and they started to drag the boat away. Just when they thought they had

properly secured the vessel, the knot for the towline came undone. To go forward to the bow to try and re-establish the link was by now too dangerous, so Aileen decided to manoeuvre the boat close enough to allow one of her crew to clamber aboard the other vessel. To do so he needed to wait for a gap between waves the height of a living-room ceiling. Then having made the crossing, and hanging on desperately, he managed to edge towards the bow and attach another rope.

The Atlantic 75 lifeboat drew away from the bank, slowly and with great care, a procedure lasting an interminable time. At last a larger lifeboat arrived, from the Mumbles an hour and a half along the coast which, because of its superior size, was able to take over and secure the fishing vessel. The whole episode had lasted three-and-a-half hours. Characteristically, Aileen Jones shies away from being made a heroine because of this, and this attitude is typical of all lifeboat crew members.

> 'These are among the bravest and most skilful mariners that exist. Let a sea run that might appal the stoutest heart that ever beat; let the lightships on the sands throw up a rocket in the darkness of the night; or let them hear through the angry roar the signal guns of a ship in distress, and these young men spring up so dauntless, so valiant and heroic. For the recollection of their comrades, whom the raging sea has engulfed before their children's eyes, let us hold the boatmen in our love and honour.'
>
> Charles Dickens, in *Household Words*, 1850

THE LIFEBOAT STORY

In many respects the story of the Royal National Lifeboat Institution is the story of men and women exercising the highest standards of bravery and selflessness seen anywhere. The story began about 180 years ago, when an idiosyncratic Quaker, Sir William Hillary, founded a charity dedicated to 'the preservation of lives and property from shipwreck'. The year was 1824 and the boats were powered and steered by oars and could only operate close to the beaches. Its affairs were managed on a part-time basis by enthusiastic amateurs.

In 1849 the Institution reached the lowest point in its fortunes. Its founder had just died, and one of the principal lifeboats had gone down with the loss of 20 of the 24 crew. Such disasters trigger considerable sympathy in the public, and it was clear that the time had come for a change in the Institution. In 1854 the Institution became the Royal National Lifeboat Institution, the name by which it is still known today. Fund-raising increased markedly, and income rose from around £5,000 in 1850 to £70,000 in 1882. In this period, sail power started to replace oars, with a corresponding improvement in speed and monoeuvrability, and by the turn of the twentieth century steam boats had taken over, shortly to be joined by petrol-driven craft.

HM The Queen with Andrew Freemantle, RNLI Chief Executive, at the Lifeboat College opening at Poole. *photo: Chris North*

MASONIC INVOLVEMENT

Masonic involvement in the affairs of the RNLI, particularly fund-raising, dates from the middle of the nineteenth century. At that time, although individual Freemasons and lodges gave their support, the United Grand Lodge of England failed to respond to editorial comments in *The Freemason*. The Editor said that his publication was 'looking forward with some impatience to the provision of a Masonic Lifeboat. Surely,' he continued' 'a body so numerous, important and wealthy as The Masonic can have little difficulty in raising the necessary funds to complete the purchase of a Lifeboat'.

In 1871 J.R. Stebbing, the Deputy Provincial Grand Master for Hampshire and a former Mayor of Southampton, took a proposal to Grand Lodge 'for a grant of £50 towards the provision of a Masonic Lifeboat'. The motion was put to Grand Lodge and carried, and so the links with the RNLI were forged. The consequence of this was that, in 1872, a lifeboat named 'Freemason' was launched at North Berwick before an array of RNLI and Grand Lodge officials.

In 1876 a special committee was set up by Grand Lodge to mark the safe return of the Prince of Wales from India. This committee proposed that the sum of £4,000 be voted for the RNLI to found two lifeboat stations 'in perpetuity'. This was passed by Grand Lodge in March 1877. The sites chosen were Clacton in Essex and Yare in Devon. A lifeboat was to be provided at each station, and they were duly named *Albert Edward* and *Alexandra*, after the Prince and Princess of Wales respectively.

So it was that the Craft moved from an impartial interest in the RNLI to a committed responsibility to maintain two lifeboats, carriages and boat houses. These boats were launched 270 times and saved 556 lives. In 1896, yet another boat was financed, to be called *City Masonic Club*. This boat was stationed at Poole, the present headquarters of the RNLI, until 1910.

RNLB of the Tyne Class off St. Helier going to the assistance of the dismasted yacht *Dodger* and two crew. *photo: Jonathon Cornick*

All these boats, and others financed by Freemasons, were from time to time replaced as the need arose. Then, in 1980, Grand Lodge voted a sum of £300,000 for the purchase of a 54ft. Arun Class lifeboat, to be named *Duchess of Kent*. This was the eleventh masonic lifeboat to be presented. Up to 1987 masonic lifeboats had been launched over 500 times and saved a total of 995 lives.

A MODEL OF EFFICIENCY

Today, the RNLI operate over 400 high-powered craft from over 200 stations round Britain and Ireland, providing a swift and efficient rescue service. Every year it answers about 6,000 calls and rescues the lives of some 1,000 people.

Although its management and administration are run in a professional and competent way, it is still a charitable organisation, with no financial support from the government. It relies on largely unpaid crew members who are all volunteers, only 5% of whom come from a maritime background.

The RNLI's annual running costs are around £119m – over £325,000 per day and, as a registered charity, the organisation continues to rely on voluntary contributions and legacies for its income. Its one clear purpose is to save lives at sea. They provide a 24-hour search and rescue service out to 100 nautical miles from the coast of the United Kingdom and Republic of Ireland and since it was founded their lifeboat crews have saved more than 137,000 lives.

HM Coastguard and the Irish Coast Guard initiate and co-ordinate civil maritime search and rescue in the UK and Irish sea regions. During maritime emergencies on cliffs, beaches, shoreline or at sea each of these authorities calls on RNLI lifeboats and hovercraft.

Crew members come from many walks of life and are prepared to exchange leisure, comfort and sleep for cold, wet, fatigue and sometimes danger. Lifeboat crews spend many hours of their own time training, and because of their willingness a very high proportion of the RNLI's money

Severn Class all-weather lifeboat The Duke of Kent at her naming ceremony, HRH The Duke of Kent on board.

photo: RNLI/Derek King

can be spent on lifeboats and equipment, not on wages. They owe a debt of gratitude to over 45,000 indispensable volunteer fundraisers, from all over the British Isles, who help to raise the money needed for the RNLI to go on saving lives at sea.

The RNLI fleet consists of all weather and inshore lifeboats and, at selected stations, hovercraft. They operate four lifeboat stations along the tidal reaches of the Thames (Tower Pier, Chiswick, Gravesend and Teddington). The charity also operates lifeboat stations covering major inland waters at Lough Derg, Republic of Ireland; Enniskillen (Lough Erne) Northern Ireland; and South Broads, Norfolk.

HOVERCRAFT

The RNLI introduced hovercraft to its fleet in December 2002, to enhance inshore search and rescue operations. The craft operate in areas of shallow water and mud, which conventional lifeboats cannot navigate. RNLI hovercraft are developed in conjunction with the RNLI's technical department specifically for search and rescue purposes. The hovercraft is 7.75m in length, carries a crew of three and has a top speed of 30 knots with a range of 3 hours at maximum speed. In 2004 the RNLI

hovercraft at Hunstanton launched 9 times, the hovercraft at Morecambe launched 21 times, and the hovercraft at Southend-on-Sea launched 15 times.

They are always searching for new ways of saving lives at sea and after a successful pilot scheme in 2001, 2002 saw the introduction of a beach lifeguard service on 43 of the country's busiest beaches in south and south west England, expanding to 59 by 2005 – a very successful service that they hope to widen over the next few years. Today more and more people are using the sea for leisure and crews are responding to an increased number of incidents relating to recreational pursuits. Last year they launched 7,656 times, an average of more than 21 times a day and saved 433 lives.

Research shows that 4 out of 10 adults in the UK don't know the RNLI is a charity, but in fact they rely on voluntary contributions and legacies from the public for income.

Grand Lodge gave £30,000 to the RNLI in 1995, but the donations from private lodges and from Provinces continue to flow: over £14,000 in 2003, £28,000 in 2004 and £27,000 in 2005. Their Royal Patron is the Grand Master, HRH The Duke of Kent, and their Treasurer for the past six years is the recently retired Deputy Grand Master, Iain Ross Bryce.

Here we have one of the outstanding examples of the best that Britain can do in voluntary work, and at the same time provide a vital national resource, vital on so many planes. It relies for its effectiveness on volunteer crew and voluntary fund-raising, and demonstrates what resourcefulness, courage and hard work can achieve.

For more information about the Train One; Save Many campaign, visit www.rnli.org.uk/crewtraining or telephone 0800 543210.

Poole Lifeboat College - how to capsize a boat . . . .

. . . and how to right it again.

photos: Sue Sieger and Derek King

FROM FRATERNAL GROUPS TO TRADE UNIONS

ANDY DURR LOOKS AT AN IMPORTANT INFLUENCE ON MODERN SOCIETY

Design created by A. J. Waudby for the Friendly Society of Operative Stone Masons. The centre shows the building of Solomon's Temple. *People's History Museum*

While we have at Freemasons' Hall in London a public relations machine to combat ill-informed reports and to proactively promote Freemasonry, we still have a rather fixed view of masonic history: that is, the history written by Freemasons for Freemasons. In itself it is harmless enough but until quite recently this was also the only history available for non-masons to get any feeling about where Freemasonry came from. However good this history is, the agenda, and the themes, explored by masonic historians today, are by and large those set over a century ago.

R. F. Gould's, *The History of Freemasonry* was first published in 1887! He and his friends had a fundamental preoccupation with the origin of Freemasonry, with the identification of the moment of its birth. While they accepted a period of pregnancy, the idea to most, that parenthood and the artisan were linked, was beyond the Pale. The Freemasons he was writing for belonged to an organisation with the Prince of Wales as Grand Master and Lodges containing the local social elite. It was an organisation which was the natural home for the Victorian middle-class male. *The London Illustrated News* published pictures of the Grand Master in his regalia. Local Press would report Masonic Balls and who were present. These were all important social events.

Gould's generation of masonic historians were men of independent means writing for the emerging late-Victorian middle-class. For them, the conception of Freemasonry in the seventeenth century was due to the interjection of their perceived social antecedents: seventeenth century gentry, intellectually associated with Rosicrucianism and other movements. But the only empirical evidence Gould has for this comes from Elias Ashmole's diary where he stated 'I was made a Free Mason in 1646' and giving the names of those who were then at the Lodge. From Gould's point of view, it established beyond doubt that there was in existence a Lodge of Freemasons composed of speculative or non-operative members.

In 1894, just a few years after Gould wrote his *History*, Sidney and Beatrice Webb produced their influential, *The History of Trade Unionism*. The Webbs came from the same sort of background as Gould, and like Gould, they had an agenda, not the least being the forming of a Labour Party, the London School of Economics, and the London County Council. Their writing of history served this end.

One might well ask, what is the connection between these two histories? Well, the Webbs argued that it appears 'probable, indeed, that the masons, wandering over the country from one job to another, were united, not in any local guild,

Apron used by the Friendly Society of Operative Stone Masons.   *Library and Museum of Freemasonry*

but a trade fraternity of national extent'. The Webbs were not aware of it but they were referring to the fraternity known to Gould as the Society of Free Masons. The Webbs added that such an association may, 'possess many points of resemblance to the Friendly Society of Operative Stone Masons'. This latter was a Trade Union formed just three years before Gould's birth in 1836.

The main sources of information which we have of the Society of Free Masons have come from antiquarians such as John Aubrey and seventeenth century scholars like Dr. Robert Plot. Plot was a product of restoration science; part of a new breed of scholars who declined to 'proceed, by repeating what somebody else had written and adding a little more.' To them, 'the Nature of Things in Metaphors and Allegories is nothing else but to sport and trifle with empty words.' They were to 'speak of things as they are'. They relied on 'first-hand observations and credible reports.' And when they wanted to learn more about stone building they spoke to 'masons, and stone-cutters'.

Plot claimed of the 'Society of Free Masons' that their Lodges were 'spread more or less all over the Nation'. Lodges were on, or near, building sites such as St. Thomas' Hospital, Southwark; St. James' Church, within monumental masons' yards; others were in quarries. Some seventeenth century quarries even displayed the Mason's

Arms at the entrance, indicating the importance of the trade, its customs and rules.

In London, a Lodge met at the Hall of the Masons' Company; we have one meeting recorded in 1682. In fact, this was the second, and only other, meeting attended by Ashmole. Those present, while important, were masons by trade. William Wilson carved the elaborate porch to Subrey Hall. William Woodman was a monumental mason at Westminster Abbey, Thomas Wise

was a stone carver, Nick Young worked at the Apothecaries Company, William Hammon[d] at the Vinters' Company and the Royal College of Physicians. John Shorthose carved the steeple door at Christ Church Newgate, and William Stanton was an important monumental mason with a yard in Holborn. The importance of this record is that it definitively kills Gould's notion of gentlemen scholars partaking of esoteric secrets, for what happened that night was that a young man who had just finished his apprenticeship was initiated, was 'made a mason'.

To become a member of the Society in the seventeenth century required that you were freeborn and of good kindred; entry requirements which were not too different from those of the Friendly Society of Operative Stone Masons in the nineteenth century. The candidate was then given a history which started from the Book of Genesis and the building of the first stone house by Jabell. It proceeded to explain how the rules of the 'craft' had been established, and later confirmed, by King Solomon at the time of the building of his Temple – and so on! This myth or legend did not disappear: in 1868, A.J. Waudby was commissioned to design an emblem for the Friendly Society of Operative Stone Masons; it was made quite clear to him that the central panel was to depict the building of Solomon's temple.

The History having been read to the candidate, he placed both hands on the 'book' – the Bible – and each rule of the Society was read, repeated and rehearsed. The Society of Free Masons saw itself to be synonymous with the 'trade' and so the new member, through his obligation to the rules, was deemed to have been 'made a mason'. Then the newly 'made mason' was

---

FROM THE DIARY OF ELIAS ASHMOLE

10 Mar. 1682

About 5H: P.M. I received a Sumons to appeare at a Lodge to be held the next day, at Masons Hall London.

11 Mar. 1682

Accordingly I went, & about Noone were admitted into the Fellowship of Free Masons,
Sir William Wilson Knight, Capt: Rich: Borthwick, Mr: Will: Woodman, Mr: William Grey, Mr: Samuell Taylour & Mr William Wise.
I was the Senior Fellow among them (it being 35 yeares since I was admitted) There were present beside my selfe the Fellowes after named. Mr: Tho: Wise Master of the Masons Company this present yeare. Mr: Thomas Shorthose, Mr: Thomas Shadbolt, [blank] Waindsford Esquire Mr: Nich: Young. Mr: John Shorthose, Mr: William Hamon, Mr: John Thompson, & Mr: Will: Stanton.
Wee all dyned at the halfe Moone Taverne in Cheapeside, at a Noble Dinner prepaired at the charge of the New-accepted Masons.

FRIENDLY SOCIETY JEWELS

Jewel of The Good Samaritans

Jewel of the Loyal United Friends

Jewel of the Oddfellows

Jewel of the Ancient Order of Foresters

These Friendly Societies grew at the same time as the Trade Unions and can be seen as parallels in terms of Working Class organisations. Andy Durr will be looking at these in a second article. Library and Museum of Freemasonry

taken to one side and given 'certain secret signs' and the 'masons' word'. Two hundred years later the Friendly Society of Operative Stone Masons, the Trade Union, would publish similar initiation rituals which they used.

William Dugdale, in conversation with John Aubrey in 1691, talked of Free-Masons being 'known to one another by certain Signes & watch-words' and of the Lodges where if any 'of them fall into decay the brotherhood is to relieve him &c'. For the travelling mason with no means of support, the notion was simple enough. Whether money was given, or gained, it gave him the ability to stop at Inns, such as the seventeenth century Inn at Cotgrove, which displayed the arms of the Society, and 'pay truly for any meat and drink'. In England, in the mid-nineteenth century, 'one fifth of the stonemasons' lodges or relieving stations' were still held in Inns displaying the 'Masons' Arms'.

In London, the Society of Free Masons, was formally integrated within the Company of Free Masons from the early seventeenth century. The practice appears to have been that you were made free and joined the livery, then paid an extra fine to be 'made masons' just before leaving the confines of the City of London; 'going abroad' to seek, or undertake, work elsewhere.

In the first half of the seventeenth century this would have been a one-way traffic but this changed after the Great Fire of London. With the passing of the Rebuilding Act in 1667, London was an open city with the Company of Free Masons losing control over labour. Masons from all around the country were allowed to work in the city. The Society of Free Masons displayed the 'names of the accepted Masons in a faire inclosed frame with lock and key'.

It was in this period in the history of London that the Society of Free Masons was operating as a labour exchange or house of call for masons coming in from the country. It has to be understood that both masters and men were members of the Society. This was still the case in the 1830s: members of the Friendly Society of Operative Stone Masons took an oath, 'that I will not work for any master that is not in the Union'.

After the Rebuilding Act's powers came to an end, work for masons started to dry up. William Preston explained some time later that the old lodge at St. Paul's, and a few others, continued to meet regularly, but had few members. To increase their numbers, a proposition was agreed, that the privileges of Masonry should no longer be restricted to operative masons but extend to men of various professions. This was the birth of Freemasonry.

By 1717 we had the forming of Grand Lodge. The mistake has always been to assume that working stone masons were not members of the new Freemasons. This is far from the case. In fact, whole Lodges of Operative Masons joined the new Grand Lodge in the Counties in the 1730s, in London in the 1760s, and in the north of England one Lodge joined as late as 1822; this Lodge returned its Warrant ten years later, the year that the Friendly Society of Operative Masons was founded.

We can see then that Freemasonry was integral with the evolution of this Trade Union and others.

Andy Durr was Mayor of Brighton and Hov,e, and currently is Visiting Research Fellow at the University of Sussex. He is a member of South Down Lodge, No.1797. This article is a summary of some points taken from a chapter of his book in progress under the working title of, The English Artisan and Fraternal Association – A Troublesome History but Common Heritage – Fraternities, Freemasonry, Secret Orders and Trade Unions.

VISION WITH THE SONG

I saw Eternity the other night,
Like a great ring of pure and endless light,
All calm as it was bright;
And round beneath it, Time in hours, days, years,
Driv'n by the spheres
Like a vast shadow mov'd; in which the world
And all her train were hurl'd.

Henry Vaughan 1622-1695

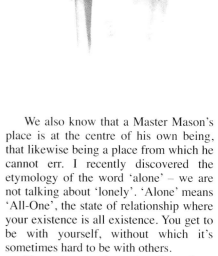

As if you needed reminding, we have been subject to serial mishaps in the past twelve months. A supersonic airliner hits a piece of metal shed by another airliner and is destroyed. The weather-shift causes flooding with disastrous consequences. Our computers are invaded by more and deadlier viruses. As if BSE hasn't been enough, we are hit by foot and mouth disease. More miscarriages of justice are uncovered. Railway lines begin to show cracks, leading to fatal disasters. And in one of the cruellest twists of coincidence, a vehicle accidentally leaves the motorway causing a collision with two trains

Technology is complex, and we only notice how complex it is when it fails. We not only expect it all to work smoothly, we demand that it does so. When our trains don't run, when the motorway seems to be one vast tail-back, we fume impotently. We inhabit a society which is very intolerant of technical failure. Simpler civilizations may have television sets and a limited number of cars and trucks, but when they stop working, society doesn't break down.

The complexity with which we surround ourselves is not even self-serving. There are so many strands, so many threads which cross each other, that they have become mutually destructive, as in the Selby crash. We even invent acronyms for both the causes and the consequences, so that we do not have to face them too squarely. Who remembers what "HIV" or "BSE" stand for? or the sinisterly-named "variant CJD"? For "variant", should we be reading "deviant"? And if we do remember what they stand for, does it aid our understanding of them?

Complexity is a peculiarly twentieth century talent. It is defined as the unpredicted result of a multitude of interreacting elements which, in themselves, are simple. It is similar in appearance to chaos, which is a system difficult to predict because of so many unknown factors (earthquakes). For me, a child of the twentieth century nurtured on this stuff, they are indistinguishable in their effects.

Chaos doesn't only reside outside us. We all have to contend with inner chaos – depression, self-doubt, despair, pain physical and mental, bereavement, anger and low self-esteem are all part of the same cosmic chaos. The good news is that, especially as Freemasons, we can answer it with a corresponding cosmic awareness, growth and enlightenment. Look at the first degree tracing board :

In all regular, well-formed, constituted Lodges there is a point within a circle round which the Brethren cannot err; this circle is bounded between North and South by two grand parallel lines, one representing Moses and the other King Solomon; on the upper part of this circle rests the Volume of the Sacred Law, supporting Jacob's ladder, the top of which reaches to the heavens . . . . in going round this circle we must necessarily touch on both those parallel lines, likewise on the Volume of the Sacred Law; and while a Mason keeps himself thus circumscribed, he cannot err.

We also know that a Master Mason's place is at the centre of his own being, that likewise being a place from which he cannot err. I recently discovered the etymology of the word 'alone' – we are not talking about 'lonely'. 'Alone' means 'All-One', the state of relationship where your existence is all existence. You get to be with yourself, without which it's sometimes hard to be with others.

There is a rather nice fact about Edward Elgar which I want to share with you. When the music was slow to come to him, or would not come at all, he went out into the country to be with himself, away from the complexities of everyday life, to discover himself and own himself, in his case to discover the song inside him, away from the chaos, whether inner or outer.

Read that tracing board lecture again. Cross the barrier. Be with yourself and find the song.

Julian Rees is available to discuss these and other matters at jrees@aol.com

In May 1940, as the Battle of Britain raged in the skies above southern England, Nazi intelligence officers in Berlin were busily preparing for the expected invasion. Yet few people today realise the hatred reserved for Freemasonry, and to what extent this would have been vented in the event of a German victory over Britain.

FASCIST ATTACK

Upon the outbreak of war, Adolf Hitler ordered the creation of an overall directorate of Reich Security, the RSHA *(Reichssicherheitshauptamt)* which was divided into six main sections, and headed by Reinhard Heydrich. The Chief of the counter-espionage bureau IVE of the RSHA, prepared the *Special Search List Great Britain*, *(Sonderfahndangliste G.B.)*, more commonly known as the *Black Book*. This list comprised some 2,820 names, and included the addresses of embassies, universities, newspaper offices and other companies to be dealt with. Freemasonry was marked out for special attention. Nazi agents listed the addresses of craft Grand Lodges in England, Ireland and Scotland, including also the headquarters of many side orders such as Mark Masons' Hall, the Provincial Grand Lodges, and specific lodges such as *Grand Masters*, *Antiquity*, and *Pilgrim*. Famous personalities known to Hitler's informants as Freemasons were also named, such as Winston Churchill, Labour's wartime minister Herbert Morrison, the exiled President of Czechoslovakia Edward Benes, his foreign minister Jan Masaryk, and the Polish pianist and statesman, Ignace Padarewski [1].

Even though the Bolsheviks in Russia had outlawed Freemasonry in 1924, the European fascist powers were driven by their belief in the existence of a Judaeo-Masonic-Bolshevik conspiracy. As the decade unfolded, the situation across Europe grew even darker, and in Italy the movement fell to the Italian fascists led by the dictator Benito Mussolini. In Germany, the Nazi newspaper *Volkischer Beobachter* long ranted about the supposed perils of the Order, before the Grand Lodges there too were forced to close due to state intolerance in May 1935. Indeed, the Nazi movement's first leader, General Ludendorff, had long before published a book condemning the Order in 1924, entitled *The Destruction of Freemasonry through the Revelation of its secrets*, which by 1940 had sold hundreds of thousands of copies and gone through many editions [2].

Left: In October 1942 an anti-Masonic Exhibition was opened by the Nazis in German–occupied Belgrade. The event was financed and commemorated by a set of charity stamps with blatant anti-Masonic/Semitic designs, one of which is reproduced here.

The exhibition was set up as evidence of a Judaeo-Masonic conspiracy for world domination. Several exhibits were from the looted masonic temples in the Channel Islands.

(Illustration and caption courtesy Yasha Beresiner)

Above: The Nazi 'Black Book' and sample showing addresses of Lodges.

Photographs: M.D.J. Scanlan

Above: General Ludendorff's book -
The Destruction of Freemasonry through the revelation of its secrets.

Photograph: M.D.J. Scanlan

Above: Spanish anti-communist and anti-masonic propoganda changed little between 1945 (left) and 1975 (right). Note the square and the dividers on the limbs (indicated in red).

Right: Samples from *The Fascist*. (Imperial Fascist League).

Photographs: M.D.J. Scanlan

In Spain, the military rebellion of July 1936 had ignited an all-out civil war, and throughout territory held by the Nationalist forces under General Franco, all masons, members of Popular Front parties and Trade Unions were arrested. Large numbers were executed [3]. In an interview conducted with the Roman Catholic *Tablet* in 1937, Franco declared quite unequivocally that "the Spanish Republic did not find itself free of obligations. For the most part the leaders were Freemasons. ...In my opinion, Freemasonry, with all its international influence, is the organization principally responsible for the political ruin of Spain.."[4]. In fact, the blood-letting was so intense during the start of the conflict that between 18 July and I September, an estimated 75,000 were executed, a figure which included a large number of Freemasons [5].

In England, Oswald Mosley's British Union of Fascists did not quite share the same white-nuckle hatred as their continental counterparts. That was left to Spencer Leese's extreme Imperial Fascist League, who regularly attacked Freemasonry in their monthly newspaper, *The Fascist*. One of their pamphlets, simply titled *'Freemasonry'*, stated : "It [masonry] is universal, and preaches the universal Brotherhood of Man, which means in practice the mongrelisation of the human species," "It is subversive in

a political sense, and was started by Jewry and is now controlled by Jewry for the purpose of paving the way for Bolshevism, as outlined in the Protocols of the Elders of Zion."[6]. Other titles included *Race & Politics - A counterblast to the masonic teaching of universal brotherhood*, and *The Growing Menace of Freemasonry in Britain*. Although the IFL was never large enough to constitute a major threat, Leese's rantings reached sufficiently outrageous proportions in 1936 to make the Crown bring charges of seditious libel against him, and he spent six months in gaol [7]. Uninhibited by incarceration, he later declared that the post-war Nuremburg trials were a "Jewish Masonic affair"[8]. Ironically, as Spain began to emerge from a struggle which left almost a million dead, the rest of Europe descended into a devastating conflict.

What exactly might have befallen members of the craft had Hitler's legions crossed the Channel can probably be best guaged by looking at events in France. Upon capitulation to German forces, the country was effectively partitioned, with the south under the collaborationist Vichy regime of Marshal Pétain. Pétain started a special bureau of investigation whose job it was to expose Freemasons, who, as a result, lost their jobs, and in the occupied north were often visited by the Gestapo. In Paris, the headquarters of the irregular but largest of the French masonic Grand Lodges was occupied and used for anti-masonic propaganda. Many French masons were active in the French resistance movements, which only goaded the Gestapo to further persecution. Somewhere in the region of 1000 members ended their days in concentration camps[9].

Ominously, the man who was to head the SS operations in Britain, and who was assistant chief to Heydrich, was SS Colonel Dr. Frank Six. Later held responsible for wholesale slaughter on the Eastern Front, Six's headquarters were to have been in London, where a number of *Einsatzkommandos* (Action Commandos) were to track down and arrest all targets. Chillingly, it was Department 4b.IVB which was given the task of dealing with Jews and Freemasons, as "enemies of the people and of the Reich", and was to be personally headed by the infamous Adolf Eichmann, better known to history as "the technician of the Holocaust". After the war, Eichmann escaped to Argentina, but was kidnapped by Israeli agents on 11 May 1960, tried in Israel, and hanged two years later. [10].

After the war, the craft in England began to keep a far lower profile than it had done previously, and it is debateable whether or not that was intentional after all that had happened. Yet today, Freemasonry is once again in an era of openness, and all members of our Order can be justifiably proud of a tradition which rigorously opposed the dogmatic intolerance of Europe's 20th century dictators.

1. *The Black Book,* reproduced by the Imperial War Museum.
2. AQC. Vol. 95, Ellic Howe, *The Collapse of Freemasonry in Nazi Germany, 1933-5.*
3. Prof. Hugh Thomas, *The Spanish Civil War.* p.165.
4. *Why the Army Rose.* Interview with General Franco, *The Tablet,* November 6 1937.
5. Thomas. *The Spanish Civil War.* p.173.
6. *Freemasonry.* p.22. Imperial Fascist League, 1935.
7. Robert Benewick, *Political Violence and Public Order.* Allen Lane, The Penguin Press, London 1969.
8. *British Fascism.* Ed : Kenneth Lunn & Richard Thurlow, 1980. Croom Helm, London. p.62.
9. Information very kindly supplied by Pierre Mollière.
10. *Introduction to the Nazi Black Book,* by Terry Charman, Dept. of Printed Books, Imperial War Museum.
11. Created in 1929 by Spencer Leese, a former member of the British Union of Fascists, Leese helped run the Stamford branch, but broke to form the IFL as his advocacy of Hitler went a good deal further than Mosley's.

Matthew Scanlan MA, is a member of CEHME, the Centre for Masonic Studies, Zaragoza University, Spain.

COMMUNITY AND BROTHERHOOD

HARRY BUCKNALL MEETS FORMER POLICE SUPERINTENDENT DAVID WEBB

Basil Clarke MBE and David Webb, both members of Lodge of Universal Brotherhood, No. 9329, West Bromwich, outside the local Sikh temple shrine.

Harry Bucknall

Toxteth, Southall, Moss Side, St Pauls, Brixton and Handsworth all send a shiver down the spine of anyone who was about in the 1980s. The list of names reads like some War Memorial to the inner city riots that swept across the country over twenty years ago: synonymous with inner city tension as our urban communities came to harsh physical terms with the then growing problem of non-integrated multi-ethnic communities.

David Webb was the Police Superintendent in charge of the Handsworth District, in Birmingham, at the height of these troubles and was one of the driving forces behind the policies, which have helped shape our multi-racial society of today. The only difference with David was that, as he was right at the coal face, he actually had to implement them the hard way.

I had arranged to meet David Webb in Handsworth; his booming voice giving me clear instructions as to where and when. It wasn't hard to identify him, an immaculately polished motor car and a trim military hair cut were a quick give-away. It was obvious that his early days in the Army had not been lost on him. A big smile greeted me at the window and a large friendly hand quickly followed.

You cannot help but like David Webb. There are few airs and graces about him. He is still very much a community man, something which has not deserted him since his time as a village bobby, on his bike, in Hertfordshire, a time he describes as 'when they knew you and you knew them and all you had for communication was a telephone call every hour'.

When I asked him what was it like when he was appointed to Handsworth, he matter of factly replied that it was

'crisis every day, you could sense the atmosphere' and in comparison to his native Hertfordshire he commented that 'you hadn't got the hostility [as] with these young guys who had no job, no employment, absolutely nothing to look forward to and no prospect whatsoever. The Police, in Handsworth, were right in the middle of that.'

And perhaps a crucial point about David Webb, is that he then remarked to me '..and I just said, no, its gonna have to alter. Lets see if we can make this into a village and say "Can we help on this, can we help on that and bring the community in"'.

Webb quickly started to galvanise the community. The current Police system of graduated response calls is 'totally unacceptable' to David – he liked his Officers to be 'out on the streets, where the Public can relate to them'. He quickly reintroduced the Permanent Beat Officer

David Webb in Handsworth.   *Harry Bucknall*

to Handsworth's streets – a tried and tested formula which had worked so well in his junior days when he himself had been on the beat in village Hertfordshire.

Defusing ethnic tensions

From his Thornhill Road Headquarters, David Webb began to build long-lasting relationships with the leaders of the local racial groups. 'We've got everybody here, the West Indians; the Asian groups - and the Bangladeshis don't talk to the Pakistanis and the Pakistanis don't talk to the Indians and the Hindus fall out with the Sikhs.' He went on to explain that 'There is a tension there between them all the time. Every action you take has a consequence elsewhere in the territory.'

By David's own admission, perhaps the key to his good fortune was that he was given complete autonomy over Handsworth, something which his successors do not necessarily enjoy. I reminded him of Warwick University's Professor John Rex's comments at a meeting of the Birmingham Community Relations Council in 1986, when Rex maintained that under David, Handsworth had effectively been a mini Police state.

'Yes, it was a mini Police state. Ok, the iron fist in the velvet glove, but it was because we were there all the time. We had relations with each of the different groups and all the different projects, which they didn't have with each other and the only organisation that could fetch them in to do things together was the Police. It was the only way we could unite them.'

With an enthusiastic programme of Police-led activities, from sport to youth groups to promoter of one of the largest ethnic community festivals in Europe, David Webb's command quickly assumed the leadership role Handsworth so desperately needed. His officers were embedded in the very heart of this culturally diverse suburb. Webb's achievements over the five years he was in command of the area were quickly acknowledged and lauded by the press. However, it cannot escape notice that it was a National Front incited riot in 1981, not to mention a well aimed brick to his forehead, that signalled a sharp exit from the district and indeed subsequently the West Midlands Police. I asked him if such an apparently ignominious departure, with all his hard work in tatters, was a sadness for him:

'Of course it was sad and I can be moved to tears now, 25 years later, as easy as I was then.' He continued, 'Yes, I had given it my all – I still have a telephone by my bed that rings at all hours of the night, and I was very upset that that was the response that had come, to see it go down the pan as, you see, I knew that it worked.'

At pains to emphasise his own personal continued involvement in the local community, David goes on to illustrate the numerous local associations he chairs and the endless list of invitations he and his wife, Betty, receive to local community weddings, not to mention their annual trips to India. David, incidentally, has recently been highly instrumental in the raising of over £100,000 for three schools in Jalinder, India, for the Valmicki Society.

Later, walking Handsworth's streets, it was clear to see that David Webb is still held in considerable respect in the town. There was hardly a shop door or window we passed where he didn't stop, have a few words or wave to a friend.

Freemasonry and the Police

David had previously told me that he had given Handsworth 'his all' and, when you hear this kindly souled man talk, it is clear to see that that is just what he meant. It is no surprise therefore to learn that David Webb, with his ably demonstrated ideals of respect, moral improvement and the promotion of brotherly love, should be a committed Freemason with over 38 years on the square.

He played a pivotal role in the 1998 Parliamentary Home Affairs Committee investigation into Freemasonry and the Police, led by Labour MP Chris Mullin. The investigation focussed on allegations of masonic wrongdoing in the West Midlands Serious Crime Squad which may have affected the investigations of the Birmingham Six (the IRA pub bombings), and later the Stalker-Sampson enquiry into an alleged shoot to kill policy. Initially, Grand Lodge were slow to divulge to the Committee the names of those officers involved who were Freemasons. Masonry was seen, in some quarters, to be defying the authority of Parliament and Webb, as the most senior masonic member and police officer in West Midlands was approached by Mullin for comment and assistance.

He appealed directly to the Provincial

David Webb and his wife Betty.   *David Webb*

Inaugural meeting of the Lodge of Universal Brotherhood, West Bromwich, 1989. David Webb

Grand Master, stating that 'we should never allow the public to think there exists some secret agenda....or pursue activities which are subversive and unlawful and to their detriment'. His action resulted in the names being published. Of the 117 names involved in the investigation, Webb was able to prove sixteen were masons and only three, all junior ranks, took part specifically in the incidents under examination. 'From that moment we hit him, saying, no way is Freemasonry involved in this and this is the reality of it, the matter has gone dead. I said to Grand Lodge, "No Way" and in actual fact if they didn't release the names I would have done it myself, but luckily it didn't come to that,' he chortled.

Lodge of Universal Brotherhood

David Webb has always been very open about his long association with Freemasonry – 'Absolutely, what's wrong in it? I am not frightened of being identified, I am proud of it' he bursts. 'Everybody will judge Freemasonry by the people they know, therefore we should be open about it. In our Lodge of Universal Brotherhood - we set it up to show there should be no barrier, if it's a white guy, a black guy – all are welcome. In Universal Brotherhood, we've got Sikhs, we have members of the Valmick community, members of the Ravidass community, the Low Caste Dalit communities in Hindu, they're all members of our Lodge. They are respectable responsible members of our community. I will not allow, the same as I didn't allow in Policing, any High Caste to say we are not having Untouchables in our Lodge. The first one that does that is out on his ear 'ole. Masons can be of any group as long as they are responsible, respectable, law-abiding, all the things that we ask questions of in interview. We judge them on their standing as people.'

When I asked him about the old adage of promotion and masonry in the Police Force he was keen to put the record straight: 'You can only get promotion if you pass the exams, and if you have recommendations from your supervisory ranks all the way up, some of whom may be masons but 99% of whom are not. In the old Birmingham City Police, where I was misrepresented to Stephen Knight (who wrote *The Brotherhood*, a sensationalised account of the Craft) by someone purporting to be me, it was alleged that you couldn't get into any rank unless you were a mason as the Chief Constable himself was a mason. I have never experienced that in my service and I have never met anyone trying to use their masonic experience to alter things in the Police. But it has happened and, there were lots of incidents that have been quoted in Stephen Knight's book and elsewhere. There are always going to be individuals in masonry who do not toe the line, just as in any other walk of life."

David Webb with colleague John Eyre and the Master of an Indian Lodge at a masonic centre in India. David Webb

It is a joy to know that David Webb's welcoming outlook on life puts those wrong doers to shame.

David Webb was a founding member of the Lodge of Universal Brotherhood, No.9329, which meets in West Bromwich, Staffordshire. He is also a member of Cloisters Lodge, No. 7100, Letchworth, Hertfordshire, Mercia Lodge, No. 3995, Aldridge, Staffordshire, and Lodge of Universal Brotherhood, No. 9329, West Bromwich, Staffordshire. He was promoted to Grand Rank in the Province of Staffordshire in 1992.

David Webb's book, Policing the Rainbow is available from www.thefreemason.com Telephone: 01299 822 333. It was reviewed in Freemasonry Today, Issue 31, Winter 2005.

MODERN ANTI-MASONRY

DANIEL SEYMOUR REVEALS A NEW VERSION OF AN OLD CONSPIRACY THEORY

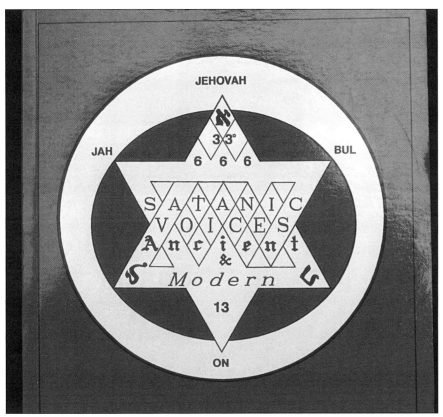

Detail from the cover of a modern anti-masonic publication available in the United Kingdom.

Ever since the eighteenth century Freemasonry has been a favourite whipping-boy of conspiracy theorists. However, in recent years a new breed of conspiracy writer has joined the traditional purveyors of this 'black legend' and a growing number of websites vent a new hatred of Freemasonry. One such site even offers two free downloadable tapes, alleging that Freemasonry is responsible for most of the world's ills. It claims that the Gulf War against Iraq in 1991 was 'engineered, controlled, and manipulated by an elite group' who had been formed in the Crusades.

This mysterious and powerful group had supposedly learned the 'dark' arts of the Hebrew Kabbalah, which the Jews had earlier learned from the pagan priests of Ancient Egypt. This group was the legendary Knights Templar who, upon their suppression in the early fourteenth century, so the story goes, sought and obtained sanctuary in Scotland. Four centuries later, in 1717, they re-surfaced under a new name, the Freemasons, under which guise they have 'engineered all the world's wars and revolutions' and 'control everything you read, hear and see'. The narrator asserts how they 'hide subliminal messages' in the works of popular entertainment such as the records of Michael Jackson, the film *Independence Day*, and even the seemingly innocuous cartoon, *The Simpsons*.

Accordingly, in association with the US military, the UN and the EEC, this organisation secretly orchestrates the spread of illegal narcotics, terrorism, organised crime, genetic engineering and even HIV AIDS, creating the constant need for higher levels of security in a quest to bring about a world super-state. The tape ends by identifying the Freemasons as agents of the *Dajjal* (the Muslim equivalent of the Anti-Christ) who, it claims, can be recognised by the symbol of the one eye, which is on the back of the US Dollar Bill.

On the face of it, one might think that such self-evidently erroneous ideas would have little currency in the modern world. Yet sadly, such conspiratorial tales are growing in popularity within the ranks of some religious fundamentalists, a phenomenon that all Freemasons should be aware of. On 25 January this year, the controversial north London Sheikh, Abu Hamza al Masri, expressed his views to *The Independent*:

> I am not saying every American government figure knew about this [September 11th]. But there are a few people [in the US government] who want to trigger a third world war. They are sponsored by the business lobby. Most of them are Freemasons, and they have loyalty to the Zionists.

Roots of a conspiracy theory

The roots of this malicious tale can be traced back to the end of the eighteenth century and the writings of a French priest, the Abbé Barruel. Barruel claimed that the medieval Templars had survived as a secret society before infiltrating Freemasonry in order to bring about the

French Revolution and an eventual world republic. A few years later Barruel added a Jewish component to his story after receiving information from an army officer J.B. Simonini in 1806. Barruel claimed the existence of a conspiracy down the ages from the heretic Mani, via the Templars to the Freemasons, which was ultimately controlled by Jews. This created a blueprint for further paranoid elaborations.

These stories re-surfaced towards the end of the nineteenth century, only this time in a slightly altered form. In the 1890s the Tsarist Secret Police in Russia, the Okhrana, concocted one of the most infamous and sinister forgeries of all time which first appeared in print in 1905 as *The Protocols of the Elders of Zion*. This document purported to be the 'secret' minutes of the first Zionist Congress held in the Swiss city of Basle in 1897 and consisted of 24 protocols outlining an imaginary blueprint for Jewish World domination. Freemasonry was implicated in this grand diabolic design as it was stated, 'Gentile masonry blindly serves as a screen for us [Jewry] and our objects ...' (Protocol 4, 2), and the entire document was allegedly signed by 'representatives of Zion of the 33rd degree'.

Although the Protocols are known to have been a sinister forgery they were fervently believed by the European Fascist powers and helped to prepare the ground for the Holocaust as well as the imprisonment and execution of thousands of Freemasons. During the Second World War, the Fascist regimes flooded the Middle East with anti-Jewish and anti-Masonic propaganda which was readily received in countries such as Iraq whose governments were openly sympathetic to the Nazis. Even the Grand Mufti of Jerusalem met and discussed such matters with Adolf Hitler. When such xenophobic tales became unacceptable in most parts of the world following the defeat of Fascism, the establishment of the modern state of Israel in 1948 offered new life to such ideas in the Middle East.

The Middle East

As relations between the new Jewish state and its Arab neighbours deteriorated successive Arab regimes began to outlaw Freemasonry which they perceived as a tool of 'Zionism'; Iraq in 1958; Egypt in 1964; Syria and the Lebanon in 1965. Indeed, the notion that the Jews, with their cohorts the Freemasons, formed part a gigantic world conspiracy grew in the aftermath of the Arab-Israeli six-day war of 1967. Consequently, when the Ba'ath

Socialist Party seized power in Iraq on 17 July 1968 the new regime unambiguously reiterated its hostility toward Freemasonry:

> Whoever promotes or incites Zionist principles, including Freemasonry, or belongs to any one of its institutions, or helps them materially or morally, or works in any form for achieving its purposes shall be executed.[1]

In neighbouring Iran a number of anti-Zionist writings also called for a holy war against the Jews. The paranoia of a number of Muslim Shi'ite authors was heightened due to the pro-Western policy of the Shah which tolerated the existence of liberal-minded groups such as the Bahais and the Freemasons. After the violent toppling of the Shah's regime in 1979 the new Islamic Republic immediately turned on Freemasonry and more than two-hundred masons were summarily executed, including Iran's former Prime Minister Amir Abbas Hoveyda.

In 1982, even though the Grand Master of the Grand Lodge of Israel was actually a Christian Arab, paranoia continued to hold sway. Article Thirty-two of the Palestinian Hamas (the Islamic Resistance Movement) Covenant of 1988 claimed that Zionism knew no bounds and that their 'scheme has been laid out in

the *Protocols of the Elders of Zion* ...'; in other words Freemasonry was once again implicated. Articles Seventeen and Twenty-two both mention Freemasonry and other groups. The latter states that 'the enemies' with their financial power 'formed secret societies, such as Freemasons, Rotary Clubs, the Lions and others...'

Hamas has openly accused Israel of controlling the world's wealth and its mass media, of instigating the French and Russian revolutions and the two world wars, in order to cynically promote Zionist objectives. A similar radical ideology also motivates the Lebanese, Iranian-backed Shi'ite Hizballah ('the Party of God'), which rose to prominence in the wake of the Israeli invasion of the Lebanon in 1982. And only last year, Egyptian state television broadcast a forty-one episode dramatisation based on *The Protocols*, despite repeated remonstrations from the Israeli government. According to Professor Robert Wistrich:

> Anti-Semitic conspiracy theories lie at the very heart of the Muslim fundamentalist and Arab nationalist worldview today linking plutocratic finance, international Freemasonry, secularism, Zionism, and Communism as dark, occult forces led by the giant octopus of international Jewry.[2]

Distressingly, such ideas have, in recent years, taken on a new and ultra-virulent form. On 27 July 1997 an English Arab-language magazine, *The Political Witness*, published an article entitled 'An in-depth look at Freemasonry and Zionism'. It began by presenting the official view as propounded by the United Grand Lodge of England before radically juxtaposing this with the teachings of Sheikh Adbul Aziz bin Baz who in the late 1970s, pronounced Freemasonry to be 'Zionist' and a 'very evil and dark fraternity'. Significantly, Sheikh Abdul Aziz bin Baz was for thirty years, until his death in 1998, Grand Mufti of Saudi Arabia, the country's highest religious authority. He also chaired the immensely powerful World Muslim League which has been described as 'the main conduit for Saudi government funds to Islamic causes worldwide' and preached in favour of the Taliban regime in the mosques and madrassahs (Sharia religious schools).

The Islamic Anti-Christ

While such high-level condemnation has gone unnoticed in much of the secular Western world an almost pathological hatred seems to be fomenting in the minds of a growing number of religious zealots.

In 1987, the Egyptian writer Sa'id Ayub published a book in which he linked Freemasonry with the *Dajjal*. Today such ideas are now being espoused by some Muslims living in the west who are being influenced by the teachings of radical preachers such as the English convert to Islam, David Musa Pidcock. In 1998, a sinister book, *Dajjal the AntiChrist*, was published in London. It baldly asserts that the *Dajjal* has taken over the world with the assistance of the Freemasons who, it says, control all large corporations, banks and Governments. Perturbingly, it also casts doubt upon the Holocaust.

Alarmingly, since September 11th 2001, an increasing number of Muslim and Christian fundamentalist websites seem to be inter-linked in a kind of unholy alliance; a sizeable number even offer complete transcripts of *The Protocols of the Elders of Zion*. They both agree on the existence of the anti-Christ and his forces and they both agree that Jesus will return to defeat the anti-Christ.

It is a tragic irony that the extremists who peddle such hatred do not ask themselves a basic question: if, as they assert, Freemasonry is in league with Zionism, how is it that thousands of Muslims have been Freemasons? Freemasons who include the Emir of Afghanistan, Habibullah Khan; the Algerian freedom fighter, Abd El Kader; and the great pan-Islamic religious reformers, Jamal al-Din al-Afghani and Shiekh Muhammad Abduh; As nonsensical as such conspiracy theories evidently are, they are nevertheless dangerous. For as Umberto Eco once noted, the gap between ecstatic vision and sinful frenzy is all too slight. ■

© Daniel Seymour, 2003.

[1] *Article 201 of the Iraqi Penal Code No. 111, amended by the Revolutionary Command Council of the Ba'th Socialist Party as amended in 1975.*

[2] *Robert S. Wistrich, Muslim Anti-Semitism: A Clear and Present Danger, The American Jewish Committee.*

The author would like to thank all those who helped in the preparation of this article.

AT A PERPETUAL DISTANCE

RICHARD LEIGH EXPLAINS HOW MYTH MIGHT DRAW US TOGETHER, OR DRIVE US APART

The remains of the famous bridge at Mostar, Bosnia-Herzegovina, which linked the town's Christian and Muslim communities. Built in 1566; destroyed by mortar fire in 1993.

AP

Since the beginning of the 20th century, Western man has become increasingly aware of the importance of what is called 'myth'. But myth is not confined to the legends of antiquity. More recent people, places, and events have assumed the status of myth – the 'Wild West' for America, Napoleon in France, John F. Kennedy and the unanswered questions pertaining to his death, and Diana, Princess of Wales.

The creation of myths is a spontaneous activity of the human psyche – as spontaneous as the generation of dreams. By means of myths, man not only seeks to understand his past, but also to shape his present and his future.

Ancient peoples did not devise myths to entertain and amuse their children. On the contrary, their myths were evolved to explain things – to account for reality. Myth was synonymous with science, philosophy, religion and history. Myth can be defined as *any systematic attempt to explain or account for reality*.

By such a definition, any system of beliefs can be described as a myth. All history, as we order it, is a form of myth. Christianity is a myth, Darwinism is a myth, psychology is a myth, atomic theory is a myth, the entire edifice of

modern science is a myth. All these things attempt to explain reality.

THE CHARGES OF A FREEMASON

Let a man's religion or mode of worship be what it may, he is not excluded from the order, provided he believe in the glorious architect of heaven and earth, and practise the sacred duties of morality...

Thus masonry is the centre of union between good men and true, and the happy means of conciliating friendship amongst those who must otherwise have remained at a perpetual distance.

We cannot escape the myth-making process. It is a necessary characteristic of

the human mind. Given this fact, it is all the more important that we recognise the myths we embrace – and recognise, too, their mythic nature. We live by myths, and we are responsible for them. We must therefore choose our myths wisely.

A myth will often supplant its prototype. It will then assume a greater reality for subsequent generations than the historical actuality which generated it. Thus, for example, the mythic figures of Richard III and Henry V, as depicted by Shakespeare, have a more vivid existence in our consciousness than the 15th century individuals who spawned them. The mythologised image of John F. Kennedy has eclipsed the man himself. The mythologised image of Diana, has eclipsed the more complex, and rather less saintly, woman.

Myths can be *personal*, or *collective*, or both. Each of us possesses a personal mythology – people, places, phases of our lives, other aspects of experience endowed by distance with a mythic status.

Personal myths may depend on the individual for perpetuation. Collective myths do not. Neither do they die. They reincarnate from age to age, re-enact themselves in a succession of new guises. The Lone Ranger – the solitary heroic individual who 'makes a difference' -- reflects the medieval knight errant, or the Japanese Samurai, or the protagonist of countless archaic sagas. The 'noble outlaw', exemplified by Bonnie and Clyde, is an avatar of Jesse James, who, in turn, in an avatar of Robin Hood.

In film and television, the modern guarantor of 'law and order' no longer rides a horse. He drives a car. But the basic pattern of his activities is essentially the same as it was centuries ago. The modern city is now the dangerous frontier between the known and the unknown, the perilous enchanted forest, where menace stalks every dark corner. Having destroyed the frontiers and forests of the past, man has proceeded to create new ones in the heart of urban existence.

If myths are constantly being re-enacted, they are also constantly being re-appraised, and either renewed or temporarily deflated. The native American Indian, once regarded as a terrifying savage, is now recognised as a tragically noble figure – the protagonist of an heroically lost cause, fighting to retain his land and his heritage. Conversely, Custer's 'Last Stand', once deemed a gallant martyrdom in a worthy cause, is now seen as a triumph of poetic justice – appropriate retribution visited upon a cruel man of foolhardy arrogance.

The process of re-appraisal, in whatever direction it occurs, reflects some degree of growth in the collective psyche. When myths are allowed to stagnate, however, it is symptomatic of cultural retardation. Such was the case in the American South prior to the 1960s. Such has been the case in Northern Ireland. Such has been the case in the Balkans.

Tribal and Archetypal Myths

Any myth possesses both *tribal* and *archetypal* aspects. Either of these can be emphasised at the expense of the other; and the myth itself will then become primarily tribal, or primarily archetypal.

An *archetypal myth* embodies universal constants of human experience and the human condition. Whatever its origins in a specific time or place, an archetypal myth will transcend such limitations and refer to something shared

Early twentieth-century illustration of Custer at the Battle of Little Big Horn. Initially a heroic figure, Custer is now seen as cruel and arrogant.

Denver Public Library, Western History Collection.

inwards towards self-confrontation and self-recognition, tribal myths point outwards, towards self-glorification and self-aggrandisement.

Such myths derive their energy from insecurity, from prejudice – and from the wilful creation of a scapegoat. Because they lack an internal core, they must fabricate an external adversary. Tribal

myths reflect an uncertainty about inner identity. In compensation, they define an external identity by means of contrast and negation. White thus becomes identified as everything that is not black, and vice versa. Everything that the enemy is, one is not. Everything that the enemy is not, one is.

It is myth of this kind, with all the attendant oversimplifications, that has operated in such contexts as Northern Ireland and the Balkans. It is myth of this kind that has generated and perpetuated antipathies there.

Tribal myths must be exposed in all their hollowness – must be stripped of their romantic aura and made to divulge the petty prejudice, self-aggrandisement, and self-deception at their core.

Each side must seek to correct something of its own respective mythic imbalances by learning something of each other's mythic mentality. In this manner, the mythic orientation that divides people can be shifted from a tribal to an archetypal basis – from the myths that separate men, to the myths that unify them, from what men extol at the expense of other men to what mankind as a whole shares.

This is an exerpt from a longer essay addressing the role of myth on Northern Ireland.

Richard Leigh is a novelist, antinomian Hermetic numinist, and co-author of a number of books including The Temple and the Lodge. *He is a co-founder and Trustee of* The Pushkin Prizes, *an educational awards programme in Ireland.*

CREATING NEW MYTHS IN LATIN AMERICA

Speaking of Latin America, writers such as Octavio Paz and Carlos Fuentes describe their continent as being 'in process of creating her origins'. In other words, it is futile to recapitulate, and thereby perpetuate, the conflicts of the past. It is futile to waste time and energy allocating blame. One must take the existing reality as a new beginning, and shape it into a future rooted in, but not determined by, the past.

It is out of this shared experience that the new myths must be created – myths which impart form and expression to a common trauma. Unless such myths are nurtured, people will continue to seek a mere 'political solution', which their very efforts will continue to render unattainable.

by humanity as a whole. Birth, coming of age, death, the traumas of war, the relationship with nature, the quest for meaning, the journey towards self-discovery – these are some of the themes that characterise archetypal myths.

They are themes that men share in all times and places. They offer a basis for mutual understanding and reconciliation. They point towards integration and wholeness.

Tribal myths, in contrast, emphasise not what men have in common, but what divides them. Tribal myths pertain to the vested interests of a specific group. They serve to exalt a specific tribe, culture or nation – at the expense of other tribes, cultures, or nations. Instead of pointing

Northern Ireland: two peoples in one land divided by tribal myth.　　PA

FOR THE SUPPORT
OF BROTHERS

ANDY DURR COMPLETES HIS LOOK AT WORKING-MEN'S ASSOCIATIONS
AND THEIR GREAT SOCIAL INFLUENCE

Late nineteenth century regalia of the Independent Order of Odd Fellows, Manchester Unity showing their colourful character in contrast

When in 1883 J.M. Baernreither, a Doctor of Law from Venice, visited Britain he got very excited. He found that 'there [had] gradually been formed an aristocracy of workmen, a kind of vanguard, which already counts many hundreds of thousand', actors in a 'gigantic' 'theatre' of 'associated life'. For Baernreither these Working-Men's Orders as he called them, were 'offshoots of, or in imitation of, Freemasonry'.

These Working-Men's Orders, Secret Orders or Affiliated Societies as they were better known, were numerous with over 150 of them recorded in 1874. They boasted an array of names, such as the Loyal Order of Alfred's, the Loyal United Anglo Saxon's, Orders of Britons, the Ancient Order of Comical Fellows, the Druids, the Foresters, the Free Gardeners, the Order of Ancient Grey Beards, the Odd Fellows, the Order of Old Friends, the Sons of Phoenix, the Rechabites, the Ancient Order of Romans, the Ancient Order of Shepherds, and more. Each, in turn, generated for themselves a mythological history; the 'Druids claimed links with Moses', the Foresters with the Garden of Eden, the Rechabites with ancient Egypt and the Odd Fellows with the Roman Empire.

The reality was that these associations had their roots in the eighteenth century but were institutions of the nineteenth. For brevity we will concentrate on the Odd Fellows, the most prolific: by the mid-nineteenth century there were over thirty-five different Orders of the Odd Fellows – such as the Nottingham Ancient Imperial, the Grand United, the Ancient Noble Order of United Bolton Unity, the Independent Order - Manchester Unity to name a few. Some were quite small, consisting of a handful of lodges but the largest, Manchester Unity, had over 4,500 lodges by the early 1890s. When compared with the Freemasons – United Grand Lodge of England at the same period mustered 2000 lodges – the numerical magnitude is impressive.

It has been argued that the Odd Fellows started to form lodges in London in the mid-eighteenth century. This may well be

Canterbury, Dover and Lewes with others in Bath, Shrewsbury, Windsor and Richmond.

Odd Fellows' Rituals

From what can be pieced together, the Odd Fellows were not 'offshoots' from Freemasonry but like many other organisations were 'in imitation of Freemasonry'. As with Freemasonry these lodges met in taverns and had food and drink at their meetings. Early reports of initiation rituals suggest that the candidate was blindfolded before he entered the lodge room. He was made to walk on 'loose planks [that formed] an imaginary road

pedestal on which was a skull and a scythe. All around him the other members of the lodge, also in white surplices, had their faces covered by 'grotesque masks'. The masks had the same effect as described in reports we have of early eighteenth century Freemasons grotesquely distorting their faces as the initiate's blindfold was removed. The importance of masks to the Odd Fellows can be seen in the images used in early nineteenth century certificates and pottery. Then, as with the Freemasons, he was given the secret signs and passwords. Following this lectures were given on the benefits of charity.

It is not until the late eighteenth century that we can get a feel of who these Odd

to the plainer regalia favoured by Freemasonry.   Andy Durr

the case since by the 1790s they were well enough known for publishers to engage engravers to produce caricatures of their initiation rites. What we do know is that by the end of the eighteenth century, they had lodges all around London under a Grand Lodge. This Grand Lodge was issuing dispensations for Lodges to be formed in the provinces; in the North with two in Sheffield, others in Birmingham, Wolverhampton and Liverpool; and in the South with lodges in Maidstone,

with rough knots left at intervals, some faggots of wood and bundles of cork, so arranged as to form rocks and forests' - giving much the same effect as early eighteenth century Freemasons being led blindfolded over a floor covered with sand. The Odd Fellow then made his obligation, his blindfold was removed and the presiding officer then confronted him in a 'long white beard and wig' and a long apron 'with the emblems of mortality painted'. This officer stood in front of a

Fellows were. In Sheffield, the Freemasons had two lodges, the first formed in 1765. By the 1790s they were joined by two Odd Fellows' lodges. The masonic lodges in Sheffield reflected the social composition that modern academic research is revealing across the country. They were predominantly composed of artisans and shopkeepers with a small tail of others: an attorney, a surgeon and some gentlemen. In this period the occupations of all four lodges mirrored Sheffield: there were cutlers, file-makers, grinders, hammer makers, silver-platers and a mix of other trades, not least working masons.

Functionally, what both the Freemasons and the Orders were doing at the end of the eighteenth and early nineteenth century was filling that gap in 'civil society' left by the demise of the Social or Religious Guilds at the end of the Reformation and the Craft Guilds at the beginning of the eighteenth century. They would bury their dead, look after widows and orphans and relieve members in distress, not least as they moved around the country from lodge to lodge seeking work. In public, they would wear their regalia at a brother's funeral and take part in the funeral rites. Both Freemasons and the Orders alike played a part in civic life. In Sheffield, at the opening of the General Infirmary in the 1790s, the thirty-five trade clubs took part, each carrying different coloured silk flags. The freemasons were preceded by two trumpeters dressed in white on white horses, a band, two Tylers with swords and, in the first of many banners, one of crimson silk depicting Faith, Hope and Charity.

Coming down another street were the Odd Fellows: 'The Most Noble Grand Master' with a scarlet sash, trimmed with silver lace, and his jewels suspended by a narrow ribbon of the same colour, carrying in his hand a gilt staff. The supporters wore green sashes, medals and gilt wands. An elegant flag, of white silk, was carried. It delineated many symbolic figures of the Order.

It was not just the large cities which held such parades: in Lewes, with the visit of the King and Queen, they had the trade clubs of the Carpenters and the South Saxon Lodge of the Freemasons and the Royal Clarence Lodge of the Odd Fellows stationed on either side of the carriage road in full regalia under their respective banners.

With the French Revolution and then war with France, the State passed a raft of legislation making national associations

Detail: centre of Odd Fellows apron.
Berkshire Masonic Library and Museum

illegal. The Freemasons only just escaped when they agreed to give the names of each lodge member annually to the local magistrates. The Freemasons then formed into the United Grand Lodge of England. Lodge meetings became separated from the eating of food and drinking. Regalia became much plainer as did the membership certificates. Gone were the glorious colour and the emblematic images. In simple terms we begin to witness perceived respectability and internalisation of English Freemasonry which helped to seduce the fast growing white-collar Victorian managerial and professional middle-class into membership.

Benefiting Society

The Orders, on the other hand, after the set-backs caused by the Napoleonic Wars, emerged in public from the second decade of the nineteenth century little altered.

What the Orders did was to recognise the down side of the astringent doctrine of laissez-faire economics which added to the

'ancestral hazards of illness, accident and old age, unaccustomed perils of unemployment and unpleasant anonymity of the new industrial centres'. To achieve their aims they needed to become legal, not least to safeguard their funds. The only route open to them was to register under the Friendly Societies Act of 1790 which, for them, was far too restrictive – it allowed the collection of funds but not the regalia, the rituals or the feasts. In the end, after a Select Committee took place at which they gave evidence, a new Bill was passed. While each lodge had to register their rules they were able to maintain their rituals of initiation, pass words and signs and their regalia, banners and other social activities that many would have liked to remove – there were complaints of the 'reckless extravagance, trumpery regalia' but as the Friendly Society actuary, Charles Hardwick, noted with some pleasure in 1856, 'no expenditure, however great, in the manner adopted by the modern "scientific" insurance companies, could have commanded much success, for the simple reason that it neither is, nor was, adapted to the education, taste, or condition of the people addressed. The "respectable" companies now generally employ an artist to design for them an allegorical emblem which they display as conspicuously as the Odd Fellows do' on their sashes and aprons.

But it was not just that. The Orders were all-round organisations with social activities, adult education classes and more. On a practical level there were a range of benefits not the least that lodges would employ their own doctor. By the late nineteenth century it would be the Odd Fellows' Hall in many towns that would be used by many different community organisations. It was the different Orders, Trade Unions, Churches, and Sunday Schools that would parade around the towns on annual Hospital Day collecting money.

These Working-Men's Orders, Secret Orders or Affiliated Societies were so important with over 12 million members that when Lloyd George started the embryo Welfare State in Britain with the first National Insurance Act of 1911, it was in partnership with these societies. If one skims through the pages of Bevridges' Report - the 1940s working document from which the Post-War Welfare State derived - so much of what these organisations had in place was a model which now forms part of our National Health Service.

Andy Durr was Mayor of Brighton and Hove, currently Visiting Research Fellow at the University of Sussex. Member of South Down Lodge, No.1797. This article summarises some points from a chapter of his book in progress, The English Artisan and Fraternal Association.

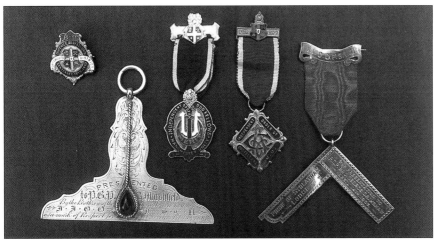

A set of symbolic jewels used by the Odd Fellows.
Berkshire Masonic Library and Museum

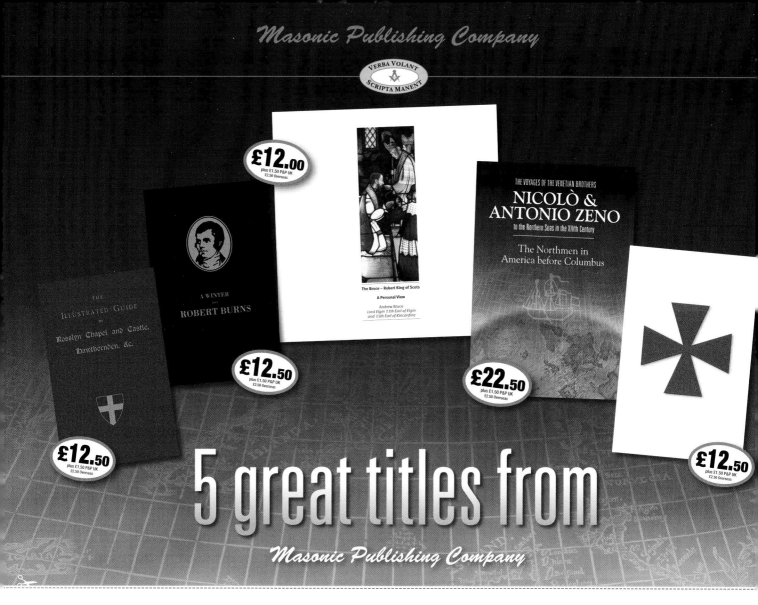

NOT A CRIME, BUT A SIN?

AXEL POHLMANN REPORTS ON DISCUSSIONS BETWEEN FREEMASONRY AND THE CATHOLIC CHURCH

The Catholic Cathedral of Würzburg, Bavaria.

For the first time in twenty years, Catholic priests and laymen met in an open and mostly friendly discussion with a representative of German masonry in November 2003.

There has been a long silence between the Catholic Church and masonic institutions in Germany since the Conference of German Bishops pronounced an unequivocal ban on Catholic membership in all masonic lodges in 1980. At the time, this came as a surprise to German Brethren, as a decade of seemingly friendly and open discussions between representatives of German and Austrian masonry and of the churches of both countries had originally led to a declaration of good will, instigated by the Viennese Cardinal König, and then carried to Rome to influence the new *Code of Canon Law*, the Catholic book of church law. The surprise was particularly bitter as the Church, in an aftermath of bad faith, styled the discussions as an inquest on masonry.

All hopes of Catholic masons then centred on the amendment of the Canon Law which until then had expressly condemned membership of masonic lodges, with the consequence of automatic excommunication and refusal of church burial. In fact, Canon Law was amended in 1983. Masonic lodges are no longer mentioned in church law, and excommunication may only strike members of any organisation which 'plots against the Church'. In fact, the Law only specifically threatens with interdiction someone 'who promotes or takes office in such an association.'[1]

Nevertheless, only days before the promulgation of the new Law in January 1983, the German Cardinal Ratzinger, head of the Congregation of the Doctrine of the Faith - previously known as the Inquisition - stated that membership in masonic lodges remained incompatible with being a Catholic.

At this point, German masons gave up any hopes of reconciliation of the Church with its 'lost Brethren'. The formula was and is: it is not we who have a problem with the Catholic Church, but the Catholic Church which has a problem with us.

Masonry and the Church

During November 2003 the Academy of the Catholic Church of Würzburg (Bavaria) held a one-day seminar, open to all interested persons, on the topic of 'Masonry and Church'. A Jesuit priest, Dr. Reinhold Sebott, professor of Church Law in Frankfurt, together with the director of the legal department of the Hamburg archdiocese, Klaus Kottmann, reported on the history of the difficult, sometimes violent, and always uneasy, relationship between Catholicism and Freemasonry, and on the current situation.

Axel Pohlmann, member of the Senate of the United Grand Lodges of Germany.

The Burkhard Haus, in the Cathedral precincts; site of the seminar on 'Masonry and Church'.

The writer, who is a member of the Senate of the United Grand Lodges of Germany and Chairman of its Committee on Foreign Relations, tried to give an outline of the many facets of masonry as a whole and German masonry in particular to an audience of 60 men and women, among them Catholic priests and a locally prominent member of the Christian Socialist Union party, the ruling political party in Bavaria.

It certainly came as a surprise to many listeners that both Catholic law experts hold the clear view that a Catholic's membership of a masonic lodge does not necessarily mean that he is not on good terms with his church. It seems important enough for Catholics all over the world to quote their result literally:

1. The Code of Canon Law as amended in 1983, in contrast to its predecessor, no longer threatens a Catholic who is a member of a masonic lodge with ecclesiastical sanction.
2. The declaration of the German bishops of 1980 on the incompatibility of membership of the Catholic Church with masonic membership was extended to the whole Church by the corresponding declaration of the Congregation of the Doctrine of the Faith in 1983.
3. These declarations mean that a Catholic's membership of a masonic lodge seems to be impossible and thus is disapproved on a moral, not necessarily criminal, basis.
4. Only by examining the individual case may the Church shed light on whether this Catholic by his convictions fulfils other criminal offences such as heresies or apostasies which might lead to consequences.
5. But when a Catholic in his conscience comes to the conclusion that the prohibition of membership (incompatibility) pronounced by the official Church is wrong, this decision

must be respected by the Church.

This statement is based on the distinction between a crime (a violation of church law) and a sin (a violation of moral law, in this case as defined by the Congregation of the Doctrine of the Faith). As church law does not specifically forbid masonic membership, and the law must be strictly interpreted, there can be no crime in being a member of a lodge - this does not include an association like the former Italian lodge P2. In contrast, a man sins if he knows that it is morally wrong to be a mason; he doesn't sin if he is convinced in his conscience that there is no moral wrong inherent in masonic

school of thinking on the subject.

Klaus Kottmann quoted the example of a Hamburg mason, a Catholic, who is a member of his local parish council. When he was elected into a council of the archdiocese, he was asked to step down by the authorities, but his membership in the parish council was never challenged.

Unfortunately, this is not every Catholic's view. Only in March this year a German lodge was confronted with the problems of one of its Brethren who is also a member of the 'CV', a Catholic brotherhood of students where you remain a member for life. The president of his local club having been advised of this Brother being a Freemason demanded immediate termination of his lodge membership, threatening to disclose his masonic connection to the public if he did not comply, a very substantial threat to somebody making his living as a sales manager with many contacts in his Catholic surroundings.

Cardinal Ratzinger, head of the Congregation of the Doctrine of the Faith, the modern successor to the Inquisition.   *Getty Images*

membership.

The statement of the experts on Church law may be rendered more comprehensible by an analogy: taking the birth-control pill is not a Church crime, but has been defined a sin by Pope Paul VI. However, the millions of Catholic women taking the pill for good reasons will not be excommunicated.

Naturally this is not the Church speaking, but two individual law experts. But they seem to represent the major

And what is in store for the future? When Father Sebott was asked whether contacts should be carried on, he said: 'Not as long as the men who made the decisions in the 1980s are in office, including the Pope.'

This statement may be negative for the present, but bears hope for the future.

[1] *The Code of Canon Law,* rev. trans. London (HarperCollins) 1997, p. 305, *Canon* 1374.

The exclusive world of the Holiday Property Bond...

The Holiday Property Bond's historic stately home in the Scottish Highlands

elegant palazzos, castles, villas and manor houses...

One of HPBs private villas on the island of Majorca

over 1,000 properties throughout the UK and Europe.

Stigliano, HPB's medieval hilltop village in the heart of the Tuscan countryside

HPB
The Holiday Property Bond

Enjoy a lifetime of rent-free holidays in beautiful places

The Holiday Property Bond allows you to buy a financial interest in over 1,000 of the finest apartments, villas and cottages in the UK and Europe. You can holiday in any of them rent-free for the whole of your life and then pass the benefit on to your children. It means that, for an initial investment of as little as £4,000, you can look forward to wonderful holidays in beautiful places, with top quality accommodation, year after year.

If you want more from your holidays, the Bond could be right for you. Browse our properties at **www.hpbforlife.com**. To receive our free brochure without obligation, clip the coupon or

CALL OUR FREE 24-HOUR INFORMATION LINE

0800 66 54 90
PLEASE QUOTE REF CODE EM19

THE MYSTERIES AND SECRETS

Our Craft is full of mystery, and has been so since the earliest recorded history of Freemasonry. In this it shares a rich heritage with many religious faiths, faiths which clothe their belief systems in mystery, so that allegory may be employed in uncovering and revealing the truths they contain. The ceremonial of Freemasonry refers to 'hidden mysteries of nature and science', by this relating to human nature, the inborn nature of each individual, and the knowledge of it, or science, which is required of each seeker after Truth. For Freemasons, the secrets guarded are not so much to do with signs and words, as with the truth in themselves that they reveal by progressing through the degrees.

Where exactly Freemasonry originated, and how, is open to much debate among historians, but one thing is clear: the forms and practices of Freemasonry contain much that has been observed in mystery systems since the dawn of time. In this section, we read of startling echos with ritual practice in ancient Egypt, and reference is also made to the mystical philosophy attributed to the legendary Hermes Trismegistus, whose name is the Greek rendering of the Egyptian God Thoth, the god of wisdom, knowledge, secrets and magic.

Many buildings throughout the world display symbols of mystery. In the following pages we learn of symbolic significance in style and architecture. We also learn of connections between medieval mystery plays and masonic ritual, both leading us to an awareness of what the allegories point to, namely insight that goes further than the surface appearance.

In these pages also we investigate ancient cultures going back almost to pre-history, to learn what they have to teach us about mysteries as old as the world itself. These mysteries came forward into ancient Egyptian and Greek philosophies, and so they have been handed down to us, lessons in the adoration of divinities, and routes by which Man may come to understand his own true nature. These were the pathways by which he came to understand, and to be in harmony with, the universe around him.

In another article we learn of other, new-world ancient cultures, and trace similarities and consonances between them and our present-day mystery pursuits. We learn of the linking of heaven and earth, the macrocosm of Divinity and the microcosm of Man. Celtic, Nordic and Mayan cultures all resonate with the same cultural harmony, indicating mysteries as old as time, and finding an echo in the masonic injunction for each individual to find his own centre.

Ancient Egy

"The usages and customs among Freemasons have ever borne a near affinity to those of the ancient Egyptians". Thus begins the explanation of the First Degree Tracing Board. Only an affinity? Or could there be something more?

The explanation continues: "Their philosophers…couched their systems of learning…under signs and hieroglyphical figures, which were communicated to their chief priests or Magi alone, who were bound by solemn oath to conceal them." (William Preston. *Illustrations of Masonry*. 1804. Reprint: Wellingborough, 1986. p.42) This does not reveal the full story. There are residues from ancient Egypt in Freemasonry, carried through the millennia by the mystical philosophy attributed to the legendary Hermes Trismegistus.

The early 15th century 'Charge', the *Cooke manuscript*, tells of "Hermes the philosopher" who, along with Pythagoras, restored knowledge to the world after the Flood, having found it written on two great pillars. (Matthew Cooke. *The History and Articles of Masonry*. London, 1861.pp 46-49) Hermes Trismegistus is the Greek rendering of the Egyptian god Thoth: god of wisdom, knowledge, secrets, magic and writing.

One of the great symbols of Hermetic thought is the *hexalpha* of two interlocking triangles. It represents the dynamic interweaving of heaven and earth, the visible and invisible. This symbol is prominent on the Royal Arch jewel. Below, on a scroll, is a Latin text which translates as: "Nothing wanting but the Key." Does this refer to something which has been lost and must be found? If so, it brings us back to Thoth-Hermes, the god of the Word.

The Greek Domination of Egypt

The Greek armies, led by Alexander the Great, invaded and defeated Egypt in 331 BC. After Alexander's death, one of his generals, Ptolemy, ruled as king, founding a dynasty

pt and Freemasonry

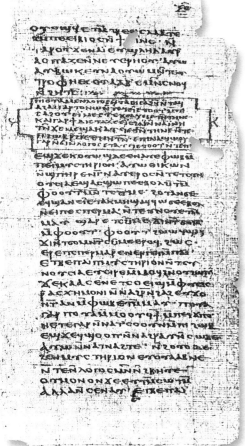

Coptic papyrus of the Hermetic *Asclepius*, buried near Nag Hammadi, Upper Egypt, in c.367AD

The Temple Mysteries

It is known that within the sacred chambers and halls of their temples, the Egyptian priests practised a technique of mystical initiation. They fostered, through stillness and silence, a deliberate incubation, a journey to the gates of death where questions might be put to the gods: a dialogue with the gods through visions and dreams.

It is clear that some of the ancient texts, rituals and spells, apparently aimed at the dead, were used to serve the living. For example, the oldest section of the Egyptian *Book of the Dead* is called "The Book of Coming Forth by Day". A more mystical rendering would be: "Instructions for coming forth into the Light". These are instructions for an initiation, not a funeral.

Shepherd and Son of God

The first of the philosophical books of Hermes is called, in its original Greek: *Poimandres*. This is a very revealing name. It means "Shepherd" and for many years scholars took this name to be the explanation: Hermes shepherding those on the way to wisdom. But there is more to it than this; it is a play on words. *Poimandres* derives from the ancient Egyptian *P-eime nte-re* which means "The Understanding, or Intelligence, of Re", the god of whom the sun is the visible presence. (Peter Kingsley. *Poimandres: the etymology of the name and the origins of the Hermetica* in the Journal of the Warburg and Courtauld Institutes, 56.1993, pp4-8.) Re was Lord of the Universe, the supreme god – and Thoth was his son, his representative.

As a result, it is now accepted that the books of Hermes reveal the inner secrets of the Egyptian temples. In particular, those concerning initiation. The *Poimandres* states bluntly to the aspiring initiate: "Now fix your thought upon the Light and learn to know it." (*Corpus Hermeticum*, Book I).

Freemasonry brings men into a more moral and more socially responsible way of life. But it does more than this. Masonic rituals gently, but methodically, guide and initiate each man through the degrees until, symbolically, the limits of mortality are brought to the forefront of

Greek copy of the *Poimandres*, brought to Florence in 1460, initiating an Hermetic Renaissance

his attention. Once there, he is confronted with the question of who he really is, and he is asked to fix his thoughts upon the glimmering ray of Light from above. This symbolic instruction is almost identical to the statement in the *Poimandres*.

We have in Freemasonry, I believe, a distant, but actual, echo of those ancient mysteries: an echo of ancient Egypt.

Michael Baigent is a Freemason, author and co-author of many best-selling books on astrology, Freemasonry, the Knights Templar and the western mystery traditions. He has just completed a new book on the Inquisition. Photographs by the author

which ruled for over 300 years, finally ending with the death of Cleopatra in 30 BC. During this era, Greek culture dominated; Egyptians feared that theirs would be lost. Accordingly, Egyptians trained in the Greek culture began recording and revealing their wisdom, so long concealed in the temples.

Out of this world, during the first and second centuries AD, came the *Hermetica*: a collection of texts supposedly written by Hermes Trismegistus. But their true origin was recorded. The Syrian Iamblichus, writing in the early fourth century AD, revealed that the books circulating under the name Hermes, although written in the Greek philosophical style, contained true Hermetic doctrines. They had been translated from the Egyptian language, he said, by those educated in the Greek philosophical tradition. (Iamblichus. *On the Mysteries*. VIII.4. Trans. Thomas Taylor, Chthonios reprint, 1989.)

FORBIDDEN TECHNOLOGY

ROBERT TEMPLE REVEALS
IMPORTANT ANCIENT ARTIFACTS WHICH ARE NOT ALLOWED TO EXIST.

Robert Temple, London, 2001. (Photo: Michael Baigent)

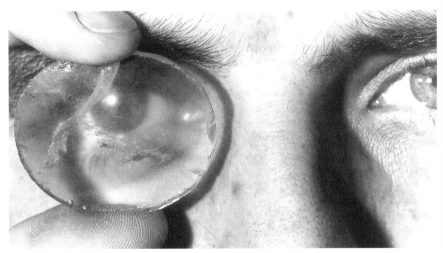

The 8th century BC 'Layard Lens' from ancient Assyria. Ground to correct for astigmatism, it was undoubtedly used as a monocle. (Photo: Robert Temple)

Technology is forbidden when it is not allowed to exist. It is easy to forbid technology to exist in the past because all you have to do is to deny it. Enforcing the ban then becomes a simple matter of remaining deaf, dumb, and blind. And most of us have no trouble in doing that when necessary.

I have discovered an avalanche of evidence proving the existence of a very remarkable ancient technology, one which is well and truly forbidden because it indicates that our ancestors were not idiots, and as we all know very well, if we ever admitted that, the illusion of progress would be seriously imperilled.

The technology I have discovered is optical. I have found in museums all over the world, more than 450 ancient optical artefacts, most of them lenses, but in any case, magnifying aids.

These ancient lenses generally magnify about 1.5 or 2 times. Heinrich Schliemann, the 19th century discoverer of Troy, excavated 48 rock crystal lenses at Troy. This is one of the largest hoards of ancient lenses ever found. These were unfortunately lost for many decades because they were with the missing Trojan gold hoard which disappeared from the Berlin Museum at the end of the Second World War. In recent years the Russians have admitted that the Red Army stole the gold and it is all in Moscow today. The 48 lenses are with these gold artefacts.

Another large number of crystal lenses exists in Crete, mostly found at Knossos. And yet another hoard exists at Ephesus, in Turkey, though those ones are very unusual because they are concave lenses used to correct for myopia (short-sightedness), some shrinking images by as much as 75%. Most ancient lenses are convex and were used to magnify. At Carthage there are 14 glass lenses and two of rock crystal stored in a drawer in the museum; they have apparently never

This pair of plano-convex glass lenses was found in a stone sarcophagus at Carthage in 1902.　*(Photo: William A. Graham)*

been displayed. Egypt too has examples one pair of glass lenses was excavated from the wrappings of a mummy and obviously were used as spectacles except that loops around the ears for modern-style spectacles seem not to have been invented in ancient times. So these may have had some kind of nose loop or may have been held as a lorgnette.

The earliest evidence of optics

The oldest evidence of a sophisticated optical capability which I have found goes back as far as 3300 BC. An ivory knife handle was excavated in the 1990s from a predynastic grave of that date at Abydos in Egypt. It belonged to a king. It bears microscopic carvings which could only have been made with, and can only be seen with, a magnifying glass.

The oldest actual lenses which I have found are from the 4th and 5th Dynasties of ancient Egypt and date to perhaps 2500 BC. These are perfectly ground and polished convex crystal lenses which are used as eyes in statues of that date. One such statue is in the Louvre, in Paris, but the rest are in the Egyptian Museum in Cairo.

There are many ancient classical texts which specifically describe both magnification and works produced under magnification by craftsmen. For instance, the Roman author Seneca speaks of magnification, and Cicero, Pliny and others described microscopic works of art. I have gathered together all of these texts in my book, *The Crystal Sun*. It is from Cicero's description of a miniature version of the *Iliad* so small that it could fit inside a walnut shell that our modern expression, 'in a nutshell', came into use, passed on by Shakespeare's *Hamlet* into modern usage.

The 'blindness' of experts.

I even own an ancient lens myself which I was able to purchase from a friend who collected ancient objects. He had no idea that it was a lens, but he bought it because it had an archaic Greek carving of a flying figure on it. In fact, that wonderful carving in no way interferes with the magnifying properties of the lens, since it is transparent. It was probably added to the lens at a later date in its history, but it offers a convenient way to provide a minimum date for the object.

I took it along to the Greek and Roman Antiquities Department of the British Museum for a dating of the carving. I was told there that the object was a 'fake' because it was made of glass. After much prodding, I got the 'expert' to say that if the object had been crystal, the carving would date from the 6th or 7th century BC. Of course, I didn't believe for a minute that the object was glass, so I took it to the Natural History Museum for an X-ray diffraction analysis. This proved that the object was rock crystal, and hence genuine. The interesting part of the comment by the British Museum expert who insisted my lens was a fake was: 'they didn't make these then, it can't be real'.

No, none of this can be real.

At the end of this article is a photo I took of a painting of an ancient Greek of the 5th century BC using a telescope. This painting is from a pot excavated at the Acropolis about twenty years ago. The pot fragment has been on display in the Acropolis Museum at Athens for many years, where no one appears to have `seen' it. Many ancient lenses are on display in museums around the world, falsely labelled of course as `counters', `buttons', `gems' and so on, and no one `sees' them either.

What is the answer to this? I call it *consensus blindness*. People agree not to see what they are convinced cannot exist. `Everyone knows' that there was no optical technology in antiquity, so consequently when you come across its,

Ancient British Lens in the Natural History Museum, London. It was originally mounted in a metal band.　*(Photo: Robert Temple)*

The Cairo lens; of Roman glass, around 3rd century AD. Now in the Egyptian Museum.
(Photo: Robert Temple)

A Greek rock crystal lens from the Mycenaean period in the Athens Archaeological Museum.
(Photo: Robert Temple)

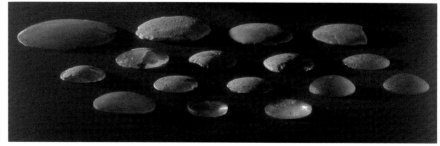

The 16 plano-convex lenses excavated at Carthage; 2 of rock crystal and 14 of glass.
(Photo: William A. Graham)

Wooden statue from the 5th Dynasty (2498-2345 BC) in the Egyptian Museum. The inlaid eyes are perfectly ground convex crystal lenses.   (Photo: Robert Temple)

A wooden statue of the 5th Dynasty Egyptian, Ka-aper, from his tomb at Saqqara. Ground and polished plano-convex rock crystal lenses form the irises of his eyes.   (Photo: Robert Temple)

Microscopic carving of a pre-dynastic ivory knife handle from Abydos, Egypt. It dates from 3300 BC and is the oldest evidence of optical technology known.

(Photo: Günter Dreyer and the German Institute of Archaeology at Cairo)

staring you in the face, you go blind. End of conflict.

In fact, optical technology in antiquity sometimes reached extraordinary heights. The Layard Lens in the British Museum dates to the 8th century BC and was excavated in the throne room of the Assyrian King Sargon II's palace in what is today called Iraq. I have carried out a full technical analysis of this lens. I have been able to demonstrate that this rock crystal lens, now cracked and considerably damaged, was originally a perfect convex lens with a flat (`plane') base, which was ground in a special way known to opticians as `toroidal', - a technique only available for the public since about 1900. Such grinding produces lenses to correct for individual cases of astigmatism. It would be possible to go out into the street today and find someone whose astigmatism was perfectly corrected by the Layard Lens. It was clearly used as a monocle. It perfectly fits the eye aperture, as we can see in the illustration. It is most extraordinary that such a high technology existed in the 8th century BC. And not a single Assyriologist has acknowledged the publication of my study of this important object except for the one who encouraged me in the first place; he was curious as to what the results would be. So it appears that the community of Assyriologists find it convenient not to `see' my book.

Viking and British Lenses

Another example of optical technology being taken to extraordinary lengths I found in Sweden. The Eastern Vikings had a very extensive crystal lens industry. More than a hundred lenses survive in Sweden and the surrounding countries. None, however, are known from Norway; the Western Vikings were apparently not let in on the secret.

The Scandinavian archaeologists were delighted at my findings, and they have translated some of my work into Swedish and published it already in a leading archaeological journal there. They had no reason to be `blind' because they loved the fact that I could show that their Vikings were even more interesting than they already thought. I discovered that the Vikings had a microscopic optical industry: they were grinding and polishing lenses the size of rain drops which could magnify three times. This is an astonishing feat and one would marvel at it even today.

There are many old British lenses as well. I found two collections of them stored in geology collections. Some of them are extraordinarily clever, and have

projecting points at the back which I termed `resting points', to enable them to be use by craftsmen for magnifying while keeping both hands free; the point does not interfere with the magnifying properties. A similarly ingenious design was produced at Troy, where one crystal lens was perforated with a central hole, through which the craftsman could insert his carving tool, while the magnification all around was undisturbed.

Ancient telescopes were not a difficult invention once they had the lenses. All you have to do is to hold up a lens in each hand and look through them both at once: thus you have a rudimentary telescope. Even though the image is inverted – it takes a third lens to flip it right way up – this makes no difference if you are, for instance, studying the surface of the moon or looking at the stars. No one can tell if a star is right way up or upside down – it all looks the same. In *The Crystal Sun* I suggest that primitive telescopes were used in ancient Britain and that Stonehenge was an observatory. I suggest that the outer trilithons may have acted as a base for a perishable dome of wood or wattle, and that the inner trilithons, which are higher, were to serve as the base for a perishable wooden observation platform facing east, for the observation of lunar risings.

Or are such thoughts forbidden?

©**Robert Temple**
Robert Temple has a degree in Sanskrit and Oriental Studies. He is the author of nine books, including, The Sirius Mystery. *He worked with Joseph Needham of Cambridge University on the history of Chinese science and wrote,* The Genius of China. *See the review of his,* The Crystal Sun, *in this issue.*

Ancient Greek painting on a pot, dating from 5th-4th century BC, revealing the use of a telescope. In the Acropolis Museum, Athens.   (Photo: Robert Temple)

TL Risk Solutions

Insurance From
A **Different**Perspective

At TL Risk Solutions, we understand that your needs are as individual as you are.

With over 40 years of experience in providing risk consultancy and tailored insurance solutions, our traditional approach to your insurance needs ensures you receive advice designed specifically to protect you.

We won't confuse you with insurance jargon or simply recommend off-the-shelf policies. What we will do is listen to you as an individual, deliver tailored and practical insurance advice, and provide you with a dedicated advisor so you always receive the personal service you need.

We believe in developing a close relationship with you, and pride ourselves on the exceptional standard and quality of our services.

We can provide cover for a variety of personal insurances, including:

- Mid & High Net Worth Homes
- Second Home & Holiday Homes
- Overseas Properties
- Residential Let Properties
- Beach Huts & Chalets
- High Value & Classic Motors
- Yachts & Small Craft
- Annual Travel & Personal Accident

Help Support a Masonic Charity

At TL Risk Solutions, our service and support goes beyond the help and advice we provide around your insurance needs – that's why whether you purchase a new policy, renewal or mid-term adjustment through us, we will make a discreet donation of half the commission we receive, to a charity supported by the Masons.

Receive High Street Vouchers With Every New Policy!

As a special 'thank you' to readers of Freemasonry Today, we are offering High Street Vouchers with every new insurance policy you purchase through TL Risk Solutions today.

To find out more about our services, receive a quotation, or apply for your insurance, simply contact one of our advisors on the details below:

 0845 671 0669

 enquiries@tlrisksolutions.com

 www.tlrisksolutions.com

Don't forget to quote reference '**Freemasonry**' in your application so we know to make our charity donation and send your vouchers!

Edfu: The initiate (Pharaoh) knocking three times on the door of the inner sanctum in order to be admitted by Horus

The Mysteries existed for a simple reason: to satisfy the desire of those who wished to know the truth of who we are, what happens at death and what Divinity is. Certain Mysteries achieved widespread fame: those of Demeter and Kore at Eleusis for example (dating from at least the 6th century BC), and those of Isis and Osiris (from perhaps thousands of years earlier). Then there were the Mysteries of Mithras, of Dionysus, Bacchus, Orpheus, the Great Mother and many others. And as evidence slowly emerges, even the Great Pyramid is being seen as a place of initiation rather than burial.

The Lovatelli Urn, Rome. It depicts scenes from the Mysteries of Eleusis. Here the candidate is veiled prior to hjs initiation

A classical writer, Themistios wrote that when death comes, "the soul suffers an experience similar to those who celebrate great initiations...Wanderings astray in the beginning, tiresome walkings in circles, some frightening paths in darkness that lead nowhere... And then some wonderful light comes to meet you..." (Burkert.W. *Ancient Mystery Cults*. Cambridge (Mass.) 1987, p.91 and p.162.n.11)

The Mysteries demanded complete secrecy from its initiates. This demand was taken very seriously at Eleusis. Those who failed to keep their vow to do so would face the death penalty. For this reason we have no direct 'inside' information giving details of the rituals, passwords, texts and inner meaning of the symbolism of the secret rites. We have only fragments from observers who saw those of the events which occurred beyond the inner sanctum and a few tantalising hints from initiates or from scholars who had gleaned a little of what the secrets involved.

Know thyself; nothing in excess; remember to keep silent. *From the Mysteries of Eleusis, Greece.*

Inside the Mysteries

The only 'insider' account is by an initiate into the mysteries of Isis, author Lucius Apuleius of Madaura. Even so, he does not violate his oath of secrecy. Nevertheless, he does reveal what occurred:

"...listen, and believe that what you hear is true. I approached the very edge of death and stood upon Proserpine's doorstep, I returned home travelling through all the elements; in the middle of the night I saw the sun, a bright shining and glittering light; I entered the presence of the gods of the lower-world and the gods of the upper-world and adored them from close by."
(from *Metamorphoses*, author's trans.)

THE MY

Veiled in allego by sy

Michae

His request for us to listen has a deeper meaning. The Latin word *audi*, translated as 'listen' has the further meaning of 'to learn' or 'understand'. Apuleius is challenging us to listen behind the words and symbolism to know the true meaning of this short 'exposure'. He travelled to the gates of death - Proserpine (in Greek, *Persephone*) was the wife of Hades, king of the

STERIES

and illustrated

bols

Baigent

The shrine or naos of the god in inner sanctum (Edfu). The reverse of this structure has been left rough and unformed

Underworld. There, in the middle of the night, he experienced the bright mystical light; he was humble in the presence of Divinity. Born again, he celebrated the next day as his birthday by a banquet with his friends.

Parallels with Freemasonry

While we cannot argue that Freemasonry directly derives from the ancient mysteries, or even that it has retained certain practices carried down through the centuries (it might have done, but we cannot point to any proof of this) we can show that many parallels of symbolism exist. In some way Freemasonry shares a symbolism in common with these ancient rites. And how much does Freemasonry share the understanding of that symbolism? We cannot answer this question definitively but it is certainly plausible to suggest that an understanding of the hidden meanings managed to survive the centuries.

The mystical rites of Eleusis lasted for three days. We can see a similarity in our own rituals: each of the three degrees in Freemasonry is a symbolic day; each is opened at sunrise in the east for work by the Master

> The cults of the Mysteries of the ancient world allowed initiates to see beyond the gates of death. And then return, bearing whatever gifts they were able.

and closed with sunset in the west by the Senior Warden. And there is a further mysterious parallel here, of course, which relates to Christian mysticism and the three days of Easter.

The Temple of Edfu

Inside, standing in front of the far wall, is the *naos*, the carved shrine for the statue of the god. This is a finely shaped and polished solid block of stone several yards high. But this *naos* at Edfu is curious, the rear of it is rough and unfinished; just as it was when it was taken from the quarry. This combination of rough unfinished stone, out of which emerges the visible smoothed and highly polished structure suggests a parallel symbolism with the rough and the smooth ashlars present in every lodge.

In Freemasonry, the rough ashlar symbolises the unrefined and ignorant man. The smooth ashlar represents the man who, by virtue of his

The rising of the sun ended the rites of initiation in the Mysteries. Temple of Karnak, sunrise

masonic progress, has become refined and perfected: able to support the harmony of society. It is reasonable to ask whether the ancient Egyptians at Edfu had in mind a similar symbolism of an initiate's progression when they carved the *naos* for Horus.

For the Mysteries touched the very centre and source of life itself; that too is Freemasonry's aim - if we take the Third Degree charge seriously. It would be very odd indeed if our symbolism did not carry some of those same hidden meanings which were most valued by the ancients.

The inner chapel in the Temple of Dendra, dedicated to the mysteries of Hathor

MYSTERY SET IN STONE

Matthew Scanlan investigates
THE TRIANGULAR LODGE OF RUSHTON

The Triangular Lodge showing the entrance in the south-east.

On the edge of the village of Rushton, in the heart of the Northamptonshire countryside stands a mysterious stone edifice. Three stories high and illuminated by three windows on each side of each story, the building forms a perfect equilateral triangle. Each face has three gables rising to three pinnacles constructed from three stone triangles, and the roof is crowned with a three-sided chimneystack: the whole building is based around the number three.

The triangular lodge was the brainchild of Sir Thomas Tresham, a Catholic recusant in the reign of Queen Elizabeth I. He was born into a landed Northamptonshire family in the mid sixteenth-century, and was only fifteen years old when, in 1559, he succeeded his grandfather to the family estates. Significantly, his grandfather had been one of the first magnates to proclaim Catholic Queen Mary on her succession to the throne on the 18 July 1553, and guarded her on her march to London.

When Mary resolved to restore the Order of St. John in England, suppressed by her father, King Henry VIII, Tresham was appointed as grand prior. However his appointment was short lived, for he died within two years, to be succeeded by his grandson of the same name.

The young Sir Thomas Tresham was raised as a Protestant, but in 1580 was converted to Roman Catholicism by a Jesuit, Robert Parsons, thereafter he received numerous visitations from missionary priests. On 18 August 1581, he was arrested, charged with harbouring Jesuit, Edmund Campion, and imprisoned. He remained in confinement for almost seven years. In 1586 many believed he would join the Babington conspirators as the ground was being prepared for a Spanish invasion, but though staunchly Catholic, he did not care for Spanish aggression. After the defeat of the Spanish Armada, Tresham was finally released on bail on the 29 November 1588, after swearing his allegiance to Queen Elizabeth, though her wily spymaster, Sir Thomas Walsingham, kept him under constant surveillance. He was correct to do so for Tresham's son was later involved with Guy Fawkes in the Gunpowder Plot; it is

The strange code, 5555, above the entrance.

A Jewish Menora and monogram of Christ on the chimney, south-east side.

The entablature on the north reads: QUIS SEPARABIT NOS A CHARITATE CHRISTI? - 'Who shall separate us from the love of Christ?' *(Romans, VIII, v 35)*, and on the gables are the Pelican in its piety and the Raven, both associated with Christ as they bring spiritually nourishing food. A Raven is typically associated with bringing a loaf of bread to holy men in the desert, such as Elijah or St. Anthony.

In medieval alchemy it symbolised the death or beginning of the work called the *"nigredo"*. The contemporaneous English alchemist, Edward Kelly (1555 - 1599) wrote, '*The beginning of our work is the Black Raven, which like all things that are to grow and receive life, must first*

said that the conspirators met in the triangular lodge.

Over the next few years, Tresham used his freedom to concentrate on a number of building projects, including the market-house at neighbouring Rothwell, alterations to the family home of Rushton Hall, and a cruciform house at Lyveden New Bield. Yet it was the triangular lodge at Rushton that was to prove his most remarkable architectural legacy.

Built between 1593-5, it stands as a testimony to Tresham's stubborn adherence to the old Catholic faith, and the repetitious use of the number three emphasised his devotion to the Trinity. Each side of the lodge measures exactly

thirty-three feet in length, and just below the gables, a frieze carries an inscription consisting of thirty-three letters. Entrance to the lodge is from the southeast and relates to the Old Testament. It carries the appropriate inscription: APERIATUR TERRA ET GERMINET SALVATOREM - 'Let the Earth open and bring forth a Saviour'. *(Isaiah, XLV, v 8)*. Above the door is the strange code 5555, which, appears to allude to Bede's calculation of the date of Creation, 3962 BC: if this is added to the starting date of the Lodge, 1593, it gives 5555. Above this are the Jewish seven-branched Menora and a hexagon containing the seven eyes of God.

An example of the ubiquitous Tau crosses.

putrefy'. The reference here is to a spiritual death of the former self, and the accompanying sacrificial symbol of the Pelican echoes this. From the early Christian centuries, the Pelican was believed to gouge blood from herself which she then gave to her offspring. Consequently medieval theologians, philosophers and alchemists likened the bird to Christ, and the alchemical stage was said to issue like 'a fountain of blood from the white stone'. Even St. Augustine had earlier stated that the Pelican had '*a great likeness to the body of Christ, whose blood nourishes us*'. Today this symbol is associated with the 'high' degrees of modern Freemasonry.

Following in thematic sequence, the southwest side proclaims, CONSIDERAVI OPERA TUA DOMINE ET EXPAVI - 'I have considered thy works, O Lord, and been afraid' - *(Habbakuk, III, v 2)*, words which derive from the Good Friday Mass. They are accompanied with the symbols of a Dove upon a coiled serpent *(Uroborus)* with a hand issuing forth from a Sun Appropriately, on the chimney above, a Tau cross rises out of a chalice which is enclosed within a pentagon, and the Tau also features on each corner of the lodge.

Below the spout, a uroborus enclosing a triangle with a point at the centre, south-west side.

A Pelican in its Piety, north gable

Evidently this mystical cross was of importance to Tresham, as he also had it carved in verse relating to the Crucifixion upon the walls of the Oratory of Rushton Hall. Once again there is no need to speculate upon its meaning as the verse reads: ECCE SALUTIFERUM SIGNUM THAU NOBILE LIGNUM - 'Behold the salvation-bearing symbol Thau, the noble Tree of Life'. On the north side of the chimney is the Agnus Dei or lamb of God with the inscription, ECCE - 'Look', while on the southwest is the sacred monogram IHS under a cross, with three nails contained inside an octagon, signifying rebirth and regeneration - themes which once again echo modern Freemasonry.

A dove sitting upon a uroborus enclosing a sphere, south-west gable.

The Builders

One might easily think that the story ends there, except that this strange edifice offers yet more surprises. Examination of the extant accounts relating to Tresham's building endeavours, reveals that he

employed a number of *'ffreemasons'* to execute his extraordinary projects. The term 'freemason' was a corruption of 'free-stone mason', and is first recorded in England towards the end of the fourteenth century as *'lathomos vocatus ffre maceons'*. All the great fifteenth and early sixteenth century examples of English perpendicular architecture, were the result of these ingenious craftsmen, and the master who vaulted the magnificent ceiling at King's College Chapel, Cambridge, bound himself to *'kepe continually 60 fre-masons workyng'*. Great changes took place as a result of the Reformation, when most craftsmen began to rely upon the patronage of rich merchants or the landed

The seven eyes of God within a hexagon, south-east side.

aristocracy, working on their country houses and monumental tombs. In spite of these changes, the term survived. In 1578, Sir Thomas Tresham contracted with the local 'freemason' William Grumbold to undertake *'certaine workes to be done at Rothwell Crosse'* market-house, and the craftsmen also employed

on the building of Rushton Hall, Liveden, and the triangular Lodge itself are all recorded as being 'freemasons'.

Clearly these craftsmen would have been familiar with the symbolism used to adorn the Lodge, however the key question remains: did they have symbolic ceremonies to accompany their ancient tradition? Many arguments have been advanced as to why symbolic or ceremonial Freemasonry cannot have existed at this time. John Hamill and R. A. Gilbert state in *Freemasonry, A Celebration of the Craft*, .. 'there is as yet no evidence of operative lodges in England after 1500.'[1] Contrary to this assertion, at Westminster in 1532 it is recorded that a lock and *'shutting plate'* were, *'set upon a dore belonging to one of the lodgies wherein certein of the masons worke.'* In 1582, a new timber bridge is recorded as on the channel at Westminster against the end of *'the masons' lodge'*, and five years later some tiling was done on *'the Masons Lodge next to Charing Crosse'*. In 1602, the rooms adjoining the Masons' lodge in Westminster were also rendered with lime and hair. Masonic manuscripts of the period, known as 'Old Charges', also refer to lodges and contain a traditional apocryphal history of the craft that typically embraces biblical and classical antecedents, including the sons of Noah, Euclid, Pythagoras and Solomon. Clearly Sir Thomas Tresham and the craftsmen he employed were both extremely interested in biblical themes. However, deciding who exactly influenced who is one of those enduring mysteries that still surround the origins of our modern craft.

[1] J.M. Hamill & R.A. Gilbert, *Freemasonry - A Celebration of the Craft* (Herts, 1992), p. 22

Text and photograhs © Matthew Scanlan, May, 2001.

Matthew Scanlan MA is a doctoral student currently completing a book on the Origins of Freemasonry and the related Templar legends. He is a member of the Duke of Wharton Research Lodge, No.18, Barcelona, and the Centro Estudios Historicos de la Masoneria Espanola (CEHME) based at Zaragoza, Spain. He is also International Editor of Freemasonry Today and editor of the Canonbury Masonic Research Centre's forthcoming transactions, *The Canonbury Papers*.

NAVEL OF THE WORLD

PAUL DEVEREUX ENCOURAGES US TO SEEK THE CENTRE

Many ancient cultures possessed the notion of there being a symbolic world centre – a "world navel" or *omphalos* as it was called in the Classical age. Although strange to us, of all the ruling themes of ancient thought, it was one of the most fundamental and pervasive.

The ancient mind perceived the world navel motif at all scales. At the largest, cosmic, level the north or pole star, Polaris, was often its symbol for peoples in the northern hemisphere, because it marks the fixed position around which the heavens appear to rotate. Even as far south as Vijayanagara, India, the axis of the ancient royal city is aligned towards Polaris, which at that latitude appears low in the sky, shining above the Virabhadra temple on the summit of a nearby holy hill.

At the next stage down, the landscape or territorial level, the world navel took many guises. The tree offered itself as one symbolic image of the motif in the form of an *axis mundi* linking heaven and earth. The Yakuts of Siberia, for instance, conceived of a magical tree at the "golden navel of the Earth", but the most famous northern World Tree is doubtless the Norse *Yggdrasil*, the mighty ash tree, where the gods met. The pagan Celts, like many other peoples, made this mythic tree tangible in the form of a pole: for example, in the Iron Age ritual landscape of Navan Fort, in County Armagh, Northern Ireland, a massive oak post 36 feet tall was erected. The tree from which it was fashioned was 200 years old at the time it was felled, and had probably been a sacred tree. The giant post would have formed a powerful ritual landmark. It is quite likely that the Christmas tree and the European maypole are latter-day reflexes of sacred trees and the ceremonial poles that derived from them.

Versions of the *axis mundi*, in the form of a pole or tree, also figured in several American traditions. The ancient Maya envisaged a mythic "Central Tree", and deep within their ritual cave of Balankanche, in the Yucatan, the Maya found its physical image in a remarkably tree-like fused stalactite-stalagmite, which they ardently venerated.

The fused stalactite-stalagmite in the depths of the Mayan ritual cave of Balankanche, Mexico. The Maya venerated it as a magical natural representation of the World Tree for centuries before a rock-fall sealed the entrance for a thousand years. When archaeologists gained entry in 1959, they found censers and offering bowls still laid out around the stone `tree'.

Hills and mountains provided another landscape feature suitable for symbolising the ancient motif of the world navel. In pagan Ireland, the hill of Uisnecht, Westmeath, has on it slopes a large boulder called *Aill na Mireann*, the Stone of Divisions. An ancient text refers to this stone as "the navel of Uisnecht". The most famous World Mountain of all, though, is Mount Meru, the mythical sacred peak of both Hindu and Buddhist cosmologies. Its physical representative is Mount Kailas in the Himalayas, which

The centre of England? Though a modest eminence, Croft Hill in Leicestershire is nevertheless prominent in the flat landscape surrounding it and extensive views are to be had from its rocky summit.

pilgrims still circumambulate, often in the arduous form of repeated prostrations.

Contemplating the National Navel

Many lands have an optimum geographical centre point which may or may not coincide with the symbolic territorial *omphalos*. Because of this, the true location of the English or British navel is an uncertain matter. The Venerable Bede identified the site of Lichfield Cathedral in Staffordshire as the centre of England, but the place often touted as the geographical centre of England today is the village of Meriden, Warwickshire. The Roman surveyors, on the other hand, identified the centre as Venonae, where they placed the crossing point of two of their great roads, Watling Street and the Fosse Way. This is now known as High Cross, an isolated point on the Warwickshire-Leicestershire border where four parishes meet.

Of all the candidates for the British *omphalos*, my personal preference is for the little-known Croft Hill, a few miles southwest of Leicester. In writing about this solitary hill in 1879, local historian, T.L.Walker, observed that in ancient Gaul there was said to have been a "mesomphalos" in the centre of the country, on the River Loire, where the Druids met. "This Mesomphalos was an isolated hill in the midst of a plain . . . The idea of such a Mesomphalos was said to have been borrowed from Britain."

Walker was sure that Croft Hill was this lost British mesomphalos. There is strong supportive evidence for his idea in that not only does Croft Hill stand near the River Soar, it is close to the village of Leir, a version of "Loire". Croft Hill was also important in past times: in A.D. 836, King Wiglaf of Mercia held a council there attended by dignitaries including the

In 1711, a pillar was erected in remembrance of the Roman centre of Britain, Venonae, but only this plinth now survives

The Stone of Divisions on the central hill of Uisnecht, Westmeath, Ireland. The pagan Celtic navel of Ireland.

FREEMASONRY AND THE CENTRE

Every Master Mason is aware of the ritual instructions that the true secrets of a Freemason are to be found in, or with, the Centre. This is visually symbolised by a point within a circle. A direct spiritual and moral interpretation is also given: that by being upon the centre, or acting from it, no erroneous actions can occur. There is a profound message here for Freemasons.

Archbishop of Canterbury and other bishops, and was also used as an open-air court as well as the site of an annual fair. Further, it sits almost exactly midpoint between the Norfolk coast in the east and the Welsh coast in the west, and only five miles from High Cross. The name "Croft" apparently comes from *Crebre*, a Celtic word comprised of two elements,

bre, "hill", and *cre*, which may derive from *craeft*, "(rotating) machine". In nearby Croft village there is an Arbor Road, and "arbor" also refers to the axis around which a wheel turns. Taken together, these clues hint at a former symbolic hub or fulcrum association with the hill. Croft Hill gets my vote as being the pre-Roman navel of southern Britain.

Town and Temple

In following a reducing scale of the world navel motif, after cosmos and landscape, we come to town and temple. The Etruscans of pre-Roman Italy dug a ritual pit called the *mundus* ("world" or "universe") when founding a city, from which point the usually grid-iron street plan was laid out. Following this tradition, the Romans also put the equivalent of a *mundus* at the centre of their towns, where the north-south (*cardo*) and east-west (*decumanus*) roads crossed (*cardo* gives us the *cardinal* points).

The classic example of a city as a world navel is Jerusalem. The Jewish perception of this is conveyed in Hershon's *Talmudic Miscellany*:

The land of Israel is situated in the centre of the world, and Jerusalem in the centre of the land of Israel, and the Temple in the centre of Jerusalem, and the Holy of Holies in the centre of the Temple, and the foundation-stone on which the world was founded is situated in front of the ark.

There was, indeed, a widespread association in the ancient world between temple and world navel. In Hindu towns

A Maibaum *in Burtscheid, Germany. Such trees, like maypoles, carry folk echoes of the ancient mythic concept of the World Tree at the centre of the Earth.*

such as Leonardo da Vinci and Dürer give the navel a *phi* (∅) or Golden Section relationship in the proportions of the body. In ancient Egyptian, Greek, and Japanese traditional canonical systems the navel is similarly associated with the *phi* division of the body.

All in the Mind

Finally, the world navel motif reaches its most fundamental level – the mind. This is particularly well revealed by shamanism, that most ancient of religious expressions still found in many tribal societies worldwide. The basic cosmological model of shamanism is of three worlds connected by a "vertical" axis: the underworld, the middle world of human existence, and the upper world of the gods. The shaman used this axis mundi to access the upper and lower worlds while in his out-of-body trance. Indeed, in some Siberian tribes, the frame of a shaman's drum was believed to have been fashioned from a branch of the World Tree.

The representation of the universal world navel motif at different scales and in differing forms is like a series of conceptual gear wheels that used to orient people in space, time, and spirit. Our modern globalised culture, which is eccentric in the literal sense that it has lost its centre, should perhaps consider re-inventing the inherent psychology of the perennial ancient wisdom of the world centre motif.

Paul Devereux is the author of many books on ancient sacred sites and traditional lifeways. The world navel is just one of four key themes of ancient thought he explores in depth in his recent book, Living Ancient Wisdom *(Rider, 2002). See the review on page 57.*

All photographs by Paul Devereux

the central temple represented Mount Meru, just as the tallest tower at Angkor Wat in Cambodia also represented Mount Meru. In Greece and the eastern Mediterranean area, temples often displayed "navel stones" or *omphaloi*. In their classic form, these were usually domed stones a few feet high. A legend associated with the oracle temple of Delphi says that Zeus released each of his two eagles from the opposite ends of the Earth, and where their flight paths met was deemed to be the centre of the world, and was marked with a stone. There are two surviving *omphaloi* at Delphi.

Body Image

If the sky and land are the macrocosm, and the city and temple the mesocosm, then the human body is the microcosm, and as such it was always regarded by the scholars of antiquity – the Greek philosopher Heraclitus said, "Man is the measure of all things". The human body is the hub of the four bodily directions of front, back, left, right. These have been conceptually projected on the outer world

as the cardinal directions. We are all at the perceptual centre of our world. In other words, world centre symbolism has a physiological basis, and that is why it is a universal motif.

At birth, the navel or belly button is at the centre of the infant's body, but in the course of maturation its relative position moves up the body. The canonical (ideal) drawings of the human form by masters

The two surviving omphaloi *or navel stones at the temple complex of Delphi, Greece. That on the right is carved with a curious lattice motif which has so far defied explanation.*

ENTERING THE ORACLE OF THE DEAD

ROBERT TEMPLE DESCENDS INTO AN ANCIENT HELL

Tunnel leading down to the underground river, the "Styx", which runs beneath the underground sanctuary of the Oracle of Baia. This tunnel, 290, branches off from the entrance tunnel 408 feet from the cliff and runs for another 150 feet down to the "Styx".

Author, Robert Temple, emerging from a tunnel entrance near to the Inner Sanctuary of Baia.

The most terrifying and dangerous of all ancient rituals for foretelling the future was undertaken by means of the descent into Hell. This took place at the Oracle of the Dead, at Baia, near Naples in southern Italy. It was not just a poetical or mythological allegory: *it actually happened.*

During the reign of the Roman Emperor Augustus, in the last decades BC, the underground Oracle of the Dead was closely packed with soil and rubble and sealed so that it could never be used again. A rough calculation shows that at least 30,000 man-journeys were required to carry the soil into the tunnels to block many of them so thoroughly. What was it that the Romans feared? Clearly they feared the infernal powers and the terrifying things which had once gone on in the Oracle.

The Roman poet Vergil lived in the vicinity, and he seems to have entered the Oracle before it was sealed off, and he probably knew some of the priestly staff. His descriptions of the descent into Hell in his great poem the *Aeneid* (Book Six) are very precise and match details of the underground complex at Baia.

In 63 AD, the entire area of Baia was destroyed by an earthquake associated with nearby Mount Vesuvius, and the entrance to the Oracle was obliterated by mounds of Roman rubble. It remained entirely lost until 1962, when a retired Englishman named Robert Paget, aged 72, discovered it when he was making amateur archaeological searches of tunnels in the area. But the Italian authorities, claiming it was dangerous, sealed it up once more, and

The entrance tunnel to the Oracle, 270, which runs due east-west for 408 feet before joining tunnel 290. It is only 21 inches wide.

Michael Baigent at the narrow cliff-side entrance to the Oracle of Baia.

View of the Inner Sanctuary, 600 feet in from the cliff face. The original entrance was bricked up by the Romans around 44 BC. A brief exploration in 1962 revealed that the sanctuary was packed with rubble behind the wall. A bundle of fresh myrtle sits in the initiate's offering niche to the lower right.

until 2001, none of the current authorities had ever entered the tunnels of the Oracle.

It was in 2001 that, after twenty years of requesting it, I was finally granted permission to enter the Oracle - if I first signed a waiver that the authorities were not responsible for my injury or death. They removed the stones they had previously put there to block the entrance, warned me that the tunnels were full of poison gas, and left me to my fate. I chose to bring my friend Michael Baigent with me, and we and our wives entered the Oracle with great trepidation. We soon threw away our gas masks because we discovered that the fear of poison gas was groundless: there was none at all, merely a shortage of air deep in the interior. We were accompanied part of the way by one Italian archaeologist and two workmen who set up a generator and cables to bring light to the initial and middle

The rubble covered steps leading to the underground river, the "Styx", 558 feet in from the cliff and 140 feet beneath the ground. The "Styx" runs beneath the Inner Sanctuary for 150 feet.

portions of the Oracle, although their hundreds of feet of electric cable proved highly inadequate in the end, as the Oracle extends deep into the solid rock for more than a fifth of a mile.

Entering this bizarre and unique place, which is so wonderfully preserved, took us far back into time. The Oracle is certainly at least 2500 years old, but more probably 3000 or even 3500, as it is mentioned in the *Odyssey* of Homer. In fact, Baia itself is named after Baius, a companion of Odysseus. Since the date of the *Odyssey* precedes the earliest Greek city in Italy (nearby Cuma), it may well be the case that the Oracle was not constructed by the Greeks (who later certainly used it). It may have been built by the Minoans from Crete, as it shows a high degree of engineering precision in its construction and could never have been built by

'locals' who did not possess superior engineering and surveying skills.

Inside the Tunnels

It appears to be astronomically oriented: the underground sanctuary is oriented towards the sunset of the summer solstice and the entrance tunnel runs absolutely straight, east to west, without deviation, for hundreds of feet, its cliff-side entrance facing sunrise on the same day. But most astonishing is the inclusion of an underground artificial river in the Oracle complex, one which we call the River Styx - of which it was a 'mockup'. It is about 150 feet long and has a landing stage at either end, and artificial underwater inlets for the water supply leading to an unknown source. How this could possibly be constructed is a baffling mystery. How would the

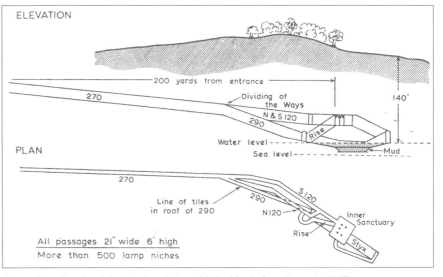

Plan of the Oracle of the Dead at Baia published by Robert Paget in 1967.

builders of the tunnel have known the water was there? Our only hope of solving this seems to be to excavate a lower layer of tunnels at the Oracle which I believe I have discovered, but could not enter. They may lead to the water source. But one must always keep in mind that the Oracle complex is 140 feet below the surface of the earth, though entered from the base of a cliff at the side.

The atmosphere inside this strange place was eerie but peaceful. One did not feel goblins at one's elbow, but rather a sense of timelessness. Although it would at one time have been a site of sheer terror, today the terror has all gone, and all that remained for us was the fear of the unknown hazards we might encounter. Certainly it is no place for claustrophobes. The tunnels are too narrow for anyone to pass, and I even had to twist slightly because my shoulders rubbed against the walls. But for some reason the tunnels which so conspicuously lack width often have much more height than is needed, culminating in an elegant arched roof.

One possible reason for the height of the tunnels is the use of torches and hoods. Although there are more than 500 lamp niches carved into the walls for light, torches would also have been carried. And we believe that behind the clients who entered the Oracle were processions of priests in pointed hoods with eye-slits, looking like members of the Ku Klux Klan. It clearly would not have done to have them rubbing their pointed hoods along a low ceiling. The procession was led by the Sibyl of Cuma wearing a scarlet cloak. There is good reason to believe that baying hounds of Hell would fill the corridors with terrifying howls, and we found places for the hounds to sit, just as at nearby Cuma we found tetherings carved out of the rock on either side of the Sibyl's oracle chamber for hounds to be tied. In fact, Cerberus, the Hound of Hell, was portrayed on coins minted at Cuma.

In ancient times, after the payment of vast sums, selected clients were allowed to descend into Hell (which most of them must have believed was real) and been rowed in a coracle along the lengthy River Styx, disembarking to go up some stairs into the Inner Sanctum where a necromantic séance would have been staged to enable them to consult the spirits of the dead. Since we know the clients were drugged beforehand by various potions and lotions of powerful drug plants such as henbane, hellebore, and belladonna, they would have been highly suggestible.

Another blocked entrance to the Inner Sanctuary of the Oracle. To the right is the tunnel leading down to the far end of the "Styx".

An Initiation Centre?

It is possible that this underground site doubled as an initiation centre when it was not being used for necromancy, especially as there is some archaeological evidence recovered from the southern Italian tomb of an Orphic initiate that there were mysterious 'ceremonies carried out underground' connected with the ancient mystery cult of Orphism. This evidence occurs in a text inscribed on a gold tablet buried with the initiate. The

After about 130 feet, tunnel S.120 inexplicably divides into two, a fact never before noted and which only excavation will explain.

Orphics were Greeks who rejected the state religion of the Olympian gods and opted for a more personal religion of a mystical nature. They were named after Orpheus, who of course made a famous Descent into Hell, where he lost his wife Eurydice, - a possible echo of the Baian Oracle. Both Michael and I were fortunate still to have our wives with us when we left. Perhaps this is because I left a bundle of myrtle sprigs in an offering niche to the underground goddess Persephone just

outside the Inner Sanctuary, which is currently still filled with soil and blocked with Roman bricks.

We hope that this archaeological site which should really be declared a World Heritage Site for its outstanding state of preservation, size and importance, can be cleared of soil and rubble and be excavated in the manner which is so urgently needed. But it can never be open to tourists, because it is impossible for anyone to pass in the long corridors extending for hundreds of feet. However I am pleased to have been able to make the exploration and become the first person living to enter the place. Between us, Michael Baigent and I have made full photographic coverage of the site, even though it often meant crawling for long distances in spaces only 18 inches high owing to the Roman blockages. One day we hope that it will be possible to walk upright throughout the whole site, and that the original air circulation will be restored by breaking open some Roman obstructions, so that people exploring the place will not be threatened with passing out for lack of oxygen, as we were. And if they pass out from terror, that is another thing, and we can do nothing to help them there.

Robert Temple has a degree in Sanskrit and Oriental Studies, is a visiting professor at universities in the United States and China and the author of ten books. The full story of the Oracle and tunnels of Baia, along with other ancient Oracle sites, is in his recent book Netherworld. *See the review on p.56.*

FROM ROLE-PLAY TO RITUAL

NEVILLE CRYER CONSIDERS THE ORIGIN OF MASONIC RITUAL IN GUILD MYSTERY PLAYS

This is, I am sure, exactly what must have happened in medieval days. The builders and stonemasons would have been fully aware of what it was that they had to produce – even if we are, in part, mystified by what they carved. Some of the symbolism may be wholly lost on us but you may be sure it was well understood by those who carved it.

The masons were aware of their work and its contribution to the education of the public who would see it and were also fully aware of their need to share in the life of the local community. Their Guild, with those of other crafts, formed the basis of town or city government and this sense of communal involvement is what led them to take part in the annual public procession of Corpus Christi plays in June.

This mobile performance of plays during one whole day took place in cities as far apart as Newcastle, York, Wakefield, Norwich, Coventry, Exeter and Chester; country-wide, in fact. And the performances continued for over 250 years – from just after 1300 to about 1575, a sizeable slice of English history.

A reconstruction of the waggon and the play of the Resurrection as performed in medieval times by the York Carpenters' Guild. This reconstruction was performed in Stonegate, Lancaster, by the Joculatores Lancastrienses as part of the 1992 York Festival waggon plays. The soldiers in the street report to Pilate that Christ's body has disappeared. Such reconstructions of the medieval Mystery plays were part of the medieval theatre course at Lancaster University directed by Professor Meg Twycross.

Not long ago the Chapter of York Minster, the governing body of the Cathedral, decided that the time had come to replace the stone-work around the arch over the main West doorway. The figures that were originally carved there had slowly worn away. The scenes to be newly carved included the Garden of Eden, the story of Cain and Abel, the dramas of Noah and Jonah, as well as three scenes of our Lord and St. Peter. To achieve this end the clergy and the architect agreed on the subjects and the drawings to be made, then the stonemasons in the Minster work-yard were informed and asked to execute the carvings required.

The Guild Performances

In each city there were two lists: one of the plays to be performed and another of the Guilds in their local order of importance. This latter order differed: in Chester and Norwich the most important Guilds were those of the Drapers and Haberdashers whilst in York it was the

Barber-surgeons. Whatever the order, the Guilds made their choice of which play they would each present, according to the local order. Once their choice was made, that play was the one which they would probably perform for year after year unless there was a change in the ranking of the local Guilds or if a Guild specially requested permission to change their play, as the York masons did in 1431. What must be emphasised is that even if, as with the Masons, a Guild was one of the lesser ones and thus had a more limited choice after several others had decided, great care was still taken over the kind of play because not only was the symbolism of the play important – as with their stone-carving – but the cost of performance was substantial. In present day values the initial outlay would be up to £4000 with an annual upkeep of £1000.

Each Guild wanted a play which related to its own Patron Saint; the Masons preferred plays involving either the Virgin Mary or the two Saints John. The other requisite was that the content of the play needed to relate to the particular craft which presented it. The Barber-surgeons preferred plays showing the fine beards of John the Baptist or the Jewish priests whilst the Watermen chose plays about Noah's Ark or Jonah and the Whale. The Masons wanted plays about the Temple, David and Solomon, the Virgin Mary, Jesus, stones or the death of the innocent – the latter referring to the ancient builder's legend that a suitable victim had to be slain and laid in the foundations before a building could be safely erected. What they chose is relevant to several degrees known in York in the 18th century.

The Masons performed in:

Aberdeen,	the Massacre of the Innocents;
Beverley,	the Temptation of Jesus on the pinnacle of the Temple;
Chester,	the Massacre of the Innocents;
Coventry,	the three Maries at the tomb of Jesus with the stone rolled away;
Dublin,	Moses causing Pharaoh's host to be lost in the Red Sea;
Newcastle,	the Burial of the Virgin Mary;
Norwich,	Cain murdering his brother Abel;
Wakefield,	the child Jesus presented in the Temple; or Cain murdering Abel;
York,	the Burial of the Virgin Mary; or the coming of the Magi and the Massacre of the Innocents; or Jesus' presentation in the Temple.

A reconstruction of the York Mercer's Guild's waggon for their play of Doomsday. The reconstruction was made by the Joculatores Lancastrienses in Low Petergate as part of the 1988 York Festival waggon plays. The illustration shows the moment when the first Good Soul rises from the grave.

Symbolic Meanings

The plays were composed in verse and the words learnt by heart since the participants might be unable to read. Severe fines were imposed for disgracing the company by failing to recite the words correctly. In addition, the verses were accompanied by formal gestures because the public, also largely illiterate, were used to the formal gestures employed by the clergy during mass. Objects were used which acquired symbolic meanings – pointed hats signified Jews; mitres represented High Priests; staves denoted prophets and a cluster of candles was a star, pots represented manna or incense and robes of specially chosen colours were used. If you want to find Solomon or David on the roof of our older churches or cathedrals you simply look for a figure holding a model temple or a harp.

Is it any wonder that from these plays men and women received impressions that persist nearly seven hundred years later – impressions that have gone very deep and affected our whole culture: the idea that God is an old man with a beard sitting on a cloud; that Matthew, Mark, Luke and John surround one's bed; that

Hell is a blazing furnace with red horned devils brandishing forks; that angels have blond hair, white robes and huge wings; that the Virgin Mary wears blue and has a halo of stars. The complete list is much longer.

If seeing the plays was able to so deeply impress the minds of the audience, and their descendants, what might it have done to those who planned and produced the plays they memorised? Furthermore, the clergy attached to the Guilds, those who read the books which coloured the contents of the plays, were as influential in affecting the city craftsmen as the monks of the monasteries had been in guiding the masons whom they employed.

I have no hesitation in asserting that, contrary to what some have claimed were the uninteresting practices of the late medieval masons, these men had a dramatic background knowledge to draw on. The operative masons were likely, over time, to weld into their traditions the words, symbols and gestures which they had so regularly displayed in their plays. When these operatives were joined, or replaced, by the new `speculatives' who, as products of the new Tudor grammar schools, were now able to read and write, then the old form of the Lodge and its acquired `traditions' could begin to be altered. Through these new and accepted Freemasons, the new Guild `lodges' could be shaped, slowly but steadily, into a style more familiar to us and the proceedings of that kind of `lodge' would begin to be not play-acting but ritual.

A period of transition

It is impossible to explain briefly the transition in dramatic presentation following the late 1500s when many of the Mystery plays ceased to be regularly staged; in York this end came in 1572. However, some places continued them until about 1620. Even so, three points are relevant to note:

1: Some fifty new plays, based on biblical themes, were produced between 1550 and the arrival of King James I in 1603; the subjects include Moses, Gideon, Jephtha and King Hiram of Tyre. In 1560 there was a special play called "The Wisdom of Solomon" which ended with the Queen of Sheba arriving at Solomon's court to admire the completion of the Temple.

2: The Globe Theatre in London was designed to be erected as a form of sacred temple in the octagon shape of what was then thought to be the form of the Holy Sepulchre. Here the plays of Shakespeare were staged still using verse with formal

This shows, in the festival of Corpus Christi in Valencia, the pageant waggon "La Purisima", the Immaculate Conception, which was constructed before 1665. These Spanish waggons are designed with a statue in the place of honour; here it is of the Virgin. The figure at the front is St Helena with the True Cross, and at the back is Judith with the head of Holofernes. In the waggon is a troupe of musicians, who play as it goes along.

gestures, symbolic dress and symbolic objects.

3: Masons like Inigo Jones and Nicholas Stone were asked to construct buildings in Stuart times based on the work of an architect called Serlio whose main contribution had been the construction of the perspective stages of the Roman theatre. Inigo Jones, the designer of the Whitehall Banqueting Hall, which was erected for Royal stage entertainments, became, with colleagues, the creator of masques and costume dramas; a presentation of "Solomon and Sheba" took place in 1607.

We can conclude that even though Guild plays were discontinued by 1580, the number of biblical themes available was actually increased. The introduction of the Geneva (or Breeches) Bible in 1560 introduced clear links with our present ritual.[1] The Freemasons links with dramatic presentations were clearly continued and revived knowledge about ancient forms of architecture was being acquired.

The Commonwealth period saw a ban on theatres, a limit on large house building and an attack on traditional beliefs and practices. But it only lasted for twenty years and many people hung on, all the more tenaciously, to what they prized from the past. It was followed by the Restoration: ideas and customs that had been disallowed burst forth and we come to this fresh age of re-building with Palladian and Vitruvian-style stone dwellings that also made use of Roman stage designs. And, it saw the

emergence of what we can begin to call Masonic ritual.

What do we find when anything resembling our present practice appears? Ritual in verse, standard biblical themes, no printed or published texts, memory learning still required, specific gestures, symbolic items – almost a complete re-run of where the Mystery Plays left off. Only now, not performed on an open wagon and in the street, but on a tavern or private house floor and in a rear or upper room.

I would dare to claim that we have come from Role-play to Ritual.

The Rev. Neville Barker Cryer, MA., formerly served as Grand Chaplain, Assistant Provincial Grand Master of Surrey, and Master of Quatuor Coronati Lodge, No. 2076. He was Prestonian Lecturer in 1974 and Batham Lecturer, 1996-8 and author of many books including Masonic Halls of England, The Arch and the Rainbow, *and* I Just Didn't Know That. *Until his retirement, he was the General Director of the British & Foreign Bible Society.*

[1] Cryer, N. B., "The Geneva Bible and the Development of English Speculative Freemasonry", *Yearbook of Grand Lodge of Scotland*, Edinburgh, 1993, pp. 52-60.

Photographs © Meg Twycross.
York Medieval Theatre project:
www.lancs.ac.uk/users/yorkdoom/welcome.htm

BEYOND THE BRAIN

IS THE MIND THE SAME AS THE BRAIN? PAUL DEVEREUX INVESTIGATES

A Zen Garden in Kyoto, Japan. When we see such a garden are we experiencing it as 'outside' our minds or are we just experiencing an internal image? When meditators look at a Zen garden, where is their mind? Is it within their brain or is it in the garden?

Photo: John Grange.

A crucial philosophical struggle is taking place within science about the nature of the mind and its place in the physical universe. The outcome of this will determine the future course of human destiny, and so should concern Freemasonry which, behind its social, secular activities, its fellowship and philanthropy, has philosophical principles as its integral guiding lights.

The side that currently has the upper hand in this philosophical discussion within science is materialistic, claiming that consciousness is purely a product of brain activity, a mere glint off the mental machinery. But those who oppose this approach argue that there is a subjective flip side, an internal aspect to physical creation experienced by us human beings as consciousness. Indeed, some scientists, such as Professor Robert Jahn at Princeton University, are arguing that there is a pressing need for a new 'science of the subjective'.

The Matter with Matter

Dominated as we presently are in our culture by the materialistic model, we find it difficult to conceive that consciousness could be integral to the physical world, which is so solid, so real, so 'out there' and so we build a false wall between mind and matter.

But let us think carefully about what we know.

First, matter: what is it? It is in fact a mirage woven by the dance of atoms and the forces that bind them. We know that the quantum-scale innards of those atoms behave in ways that belie the stable appearance of the world of human experience. We are nowadays becoming increasingly familiar with baffling observations in quantum physics such as the 'uncertainty principle' whereby it is impossible to precisely measure the position and momentum of a quantum entity simultaneously or the 'double-slit experiment' which proves that an electron can travel through two apertures simultaneously.

But the most startling revelation of all is 'quantum entanglement'.

A series of experiments in the 1980s demonstrated that if one of a pair of electrons emitted in different directions from a suitably stimulated atom is measured, the other, distant one will *instantaneously* conform to whatever state the monitored electron adopts. This bizarre phenomenon is also referred to as 'non-locality' but was more colourfully described by Einstein as 'spooky action at a distance'. In fact, he never believed it to be possible, and died before the theory was confirmed experimentally.

Physical reality only appears solid to us because we are part of the same mirage, the same atomic dance. Even the very space within which that dance takes place is not empty, for it seethes with mysterious quantum-level fluctuations referred to by physicists as 'vacuum energy'. Many people, including some of those physicists, are asking if consciousness is already there, in that ground-state shimmer of our universe.

Is it that subtle but all-pervading level that which mystics variously describe as the Tao, the void, oceanic consciousness, Mystical Union, or the Godhead? This brings us to the other side of the conceptual wall – mind.

Wired to the Source

Convinced that raw, unstructured consciousness exists at the deep, sub-atomic quantum level, at the roots of both mind and matter where time and space smear into one another, some scientific researchers are actively seeking the actual, physical doorways in our brains through which we can directly access that primordial level, as the accounts of the mystics indicate is possible.

In other words, the researchers are trying to identify brain structures that may facilitate sub-atomic, quantum, effects.

Possible candidates include "microtubules" belonging to the skeletal structure of brain cells. These are being investigated by Roger Penrose, a celebrated professor in mathematical physics at Oxford University, and Arizona-based scientist, Stuart Hameroff. If these two or the several other scientists studying such possibilities are proven correct, then it will be the case that our minds are directly 'wired to the source'.

It is salutary to recall that decades ago the great Swiss psychologist, C.G. Jung, argued that the collective unconscious, his hypothesised vast, transpersonal 'species mind' of humanity, resides in the very molecules and atoms of the material world. He insisted that 'psyche and matter are two different aspects of one and the same thing' A similar sentiment was expressed by the astronomer, Sir James Jeans: 'Mind no longer appears as an accidental intruder into the realm of matter…'. Physics is only now beginning to catch up with such prescient observations.

The Magic Theatre

Our personal experience of even the most concrete of material realities is in fact put together for us in the moist darkness within our skulls. We are immersed in, or part of, something-or-other whose energies impinge on our sense organs and are then translated into electro-chemical signals that are whisked along nerve fibres and across synaptic connections into various parts of our brain where by some miraculous process in the magic theatre inside the cranium they are made to coalesce into a three-dimensional production we take to be the

external world. We never see the world as it actually is, only the representation of it conjured by brain activity.

Everything we know, inner or outer (if either state truly exists), is a product of consciousness. As difficult as it is for us to appreciate, even our bodies (including our brains) are an 'inner' construct of the 'outer' world. It is hard for us to accept, but it is nevertheless true: we literally put this inconvenient fact to the 'back of our minds'. As an oriental sage once said, we can only be certain of one thing – that there is existence. Everything else is virtual reality.

Meeting with the Octopus

If mind extends beyond the brain, then parapsychology takes on fresh importance. A new science of the subjective would be able to find a framework of understanding in which phenomena like telepathy or remote viewing - 'clairvoyance' - can be legitimately included rather than being dismissed by mainstream thought as is the current situation. The evidence for such phenomena is, in fact, much stronger than publically acknowledged, and parapsychological research is advancing.

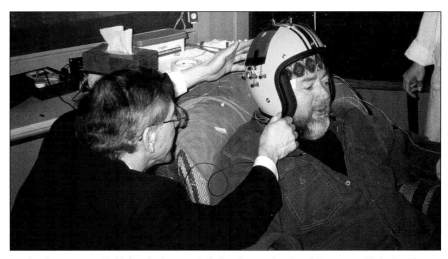

Michael Persinger (left) fits the 'magnetic helmet' to author Paul Devereux. Units inside the helmet send programmed bursts of magnetism into the brain that can, among other things, mimic the effect of various drugs. Persinger's main aim with the device is to find a non-pharmaceutical analgesic - an electronic painkiller as a substitute to the standard chemical ones.

Photo: Paul Devereux

As a prime example of this, Bob Morris, Koestler Professor of parapsychology at Edinburgh University, has produced a string of students with doctorates in parapsychology who are now active as faculty in several university departments.

The work of Morris and his colleagues in telepathy and remote

viewing is meticulous and proving statistically significant: the countdown to unavoidable mainstream acceptance is well under way.

In fact, the argument may already be won, as I found out for myself when visiting the laboratories of another tireless worker in parasychology, brain scientist Professor Michael Persinger.

Persinger is based at Laurentian University in Sudbury, north of Toronto in Canada. I visited him in 1998, initially to experience his famed 'magnetic helmet' which I had heard could produce altered states of consciousness.

Persinger's primary purpose for the device, though, is to find the magnetic signatures of drugs in the brain, so that analgesics, for instance, can be administered in a safer, non-pharmaceutical manner. It applies carefully designed and directed magnetic field patterns to the temporal cortex, a part of the brain sensitive to magnetic field changes and associated with functions such as memory and dreaming. I had an intriguing session under the helmet, but a more significant experience was to follow: Persinger asked if I would like to try out a prototype device they nicknamed the 'Octopus'.

The Octopus itself was well-named, consisting of a headband linked to the computer by a profusion of leads. The prototype contraption was fitted around my cranium as I sat down in a chair. It was explained to me that the headband was fitted with solenoids that would be activated in computer-controlled sequences causing a magnetic field to shift in various configurations over and around my cranium. My eyes were covered with gauze and dark goggles, and the session began.

It continued for about forty minutes, during which time I was encouraged to give a running commentary describing any impressions that came to me. This was not difficult as there were two recurring images that came without bidding. One I described as like two telegraph poles silhouetted against a sunset, and the other, even more persistent image, was like a complicated piece of fairground equipment with its various parts painted in different, vibrant colours – I was particularly aware of a bright green. I say the images were 'like' these things, because the images were not pictures as such, but more like information I had to interpret.

Completely unbeknown to me, my wife had been taken into an adjoining room by the lab technician and asked to select one envelope from several, each containing a picture. She chose one and was asked to write a description of the picture it contained that she felt I might produce if I was looking at it. She did not see the pictures in the other envelopes.

After my session, my wife and the envelopes were brought into the laboratory. All the pictures were displayed and I was asked to pick anything that related to the impressions I had received under the Octopus. I identified two. One was of two very tall smokestacks that mark the Sudbury skyline silhouetted against a sunset sky (my 'telegraph poles' image), and the other was the picture my wife had actually selected – it showed an old-fashioned railway locomotive painted in variegated colours with a bright green cow-catcher at front. I had 'seen' it repeatedly while under the Octopus, yet at that time I couldn't directly conceptualise what it was. I was dumbfounded.

Although having no natural psychic ability, there was no doubt that I had achieved remote perception; I felt privileged to have been able to observe the process 'from the inside'. I could now understand why psychic research so often produces infuriatingly vague and apparently inconsistent results – the problem, the skill, was in the left-brain interpretation of the right-brain information or impressions.

I couldn't account for the 'leakage' of the smokestacks image, which had never been taken out of its envelope while my wife was present, but I supposed it to be some effect of 'mind at large' caused by the actions of the Octopus on the brain that will become fully understood in time. I later asked a colleague from a scientific research group I am part of to visit Persinger and experience the Octopus. A highly trained and accomplished psychologist, she duly did so and had an identical experience to my own.

Persinger and colleagues have now conducted much more work with the Octopus, and it is producing remarkable and repeatable results. He is looking at quantum entanglement as a model to explain some of the device's effects; for me, though, the Octopus has provided something more immediate than statistics or the explanatory powers of quantum physics – it has proven that mind can roam beyond the brain.

Paul Devereux is not a Freemason but maintains a strong interest in the spiritual and its links with science. He has written some twenty six books including Stone Age Soundtracks *(reviewed in this issue),* Living Ancient Wisdom *(reviewed in* Freemasonry Today, 22, Autumn 2002 *and* Mysterious Ancient America. *Website: www.pauldevereux.com.*

MASONIC TRADITIONS FOR THE TWENTY-FIRST CENTURY

DENNIS CHORNENKY DISCUSSES MASONIC DECLINE AND THE INITIATIC TRADITION

Individual initiation was at the heart of Freemasonry at its beginning and, after hundreds of years, remains the focus of the rituals.

Reports and comments critical of mass initations in the United States have been regularly carried in the pages of Freemasonry Today. The large majority of the American Brethren who responded have given their wholehearted support to our stand. Partly as a result of the spread of mass initiations, but also as a result of other evidence of a decline in masonic practice in the United States, the Masonic Restoration Foundation has come into being. Its stated purpose is to re-awaken and re-invigorate the spiritual and philosophical traditions of Freemasonry. The Masonic Restoration Foundation is receiving the support of Freemasonry Today and also of The Cornerstone Society. In this article, the President of the Masonic Restoration Foundation outlines the problems and gives some suggestions for renewal.

Considering the Craft's current decline in most English-speaking jurisdictions, it is important that we understand what is at stake if the organization is to be preserved in its original form and its traditions are to continue to have a meaningful impact on the lives of its members.

Masons must be able to answer three questions if Masonry is to be successful:

What is Freemasonry?

What is its historical purpose?

And what makes it different from other fraternal organizations?

The answer to the first question is that Freemasonry is a traditional initiatic order. While it has taken its modern form during the Enlightenment, its traditions, symbols and lessons reach back to pre-modern times. If we closely investigate the lives of the individuals who were active in shaping speculative Freemasonry out of its operative roots, and particularly examine their connections to older occult societies and traditions, it becomes clear that speculative Freemasonry was designed to be foremost an initiatic institution through which men could recognize their true spiritual potential.

The courtly philosophical climate of sixteenth and seventeenth century Britain, where it did not follow strictly Puritan or Anglican trends, was strongly influenced by the underground tradition sometimes referred to as Arcadia, which encompassed within its philosophy elements of Gnostic, Neo-Platonic, Hermetic, and Kabalistic thought. As Rosicrucianism surfaced in the early seventeenth century it also showed an affinity to the Arcadian stream of thought.

Custodian of initiatic tradition

A close study of the literary works produced during this period reveals a distinct current of symbolism embedded inside seemingly mainstream publications. And to those well versed in masonic symbolism the central themes of the initiatic tradition become quickly evident upon examination of this literature.

It was precisely out of this philosophical climate, united through organizations such as the Royal Society, and through extensive correspondence that is now well documented, that the most well-known proponents of seventeenth and early eighteenth-century Freemasonry emerged; men like Sir Robert Moray, Elias Ashmole, John Desaguliers, James Anderson, and their numerous friends and counterparts from all across Europe. Even if some of their writings regarding the history of the Craft may appear questionable to us in light of the evidence now available, it is clear that they viewed Speculative Masonry as a custodian of the initiatic traditions of the past, charged with their propagation and preservation.

The general work associated with the initiatic tradition, and the purpose of Freemasonry, put simply, is to provide an environment where good men can unite together to assist one another in self-improvement and the realization of their true potential. One of the underlying tenets of this initiatic tradition is the belief that if even one individual becomes a better person the entire world profits thereby.

Initiation into the mysteries

Being part of the initiatic tradition is what distinguishes Freemasonry from purely social or philanthropic organizations. There are many organizations that contribute large sums of money to charity; there are many organizations that offer fellowship with like-minded men and there are many organizations that exist for the purpose of providing education. But there are far fewer organizations that offer a traditional initiation into the mysteries of life and death.

Freemasonry is special in that it combines all of the things just mentioned. However, it is essential that we recognize that the initiatic tradition is the core, defining characteristic of Freemasonry. Attempts to make Freemasonry as accessible as other organizations by reducing or eliminating the initiatic elements are likely to bring ruin to the Craft. Without the initiatic tradition there would be nothing to differentiate Masonry from other social or philanthropic organizations. One could call the new organization which would emerge from such a process anything one likes, but it would no longer be masonic.

A general decline

Much of our dilemma arises from the fact that too many men who join are not properly educated about the fraternity. Rather than coming to an understanding of the Craft based on diligent study and thinking, new candidates tend to form their opinions based on the behavior of fellow Masons, who are themselves too often poorly educated about the fraternity's history and philosophy. A

disproportionately small number of serious and scholarly men within the organization has led to a general decline over the last several decades.

In efforts to arrest the decline in numbers, many jurisdictions in North America have sought to make Masons faster and to make it easier for them to join by reducing the requirements for membership. Unfortunately, in order to appeal to the greatest amount of people possible things must generally be reduced to the lowest common denominator. It must be considered, however, that Freemasonry is designed to appeal to what might be called the highest common denominator, that is, good men seeking to improve themselves. Selling ourselves cheap is a sad sign of a desperate organization. If an organization is vibrant and has a strong sense of purpose it will attract good men naturally. Based on the facts, we know this to be the case in most Continental European and South American countries, where Freemasonry does not advertise itself to the public yet its membership continues to grow or remains stable.

This is one of the masonic traditions that must be considered – Masonry works best when lodges are smaller. Granted, for smaller lodges to be viable economically, they must adopt higher dues, but if quality is to be had it must be paid for, and men should not be afraid to show that the fraternity is important to them.

Limits on initiation

Unfortunately, North American Freemasonry has taken a different route for most of the twentieth century. When it swung its doors wide open the organization quickly swelled, but it was filled with men who had not taken the time to learn about the real purpose of Freemasonry. Nor could they have done so, as there was no way the lodges could have so quickly incorporated so many men into the masonic culture. This is one of the keys to understanding our dilemma – the number of men that any given lodge can effectively initiate and educate is naturally limited.

Initiation is a slow and sensitive process and requires great effort on behalf of both the candidate and the existing members of the lodge. For initiation and masonic growth to be meaningful and enriching, great care and attention must be afforded to each individual candidate. He must understand that the organization is highly selective, allowing him to feel self-worth and leading him to respect the high standards of the Order. Great time

Dennis Chornenky, President of the Masonic Restoration Foundation.

must be spent to educate him about the history, symbolism and philosophy of the Craft if he is to become a Freemason worthy of the title.

Therefore, another tradition that we seem to have lost, and which should be emphasized, is the thorough investigation of candidates and meaningful preparatory period. Indeed, this is a demanding tradition that limits the number of candidates that any given lodge can initiate successfully. Doing otherwise, that is, filling up the fraternity with members who have not been properly educated about the purpose and history of the Craft, seems only to have led to the deterioration in masonic traditions and values.

This, along with the rise of popular culture and high-technology, has left Freemasonry in North America unprepared to respond appropriately to the social changes that were quickly coming upon the institution. Nor could there have been a proper response, since much of the leadership, poorly versed in masonic history and the initiatic tradition, could not understand what it was that it should be endeavoring to preserve. Even now, much of what is introduced with the best intentions seems too often to result in further deterioration. The monitors warn us against innovations with good reason.

A kind of denial

The facts tell us that we are going to become a much smaller organization over the next decade. But rather than accepting this inevitable fact and making preparations for Masonry to succeed with a smaller membership, it seems that we are too eager to adopt anything that could possibly delay the inevitable, that is, anything that has the potential to bring in members in large numbers. In a sense, this is a kind of denial, and unless it is shaken off soon it is likely to leave North American Masonry unprepared once more for the challenges of the future. But if the right preparatory steps are taken, as Masonry becomes a much smaller organization, it can also become a much stronger organization.

One important thing to understand is that simply adopting one traditional practice here and another there is not going to turn the whole organization around. What is necessary is an all-encompassing approach to the way our lodges can be improved. We know that European Masonry has been very successful in working as small lodges. And we know, whether we like it or not, that our own lodges are also going to become relatively small in the near future.

Focus on quality

While it is true that we can consolidate lodges as a means of keeping the dues low, this approach is only going to work for a limited time and does not address the more fundamental problem of having lost our focus and traditions. If we want Masonic traditions to continue to have an impact on the lives of Masons, we need to focus on quality and working out viable models for smaller lodges.

A mass initiation for 2,100 'initiates' held in New York, 2003.

Uniting good men in the pursuit of virtue

We need higher dues and dress codes as a means of returning dignity to the institution. We need festive boards and more engaging masonic programs in order to provide higher-quality fellowship. And we need more thorough investigations and more meaningful preparatory periods for candidates if we are to rediscover our original purpose, uniting good men in the pursuit of virtue. We cannot afford to forget that the initiatic tradition is what defines us as Masons.

Keeping these things in mind, Masonry will doubtless overcome its future challenges and survive for many years to come. But the North American masonic experience of the last century must teach us that Masonry cannot go wholesale – that the number of men entering the fraternity must be limited to how many men can effectively be initiated and educated. We must learn and understand that Freemasonry, if it is to be true to its designs, does not lower its standards but demands that individuals raise theirs.

Aims of the Masonic Restoration Foundation

Dennis V. Chornenky is President of the Masonic Restoration Foundation (MRF), a non-profit organization providing education and support for Masons and lodges in recognized US jurisdictions interested in practising traditional Freemasonry and promoting its study and understanding. The MRF seeks to foster a network of lodges and individuals of strong spiritual and intellectual character that will help preserve the initiatic tradition within American Freemasonry for future generations.

Having studied the decline in Freemasonry in the United States, Mr. Chornenky traveled to Europe to better understand the history and structure of European Freemasonry and the reasons for its success. After visiting numerous lodges in close to a dozen European countries he returned to the United States and based on the knowledge and experience that he gained founded the MRF with the support of well-known and respected American masonic leaders and scholars.

Dennis Chornenky continues to regularly travel throughout the United States and Europe as part of his commitment to gathering accurate information and promoting discourse on the initiatic tradition of Freemasonry. If you are interested in learning more about the Masonic Restoration Foundation and its work please visit the website at www.masonicrestoration.com

HEART AND MIND

ANNE BARING DESCRIBES WHY THESE NEED TO BE IN BALANCE

The sacred marriage of the King and the Queen symbolising the essential identity of spirit and nature. From the sixteenth century alchemical manuscript by Solomon Trismosin, Splendor solis

The British Library

We are living now in a crucial time of choice – a time of stupendous scientific discoveries which are enlarging our vision of the universe, shattering our old concepts about the nature of reality. Yet the delicate organism of life on our planet and the survival of our species are threatened as never before by technologies driven by a need to conquer and control nature, technologies applied with an utter disregard of the perils of our interference with the complex web of relationships upon which the life of our species depends. This time of choice asks us to bring heart and mind – the feminine and masculine dimensions of our nature – into relationship, harmony and balance.

The feminine dimension of our nature carries the instinctual feeling values traditionally associated with the heart; the masculine dimension carries the questing, goal-defining, ordering, discriminating qualities generally associated with mind or intellect. For millennia women have been associated with the values of the heart; men with the power of the mind. But now, there is a deep impulse to "marry" these two great principles within ourselves and our culture. To understand what a tremendous endeavour this represents, we need to go back several thousand years.

In the ancient world the Great Mother or Great Goddess stood for the principle of relationship – the hidden connection of all things to each other. Secondly, particularly in Egyptian and Greek culture, she stood for justice, wisdom and compassion. Thirdly, and most importantly, she was identified with the unseen dimension beyond the known world – a dimension that was imagined as an invisible cosmic matrix or womb. The feminine principle personified by the Mother Goddess offered an image of life as an organic, living and sacred whole; the earth and the cosmos were sacred entities. Gaia, in Greek culture, was mother of all.

The Supreme Creator

However, with the development of Judeo-Christian culture, the influence of the feminine waned. The Father as supreme creator became the paramount image presiding over Western civilization. In Christianity, the Virgin Mary carried forward the feminine principle but she was not a goddess and therefore not representative of the earth or nature. Nature and matter slowly lost the sacredness once associated with the immanence of the divine in the manifest world. Because of the powerful influence of this long formative experience on the development of Western religion and science as well as cultural beliefs and patterns of behaviour derived from it, Western civilization developed on a foundation that lacked a feminine principle equivalent in value to the masculine one. Everything traditionally associated with the feminine – nature, matter, woman and body – was devalued in relation to the masculine.

Specifically, the idea developed that spirit was distinct from and "above" nature; that man was spiritually and mentally superior to woman, that thinking was superior to feeling and that mind should rule over and control body. Inevitably, with the rise of science, it was believed that man should vanquish and control nature. Over many centuries, these cultural beliefs created a deep imbalance in the culture as a whole as well as in the human psyche. It is not hard to see why mind came to be given precedence over heart. We can see the legacy of these beliefs in the ethos of conquest and dominance which still characterizes modern Western culture, particularly in the sphere of politics and science.

Where there is no balance between the masculine and feminine principles, the masculine principle becomes, over time, pathologically exaggerated; the feminine principle pathologically diminished. The symptoms of a pathological masculine are rigidity, dogmatic inflexibility, the drive for omnipotence and an obsession with power and control. The horizon of the human imagination is restricted by an overt or subtle censorship. We can see this imbalance reflected today in the ruthless values which govern the media, politics, and the technological drive of the modern world. We can see the predatory impulse to acquire or to conquer new territory reflected in the drive for global control of world markets, in the ideology of perpetual growth, and in the belief that technology – including the invention of ever more powerful weapons – can solve all our problems.

We see exaggerated competitiveness – the drive to go further, grow faster, achieve more, acquire more, elevated to the status of a cult. There is contempt for the feeling values grounded in the experience of our profound relationship with others, with other species, and with the environment. There is a predatory and compulsive sexuality in both men and women who increasingly lose the capacity for relationship with each other. There is continuous expansion in a linear sense *but no expansion in depth, in insight.*

The result? Exhaustion, anxiety,

The Egyptian cow-eared Goddess Hathor, the "mother of the light", at her temple at Dendera. She is one of the most ancient Egyptian deities, worshipped from predynastic times.   *Michael Baigent*

depression, and the breakdown of marriages. There is no time or place for human relationships. There is no time for relationship with the dimension of spirit. Men and women and, above all, children, become the victims of this harsh, competitive, uncaring ethos: women, in their desire to be accepted in a world ruled by men and because the feminine value has no clear definition in our culture, are drawn to copy the pathological image of the masculine which itself incorporates fear of the feminine. So there is a double rejection of the feminine, by women and by men.

Seeking Balance

How could we help to redress the balance between the masculine and feminine in ourselves and in our culture? The priority is to bring this whole subject into our awareness, making the imbalance between heart and mind a focus of discussion. It might be helpful to ask where we ourselves may be out of balance. Are we driven by the cultural ethos of achieving power, material success and control, ignoring feelings of anxiety and depression and the symptoms of our

body's distress? Do we allow enough time for relationships with our family and friends, enough time for being rather than doing? Or for connection with a deeper dimension of reality?

There are many areas where deeper insight and the need for a better balance between heart and mind could be addressed: in religion, in science, in politics, medicine, the care and education of our children, the proliferation of crime and our overcrowded prisons. Each of these invites a more comprehensive approach to the very great problems of our time. As Ervin Laszlo says at the end of his recent book *Macroshift*, "Planetary consciousness is knowing as well as feeling the vital interdependence and essential oneness of humankind and the conscious adoption of the ethic and the ethos that this entails. Its evolution is the basic imperative of human survival on this planet."

The choice is between clinging to an outworn and unbalanced ethos and maturing beyond it towards a greater sensitivity in our relationships with each other and with our wider environment. If we are unable to develop this empathic capacity to relate, we will surely destroy ourselves and the environment that sustains our life.

FREEMASONRY AND THE HEART

Freemasonry embraces the heart: brotherhood and charity towards others. Our Third Degree ritual states explicitly that the mind, "human reason", cannot penetrate that "mysterious veil" which shields the future and it urges us to forge a deep relationship with things of the heart: "Continue to listen to the voice of Nature…" it stresses, for this voice reveals our inner immortality. Yet balance is implicit: two of the three great pillars are the *Ionic*, Wisdom (the Mind), the *Corinthian*, Beauty (the Heart), nurturing the spirit in conjunction with the third pillar of Strength, the *Doric*.

©*Anne Baring, 2002.*

Anne Baring is a Jungian psychotherapist and teacher, author and co-author of 5 books including, The Myth of the Goddess *and* The Mystic Vision. *Website: www.annebaring.com*

DREAMING OF TIME PAST

PAUL DEVEREUX CONTINUES HIS STUDY OF SACRED DREAMS

The rugged summit of Carn Ingli, Preseli, Wales. The only open-air site selected for the Dragon Project site dreaming study.

In the last issue of *Freemasonry Today* we looked at the practice of 'temple sleep', conducted at selected sacred sites by numerous ancient cultures in order to obtain dreams for initiation, divination, or healing purposes. It was noted that 50 years ago the novelist and poet Lawrence Durrell had found evidence that modern people sleeping near ancient Greek dream temples experienced unusual, powerful, and disturbing dreams, causing him to wonder if the ancient dreams experienced at those places were somehow able to linger and be picked up, if in a garbled fashion, by dreaming minds much later on.

To mainstream modern thinking such an idea seems laughable. Dreams are supposed to live only inside the head – aren't they? Well, perhaps not if some current theorists are correct. They argue that mind is a *field* rather than a kind of buzz produced by brain activity, that our neurons process a raw mindstuff inherent in the fabric of the universe creating what we call human consciousness. Some scientists are actually attempting to identify specific neurophysiological structures that could enable this process.

Biologist Rupert Sheldrake has proposed a controversial theory he calls 'morphic resonance' which states that a person or any individual organism is informed by a memory field belonging to the species as a whole.[1]

In 1990, a multi-disciplinary research group entitled the Dragon Project Trust wondered if *places* could also have 'memory fields'. If so, how and where could they be accessed? The group reasoned that the dreaming mind, operating in the deep unconscious realms of the psyche, was the most likely candidate for picking up information at this subtle level if it existed at all, and that the place being used should be sacred, in that it might hold more information than a secular one due to intense spiritual and purposeful usage. Sacred and *ancient*, so it would have been deeply imbued with what C.G. Jung called 'numinosity'. So the trust set up an ancient sites dream research programme, and enrolled Dr. Stanley Krippner, a renowned professor of psychology at the Saybrook Graduate School in San Francisco, as its consultant.

Dreaming in Action

The Dragon Project Trust effort was aimed at making on-site dreaming as transpersonal and objective as possible. It was decided to use four ancient sites and have as many people as possible dream at them in order to see if there arose *site-specific* elements in the dreams – themes, sequences, images, motifs, symbols, even colours. The selected sites consisted of one natural and three monumental examples. The natural location is Carn Ingli, 'The Hill of Angels', a rugged ridge in the Preseli hills of south-west Wales, source of the Stonehenge bluestones. People resorted to it from at least as far back c.5,000 B.C. up until the sixth century A.D., when it was used by St. Brynach as a place of meditation and fasting. It was his visions of angels there that gave the peak its name. It also possesses a magnetic anomaly strong enough to spin compass needles.

The monumental sites are all in the Land's End district of Cornwall: Chûn Quoit, an isolated moorland dolmen dating to c.3,000 B.C., Madron Well, located in the ruins of a tiny medieval chapel where an ancient healing ritual involving sleep was carried out up until recent centuries, and Carn Euny, an underground passage and chamber complex of unknown purpose whose origins date to c.500 B.C.

The five thousand year old Chun Quoit dolmen, Cornwall, by night. This is one of the sites selected for the Dragon Project site dreaming study.

Carn Ingli has many magnetic anomaly spots on it. Here, in the summit rock, we see the red (north) points of the compass needles pointing in opposite directions. In fact, true north is in yet another direction.

The volunteer dreamers who became involved in the exercise came from many walks of life and various countries, ranging in age from teenagers to senior citizens, though most were in their thirties and forties. They were asked to record six dreams obtained in their familiar home environment for comparison with any on-site dreams they had. A local Dragon Project Trust facilitator then took them to the site they had volunteered to dream at. Dreamers would snuggle into a sleeping bag and generally fall asleep a little before midnight. Using a shaded or red-filtered flashlight, a helper checked periodically for REMs - *i.e.* Rapid Eye Movements visible beneath closed eyelids denoting dreaming sleep. Dreamers were awoken when these occurred and had their dream reports immediately tape-recorded. These were later transcribed.

Because of the sporadic, volunteer nature of the exercise along with limited resources, daunting logistics, and often harsh on-site conditions, it took until 2000 to assemble sufficient dream data for scientific analysis. The transcripts were then sent to Krippner in San Francisco. There they were re-typed onto standardised forms so work could commence on processing their data; this involved tabulating the dream elements according to a professionally-accepted analytical tool called the Strauch Scale.

Subsequently, The Dragon Project Trust and Saybrook sought further funds to enable a more sophisticated and complete system of content analysis (the Hall-Van de Castle analytical tool) which would provide a much better way of determining if the home dreams and site dreams differ significantly. This analysis was conducted independently and the raw results came in to Saybrook at the end of 2004. Krippner immediately noted that there are 'lots of statistically significant differences between the home and site dreams'. For example, 'home dreams had more familiar persons, less aggression, more friendliness, more success but also more failure, and less striving.' The

ANCIENT HEALING PROCEDURES AT MADRON WELL

Madron Well was locally famous for both its prophetic, oracular, powers and its healing properties. Although Madron Spring itself is a few hundred yards from the now ruined chapel, the healing rituals seem always to have taken place within the chapel to where the waters were carried by conduits. It was the tradition for ailing children to be brought to the chapel on the first three Sunday mornings in May, where they were plunged naked three times into the water in the granite basin or reservoir. In the 17th century, a celebrated and well-documented case involved John Trelille, who had been a cripple for 16 years. His ritual treatment consisted of being bathed in the waters once a week for three weeks, and after each occasion being encouraged to sleep on a slight mound before the rude altar in the tiny chapel. He became fully healed, and went on to live an active life as a soldier. Author Paul Devereux once slept at this site, and was rewarded with a vivid dream of a pair of hands displaying the particular way the waters should be applied to the face and eyes. The dream awoke him and he was able to go over to the reservoir basin in the chapel and immediately rehearse the procedure before he forgot it.

The reservoir for Madron Well in the corner of a now-ruined woodland chapel, Cornwall.

processing of this raw analytical data is now under way to enable an evaluation of what the differences signify, and there will also be an analysis site by site. This latter is most important, as the original main aim of the dream programme was to provide a systematic analysis of any site-specific dream content. Unlike the analysis comparing on-site with home or control dream data, this will be able to use the full range of the on-site dream report data.

With Place in Mind

While this final processing is taking place, simple 'eyeballing' of the data proves interesting, for some tantalisingly site-specific elements do appear in the dream report transcripts. As one brief example of this, here are a few snatches from just seven people's dream reports obtained at Carn Euny. It is important to remember these reports were made at different times – there was no cross-communication. The reports' sometimes

A dream study volunteer enters the Carn Euny tunnel to prepare for her overnight sleep session.

Inside the main tunnel of Carn Euny where some of the sleep sessions took place.

these people who were hikers or going somewhere ... a very friendly bunch of people ... Definitely the bustle of people going somewhere ...
BH: ... something to do with walking. It was sort of flattish sort of countryside ... I'm definitely walking around in this countryside ... I don't

GH: ... little boy with an old face, deformed face or something ... It was slightly nightmare-ish...
BH: ...stuck on the wall... was a big round thing and it had a face on it ... It wasn't really a human face ... It had big eyes, roundish eyes...
THS: ... I'm in the audience ... there's someone else who's just finishing an act. A singer or something...
BH: ... watching a show that was going on, sort of play thing but it was also something people sort of partook in ... we were sitting in the audience....

Allowing for a general sense to flow from this material, are we glimpsing some transpersonal, site-associated memories showing dimly through the distorting glass of personal dream recall?

If this is so, it will take the pending systematic analysis to make this scientifically credible. If that should prove the case then a paradigm shift in our understanding about the nature of consciousness will have been signalled by this modest pilot study, and Durrell's intuition at the Greek dream temple sites will have been strengthened. If not, the exercise will at least have produced a unique body of dream reports that will provide a valuable database for future researchers.

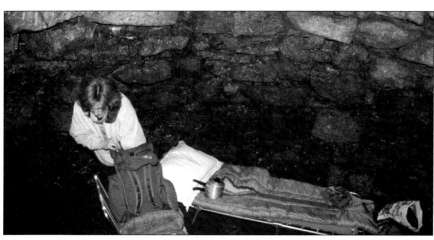

A dream study volunteer prepares for her overnight sleep session inside the chamber of the Carn Euny site.

slightly disjointed quality is accounted for by the fact that they were made verbally directly on awakening from REM sleep. The excerpts have been arranged so as to better highlight content similarities.

MS: I dreamt that I was awake ... and these people turned up and they had this dog with them ... a beige dog. And there was a cat ...
AR: ...I turned off for the Carn Euny turning ... Something went across in front of the bull-bar on the jeep ... I assumed it was a cat. It was big and beige ...

MVB: ...a sense of processing ... of going from one place to another ...
AR: ... on this flat lane, walking with

think I knew of any of these people ... It was a crowd of about five or six people ... we were walking around the area...
DS: They're holding my hands ... [Helper: "The people?"] ... Yeah ... I think they're going to take me somewhere ... It was all right though ... They were nice...
BH: There was quite a lot of people and it was something to do with food ...
AR: ...This person had set up selling ice creams and things...
MVB: ...A very tall chocolate cake ...
DS: I dreamt that we broke into a new tomb somewhere near here ... this enormous great carved ... with huge tusks and eyes, painted eyes ....

[1] See A New Science of Life, 1981, or The Presence of the Past, 1988.

Paul Devereux lectures widely, broadcasts occasionally and has written many articles, academic papers and some twenty-six books. Recent titles include, The Sacred Place *(Cassell),* Stone Age Soundtracks *(Vega),* Living Ancient Wisdom *(Rider) and* Mysterious Ancient America *(Vega). Website: www. pauldevereux.co.uk*

All photographs by Paul Devereux, © 2005

ORDER LINE 01243 790 203

Email: chichester@rohdeshoes.co.uk

Open: Mon - Sat 9am-5pm Sun 10am-4pm

ROHDE
Be comfortable.

DANIEL HECHTER
PARIS

463

- Calf leather
- High shine upper
- Stylish slip-on
- Sizes 41 - 46

R.R.P. £70

Anniversary offer ½ price £35

DANIEL HECHTER
PARIS

460

- Calf leather
- High shine upper
- Popular lace up style
- Sizes 41 - 46

R.R.P. £60

Anniversary offer ½ price £30

ROHDE
Be comfortable.

9626

- Soft leather uppers
- Full length padded leather insock
- Padded top line
- Sizes 7 - 10 (inc ½)

R.R.P. £50

Your price £45

DANIEL HECHTER
PARIS

941

- Soft lace up
- Calf leather lining
- Leather insock
- Rubber sole
- Sizes 41 - 45

R.R.P. £75

Your price £67

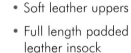

BARKER ENGLAND **Clive**

- Also available in black
- High shine leather
- Leather sole
- Goodyear welt
- Sizes 6 - 12

R.R.P. £120

Your price £108

BARKER ENGLAND **Jefferson**

- Genuine moccasin construction
- Generous width fitting
- Soft leather upper
- Sizes 6 - 12

R.R.P. £100

Your price £90

BARKER ENGLAND **Chesham**

- Black high shine leather
- Leather sole
- Wide fitting
- Sizes 6 - 11 (inc ½)

R.R.P. £125

Your price £112

BARKER ENGLAND **Chesham**

- Brown high shine leather
- Leather sole
- Wide fitting
- Sizes 6 - 11 (inc ½)

R.R.P. £125

Your price £112

All stock offered subject to availability.

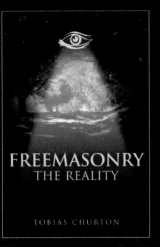
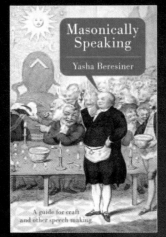
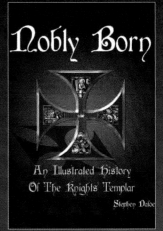
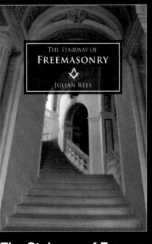

THE HISTORY

Freemasons are certainly more interested in what is happening in the world today than in the ancient origins of their Craft. But a study of how Freemasonry has evolved over more than four hundred years does provide a fascinating insight into how masonic structure and practice have been shaped by society, and how society in its turn has been shaped by Freemasonry. We live in an increasingly secular age, where spiritual aspirations are more and more being set aside; it was not always so, and Freemasonry, by its history, can claim to show us a more considerate, more caring era in the world's history, when harmony and the insights of the human heart were promoted more than they are today.

Nobody can say with certainty how Freemasonry came into existence, but that is not to say that we have lost the thread of its history, a very rich history. The story of the many men, some prominent in society and some not so well-known, who have illustrated masonic precepts by their lives and their examples, would fill several large tomes. The events in history in which Freemasons have played a part, directly or indirectly, are too numerous to catalogue.

So in this section we have assembled articles dealing with subjects as diverse as Christopher Wren, Rosslyn Chapel, a murder trial involving Freemasonry, a prominent masonic photographer, the Spanish Civil War, Freemasons in the gold rush in the Yukon, French Freemasonry in the Resistance and Freemasons in the Mounties.

Once we delve into the known history of Freemasonry, we should perhaps not be surprised to learn that many of the most prominent architects in London in the Age of Enlightenment were Freemasons – Nicholas Stone, Inigo Jones, Nicholas Hawksmoor, and possibly Christopher Wren himself. Some aspects of masonic history have a distinct flavour of having been contrived – Rosslyn Chapel is a case in point, yet it is too rich in fascinating symbolism to ignore. Then again, we learn that Mozart's music was influenced by Freemasonry, and he in turn composed music for Freemasons. Henry Wellcome, who has given his name to The Wellcome Institute for the History of Medicine, brought tolerance and philanthropy to bear on his business and on his research.

In areas of conflict we see the influence and example of masonic principles. The part played by Freemasons in the French Resistance was not inconsiderable, and many Freemasons in many countries lost their lives defending liberal ideals, not least in the Spanish Civil War.

While it has not been possible to cover the whole range of subjects included in masonic history, we gain here an insight into how history and Freemasonry have often been fellow travellers along the way of life.

The Apprentice Pillar

ROS
Chapel of t

As international interest in Scotland's Rosslyn Chapel grows, Matthew Scanlan attempts to sort out fact from fantasy

If ever a church could audition for Hollywood, Rosslyn Chapel would get the part. Recently dubbed Scotland's answer to the Pyramids, the chapel attracts almost as wide a clientèle as those other mysterious wonders of the world - scaled down somewhat but, for enthusiasts, no less fascinating. On the 2 April 1998, H.R.H. Prince Charles officially opened a new visitors centre, housing not only an exhibition on the chapel but, in due course, a section dedicated to masonic and Templar *aficianados*, along with a purpose-built car park. Yet amid all the hype and speculation, many will wonder just what exactly is the truth behind this mysterious edifice? Was this really the final resting place for a hunted order of medieval warrior monks escaping from the east? Did the Knights Templar really place secret heretical scrolls pertaining to the true identity of Christ in its subterranean vaults? And what lies behind the Chapel's famous *Prentice Pillar* and the tale of the murdered apprentice mason?

Interest in Rosslyn Chapel is itself a phenomenon and, as Stewart Beattie, Director of the Rosslyn Trust, says, everyone is free to project their own ideas onto the structure. To some it has become a beacon for extra-terrestrials, while

slyn

he Century

a new book is reportedly coming out stating that Christ's skull is under the chapel! People need a place of pilgrimage and Rosslyn has glamour : hints of masonic secrets and Templar-involvement, undeciphered imagery, and

Green Men - over 120 of them. (Psychologists note that we do have a goodly number of 'green men' these days, popping up from under prospective road and airport sites, earthy matter pouring from the nostrils in quixotic efforts to forestall the machinery of 'progress'). As if all this were not enough, there may well be 20 Rosslyn barons buried beneath the chapel. Beattie says : "I have no particular belief one way or the other." A few years ago, a sonar scan was done on the chapel, but the readings did not reveal anything. "If any future excavation is undertaken, it will be after consultation with the Trustees and Historic Scotland." So what do we know for sure?

William Sinclair

Roslin (current spelling for the village) is an old mining centre south of Edinburgh, lying half-way between Penicuik and Lasswade. The chapel stands at the end of a small lane, where the land rises to greet the Pentland Hills. The foundation stone was laid in 1446 by William Sinclair, the third and last Prince of Orkney. The construction work continued for forty years. William Sinclair appears to have acted as the Master of Works himself, as it was recorded how he caused the drafts to be drawn upon East-land boards, so the carpenters could make templates from them, before the masons could reproduce the tracings in stone. (Tracings can still be seen in the crypt or sacristy.) It is believed that the Chapel was intended to be a part of a much larger edifice but, most probably for financial reasons, it was never completed.

Inside, from its barrel vaulted ceiling, to every roof rib, capital, corbel, boss or arch, the chapel is encrusted with sculptured freestone, the eye being constantly drawn to yet another biblical allegory, strange shaped star or leering Green Man. The damp air seems conducive to their growth.

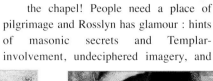

The eastern end is distinguished by three unusual pillars, reminiscent of Wisdom, Strength and Beauty, although lunar symbolism may have been intended, as arrangements such as this can be found at Carthage, representing the great mother goddess and the three phases of the moon. It is the strikingly ornate pillar standing in the south that captures the eye, spiralling upwards from the eight dragons about its base.

According to legend, the master mason who intended to carve it travelled to Rome with plans of its proposed design, only to discover upon his return that his apprentice had completed the work in exquisite fashion (an allegory for the Reformation?). In a furious rage of jealousy, the master slew the apprentice, from whence the *'Prentice Pillar'* is alleged to have earned its name. Despite this tale, the origins of the name are unclear. There is evidence of *'alabastermen'* working in the north of England in the 15th century, attached to various workshops. One of the best known ateliers for such work was the firm of *Prentys and Sutton* of Chellaston, who possessed their own quarry and workshop.

In the recent work *The Hiram Key*, the authors suggested that the pillar, together with a head carved in the chapel displaying a gash on the forehead, is related to Freemasonry's legendary figure, Hiram Abiff, the martyred craftsman of Solomon's Temple. However, the biblical Hiram does not die, and the earliest known appearance of the Hiramic legend is in 1730. The idea itself was

not uncommon, and was perhaps employed to express an archetype of sacrifice and rebirth, the ritual murder of father, master or king in fertility rites. The famous rose window at Rouen Cathedral is said to have been executed by an apprentice whose master, out of jealousy, knocked his brains out with a hammer. Other tales include an apprentice bracket at Gloucester Cathedral, an apprentice minaret at the mosque in Damietta, and I was told of another version during a recent visit to the great mosque in Damascus. Speculative possibilities are not exhausted.

Rosslyn's pillar may depict the world tree of Nordic legend, Yggdrasil, the fountain of eternal life and immortality. In the boughs : the eagle and serpent, forces of light and darkness, in perpetual conflict. Odin sacrificed himself and hung for nine nights from Yggdrasil, which represented a regenerative and sacrificial tree, thus forming an obvious parallel with Christ upon the cross - both were pierced with a spear. The capital above the pillar echoes the myth, being carved with the figure of Isaac. The serpents at its base may then represent Nidhogger the 'Dread Biter', gnawing at its root, symbolising the malevolent forces of the universe. For the Sinclair family with their Norman and Scandanavian roots, such parallels may have been congenial. Adjacent to the capital is a lintel, relevant to various masonic side degrees, carved with an inscription from the Book of Ezra and telling of the rebuilding of the second Temple under Zerubbabel, the inscription derived from his speech to Darius which earned the right to rebuild the Temple : *"Wine is strong, women are stronger, but truth conquers all"'*.

Despite recent speculation, there is no evidence for a Templar connection between the chapel and the Sinclair family, although there was a much older chapel once on this site, of which very little is known. The St. Clairs came from Normandy, and held land on the Pentland Hills from the the twelfth century. By 1500, the family were viewed by craft organisations in Scotland as hereditary

patrons. Thirty years after the split with Rome, the Catholic owner of Rosslyn resisted pressure to tear down his altars, a move eventually forced upon him in 1592. Yet, despite opposition to the Presbytery, William was still claiming patronage of the masons' craft many years later, as can be guaged from two 17th century charters. In the 1690's, the bond between the Sinclairs and the masons illuminated a famous letter :

"They are obliged to receive the masons' word and which is a secret signal masons have throughout the world to know one another by."

In November 1736, when the Grand Lodge of Scotland was formed in Edinburgh, with Sir William Sinclair becoming the first Scottish Grand Master, he was obliged to sign a declaration, as head of the family at Roslin, resigning in perpetuity the family's hereditary patronage of the Scottish craft.

The chapel is currently undergoing a programme of conservation which, as Stewart Beattie informed me, will continue for the next five years. Despite the scaffolding, the chapel's interior remains serene, and for masons and non-masons alike, Rosslyn Chapel offers a tantalising journey into the elusive minds of the craftsmen who built it. God knows what they were trying to achieve.

Matthew Scanlan would like to thank Michael Baigent, Robert Brydon and Stewart Beattie for their help in producing this article.

ALVIN LANGDON COBURN: ARTIST – PHOTOGRAPHER

A Major new Exhibition Reveals the Mysticism and Masonry in Coburn's Life and Work

Sphinx, 1905

"Searching for beauty to photograph opens our eyes to a new world of beauty; this is perhaps one of its most valuable gifts to us, it makes us increasingly mindful of an ever-richer and more glorious beauty in men and things, and in the panorama of the universe. Yet, behind the ever-changing beauty of the material world, there abides, immutable and serene, an Eternal Beauty which is its Cause, and the guarantee of its perfection."

So wrote Alvin Langdon Coburn in his autobiography published in 1966. And, referring to this Eternal Beauty, he added,

"We cannot photograph this, but, if we glimpse it with the eyes of the soul, life is changed for us, and we can see even the manifested earthly beauty in a richer splendour and with a fuller significance."

Coburn was born 1882, in Boston, United States. He became one of the leading photographers of the twentieth century. He first travelled to England in 1899, returning in 1904 when he photographed George Bernard Shaw. For the next few years he travelled between the United States and England but in 1912 settled in England and never again crossed the Atlantic. In 1918 he moved to Wales where he spent the rest of his life; and where he was to become initiated into Freemasonry.

For the first time a Summer exhibition is being mounted at Freemasons' Hall in Covent Garden, London, devoted to his photography. His photographs are linked with comments which touch upon the profound vision he sought to express.

Coburn experts and guest curators, David Bellman and Meirion Evans, working with the staff of the Library and Museum of Freemasonry, have arranged this display of photographs and linked texts which reveal, both visually and intellectually, the intimate relationship which existed between Coburn's photography and philosophy; which reveal how each informs and infuses the other.

The Art of Photography

For Coburn, photography was an art form able to stand side by side with painting, drawing and sculpture. Yet in the beginning – when he held his first "One Man Show" at the Royal Photographic Society in Russell Square, 1906 – this perception was not so. Coburn knew that photography had to fight to be accepted but knew that it had to fight from its own unique advantages – the great subtlety of

Penmaenmawr Circle, Wales, 1937
International Museum of Photography George Eastman House,
Rochester, NY.

Coburn's revolutionary photograph, The Octopus, New York, 1912.

Portland Place, London, 1906.

Coburn's portrait
of George Bernard Shaw,
1904

A Passage Between Tall Lands, Edinburgh, 1905

tonal range possible in photographs and its ability to reveal the "infinite gradations of luminosity" instead of attempting to imitate existing drawing techniques.

He pointed out that "whilst it is impossible to re-arrange trees and hills in the manner of the painter, it is possible to move the camera in such a way that a completely new arrangement is achieved, a few inches sometimes changing the entire design. For the creation of a picture, vision is of prime importance, and patience, and discrimination, and even marksmanship are decisive factors".

But the photographer seeks fragments of the beyond:

"The artist-photographer must be constantly on the alert for the perfect moment when a fragment of the jumble of nature is isolated by the conditions of light or atmosphere, until it becomes a perfect expression."

And he sought to push beyond the limits normally accepted in photography. His photograph, "The Octopus", 1912, was taken in New York looking down upon Madison Square where the pattern of paths indeed reminded him of that creature. He was aware of its weirdness to his contemporaries, "Depending, as it does, more upon pattern than upon subject matter, this photograph was revolutionary in 1912."

He continued to push beyond the boundaries. An aspiration which led him,

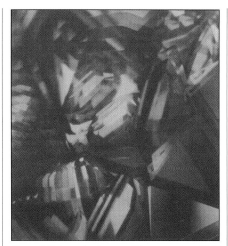
One of Coburn's abstract Vortographs, 1917

in 1916, to develop what he termed "Vortographs". He built an instrument of three mirrors fixed together as a triangle which acted as a prism splitting up the image in the lens. His exhibition in February 1917 was the first showing of purely abstract photographs, in fact, they were the first deliberately abstract photographs ever made. The poet Ezra Pound wrote in the preface to the catalogue of the exhibition that this technique had "freed photography from the material limitations of depicting recognizable natural objects".

Coburn and Freemasonry

Aged 34, Coburn was initiated into Freemasonry in 1919, into Lodge No. 1988, Barmouth, North Wales. He was passed and raised later that same year. In 1920 he joined a Royal Arch Chapter and the next year he joined both Mark and Rose-Croix. His mystical perspective was nurtured and augmented in his masonic career; Freemasonry became central to Coburn's life,

"Freemasonry is not a thing apart, cut off from life, it is interwoven with it, a thing to be understood and then to be lived, and the more it is studied with a view to spiritual progress,

Under Dark Arches, Edinburgh, 1905.

the more enlightened one becomes, and the richer in consequence are our lives".

He continued working within the masonic world, in 1922 joining the Royal Order of Scotland, the Royal Order of Eri and the Rosicrucian group within Freemasonry, the S.R.I.A. (Societas Rosicruciana in Anglia). He meanwhile progressed within the various Orders becoming Master of his Lodge for the first time in 1929-30. In 1939 he joined the Manchester Lodge of Research, No.5502, and also the Lodge of Living Stones, No. 4957, Leeds, which maintained a very individual and mystical ceremonial.

During this period he was advancing in the Ancient and Accepted Rite: he reached the 30° early 1927 and by 1939 had been initiated into the 32°. In March 1946 he was appointed Inspector General, 33°, of the District of North Wales a position he held until his death in 1966.

Coburn was well aware of the need for experience in the search for wisdom, aware that empty ritual and passive perambulation would not communicate anything of value:

"...self knowledge is a difficult thing, and yet it is for all who resolutely endure. This knowledge, as the founders of all Mysteries have realised, cannot be communicated unless there is an ardent effort to understand, on the part of the candidate. The Mysteries may not be imparted exclusively by any external rite or ceremony. The inner must reflect the outer, the symbol must be made alive, deep must answer unto deep."

The Artist and Beauty

Coburn described well the dedicated aspiration of all artists who seek to express that alluring ultimate beauty behind all life,

"It is a wonderful and inspiring thought to become one with beauty. All the artists of the world have knowingly or unknowingly engaged in this endeavour, the upward rush of their aspirations, the thrill of pleasure which has come to them with achievement, however slight and ever just ahead, luring them on; with this goes the glittering promise of the ultimate, the rainbow of perfection reflected and thus completed."

And he commented succinctly,

"We are comets across the sky of eternity".

All photographs, with the exception of the Penmaenmawr Circle, with permission of the Library and Museum of Freemasonry.

NICHOLAS STONE ACCEPTED FREEMASON

MATTHEW SCANLAN LOOKS AT THE MYSTERIOUS 'ACCEPTION'.

The Banqueting Hall, Whitehall, London.

photo: Matthew Scanlan

In the summer of 1718, one year after the formation of the London Grand Lodge, the second Grand Master, Mr. George Payne, requested that Brethren donate 'any old *Writings*' concerning masonry. Accordingly, several manuscripts were produced. However, it was subsequently reported that, sometime in 1720, 'several very valuable Manuscripts... concerning the Fraternity... particularly one writ[ten] by Mr. Nicholas Stone the Warden of Inigo Jones' were tragically 'burnt'.

Although little is known about the circumstances of this calamitous loss, the fact that 'Nicholas Stone' (1586-1647) is mentioned is significant; for he was not only the King's Master Mason and England's greatest seventeenth-century sculptor, but new research shows he was also made an accepted 'ffreemason' eight years before the well-known antiquary Elias Ashmole.

Nicholas Stone was born in 1586, the son of an Exeter quarryman. At a tender age he made his way to London and was apprenticed to the Flemish mason, Isaac James. Several years later he was introduced to the Dutch mason and sculptor, Hendrick de Keyser, with whom he returned to the Netherlands, and subsequently married his daughter, Maria.

By Dutch law Nicholas required the consent of his father in order to marry and this appears to have been attested by John Bury, the vicar of Sidbury, where Stone's father is believed to have once resided. Sadly the records of Sidbury church cannot be consulted as they were destroyed by fire in the nineteenth century. However, there is an interesting wall plaque in the chancel of the local St. Giles Church, making a play on the word 'Stone':

An epitaph upon ye Life and Death of
JOHN STONE, FREEMASON,
who, Departed Ys Life ye
first of January, 1617,
and Lyeth heer under buried.
On our great Corner Stone
this Stone relied,
For blessing to his building loving most,
to build God's Temples, in which
workes he dyed . . .

Soon after his wedding, Nicholas Stone returned to London with his bride. There he joined the 'London Company of ffreemasons', established a craft workshop in Long Acre, and rapidly secured a string of lucrative commissions. In June 1619 he secured a career-defining opportunity: he became the master mason responsible for rebuilding the State Banqueting House in Whitehall which meant he had to work in close consort with the Surveyor-General, Inigo Jones.

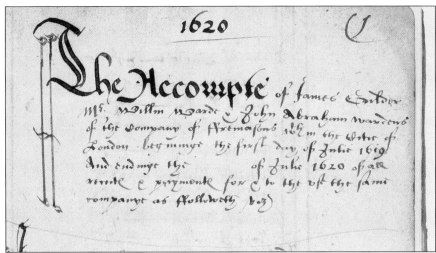

The text reads: 'The Accompte of James Gilder M[aste]r. William Warde & John Abraham wardens of the company of ffreemasons within the citie of London begininge the first day of Julie 1619 and endinge the' [gap in text] 'of Julie 1620 of all receite & paymente for & to the use the same companye as ffoloweth viz.'.

THE ACCEPTION

During the 1620s Nicholas Stone's reputation grew and in April 1626 he was appointed 'Master Mason and Architeckt' at Windsor Castle. The following year he served as Renter Warden of the 'London Company of ffreemasons' and in 1630 he progressed to the post of Upper Warden before finally being elected Company Master in 1633. Several months after this election he was also appointed Kings' Master Mason, making him the most senior mason in the country. Yet, curiously, four years after stepping down as Master of the London Company, its minutes record that, in 1638, Stone and four other men were 'taken into the Accepcon', evidently some sort of exclusive body within the Company.

Nothing like the Banqueting House had ever been seen in England before and its construction heralded a turning point in British architecture, marking the introduction of classicism. A special 'tracery-house' was even erected in Whitehall to provide a place where the planned masonry could be set out. The building proper formed a perfect double cube, a symbolic form which was in keeping with the ideas of the Roman architect Vitruvius who had stipulated that a basilica should be twice as long as it is wide. The ceiling was later decorated with paintings executed by Rubens. Intriguingly, Charles I instructed Rubens to paint his father, King James, in the manner that he most liked to see himself – in the guise of Solomon seated between the pillars of the temple.

Traditionally, researchers have described the accepted masons as non-stonemasons, yet Nicholas Stone was clearly a practising stonemason and so too were the others who joined the Acception that day. They were all described as 'ffreemasons' and one, Edmund Kinsman, was, like Stone, also a Past Master of the Company.

So what exactly was this mysterious practice? Was the Acception connected somehow with the symbolic side of architecture?

Stone certainly mixed in sophisticated and fashionable circles and his works evidently display a range of symbolism now found in modern Freemasonry: an hour-glass over a death's head, Time with a scythe, chequered pavements; figures representing Faith, Hope and Charity; the Four Cardinal Virtues (Prudence, Fortitude, Temperance and Justice), as

The Benefits of James I's Government by Peter Paul Rubens. The painting, designed to hang over the royal throne, depicts King James I in the guise of Solomon seated between the two pillars of the temple, with both Minerva (patroness of the arts and crafts) and Hermes (the bringer of knowledge and wisdom) at his feet (right and left respectively).

photo: Matthew Scanlan

well as numerous carved figures extracted from classical mythology. One of his monumental tomb designs bears the Latin inscription, 'You are the Agriculture of God'. A serpent winds round a rock, down which runs a stream, and a riband woven through the corn carries the words, 'If one were not to die, one could not be resurrected'. Building metaphors were by no means uncommon at this time. In 1609 a publication included the verse:

> As the Freemason heweth the hard stones ... even so God, the Heavenly Free-Mason, buildeth a Christian Church.

It is not known when Nicholas Stone joined the Company because the Company minutes before 1619 have been lost. However, in a separate building contract of 1615 Stone is described as a 'citizen and ffreemason of London', quite normal for the time. There are also later accounts which show Stone at various stages of progression within the Company; some of these are contained in the Company records and some derive from separate building accounts.

A similar example can be found on a mason's grave at Abbots Kerswell, Devon, dated 4 May 1639; the lines of poetry run lengthways along the tomb:

> Christ was thy Corner-stone,
> Christians the rest,
> Hammer the word, Good life thy line
> all blest,
> And yet art gone, t'was honour not
> thy crime,
> With stone hearts to worke much in
> little time,
> Thy Master saws't and tooke thee off
> from them,
> To the bright stone of New
> Jerusalem,
> Thy worke and labour men may
> esteem a base one,
> Heaven counts it blest, here lies a
> blest free-Mason.

THE DIARY OF NICHOLAS STONE JUNIOR

In the year of Stone's joining the Acception, his two eldest sons, Henry and Nicholas junior, both trained freemasons and sculptors, travelled to Italy to further their knowledge of continental art and architecture. Nicholas kept a diary of their travels and in Florence he recorded how they met the Duke of Tuscany; the Duke even expressed an interest in the brothers' drawings. They also met the great sculptor, Gianlorenzo Bernini, who evidently rated the work of Nicholas the younger, as he invited him to come and watch him work and encouraged him to continue drawing in chalk. In Rome, Nicholas mentioned the Church of Santa Maria del Popolo and a 'great piramide' that stood before it, which was engraved with 'Egyptian caracters', as well as temples dedicated to various gods such as Venus, Jupiter and Ceres. Yet the most remarkable aspect of the diary undoubtedly concerns the brothers numerous purchases, as it demonstrates that the leading master masons of the seventeenth century were not the simple, untutored, craftsmen they have often been portrayed as by masonic researchers. On the contrary, many were well-educated and perfectly capable of understanding every facet of modern symbolic Freemasonry.

And intriguingly, on 30 June 1639, Nicholas Stone junior recorded that his father requested a 'booke of [the] Archytecture of Domenico Fontana to be sent for England for Mr Kinsman' – the same Edmund Kinsman who had joined the Acception in 1638.

Nicholas Stone senior died in 1647 and was buried in the parish church of St. Martin-in-the-Fields. In a

He also left five central London houses, and his oldest son Henry inherited the family business. It was Henry who carved a wall-tablet to his father's memory in St. Martin's Church which, though later destroyed, was described as consisting of 'several Tools for Sculpture-work' as well as 'a Square, and Pair of Compasses'.

Two-and-a-half years after his passing another mysterious meeting of the Acception took place on 25 January 1650 and on this occasion five men joined, one of whom was Stone's eldest son, Henry. Henry was not only a trained Freemason, but was also a well-known copy painter, who worked for a time as assistant to the celebrated artist Van Dyck. He made numerous copies of famous paintings and later commissioned the English artist, Sir Peter Lely, to paint his own portrait.

Upon Henry's death in 1653, and with Nicholas junior already gone, the family business reverted to his younger brother John, who was also a qualified Freemason and probably the most educated of all. He had been educated at Westminster School and Oxford University, and worked as Bible Clerk and Librarian at University College, Oxford, from 1644 to 1648, before being expelled by Parliamentary forces. Unfortunately it is unclear whether John joined the Acception like his father and elder brother. Nonetheless, the evidence

The purchases in Rome included:

'The booke of Euclides geometria'

a 'booke of the ruines of Roome';

'Eosopes fables in Italian';

'two plaister heads of Venus and Cicero';

'prints of the roofe in the Popes Chapple in the Vatticane';

'a booke of the perspective of Vignolo';

'5 pound 2 ounces of wax for baking of a modell of the Satyre Martius';

'a book of the fountains of Rome';

a book of the 'Archytecture of Vitruvius';

'a plaister figure representing a Bacchus moulded from the antique';

prints of Albrecht Durer;

'113 small peeces of severall sorts of marbles to send for England according to my fathers commaund';

An Apollo made of wax;

a 'Mercury of plaister';

and a book of the 'Archytecture [of] Leo Battista Alberti'.

distinguished career, it is known that he earned well in excess of £11,000 which, for the time, shows a man of considerable standing, and in his Will he was tellingly referred to as 'Esquier'.

surrounding the Stone family unquestionably offers a rare insight into the world of our working forebears, a world which was sophisticated by any standard, then and now.

FRENCH FREEMASONRY AND THE RESISTANCE, 1940-1944

KEITH DONEY REMINDS US OF THE HEROISM OF FRENCH MASONS

Notice issued by the German authorities proclaiming the execution of Freemason, José Roig, for Resistance activities, 1 August 1941.

Photo: Collection of Keith Doney

The first active 'Résistant' shot during the Second World War by the German authorities was a Freemason. Brother José Roig was executed at Ivry, 1st August 1941, for supporting, and recruiting for, General de Gaulle and the Free French Government in exile.

The French Government's Act of 13th August 1940, which proscribed Freemasonry, led to the dismissal of all Freemasons serving in the Civil Service, Local Government and Teaching. Naturally, this caused much resentment against the Vichy Government and their masters, the occupying Nazi forces. This resentment, coupled with the ideals of Freemasonry – of liberty of speech and thought – could easily be channelled into both active and passive resistance. Furthermore, Freemasonry, with its implicit trust in fellow masons, was already organised into Lodges and "Triangles" of three Brethren (according to French masonic practice), and was thus ideally suited for clandestine activities.

In addition, many Freemasons had served in the Armed Forces and had returned to civilian life disillusioned with the French Authorities. They felt that the unthinkable collapse of France was the result of poor strategy by the leaders and the low morale of the troops. They were eager to redeem the reputation of France, by combatting the oppressive measures of Vichy and the occupying power. Their specialised knowledge was very useful in intelligence gathering, and organising networks and the necessary administration. As the Occupation continued,

Freemasons were to be found in almost all the main Resistance networks: *Libération, Combat, Franc-Tireur, Marco Polo, Coq Enchâiné, Comète, Atelier de la Bastille, La Bonne Foi* and many others.

The Organisation of the Resistance

Though officially dissolved, masonic ideals and beliefs were continued by individuals and small groups of masons. They continued to meet in houses or cafés and as early as the 7th January 1941, one group, foremost amongst whom were Eychène, Kirchmeyer and Bonnard, formed the *Grand Conseil Provisoire de la Maçonnerie Française* (Provisional Council of French Freemasonry). This was later to become the *Comité d'Action Maçonnique* or C.A.M.

Between 1941 and 1944, 211 clandestine masonic lodges were to enter into contact with it. These lodges – sometimes merely 'triangles' – were numbered according to the number of their "Départment" plus the number of precedence that they would assume in the "New Freemasonry" after the liberation of France. These 211 lodges encompassed sixty "Départments".[1]

It was an energetic ex-officer of eighty years of age, Colonel Eychène, who chose the name *Patriam Recuperaré*, a lodge and a movement formed almost wholly of Freemasons, which was to become the most famous of the masonic networks. In 1945, Bonnard, one of the founders of the lodge, summed up its raison d'être thus:

> In action, Masonry and Resistance became practically synonymous. Men are needed with "le cran courage" of Kipling, himself a mason, expressed in the poem *If*, 'Then my son, you are a Man'.

Seal of the Patriam Recuperaré *Resistance network*.   Photo: Archives of the Grand Orient, Paris

German destruction of a masonic temple in the Grand Orient, Paris.
.   *Photo: Archives of the Grand Orient, Paris*

Resistance, being a moral virtue, albeit a new one, the 'morale d'honneur' becomes a virtue also. To retain one's dignity and self-esteem, a true mason cannot help but resist. A resistance which ennobles the individual, ennobles also the nation.

Using Kirchmeyer's flat at 123 rue Saint-Antoine, Paris, as a base, and maintaining contact with London from 1942, the activities of the Resistance groups under Kirchmeyer's auspices expanded to include non-masons. Their roles were varied: information gathering, propaganda, parachute drops, aiding escaping airmen, refugees, Jews and those avoiding forced labour, clandestine newspapers, forged documents of all types, indeed, they provided all the needs of a clandestine resistance movement.

The Blow Falls

All was proceeding smoothly when suddenly the blow fell: Kirchmeyer was arrested, 3 March 1943. A trap had been set at rue Saint-Antoine and any visitor was taken into custody. Sufficient incriminating documents had been found there to fill two rooms. However, the police, through ignorance or connivance, did not appear over-thorough in searching the innumerable files kept by such a meticulous man. But ample evidence was found to connect Kirchmeyer with being the head and co-

ordinator of a vast Resistance network. The punishment was death!

Under questioning by the infamous *Commissaire* David, Kirchmeyer admitted the possession of documents of military value and of being a supporter of De Gaulle. David informed him of the seriousness of his position – he was held to be the leader of the Freemason's network, his second in command being Colonel Eychène.

Fortunately, by the time the Germans

123 rue Saint-Antoine, headquarters of the masonic Resistance network, Patriam Recuperaré   *Photo: Pascal Bajou*

Antimasonic exhibition of looted artefacts and documents mounted in the Petit Palais, Paris, 12 October 1940   Photo: *Archives of the Grand Orient, Paris*

came to take Kirchmeyer to prison, several incriminating documents had mysteriously disappeared. Enigmatically, these were returned to him by the examining magistrate after the Liberation! Kirchmeyer was kept in solitary confinement from April 1941 until 19th January 1944 when he was deported, first to Buchenwald and then to the extermination camp at Mauthausen. Interrogations revealed nothing; he gave nothing away. And he survived to return to France at the end of May 1945.

Similarly, a search at Colonel Eychène's house revealed nothing. The Germans disregarded an old man of eighty, yet he was to carry on Kirchmeyer's work at rue Saint-Antoine with the help of Kirchmeyer's family. The group ceased all its activities at the end of hostilities after having been one of the most important groups of the Resistance.

Brothers of Resistance

In addition to *Patriam Recuperaré*, in which Freemasons formed almost the total membership, masons of many lodges were involved in the Resistance as the following extracts from lodge histories reveal:

Loge de L'Enseignement Mutuel

Several Brethren continued to meet secretly in the café "Le Dercy" owned by a Freemason, and all took part in resisting the enemy in some form or another. Their losses were heavy: two Brethren, Jacques Lévy and Brother Blum, were killed in concentration camps whilst Brother Gorwick died in a camp. Brothers Voronoff, Gauthier and Poittevin died in prison; Brother Gosselin fell in action on the Alsace front and Brothers Lacroix and Rogannet fought and were wounded in Paris while evicting the Germans at the Liberation.

Loge Artistes Réunis

Brothers Perrin and Dutreix founded the Resistance network *Libération* and, with Brother Lemoine, were arrested 17th April 1943. After harsh treatment and torture, Perrin and Dutreix were shot as hostages at Romainville, 2nd October. Lemoine was finally sent to Dora camp where he died from typhus and maltreatment. Another lodge member, Brother Maugenest, died in Buchenwald, 1945; Brother Bonneau, a professor dismissed from his post in accordance

with the anti-masonic laws, also died in the same concentration camp.

Loge Etoile Polaire

Of the seven Brethren of this lodge who died as a result of the war, three were beheaded and three died in deportation to German concentration camps.

Other Lodges in the North of France

Brother Louis Lemaire, a high-ranking Freemason, was rather fortunate compared to many of his Brethren. A builder by trade, he hid escaping soldiers in the piles of material in his yard. Inevitably, he was denounced and brought before an elderly German officer. He was asked his age; he realised that he was being asked his masonic age (how long he had been a mason). On giving this information he was dismissed - and given the informant's name for good measure!

Brothers Paul Lisfranc (Lodge *Les Philadèlphes and La Lumière du Nord*) were shot on 27th December 1943 at Fort Bondues. Brother Raoul François (Lodge *Conscience*) was shot on 5th April 1944 in the moat of the Citadelle d'Arras. Brother André Serrure (Lodge *La Lumière du Nord*) was deported to Germany and decapitated at Munich on 28th November 1944 along with eight of his comrades.

On 3rd May 1942 eighteen members of a Resistance group named *Action 40* were arrested. They included two Freemasons, Brothers Guislain and Lavaud, both of Lodge *La Fidelité*. Twelve were condemned to death - including Brother Lavaud who was decapitated at Dortmund, 10th April 1943. Brother Guislain, after deportation and imprisonment, survived to be repatriated in 1945.

Lodges in the Dauphiné

Two Brethren, Oudinos and Courtot, were shot and twenty other Freemasons from Lodges in the area were killed in concentration camps or in action with the Resistance. Many others were arrested, tortured, or imprisoned, amongst whom were Alix Bertlet and Jean Pain. The latter's body was found, horribly mutilated, in a ditch. Brother Metral, the Mayor of Viziville, was about to be hanged when he was miraculously saved by a shell-burst from the Allied Forces.

The above accounts of the part played by lodges in the Resistance reveal the general commitment of Freemasonry in the struggle against oppression. However, the contribution of several individual masons, amongst the many, is worthy of a closer examination.

Masonic Heroes of the Resistance

Pierre Brossolette is such a hero. Born in 1903, he was initiated into Freemasonry in 1927. He returned from the defeat of the French army determined to continue the struggle against the Occupying Power. Unable to obtain a position in Education, he decided to buy a bookshop as a cover for his work in the Resistance. He was an active member of the networks, *Musée de l'Homme* and *Confrèrerie Notre Dame*. In 1942 the networks established links with London. His role was to co-ordinate all Resistance movements and to liase with London. He succeeded in sending his family to safety via Gibraltar and made several dangerous trips to London where he broadcast to Occupied France on the BBC World Service.

On the arrest of Jean Moulin, De Gaulle's Resistance co-ordinator, Brossolette returned to France to take over Moulin's role. While he operated under the cover of many aliases, it was when attempting to escape to England that he was arrested in Brittany by the Gestapo for failing to hold the correct pass for the area. At first the Germans did not realise the importance of their prize but once his true identity was known, he was transferred to Gestapo Headquarters in Paris. He was badly tortured and on 22 March 1944, taken from Fresnes Prison to No. 84, Avenue Foch, for further interrogation. He summoned up the strength to throw himself to his death from a fifth floor window. He thus denied the enemy the information in his possession.

He was awarded the *Croix de Guerre* and the *Croix de la Libération*. His citation, signed by De Gaulle himself, read:

An officer possessed of a rare energy and remarkable tenacity. He showed a total disregard for danger and contributed with great success to the organisation of the Resistance in France and to the union of all Frenchmen against the invader.

Another Freemason of note was Martial Brigouleix. Born in 1903, he trained as a teacher but after his Army service in 1940, he was, in 1942, dismissed from his post according to Governmental decree. This unjust dismissal was the spur needed to steer him into the Resistance. However, in 1943, he was denounced and arrested by the Gestapo. In the five and a half months of life which remained to him, he was severely tortured by his captors but none

Memorial to masonic Resistance hero, Martial Biqouleix and other martyrs at Tulle (Corréze)

Photo: Archives of the Grand Orient, Paris

of his colleagues in the Resistance was arrested by the Gestapo from information which he possessed but never revealed. Placed amongst a group of hostages at Romainville, he was shot at Mont-Valérien on 2nd October 1943, in reprisal for a German killed in Paris.

Rolf l'Hermite and his brother, Serge, returned from military service determined to carry on the struggle against oppression. Quickly, the group of which Rolf was a member, merged with other groups to form the *Mouvement National de Résistance*, or M.N.R., one of the earliest Resistance networks. Armed groups were organised, links with London were forged, and a clandestine newspaper was published.

In 1942, the brothers created the movement *Milice de la République* and later joined with *Libération Est* and *Libération Nord*. In 1944 Rolf formed an armed band of some sixty men and went on the offensive against the Germans causing much loss to them in both men and material. Both masons were decorated for their work in the resistance.

Like many other Freemasons, Georges Lapierre, a respected Headmaster, was dismissed from his post in 1941 at the age of fifty-five years. In 1942, he joined the network C.N.D. Castille. Denounced in 1943, he then travelled a horrific journey from Fresnes prison to the concentration camps of Sachsenhausen, Notzweiler-Struthof and finally to Dachau, where he died on 4th February 1945. Beloved by all who came into contact with him, he devoted his life to helping those in even worse circumstances than himself. Physically weakened by his privations although still strong in mind and spirit, Georges Lapierre became yet another victim of Nazi persecution.

LEST WE FORGET!

[1] For more information on the C.A.M., see Historique Sommaire du Groupe de Résistance Patriam Recuperaré, *Grand Orient de France*.

Dr. Keith Doney is a linguist and historian. His PhD, Freemasonry in France during Nazi occupation and its rehabilitation after the war, was probably the first awarded in England for research into Freemasonry. He is Past Master of Bridge Trust Lodge, Birmingham.

THE MOUNTIES AND FREEMASONRY

CANADIAN, NELSON KING, REVEALS THE MASONIC INFLUENCE FROM THE BEGINNING

An unknown member of the Mounties in his masonic regalia.

Like every little boy growing up in Canada, I had a great fascination with the Mounties. With their dress uniform of a low, broad-brimmed hat, scarlet jacket, and blue trousers with a yellow stripe, their Musical Ride, their horses, everything associated with them. They had dogs called King and saved the world from all types of dastardly deeds and they 'always got their man'. Imagine my joy when I learned that the Mounties had been associated with Freemasonry from their inception.

Early in the 19th century, residents of British North America began to fear that the United States wanted to absorb all of North America. As a result many colonists sought to unify the British colonies. In 1867 the British Parliament passed the British North America Act which formed the colonies into a union called the Dominion of Canada: the first four to join were New Brunswick, Nova Scotia, Ontario and Quebec.

By 1873 the Canadian people and their government were stirred by the prospect of a greater Canada. A new era had dawned, expansion and unity had become the foremost topic of discussion, a call to adventure had been sounded. That same year the government's attention was drawn to an Imperial proclamation of 1870 by which Rupert's Land and the North-West territories had been added to Canada and further, that it pledged the Dominion of Canada to care for, and protect, the thousands of Indians who lived there. This was in strong contrast to the situation south of the border where a state of war against the Indians prevailed.

A Police Force for the Territories

The Canadian Government had, from time to time, contemplated the patrol of the Western frontier with a small number of mounted men but it was felt that something more comprehensive was essential. An adequate application of the law, without show of aggression, was the

Lieutenant-Colonel George French, First Commissioner of the Mounties, 1873-1887.

primary requisite. On 28 April 1873, the Prime Minister, and Freemason, Sir John Macdonald, gave notice of a Bill: 'Respecting the Administration of Justice and for the Establishment of a Police Force in the North-West Territories'. The following day an invasion from Montana culminated in an outburst of frontier depravity. In Battle creek in far off southern Saskatchewan, blood lust and liquor had combined to wipe out a hapless band of innocent Indians wrongfully accused of stealing horses. Wholesale murder on the part of the Missouri River gangs had reached an outrageous climax on Canadian soil.

As news of the 'Cypress Hills Massacre' spread, indignation and anger exploded on the front pages of Canada's Eastern Press and when warnings of further trouble arrived arrangements for the guardianship of the far away territories were speeded up. On 23 May 1873 Royal assent was given to the bill and the North-West Mounted Police became a reality. Its first 150 men were sent to the West and they spent the next winter at Lower Fort Garry. It was quickly realised that more men were needed and 150 more joined them

the next year. This enlarged force travelled into the foothills of the Rocky Mountains where a barracks was built at Fort MacLeod.

Uniforms worn by the original Mounties in 1874. Sitting, Sub-Inspector John French, behind him with a beard is Sub-Inspector Francis Dickens, son of Charles Dickens.

The Commissioner, Lt.-Colonel French, and half the men then moved east leaving Colonel MacLeod in command of the barracks. The latter was soon fully engrossed in pacifying thousands of Indians, including Chief Sitting Bull, who had moved into Canada after the Battle of the Little Bighorn in which Custer and his regiment of the Seventh Cavalry were annihilated. MacLeod and his men routed out the American whisky traders and smugglers and assisted in the forging of treaties with the Indian tribes.

Freemasonry and the Mounties

Some three months earlier the North-West Mounted Police Headquarters were set up in Regina, the capital of Saskatchewan. The Grand Lodge of Manitoba, which had jurisdiction over all the North-West Territories, granted a dispensation for the formation of a masonic lodge there. This became Lodge Wascana, No. 23. Among the members of the North-West Mounted Police were several Freemasons. Most of them became affiliated with the new Lodge; others were initiated into it. By the mid 1880s it was decided to found a new Lodge solely for members of the

Mounties. Eventually, on 24 August 1894, a meeting was held of fourteen Freemasons – eleven came from Lodge Wascana, one from Ancient St John's Lodge, No.3, one from Bow River Lodge, No. 28 and one from the Lodge St. John, No. 175, in Greenock, Scotland – who put their signatures to a petition to the Grand Lodge of Manitoba at Winnipeg. They became the founder members of the new Lodge: North-West Mounted Police Lodge, No. 61. The first bylaws of 1895 contained an historical introduction:

> In a large body of men such as the North-West Mounted Police, whose members are scattered over such a vast extent of territory, and who are gathered from almost every civilised country in the world, a certain percentage of Masons are bound to be found, and it would not have been consistent with the usual perseverance and enlightened teachings of Freemasonry had the members of the Order failed to organize a Lodge among themselves, and so be in a better position to carry out the precepts and tenets of the Order than could otherwise have been done while so many different Lodges were represented by them.

Lieutenant-Colonel James Macleod, Second Commissioner of the Mounties, 1875-1880.

The first Master was the third most senior officer in the Regiment, Robert Belcher, who had joined the Mounties in 1873, rose through the ranks and was commissioned in 1893. The altar, Warden's pedestals and columns were made at the Regina Barracks. They were painted white and trimmed with the Mounties' colours of blue and gold. The pillars can still be seen in the Regina Masonic Temple. The original sword was presented by Inspector Church who originated the famed Musical Ride. His father had carried it in the Charge of the Light Brigade at Balaclava. Also at the Temple in Regina may be seen the original rough and smooth ashlars, hewn by the first members of the lodge.

As the Mounties grew in stature so too masonry flourished in it, and more and more members became initiated into Freemasonry. This was a natural development as the high ideals of the one are similar to and intermingled with those of the other.

With the huge Dominion Government immigration policy starting in 1896, the discovery of gold in the Yukon in 1898, and the Boer War, members of the North West Mounted Police were exceedingly busy serving in all spheres and assuming manifold responsibilities. The number of members

The Mounties' town station, Regina, capital of Saskatchewan, in 1885.

A Church Parade held at the Mounties base, Regina.

at Regina H.Q. became comparatively small, and of these only two Masons remained to keep the Lodge alive. The Grand Master of Manitoba moved to arrest the Charter. But the brethren wished to save the Charter, and to do so relaxed the custom whereby only police members could enrol in the Lodge.

Thus in 1906 it was decided to hold future meetings in the City of Regina. Deputy District Grand Master Isaac Forbes, himself a member of the Force, reported to Grand Lodge in the following words:

N.W.M.P. Lodge No. 11 (G.R.S.), Regina. I paid my official visit to this Lodge on May 2nd. This being my own Lodge, and attending regularly myself, I take a great interest in it. Owing to the fact that all the members belonged to the N.W.M. Police, and that the majority of them had been transferred to different places, leaving the Lodge short of members with whom to hold meetings, for the last four years it has been going down hill. I am pleased to say that this is now a thing of the past. The removal of the place of meeting from the N.W.M.P. Barracks to the City of Regina, which took place on October 4th, 1906, has proved to

be of great welfare to Masonry. Since the meeting on October 4th the Lodge has increased from sixteen to fifty. The Lodge is now N. W. M. Police in name only, but the name will be a landmark when the Police have gone from the Province of Saskatchewan.

In 1904 King Edward VII honoured the Force by conferring the title 'Royal' so that the force was known as the Royal North West Mounted Police. The Lodge, however, retained the name N.W.M.Police.

By 1920 the Force was Canada-wide and was renamed the Royal Canadian Mounted Police. A few years later the Provinces asked them to take over their police work and by 1932 the Mounties policed six Provinces; in 1950 the remaining Provinces of Newfoundland and British Columbia followed suit.

For many years a Degree Team of the Royal Canadian Mounted Police annually performed an average of ten Degree ceremonies and two or three exemplifications. The 'team' performed in many lodges in Canada as well as in the United States: in Indiana, Ohio, Massachusetts, New York and Vermont. In recent years however the team has disbanded, for however many Mounties remain active Freemasons, any official support or encouragement for their involvement has now vanished. ■

Nelson King is Editor of the prominent American journal of masonic research, The Philalethes. *He is also an author and a well-known speaker to masonic groups in North America.*

MOZART'S GENIUS AND MASONRY

BRUCE YOUNG TRACES THE CONNECTIONS BETWEEN MUSIC AND MASONRY

Mozart in his lodge c.1784 in a painting ascribed to Ignaz Unterberger. The figure on the bench extreme right is assumed to be Mozart.

photo: akg images

This year Austria is celebrating the 250th anniversary of the birth, on 27 January 1756, of Wolfgang Amadeus Mozart, one of the greatest composers of all time. In Salzburg, the city of his birth, celebrations include performances of all of his operas; in Vienna, celebrations under the banner of *Mozart Year 2006* are taking place, including substantial exhibitions at the refurbished house in the *Domgasse* near the cathedral, where he wrote *Figaro*, and a comprehensive exhibition at the *Albertina* Art Gallery: 'The Enlightenment: An Experiment'. The Austrian Post Office has issued a commemorative set of postage stamps depicting Masonic artefacts, and Mozart at his lodge in Vienna.

Mozart was the youngest child and only surviving son of Leopold Mozart, who was himself a distinguished musician. But Leopold was a dictatorial man, not easy to get on with, as can be seen from the extensive correspondence between father and son, and he was also ruthless in promoting his young prodigy. Wolfgang travelled the length and breadth of Europe as a very young man, playing in many courts and distinguished venues under the guidance of his father. Before the age of ten he had visited Munich, Augsburg, Milan, Naples, Paris and London. Mozart's mother died while travelling with him in Paris, in 1778 when he was 22 years old, and this was a bitter blow to the young man. Eventually he married Constanze Weber, without his father's approval, whilst in Vienna.

This signalled the point at which Mozart seemed to shake off the overbearing influence of his domineering father. His marriage to Constanze marked not only a break with his father, but with much of his past life. Up to this time, he had been Concert Master in Prince-Bishop Colloredo's entourage in Salzburg, but his move to Vienna then gave Mozart an entrée to a bustling imperial capital of over 200,000 people, of whom no less than 600 described themselves in the census as 'composer'.

Mozart found that he was able to cross the social divide and mix freely and to get work, the highest-paid in society. His fee from a single concert equalled half his annual salary in Salzburg. His status also improved, as he wrote to his

MOZART AND LONDON

It was in London in 1764 when he was 8 years old that Mozart performed for George III, whose son, HRH The Duke of Sussex, would later become a member of Pilgrim Lodge, No. 238, the only German-speaking Lodge in London, much frequented by gentlemen of the Royal Court. Another member of this lodge was Johann Zoffany, the renowned portrait painter, who was later to paint Mozart himself.

Mozart wrote the aria *Ch'io mi scordi di te*. (How can I forget you?) K.505 in 1786 for soprano Nancy Storace, who had sung Susanna in the first performance of *Marriage of Figaro*. Mozart composed this most exquisite farewell gift, penned for Nancy prior to her departure from Vienna in February of 1787, and played the piano part as she sang at its premiere. It was considered an intimate expression of his love and esteem for Storace.

Nancy returned to London becoming a family friend of Sir John Soane, architect of the Freemasons' Hall of 1831, who designed a funeral monument for her at St. Mary's, Lambeth. Sir John, born just before Mozart in 1753, became a distinguished Freemason with the rank Grand Superintendant of the Works [sic] (1813-1836), serving under HRH The Duke of Sussex as Grand Master.

father: 'All possible honour is shown me' and he eventually, in 1787, became Court Chamber Musician, as a result of which a substantial corpus of delightful minuets, German dance and contredanse written for the Court balls has come down to us.

FREEMASONRY AND VIENNESE SOCIETY

Mozart was proposed, and initiated, in the Lodge *Zur Wohltätigkeit* (Beneficence) in December 1784, and passed to the second degree in the Lodge *Zur Wahren Eintracht* (True Concord) in January 1785. This was the most prestigious Austrian lodge of all. Shortly after that, he was raised to the third degree. In his letter *On Genuine Concord*, addressed to the Vienna Lodge, Mozart confessed 'It has always been my ardent wish to join the ranks of those who set themselves as the goal of their endeavour to work for the enlightenment and well-being of their neighbours – I am confident to have found in Freemasonry exactly such people striving for the triumph of good'.

The Empress Maria Theresa's husband was a Freemason although she disapproved of Freemasonry: she nevertheless chose to ignore the Papal edict outlawing Freemasonry, as impinging on her imperial authority. When she died and Josef II acceded to the throne as sole ruler in 1780, several years of liberalisation ensued, but on 11 December 1785 an imperial ordinance on the control of Freemasonry was announced to limit the number of Viennese Lodges. Eight Viennese Freemason lodges were condensed into three and were obliged to submit their membership lists and the minutes of the proceedings periodically to the police. The lodge Beneficence had to restart as the Lodge *Zur Neugekrönten Hoffnung* (New Crowned Hope) together with the lodge Crowned Hope and the lodge Three Flames. This ordinance had a great impact not only on Freemasonry in Vienna but also on Mozart himself, since his own lodge was dissolved, and he had to join the new composite lodge, New Crowned Hope. Whilst it has been estimated that some 80 percent of the Austrian higher bureaucracy were masons at this time, the number of masons in Vienna decreased from 950 in 1785 to 350 in 1786.

The courtyard of the Summer Palace of Prince Bishop Colloredo in Vienna from where he famously dismissed Mozart in 1781.

photo: Mark Dennis

FREEMASONRY AND ENLIGHTENMENT SOCIETY

The impact of Freemasonry on Enlightenment Society cannot be overestimated. The French dramatist and Freemason Beaumarchais' play *Figaro*, having been banned in Paris, was performed as an opera by Mozart in 1786, several years prior to the French Revolution. Significantly, but also most poignantly, it reveals a profound change in social attitudes which arguably resulted from masonic influence, when the Count humbly kneels before his Countess in front of all his staff – unheard-of in the contemporary social context – and sings *Perdono Contessa* (Forgive me

Mozart in 1764 at eight years old, holding a bird's nest. Painting by Johann Zoffany, a member of Pilgrim Lodge, No. 238, in London.

photo: akg images

Countess) for having humiliated her in front of the staff. We have here a hint of the social levelling which was yet to come.

The central meeting place of the Viennese intelligentsia in the 1790s was the Lodge True Concord, the lodge in which Mozart had been passed to the second degree. In 1781 the distinguished metallurgist, actor-manager and director Ignaz von Born, became the Master of this lodge. He was advisor to Freemason Emanuel Schickaneder, who wrote the libretto of *The Magic Flute,* and who played the part of Papageno in the first performance. From shortly after Mozart's death until the conclusion of World War I, Freemasonry was forbidden in Austria, and so for a period of more than 120 years Viennese society turned its back on the Craft.

MASONIC MUSIC

Communal music plays an important part in many masonic gatherings: some influential composers, notably Liszt, Sibelius and Haydn were Freemasons. Sibelius was the only composer other than Mozart to have written anything of masonic significance.

Having been initiated in 1784, Mozart was only a Freemason for seven of his thirty-five years, but wrote a considerable body of masonic music. Whilst in Salzburg, there had been considerable religious output for Prince-Bishop Colloredo, the Archbishop of Salzburg, but as Mozart was not affiliated to any church in Vienna, he concentrated instead on Freemasonry after arriving there.

Masonic influences are alluded to in many of Mozart's works, but some of those more important specifically

Staging of the opera The Magic Flute *Act I, scene iv. Set design for the Berlin production, Opera House 18 January 1816. Coloured aquatint by C.F. Thiele after Karl Friedrich Schinkel.*

photo: akg images

composed for Freemasonry are:

- *Gesellenreise* (Fellow Craft's Journey, K.468). Brother Franz Joseph v. Ratschky's verse on the journey to greater knowledge, first performed in Lodge True Concord on 16 April 1785 for Mozart's father's Fellowcraft Degree. *Die ihr einem neuen Grade* (You who are proceeding to a new degree).

> *You, who now are risen higher*
> *Unto Wisdom's high abode,*
> *Wander steadfast, higher, higher*
> *Know, it is the noblest road.*
> *Only spirit without blight*
> *May approach the source of Light.*

- *Cantata: Die Maurerfreude* (Masonic Joy, K471). Words by Franz Petran, composed on 20 April 1785 and first performed in the Lodge Crowned Hope on 24 April 1785 to honour Freemason Ignaz von Born, the famous scientist. He was a putative model for the character of High Priest Sarastro (Zarathustra) in *The Magic Flute*. It was performed at a festive dinner held at the Freemason Casino, which was a lodge room in the Kaffeehaus Mayer on the Danube Canal, in the presence of Leopold and Wolfgang Mozart on 24 April 1785.

- *Eine Kleine Freimaurerkantate* (A Little Masonic Cantata, K623). Composed in Vienna on 15 November 1791 with the text by Brother Emanuel Schikaneder. Written for the dedication of the Lodge New Crowned Hope. Performed 18 November 1791 and conducted by Mozart personally. This was the last work completed by Mozart.

- *Maurerische Trauermusik* (Masonic Funeral Music, K477). Composed in Vienna on 10 November 1785 for a Lodge of Sorrows held by the Lodge Crowned Hope a week later for the funerals of Freemasons Georg August, Duke of Mecklenburg-Strelitz, and Franz, Count Esterhazy of Galantha.

- Chorus: 'Lasst uns mit geschlungenen Händen' K623b.

> *With clasped hands, Brethren, let us end this work in sounds of glad rejoicing.*
> *May this bond tightly embrace the entire globe as it does this holy place.*
> *To honour virtue and mankind, and teach ourselves and others love, let our first duty ever be.*
> *Then not in the east alone will light shine, not in the west alone, but also in the south and in the north.*

Following the assumption by Germany of Joseph Haydn's *Kaiserlied*, which had been the Austrian national anthem till 1918, this music (K623b) was incorporated into the present Austrian national anthem.

- *Die Zauberflöte* (The Magic Flute, K620) (1791)

Often referred to as a masonic opera: suffice to say that the opera was scripted and produced by Mozart's masonic companion, Schikaneder and includes tests of fire and water, used in many continental masonic rituals. The opera is a masonic and alchemical allegory, reflecting the great interest in alchemy amongst Freemasons at the time – the Lodge Crowned Hope, for example, had its own alchemical laboratory. The opera is, according to an expert on its symbolism Dr. van de Berk, an 'initiation into Initiation'. Tamino is initiated into the mysteries of Isis: his guide is Papageno, representing Hermes, the guide of souls. Interestingly Pamina, the principal female, leads Tamino through his initiation. Unsurprisingly, its original title was 'Egyptian Mysteries'. Masonic principles are expressed by the lead character Sarastro (Zarathusta) and the rhythm of the opening bars of the overture are of course well-known to Freemasons as the knocks of one of the three Craft degrees.

MOZART'S DEATH

Mozart died at fifty-five minutes past midnight, on December 5, 1791. Only the day before, there had been a rehearsal of the Requiem composed by him which, it is speculated, Mozart thought to be his own Requiem. At this rehearsal Mozart sang alto, although he had less than twenty-four hours to live. A Lodge of Sorrows was held in his memory, and the oration there delivered was printed by Ignaz Alberti, a member of Mozart's own lodge, who had published the first libretto of The Magic Flute.

The funeral was held two days later at St. Stephen's Cathedral, where Mozart had married his wife Constanze only nine years earlier. His body was never autopsied although Eduard Guldener von Lobes, the physician who examined it, found no evidence of foul play. Contrary to popular romantic belief, Mozart was not given a pauper's funeral. His widow had purchased a third-class funeral which, although certainly the cheapest, was the most common in Vienna. Far from being destitute and ignored, a great number of people, fans and admirers of the great composer, showed up at Wälscher Platz and St. Stephen's to pay their last respects.

There has been much speculation as to a conspiracy theory, and a theory that Mozart may have been poisoned. The Register of Deaths of St. Stephen's Cathedral, clearly gives 'severe miliary fever' as the official cause of Mozart's death. There is also mention of renal failure.

It is perhaps fitting that Mozart died in a house in the Rauhensteingasse ('Rough-Ashlar-Street') in which, down the road at No. 3 is the current home of the Grand Lodge of Austria.

Bruce Young is Treasurer of the German-speaking Pilgrim Lodge, No. 238, meeting in London. He has devoted much study to Mozart, and is a graduate in music.

MURDER AND MASONRY

BERNARD WILLIAMSON INVESTIGATES THE INFAMOUS SEDDON MURDER CASE

The accused, Freemason Frederick Henry Seddon, in Court at the Old Bailey, London, at the moment he was sentenced to death by Freemason, Mr. Justice Bucknill.

Illustrated London News

In the sparse, hushed courtroom, the judge prepared to pronounce sentence of death. Looking straight at the prisoner, he said; 'We both belong to the same Brotherhood,' (he faltered here) 'and though that can have no influence with me, this is painful beyond words for me to have to say what I am saying, but our Brotherhood does not encourage crime, it condemns it.'

This was the culmination of a sensational trial, sensational not only because of the nature of the crime committed, but because it was clear that the accused man had made an appeal for leniency in the name of the fraternity to the Judge, a fellow Freemason. In the course of the trial he had siignalled to the Judge that he was in distress, and thus was born a legend of masonic collusion between crime and justice.

Frederick Henry Seddon was an insurance agent and a mortgage salesman, who had been initiated in the Stanley Lodge No. 1325 in 1901, later becoming a founder of Stephens Lodge, No. 3089 but resigned from both in 1906. In 1909 he purchased a fourteen-room house at 63 Tollington Park, by the Finsbury Park area close to Seven Sisters Road in London, for the then princely sum of £220.

The following year he made the acquaintance of a forty-nine year old spinster, Miss Eliza Barrow, who had been left a legacy enabling her to have investments in property and stocks. She and Seddon had at least one thing in common – they were both very mean and difficult to get on with. She lived in lodgings with her cousin, Mr Frank Vonderahe, but in a conversation with Seddon let him know that she was having difficulties with living expenses. Miss Barrow, who suffered from miserliness bordering on eccentricity, did not trust banks, and kept as much as three hundred pounds in her rooms.

The Lodger

Seddon was not slow to see the possibilities, and had already sized up the advantages of having a well-heeled spinster for a lodger, whose rent payments could be relied on and settled in cash. He was persuasive and personable, and convinced her that it would be to her advantage to come and live with him. Accordingly, Miss Barrow came to live at number 63 on 26 July 1910, bringing with her an adopted boy, Ernest Grant, together with his uncle and aunt, Mr and Mrs Hook from Edmonton. She immediately proved to be an ideal tenant, who kept to her rooms, only sitting in the kitchen occasionally chatting to the charwoman.

A few weeks went by and she seemed to have settled in well when one morning, out of the blue, Miss Barrow handed a letter to the Hooks. This letter, which was probably from Seddon, told them to pack their things and leave the apartment. This resulted in a furious row, which culminated in the Hooks accusing Seddon of trying to grab Miss Barrow's

Sir Thomas Townsend Bucknill was probably initiated in Lodge of Good Report, No.136, in 1869 and was Provincial Grand Master for Surrey from 1903 until his death in 1915. He was an admirable Judge, intelligent, careful and conscientious, a man with considerable charisma, who inspired admiration in all who came into contact with him.

Frederick Henry Seddon together with his wife, who was eventually aquitted, in the dock during the trial.   Illustrated London News

estate. But relations had now broken down completely, and the Hooks left in a most acrimonious atmosphere.

With the Hooks out of the way, the devious Seddon seems to have manoeuvred Miss Barrow quite cleverly. When she expressed concerns at the value of the investments in her properties, Seddon was most solicitous, and for an annuity and a remission in the rent, offered to oversee these investments. Early in 1911 he persuaded Miss Barrow to sink her £3,000 capital into an annuity which, he told her, would provide an income of three pounds a week for life. He made all the arrangements himself, paying her out each quarter in gold, but in fact the £3,000 had gone into Seddon's own pocket and not to the insurance company.

The Death

In September 1911, following the outbreak of an epidemic in the area, possibly cholera, Miss Barrow became very ill. The doctor was called, who prescribed bismuth and morphine for the complaint. On Saturday the ninth he visited her again, and by the following Monday she was weaker. Nevertheless, she refused to go to hospital. She

improved slightly for a few days, but was confined to her bed where on 13 September she made a Will dictated to and administered by the ever-helpful Frederick, witnessed by his relatives. At 6.15 on the morning of 14 September, whilst being attended to by Mrs Seddon, Miss Barrow died. Seddon went to the doctor, who issued a death certificate without seeing the body, claiming overwork brought on by the prevailing epidemic.

The very next day Seddon visited the undertakers and arranged a cheap funeral for £4.10s of which he pocketed 12/6d commission. The burial took place in a common burial plot, despite there being a family vault in Islington, and she was hardly cold in her grave when the Seddon family left for Southend for a fortnights' holiday. Shortly after Seddon's return Mr Frank Vonderahe, on arriving to visit his cousin, was dumbstruck to hear of her sudden death, and to learn that everything had been made over to Seddon. The Vonderahes demanded fuller explanations, but none were forthcoming, whereupon they voiced their suspicions to the authorities. On 15 November 1911 Miss Barrow was exhumed and examined by Sir William Willcox, who discovered two grains of arsenic in the body which, by his calculations, pointed to there being at least five grains present at the time of death. The inquest was adjourned on 29 November, Seddon was arrested on 4 December, and his wife six weeks later. They were both committed for trial at the Old Bailey in March, under Mr Justice Bucknill.

The Trial

The trial commenced, the prosecution lead by the Solicitor General, Sir Rufus Issacs, who started his case by noting that although the case lacked hard evidence, who else in the world had anything to gain by the death of Miss Barrow? He tried to demonstrate that Seddon was a devious, callous and ruthless person, who would be perfectly capable of murder, and who had appropriated money and valuables belonging to Miss Barrow.

The renowned Barrister Marshall Hall opened for the defence, trying to cast doubt on the evidence referring to the arsenic found in the body, which Sir William Willcox had given. He proposed that the amount could have been smaller and ingested over a period of time in the normal course of nursing, rather than in

Large crowds gathered outside the Old Bailey, London, drawn by the public notoriety of the Seddon murder trial.   Hulton Archive

Seddon photographed wearing the regalia of the Holy Royal Arch although there is no evidence that he was ever actually a member.   *Bernard Williamson*

one dose designed to kill. Seddon was advised not to give evidence, but he ignored this advice, and his conceited and condescending demeanour lost him sympathy with nearly everyone in the courtroom.

When Mrs Seddon went into the witness box, the image she presented was of a woman whose passage through life had made of her a drudge. She looked much older than her 34 years of age, and one commentator wrote; 'The impression that she gave was that she didn't know why she was there, and that she neither attempted to seek her way out nor evade dangerous questions. I think this is what really saved her. As Mr Justice Bucknill summed up he left the jury a loophole for her by saying "I should be astonished if you do not acquit her."'

Seddon himself had proved to be his own worst enemy, and by giving evidence had provided the prosecution with their best witness.

It took the jury one hour to find Frederick Seddon guilty and acquit his wife. On hearing the word 'guilty', Seddon turned pale but was unmoved. On hearing that his wife was free he kissed her, and with that he finally earned the sympathy of those present in the courtroom, but of course by then it was too late.

The Sentence

Before sentence was passed, Seddon was asked if he had anything to say, and according to the records gave 'a carefully and well prepared speech, during which he appealed to the judge, as a brother Mason, for a reversal of the jury's finding'. Bucknill suddenly looked utterly bewildered, and staring straight at Seddon, broke down completely.

Seddon concluded his speech with the words; 'I declare before the great Architect of the Universe I am not guilty' and at this point he raised his arm and gave a Masonic sign.

The report continues 'The silence which followed these most unusual events was total and seemed to last forever when . . . Mr Justice Bucknill, in a stilted and emotional manner, pronounced sentence of death'. When, some half an hour after the Court had been cleared, the Clerk to the Court went to meet the Judge in his chambers, he found that Justice Bucknill, fully robed, was sitting at his table and 'his eyes were red with weeping'.

No reprieve came and Seddon was hanged by John Ellis and Thomas Pierrepoint at Pentonville Prison, just a short walk from his home, on 18 April 1912 with over 7,000 people assembled outside.

The crowd would undoubtedly have been larger, were it not for the fact that news of the sinking of the Titanic three days earlier was uppermost on everybody's mind.

Bernard Williamson is a freelance journalist, and an initiate of Strong Man Lodge, No. 45. He is a founder member of the Goose and Gridiron Society, an organisation researching masonic inns and taverns, has written several papers on masonic subjects and had papers published in the transactions of Quatuor Coronati Lodge. He lives in a quiet village in Essex, where he devotes his time to masonic research,

FREEMASONRY AND THE SPANISH CIVIL WAR

PART II: FRANCO'S MASONIC OBSESSION

MATTHEW SCANLAN COMPLETES HIS REVIEW OF THE HORRORS FACED BY FREEMASONS UNDER FRANCO'S RULE

A view towards the 'East' inside the lodge created by Franco in Salamanca to show the evils of Freemasonry. It was originally created to be the major exhibit in an anti-masonic museum but was never opened to the public.   Matthew Scanlan

The Spanish Civil War was really a foretaste of a much larger conflict to come, but in many respects was no less savage, as terrible atrocities were committed on both sides. As so often happens in times of violent flux the situation polarized, the moderates were pushed aside, and the extremists gained the upper hand. On 15 May 1937 Largo Caballero (a Freemason) resigned as Prime Minister, and Dr Juan Negrin (a non-mason) became Prime Minister until 31 March 1939, and his Government was dominated by Communists.

On 18 July Franco made a broadcast on the National Radio of Salamanca to mark the first anniversary of the military rising. He ranted about the burning of churches, the assassination of businessmen and the interference of 'foreign powers and lodges'. He accused the chief military masons of 'vacillation' and denounced the peaceful overtures made by Diego Martinez Barrio on the eve of the rising as 'the treason of the lodges'. In November he explained his actions to the Spanish journalist Nena Belmonte:

> ... the Spanish Republic did not find itself free of obligations. For the most part the leaders were Freemasons. Before their duty to their country came their

A view of the 'West' in the lodge exhibit.

Matthew Scanlan

J. Boor is a pseudonym of Franco himself who published this collection of anti-masonic articles in 1952. He was convinced that masons had bought all the copies to prevent it from being read.

obligations to the Grand Orient. In my opinion, Freemasonry, with all its international influence, is the organization principally responsible for the political ruin of Spain, as well as the murder of Calvo Sotelo, who was executed in accordance with orders from the Grand Secretary of Freemasonry in Geneva.

The Republican government meanwhile had retreated north to Barcelona, and within a year, a fierce battle raged for the city. By January 1939 Franco's stranglehold on the remaining Republican pockets was all but complete, and on 27 February, the British Prime Minister, Neville Chamberlain, recognised Franco's government. With the republic all but lost Manuel Azaña resigned as President. Within a month the Nationalists entered Madrid and Franco announced that the war was over.

However the war was not over for Franco. In March 1940 he issued a decree banning Freemasonry and Communism. All Masonic assets were to be 'confiscated immediately' and anyone deemed to be a mason would be subject to a minimum twelve-year jail sentence. It was further declared that 'any mason or communist' must 'notify the

Government of his affiliation within two months', and a Special Tribunal was subsequently established to enforce the law. Masons of the 18° and above were deemed guilty of 'Aggravated Circumstances', and usually faced the death penalty.

Alarmed by the draconian nature of the law, the British Ambassador in Madrid, Sir Maurice Peterson, wrote to Lord Halifax in London and drew his attention to the plight of the Anglo-Scotch lodges:

I should endeavour to persuade the competent authorities of the essential difference between British Masonic Lodges and the more political Lodges of the Continental type. But I fear that the new law may increase the difficulties with which the British community in Spain are already confronted.

A number of Spanish masons, such as Diego Martinez Barrio, did manage to escape but were tried and sentenced in absentia. Others were not

so fortunate. The former Catalan President and organiser of the Workers Party (POUM), Luis Companys, was arrested by the Gestapo in northern France and sent back to Spain where he faced a firing squad.

Franco's Obsession

As part of his overall campaign against Freemasonry Franco had a masonic lodge constructed in Salamanca, complete with three hooded black manikins occupying the chairs in the East, to illustrate the supposed evils of the movement in three-dimensional form. Originally intended as the showpiece exhibit in an anti-masonic museum, it never actually opened to the general public and today forms part of the official government archives of the Spanish Civil War.

On 17 July 1943 Franco circulated a secret letter to three of his military chiefs announcing that a secret international masonic plot had been uncovered. He claimed that the plotters were attempting to re-establish the monarchy in Spain with the heir to the throne, Don Juan de Bourbon (father of the present King, Juan Carlos), but Franco claimed this would only return Spain to its pre civil war chaos. He repeatedly referred to foreign pressure for democratic change as 'the

BRIGADE No. 33 IN THE REPUBLICAN ARMY

Museum of the Grand Orient de France, Paris.

Blood-stained Spanish Republican flag now held in the museum of the Grand Orient de France, Paris. It was donated by a lodge in the south of France which had many members who were Spanish Republican refugees. This was the flag of a brigade, No. 33, of which oral tradition records that almost all its soldiers were Freemasons and that the blood on it is from one of its last officers, killed a few weeks before the final collapse of the Republican army. There is every reason to accept this tradition as true.

masonic offensive', and assured a cabinet meeting that there were fifteen million Freemasons in England who all voted Labour. Yet he was also wary of the probability of an allied victory, and subsequently informed the German Ambassador that he was recalling the Spanish Blue Division from the Eastern Front whilst assuring him of his unerring resolve to continue the struggle against Bolshevism, 'Jewry and Freemasonry'.

On 11 September 1945 Franco told the women's section of the Falange in Madrid: 'We have torn up Marxist materialism, we have disorientated masonry,' and thwarted the 'satanic machinations' of 'the masonic super state' which, he alleged, controlled the

Published in 1979, this work asserted that all events in the new democracy of Spain had been predicted in the Protocols of the Elders of Zion *– known to the rest of the world as an antisemitic forgery.*

world's press and many international politicians. He described Spain's struggle as a 'crusade' because it carried the evangelism of the world and that its men were the 'soldiers of God'.

On 14 December 1946, using the alias *Jakin Boor*, after the degrees of Freemasonry, Franco embarked on a series of forty-nine articles for the Falangist Madrid diary *Arriba* ('Forward'). In his first article, 'Masonry and Communism', Franco asserted:

The whole secret of the campaigns unleashed against Spain can be explained in two words: masonry and communism . . . . we have to extirpate these two evils from our land.

He alleged that, although deadly enemies, Freemasonry and Communism had united and were allied against Spain. He asserted that the United Nations Secretary-General, the Norwegian, Trygve Lee, the Belgian President of the General Assembly, Paul-Henri Spaak, and the Spanish Republican refugee and former Minister, José Giral, were all thirty-third degree masons in the clandestine service of Moscow and this was why the UN had condemned his regime in its opening session.

Franco naïvely believed that his alias hid his true identity but Washington was well aware who was behind the articles. In 1949 he mooted the idea of having his articles translated into English but his Minister of Foreign Affairs cautioned against it reasoning that it would annoy the allies, most especially President Harry Truman who was a 33° mason. Yet Franco continued to regularly sound-off about masonic plots. The following year he hosted a meeting of television media in Madrid at which he ranted about the evils of the masons and how they controlled the BBC. And when, in 1952, he published his articles in a book entitled, *Masoneria*, once again under the pseudonym *Jakin Boor*, he convinced himself that the masons had bought all the copies to prevent it from being read.

For the remainder of his life Franco remained paranoid and obsessed. In 1959 the secret policeman Mauricio Carlovilla published *Anti-España* and denounced the monarchist cause as a tool of Freemasonry accusing Don Juan de Bourbon of being a Freemason. Franco warmly greeted the publication of the book as he similarly believed Don Juan was so 'tainted'.

On 20 December 1973 the President of the government, Admiral Carrero Blanco, was assassinated by the Basque separatist group ETA. Franco was so distraught that he cancelled all his engagements and went into retreat in order to spend time analysing the attack. In his self-imposed isolation Franco privately told a friend that the assassination had been a 'masonic' revenge killing, a claim later repeated in Leo Ferraro's *El Ultimo Protocolo – Las Claves Secretas de Sionismo Mundial* ('The Last Protocol - The Secret Keys of World Zionism'), published in Madrid in 1986. And even in his farewell address to the nation on 1 October 1975 a tearful and infirm Franco told huge crowds that the two greatest enemies that confronted

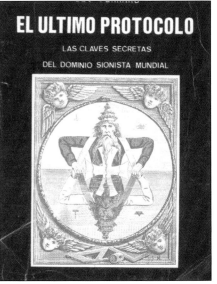

This book, published in 1986, repeated Franco's claim that Freemasonry had been responsible for the assassination of Admiral Carrero Blanco in 1973.

Spain were Communism and Freemasonry and he warned that the EEC was a conspiracy of 'left-wing masonry'.

Franco died on 20 November 1975. His chosen successor, Juan Carlos de Bourbon, was crowned king and Spain began a peaceful transition to a constitutional democracy. However, when voters failed to choose the candidates of the Right, the latter claimed it was due to 'Jewish-Masonic-Communist' propaganda. In 1979 César Casanova in his, *Manual de urgencia sobre el sionismo en España* ('Urgent manual on Zionism in Spain'), asserted that everything happening was predicted in the *Protocols of the Elders of Zion*.

In 1981 a military coup attempted to halt the return to a liberal democracy. Curiously, in the same year, Franco's *Masoneria* was also republished, only this time under his own name and by the National Foundation that bore his name.

Today Freemasonry is once again free to practise in Spain. In 1987 the United Grand Lodge of England recognised the Grand Lodge of Spain, and on 3 March 2001 the Grand Lodge officially merged with the Spanish Grand Orient, bringing one of the darkest periods in Freemasonry's long history to a peaceful close.

© M. D. J. Scanlan 2004.

Photographs of book covers courtesy of Professor Ferrer Benimeli/CEHME, Zaragoza

Matthew Scanlan MA, is a member of the Duke of Wharton Research Lodge, No. 18, Barcelona and of the Centro Estudios Historicos de la Masoneria Espanola, Zaragoza.

GOLD AND FREEMASONRY

DENNIS EVE RELATES AN EXTRAORDINARY ACCOUNT OF FREEMASONRY AND THE YUKON

Hopeful Argonauts at Lake Bennett bound for Dawson.

The mighty Yukon River, from its source at the Llewellyn Glacier high above Atlin Lake in north western British Columbia, runs about 2,300 miles, northwards through the Yukon territory, the Cities of Whitehorse and Dawson, continuing westwards across Alaska to the Yukon Delta, where it empties into the Bering Sea. In 1896 prospector George Carmack and his Indian brother-in-law 'Skookum Jim' Mason, and another Indian relative named 'Tagish Charlie' were panning for gold far up north on the banks of the Klondike river. Carmack lifted some sand from Rabbit Creek a small stream running into the Klondike River, and discovered the precious metal, thereby unwittingly creating the greatest goldrush in history.

Fortune hunters in their thousands disgorged themselves from ships at Skagway in Alaska. A shantytown of saloons and gambling dens grew up as they prepared themselves for their journey into the Klondike region over the infamous White Pass. Those with horses blindfolded them; even so, thousands of dead horses lay sprawled at the foot of Dead Horse Gulch.

The Chilkoot Pass, about 3,000 feet in height at its summit, with temperatures reaching -60C degrees in the winter, snaked along a trail of ice and rock no more than four feet wide that was permanently packed with a line of prospectors. It was an ant-like black army crawling up the icy pass, each man with a huge pack on his back, clinging to its slippery face. Their sleds, carrying a years supply of food and weighing up to 2,000 pounds, traversed the canyons that lay ahead, with the aid of the 'Jacob's Ladders' that were carried with them. Men dropped, and the gaps closed up; the march went on. 'Klondike or bust' was the slogan that bound together these men of the High North, the Arctic Brotherhood

Of those who had managed to traversethe Chilkoot Pass before the freeze-up in the winter of 1898/9, arrival in the town of Atlin, British Columbia, gave them the determination to build on their fraternal beliefs, both masonic and, at times, somewhat more whimsical. Some of these

Climbing the ice path of the Chilkoot Pass with heavy packs. Many made it, and many didn't.

brought with them their initiation rituals. The badge was a beer bottle cork and the dues a bottle of beer. In 1905 another camp was established in Discovery, British Columbia, seven miles east of Atlin, and a hall was built next to the Nugget Hotel. By this time whimsy had given way to Freemasonry, and the membership rose to 182, including Discovery and Atlin's most prominent citizens.

Dating from the summer of 1899, there are regular reports of meetings of the masonic brotherhood in Atlin and in Discovery. It was in July 1899 that seventy five 'sojourning brothers' gathered in Atlin with one aim in view, to form their own masonic lodge. The Grand Lodge of Manitoba was not convinced of the permanence of the town of Atlin, and Atlinto Lodge No. 42 was not founded until December 1904 and its charter issued in June 1906.

The history of Atlinto Lodge and the town of Atlin are closely linked. The town came into being as the result of gold being found in the adjacent creeks during the latter part of the 1890s. Many of the social events in the town were organized by the masonic lodge and were not restricted to 'members only' but were designed to include everyone who wanted to attend. The annual picnic to Ben-My-Chree, on Tagish Lake on the steamer Scotia, marked the end of the summer season. Attendance at lodge meetings was looked upon as mandatory for members living in the district, and it was a regular occurrence for many to walk from the creeks where they worked and lived, to Atlin on a lodge night. Distances varied but for some the round trip would be fifteen miles.

Although gold was discovered in the Klondike in August of 1896, it was not until July 1897 that this news reached Seattle and San Francisco. Most 'argonauts' remained frozen in for the winter, on trails over inhospitable mountain passes and it was only after the ice on the lakes 'went out' that the gold-seekers were able to continue their journey. They hiked treacherous mountain passes, rafted wild rapids and sailed storm blown lakes, in all directions. Vancouver and Seattle doubled in size almost overnight; the capital cities of Victoria and Edmonton tripled.

In one day alone in 1898 7,000 homemade boats and rafts of all descriptions set forth from Lake Bennett, where they had spent the remainder of the winter, to complete the last part of their journey via the Yukon river to Dawson City, a distance of six hundred miles. In fact the earliest existing account of Freemasonry is of a gathering at Lake Bennett in the spring of 1898, while waiting for the ice to break-up. The following is an extract from a letter written by Brother W. Galpins describing what he saw :

Dawson, January 9th,1906

The first sign of Freemasonry I met with in the Yukon was on Lake Bennett in May 1898, while thousands of hopeful Argonauts, bound for Dawson on the opening of the ice-bound rivers and lakes, were waiting at Bennett. Many formed themselves into committees for various objectives, such as the commemorating of [Queen Victoria's] birthday or gathering information concerning the navigation of the little known Yukon River, or assisting the sick and needy. From these committees an invitation was sent out to Masons to attend meetings in a large tent used for religious services. Sometimes as many as 200 Masons attended and partook of the brotherly feeling and sympathy for which so many craved, cut off as they were from home and relations. Sweet Charity had many an opportunity to show herself and many a brother too, was with loving care, attended in sickness and not a few succumbed to the combined influences of fatigue and spinal meningitis, and were sorrowfully laid to rest with Masonic rites.

On about the 1st June 1891 we had our final meeting, when Bro. Lisle presided, who reminded the

The White Pass in 1899 at the half-way point - the gateway to hell and back.

brethren of the duties they owed to one another, laying stress on the necessity for assistance in the case of misfortune on the journey to Dawson. It was decided to tie a flag or paint the bows of our boats with the symbol known to Freemasons the world over.

The challenges that could await the intrepid stampeder were extreme, and one of these was a journey assumed to have been made by Robert William Service, a great poet and author who did so much to bring the 'insiders', the Yukoners, to the outside world, with works such as 'The Shooting of Dan McGrew', 'The Cremation of Sam McGee', just two of about 1,000 poems that were written with much drama and intensity, of his time spent in the Yukon.

His poetry was proving so popular that he became financially independent and made a short visit to the United States. However, he yearned again for the Yukon and decided by 1911 to return the hard way, by the 'Edmonton Trail', a journey by canoe down the Mackenzie River, over the Mackenzie Divide via the Rat, and down the Bell and the Porcupine to the Yukon River. The journey he undertook was hazardous in the extreme - one observer mentioned that 'no one in their right mind would do that today; foolhardy would be the mildest term that I could think of'.

Once back home in Dawson, Robert Service became attracted to Freemasonry and in 1912 he was initiated into the Yukon Lodge No.45. By the end of his life in 1958, having been sixty years a bard and penned thirty thousand couplets, he had introduced the world to the Yukon, a country that had tested to the full the endurance and indomitable spirit of the Klondikers.

When these intrepid explorers of 1898 did eventually arrive in Dawson in July, after arduous months of travel and a harsh winter, they found that all the best claims

Brethren of the Yukon Lodge on the occasion of the lodge dedication in 1901.

had long since been staked by experienced prospectors who had been in the Yukon for years seeking their own Eldorado. The law of survival decreed that the people should start to build their own lives, and in the years of 1897 and 1898 Dawson City, with a population of around 30,000, became the biggest City west of Chicago and north of San Francisco.

The lodge historian of Whitehorse Lodge No. 46 wrote:

'The life story of Dawson City is much like that of a beautiful butterfly, in that it matures fully in one year and then dies. You could get anything you wanted - the finest French Champagne at $20 to $40 a pint, Paris fashions, the best foods. Prices were sky high, a shave was $1, haircut $1-50, bath $2-50. Diamond Tooth Gertie was a Yukon dance hall queen. Her nickname came from the sparkling diamond wedged between her front teeth. She made a fortune unloading the miners of their golden nuggets. Martha Louise Black, abandoned by her husband en route to the Klondike in 1898, hiked the Chilkoot Pass, sailed pregnant down the Yukon River in a home made boat to Dawson. She later became Canada's

second woman Member of Parliament.

By early 1898, all the usual amenities of city life were available including the telegraph, electricity sidewalks, a police force, banks, the Lodge of course, a post office, theatres, and many bars. The saloons of Dawson were magnificent; a man could get a drink of anything he wanted, providing that he had the money. Whiskey flowed faster than the Yukon River, and legendary ladies like 'Klondike' Kate Rockwell were in demand. For many, payment was in gold dust only, at about $16 per oz. Barkeepers let their fingernails grow long to pick up a little dust. One enterprising youngster swept the sawdust off the floor every morning and panned the gold droppings out of the sawdust.'

So it was that by 1905 the Yukon Lodge No 45, the Whitehorse Lodge No 46 and the Atlinto Lodge No 42 were actively contributing to the community. The tenacity and the brotherhood of these men ensured the survival of the area and its populace. They lived hard and fast, never knowing if tomorrow would bring fortune or disaster, and the saga of their survival remains a legend of the area, and a testimony to endurance. ∎

Dennis Eve is the current Master of Temple of Athene Lodge No. 9541, the Research Lodge of the Province of Middlesex, and a member of Earsdon Lodge No. 6219 in Northumberland amongst others. He has travelled extensively in the Yukon Territory and Alaska.

The present day Masonic Hall of Whitehorse Lodge.

ADVANCING MEDICAL SCIENCE

JULIAN REES TELLS THE STORY OF HENRY WELLCOME AND HIS INSTITUTE

The Wellcome Institute in Euston Road, London.

Photo: Wellcome Institute

The years between 1830 and 1860 were rich years for Freemasonry, since in that period many of the men were born who later shaped the Craft. But one man, Henry Solomon Wellcome, who was born in that period, went on to be not only an exemplary Freemason, but also the leader of what became a world-wide pharmaceutical empire, and an extraordinary collector and archaeologist.

Henry Wellcome was born in Almond Wisconsin, in 1853. The Wellcomes were a poor farming family and Henry's early life was a hard and eventful training-ground. By 1861 his parents had moved to the newly-founded State of Minnesota. It was there, during the Civil War, that he helped his uncle, a medical professional, to treat men wounded in the Sioux uprisings, and it was the influence of his uncle which played the largest part in forming Henry's later career in pharmacy. The brutal treatment received by the Sioux at the hands of the white settlers made a lasting impression on the young man, who in his early years already saw the inner nobility of the Indian culture.

In about 1877, Henry made the acquaintance of Silas Mainville

Burroughs, an employee of the pharmaceutical company John Wyeth in Philadelphia. Burroughs was gregarious and likeable, certainly Wellcome found him so, and when Burroughs moved to Europe to work for Wyeth there, the two remained firm friends. Burroughs had set his sights on founding his own firm, and repeatedly asked Wellcome to come and join him in a new endeavour. Wellcome at first proved hard to get, but finally gave in, and the full partnership between the two men commenced in London in 1880.

By that time, Burroughs had made a number of appointments to his fledgling firm. The first name on the register of employees dated 1879 is that of Robert Clay Sudlow, who two years earlier had been initiated in East Surrey Lodge of Concord, No. 463 (today Croydon Lodge of Concord). It seems almost certain that Sudlow, who had been Burroughs' right hand man, was instrumental in bringing Wellcome into Freemasonry. Wellcome was initiated in Fidelity Lodge, No. 3 in 1885, and Sudlow was present. The third degree was conferred on Wellcome in Eastes Lodge, No. 1965, by Sudlow himself. One year later, Sudlow initiated the man whose name was second on the register of employees, William Henry Kirby.

Wellcome, although in many ways difficult to get on with, and at times diffident, liked to play the bon viveur, the man about town, and was eventually a member of several clubs, lodges and chapters. But it would be wrong to suppose that with all this social activity, he neglected the business. His devotion to the interests of Burroughs, Wellcome and Co. was untiring. He travelled widely, selling the products of the company, and was its best publicist. Indeed, when Burroughs later accused him of spending too much time socialising, Wellcome was quick to point out how much business he was bringing in through social contacts, and this certainly was the case.

In the 1880s the company worked on an idea by Wyeth to compress medicines into the form of tablets, and eventually developed their own compressing machines. Burroughs also had an interest in Freemasonry, having been initiated in Clapham Lodge, No. 1818. In 1884, the year that Burroughs became a joining member of

The Library at the Wellcome Institute. *Photo: Wellcome Institute*

Fidelity Lodge, Wellcome registered the company's famous trademark 'Tabloid', applied to a variety of products. The name 'Tabloid' in those days had of course nothing to do with newsprint. This development gave an enormous boost to the fortunes of the company, but by then Burroughs and Wellcome were locked in an unseemly quarrel over various aspects of the partnership. Burroughs' greater financial interest in the firm meant that he earned more from it, and Wellcome, in view of the amount of work put in to further its interests, felt this to be unjust. The quarrel was long, did not reflect much credit on either partner, and finally came to a head with a hearing in the Chancery Division of a petition to wind up the partnership. The year was 1889, the same year that a number of Burroughs Wellcome employees formed, with others, the Clarence Lodge of Instruction, meeting at Tupps Restaurant in the Tottenham Court Road. Wellcome was Treasurer.

The Chancery Division hearing proved a victory for Wellcome, when the judge threw out the action and decreed that the main part of the costs should be borne by Burroughs. But despite the efforts of others in the firm, there was to be no rapprochement between the two men. In fact, in all the litigation between

Henry and Syrie Wellcome. *Photo: Wellcome Institute*

Henry Wellcome in 1902. *Photo: Wellcome Institute*

them, Wellcome leant heavily on his two most trusted masonic friends, Clay Sudlow and Will Kirby.

However, there was a most unexpected turn of events when, in 1895, Burroughs caught a chill which turned to pneumonia, and within a few days he was dead. Wellcome observed the proper formalities on the death of his partner but, despite the battle now waged with Burroughs' widow over control of the firm, it was clear that Wellcome was now free of the constraints which the partnership had placed on him.

The Kirby memorial in High Wycombe in the form of the rough and smooth Ashlar.

photo: Julian Rees

Now Wellcome, who believed in research for its own sake, planned and staffed his own chemical research laboratories, and in addition, fulfilled another lifelong ambition: the assembly of books and artefacts relating to the history of medicine and pharmacy. Now that he had the means, it became an all-absorbing passion.

In 1898 Kitchener had conquered Sudan, and Wellcome decided to go and see the country for himself. He was received by Kitchener, and found the country ravaged by disease and malnutrition. He proposed, and eventually set up, a tropical disease

research laboratory in Khartoum. This laboratory proved to be at the cutting edge of medical science. Together with Wellcome's other research laboratories, it was instrumental in developing and manufacturing anti-toxin serums for diptheria, typhoid, dysentery and tetanus to name but a few. Many years later in 1935, when the Sudan government closed it down without consultation, Wellcome felt the blow keenly.

On leaving Khartoum, Wellcome returned to Cairo, where a party newly arrived from England included the vivacious and high-spirited Syrie Barnardo, daughter of the celebrated Dr. Thomas Barnardo. Wellcome had met her some years earlier, but the two now fell in love, and married in 1901.

Although they had a son, who was born in 1903, the marriage was not a happy one. Wellcome was 48 at the time of the marriage, Syrie was 26, and the age difference doubtless had an adverse effect on their marriage. Syrie never became attuned to Wellcome's many interests, and was profoundly bored by all the travelling and collecting of artefacts. The marriage coincided with the flowering of Wellcome's many interests, and by 1911 those interests had taken over to the extent that Henry and Syrie separated amid bitter recriminations.

At the outbreak of the Boer War, Wellcome had seized the chance of being of service to his adoptive country in ensuring adequate medical supplies to British troops in South Africa. The Royal Army Medical Corps had been proved to be utterly incompetent – of the 22,000 troops who died in the war, a staggering 16,000 had died of disease, and Wellcome's intervention was a much-needed one.

At this time also, Wellcome had planned a suitably generous gift to Grand Lodge in London, of a portrait, commissioned by himself, of George

Washington in masonic regalia. This was intended to mark, in 1899, the centenary of Washington's death, and to cement relations between America and Britain. Although the artist, Robert Gordon Hardie, had been commissioned to produce the portrait in 1898, due to his illness the painting was only presented in 1902. It hangs today in the Drawing Room on the first floor of Freemasons' Hall in London.

Wellcome, Sudlow and Kirby were all members of the Clarence Lodge of Instruction, and in addition worked sections of the Emulation lectures at Festivals of the Emulation Lodge of Improvement. Kirby, although the junior of the three, distinguished himself as the Preceptor of the Clarence Lodge of Instruction, but was tragically killed in a gas explosion in 1895. In tribute to his memory, the Lodge of Instruction's name was changed from 'Clarence' to 'Kirby', and Wellcome, together with the Lodge of Instruction members, paid for the erection of a handsome memorial to Kirby in High Wycombe Cemetery.

Five years after Kirby's death, the Kirby Lodge, No. 2818 was founded, all of the founders being keen Emulation Lodge of Improvement workers. The only name missing from the list of founders was that of Henry Wellcome, who had become embroiled some years earlier in a quarrel with members of The American Society in London, a quarrel which spilt over into his masonic and social life. Nevertheless he was a member of a number of lodges and chapters in London, notable amongst them the Columbia Lodge, No. 2397, which had been formed for expatriate Americans living in London, and which counted Gordon Selfridge amongst its members.

Wellcome was knighted in 1932, by which time the imposing Wellcome Institute building in Euston Road London had been completed, and so his pharmaceutical empire was complete. He died of cancer in 1936 at the age of 83.

At the end of his life, he had every reason to be proud of his achievements. He had achieved many advances in medical science and pharmacy. He had done more than any other man before or since to promote the history of medicine, and had left a legacy, public and private, which has enriched the lives of many, and on many different levels.

With acknowledgment to Tom Howes of Fidelity Lodge, No. 3

Further reading – Henry Wellcome, Robert Rhodes James.

THE MASONIC REBELLION IN LIVERPOOL
AND THE WIGAN GRAND LODGE

DAVID HARRISON REPORTS ON A LITTLE-KNOWN MASONIC REBELLION

A Grand Lodge Certificate issued by the Wigan Grand Lodge.

On 22 December 1823 at the Shakespeare Tavern in Williamson Square, Liverpool, a gathering of masonic rebels took place. The door to the lodge room was closed and guarded by the Grand Tyler, the masons present settled and watched as Brother Michael Alexander Gage took the chair. The lodge was opened in the third degree, and the minutes of the previous meeting were read. That last meeting on 21 July had been adjourned, but now their business could be concluded, and it was hoped this meeting would change English Freemasonry forever.

The reason for re-convening the adjourned meeting was to allow the rebels to install the first Grand Master and Officers of their new Grand Lodge. The Grand Master and his Officers were elected, and then the newly written 'Magna Charta of Masonic Freedom' was read aloud to an eager audience. The document resounded to the theme of a new dawn, free from the despotic power of the United Grand Lodge. The causes which led to this re-establishment of the Antient Grand Lodge were to be advertised in the London newspapers, a public declaration, guaranteed to reach the eyes of the leaders of the United Grand Lodge. The rebellion had succeeded, but the grievances which re-established the Antient Grand Lodge, which was based on the Old York Constitutions, had its roots over a century earlier.

With the revision of the ritual under the Rev. Desaguliers and James Anderson in the early 1720s, many of the more traditional Freemasons became alarmed at the drastic changes in the ritual. A main concern was the way that the two masonic degrees, which had existed in the seventeenth century had, since the 1720s, been made into three main degrees by the Premier Grand Lodge, using the same material[1].

One of the first localities that declared itself separate from Grand Lodge was York, and on 27 December 1725 they formed the 'Grand Lodge of all England held at York', based on a tradition that the Saxon King Edwin had supposedly presided over a meeting of masons in York. The York Grand Lodge continued until 1792, and may have even survived into the early years of the nineteenth century.

The formation of 'The Grand Lodge of England according to the Old Institutions', otherwise known as the 'Antients', took place in 1751 in London, the Grand Secretary being

A Master Mason's apron of the Wigan Grand Lodge.

Laurence Dermott. The differences developed into a bitter feud, and were only reconciled in 1813 when the Duke of Sussex, with the help of his brother, the Duke of Kent, merged both the 'Moderns' and the 'Antients', creating the United Grand Lodge of England.

Continued opposition to the Union

In spite of the Union, discontent lingered and concerns about changes in ritual caused heated discussions in many lodges. Lancashire, a Province which had been neglected by their Provincial Grand Master, Francis Dukinfield Astley, suffered during this period. It was a large Province, and the majority of the masonic workload was left to the Deputy Provincial Grand Master, Daniel Lynch, who had to mediate with the lodges that had witnessed disturbances in the wake of the Union.

It was a Liverpool Freemason who was to instigate the rebellion. Michael Alexander Gage was a Liverpool tailor[2], and had been a Past Master of No. 31 Lodge, an Antient lodge based in Liverpool. In an open Provincial Grand Lodge meeting in 1818 in Hanging Ditch, he had put forward a motion regarding the rules of a lodge. When this motion was ignored by the

Grand Master of the United Grand Lodge, Gage instigated the cause for

An example of a Royal Arch apron.

independence, with a speech at the Provincial Grand Lodge, which played on the arrogance of the Duke of Sussex and the lack of interest of the United Grand Lodge.

By 1822 the United Grand Lodge had decided that William Meyrick, the Grand Chancellor of the United Grand Lodge, should be placed in charge of the Province as Acting Provincial Grand Master. Curiously, Astley still retained his title as Provincial Grand Master, and Meyrick actually paid little attention to the Province. Gage's lodge, Lodge No. 31, was erased from the list of lodges, its Warrant forfeited after their continued misconduct, and Gage and his followers were suspended.

Dissent in Lancashire started to spread, and a bitter exchange began between the United Grand Lodge and the dissenters. On 5 March 1823, the United Grand Lodge finally expelled twenty-six Brethren, stating that the rebels had 'been found guilty of various Acts of insubordination against the Authority of the Grand Lodge, and . . . have not sent any sufficient apology for their late misconduct'. Their rebellious activities were described as an 'insult', and the Brethren having 'violated the laws of the Craft', were ostracized[3]. Gage and his followers were now free to resurrect the Antient Grand Lodge.

A New Grand Lodge

The 'Grand Lodge of Free and Accepted Masons of England According to the Old Constitutions', first met in Liverpool in July 1823, and the 'Magna Charta of Masonic Freedom' was read out in the meeting

A further example of a Royal Arch apron.

in the Shakespeare Tavern in December. The Grand Lodge first met in Wigan on 1 March 1824, and was to meet only in Wigan from 1825. At its height in the early 1840s, it had lodges in Warrington, Ashton-in-Makerfield, Wigan, Liverpool, Barnsley, and had been in close contact with an Antient lodge in Lynn Regis in Norfolk, probably because Gage originated from there and had links with the town[4].

New Warrants issued

As the Wigan Grand Lodge slowly began to spread its influence, new Warrants were issued, with the lodges under its sway being numbered. As there were only five lodges, they were

subsequently numbered one to five, though the Barnsley lodge opted out of the Wigan Grand Lodge, and the Warrington lodge was relatively short lived.

The issue of Warrants upset Gage, who, though not having attended the Grand Lodge, or any other regular lodge for fifteen years, had always been given the title of Deputy Grand Master, enjoying the task of overlooking the activities by correspondence.

Gage was also upset that the 'Magna Charta' had been breached, as it stated that on the creation of the Wigan Grand Lodge, all the numbers of the lodges reverted to their pre-Union numbers. In 1842, Gage wrote a lengthy letter of resignation, in which he outlined his feelings at not being asked to review the decision of the new Warrants. He was a proud man, and as he was the person who had instigated the Wigan Grand Lodge, he appears to have been hurt by the decision. Despite Gage's coldness, he was still the spiritual leader of the 'Antients', and in the reply to his resignation, Gage was described by the Grand Master as a man whom 'the tyrants in the masonic world would have always looked upon with dread'.[5]

The Grand Lodge had moved on, and had become firmly seated in Wigan. Gage was based in Liverpool, and though seemingly showing a lack of interest in masonry, he held a sense of importance when it came to his position within the Wigan Grand Lodge. His lack of interest may have resulted from the re-location of the Grand Lodge to Wigan, or may have been down to Gage having a family and changing his career[6]. He remained a rebel to the end however, effectively rebelling against the rebels. He was always an obstinate man, passionate and arrogant in the face of opposition. He held the respect of his fellow rebels, and without Gage, there would have been no Wigan Grand Lodge. The rebels could channel their anger through the formation of the Wigan Grand Lodge, and its success was manifested in its effect on the United Grand Lodge.

After Gage's resignation, the Wigan Grand Lodge continued to meet until 1866, when only one lodge remained. Gage died the following year, and it is tempting to suggest that, like the York Grand Lodge before it, the Wigan Grand Lodge only survived as long as its founder. The surviving Sincerity Lodge stubbornly held on as the only remaining lodge, isolated and alone. It only surrendered in 1913, re-joining the United Grand Lodge, finally laying to rest the ghost of Michael Alexander Gage.

All photographs courtesy Library and Museum of Freemasonry, London

[1] *Knoop, D., & Jones, G.P., 1940. A Short History of Freemasonry To 1730, Manchester University Press, p.137.*

[2] *Gore's Liverpool Trade Directory, 1825. Liverpool Library. Ref: H942.7215 & Church records for St. Nicholas, Liverpool; Baptism of Michael Alexander, son of Michael Alexander Gage, Tailor & Draper, & his wife Sarah, 18 September, 1823. Liverpool Library. Ref: 283NIC2/2.*

[3] *Beesley, E.B., 1920. The History of the Wigan Grand Lodge, Manchester Association for Masonic Research, Leeds, pp.16-19.*

[4] *1851 Census for Liverpool, Lancashire. Liverpool Library. Ref: 153/2183.*

[5] *Beesley, E.B., 1920. The History of the Wigan Grand Lodge, Manchester Association for Masonic Research, Leeds, pp.83-88.*

[6] *1851 Census for Liverpool, Lancashire. Liverpool Library. Ref: 153/2183 and Church Records for St. Peters, Liverpool; Baptism of William Henry, son of Michael Alexander Gage, Land Surveyor, & his wife Sarah, 25th of December, 1833. Liverpool Library. Ref: 283PET2/21.*

CHRISTMAS PARTIES
at the New Connaught Rooms

The venue where

Anything &
Everything
is possible

Situated at the heart of London's fashionable West End, the New Connaught Rooms has been welcoming party goers since 1786. With 29 different function rooms available for hire, (and over 200 years of experience of holding great parties!) the New Connaught Rooms is still one of London's best venues in which to celebrate!

Why not bring your Christmas party to the New Connaught Rooms this year? There are two special hire packages to choose from.

PACKAGE A - JUST £35 PER PERSON

Our standard package (A) is available from just £35 per person for bookings of 20 people and over and includes:

- Room hire
- Welcome cocktail
- Three course menu and coffee
- Crackers and seasonal novelties

PACKAGE B - JUST £79.50 PER PERSON

Our most popular package (B) is available for bookings of 60 people and above for just £79.50 per person and includes:

- A welcome glass of Bucks Fizz
- Three course Christmas menu with coffee
- Half a bottle of wine per person
- Crackers and seasonal novelties
- After dinner, a bar package for 3 hours including unlimited beer, wine and soft drinks
- Room hire

We offer a wide range of additional menus, fine wines and drinks packages and entertainment options. Our reservations team will be delighted to discuss your requirements with you.

For more information or to make a booking, call our Reservations team on 020 7405 7811

As these are dining packages, Option A is for minimum numbers of 60 and above and Option B for minimum numbers of 20 and above. For smaller numbers, speak to us about other options. Menus/package content subject to change without notice. Prices are per person, and are subject to promotional availability.

Valid between 16th November and 31st January.

17.5% VAT included where applicable.

THE SYMBOLISM

An allegory describes a subject under the guise of something else, something which aptly suggests it by its resemblance. The figure of a holy person, or of the Divinity, is often painted with a halo over its head, to indicate sanctity. The halo is hence meant to indicate that which words cannot, nor can a mere pictorial representation. We are led to understand that this subject has qualities that set it apart, in a way that requires our own input in decoding it and interpreting its message.

Freemasonry has always engaged the minds and hearts of its members by means of symbols, applying to them the allegories necessary to unfold the truths which they represent by their nature, whether we speak of symbolic inferences in prose or poetry, in legend, in art and architecture or in music. Symbolism lies at the very core of Freemasonry, and enables the language

of the message in Freemasonry to unfold in a way that goes beyond words.

There are strong links between the symbolism of the old Craft Guilds and Freemasonry, indicating the closeness of their development in history. Here again, the mystery plays of medieval Christianity provide intriguing clues about how symbols and allusions were used in furthering morality.

The oneness of man with divinity and the consciousness of nature is emblematically represented by the many instances of the Green Man which are apparent in architecture. In the ancient carvings of Egypt there are also emblematic connections between the 'above' and the 'below'. In fact, architecture through the ages has provided a platform for the display of symbols, both those of the masonic fraternity and others. Early stonemasons, skilled in working on cathedrals and

churches for many centuries, were very probably the earliest operative practioners of what we know today as speculative or symbolic Freemasonry.

But earlier than that, the pre-socratic Greek philosophers were working with symbols in the same way that modern Freemasons do, and in the following pages we gain fascinating insights into those connections. Such philosophies have given birth to modern-day philosophy; much of what we read here regarding alternative medicine, near-death experiences and initiatory practices owe their inspiration to previous millennia.

Symbols used by Freemasons in the use of allegory and allusion have for centuries been part of everyday life. The outer forms, seen in many buildings and works of art, serve only to mirror the inner truth which each Freemason unfolds in regard to the centre of his own being.

In those days the Masters • Carried Swords

Best-selling author Michael Baigent gets to grips with something big in Fife.

Scotland holds some of the most mysterious masonic and chivalric remnants in the world.

Yet many of these residues remain enigmatic because much of Scotland's history can never be recovered. In particular, that of the important thirteenth and fourteenth centuries when chivalry flourished and the Craft Guilds were organizing.

The majority of Scotland's historical documents for this period have vanished entirely : destroyed by war or fire; lost by incompetence or accident. The first great loss came in 1291 when English king Edward I gathered together all official Scottish documents : charters, writs and letters. This last collection was last noted in 1296, following which it vanishes utterly from the historical record.

Later depredations have left us with documents covering only eight years of the reign of king David II (1331-1371) and only the first two years of the reign of king Robert II (1371-1390). As a final blow, the last major archive of Scottish records, taken to London by Cromwell's army, was lost in a violent storm at sea in 1660, while being shipped back to Edinburgh.

In order to recover even a small part of this history we must make do with family papers, medieval inscriptions, local legends and tombs. It is of particular interest to Freemasons that in many Scottish graveyards we can still see the symbolically carved grave-slabs attesting to some early organization of chivalric orders or trade guilds.

The Enigmatic Grave-slab of Culross "West Kirk"

Culross, in Scotland, sits just across the Forth from Falkirk. To the north-west are the remains of the old parish church, the "West Kirk". This church is now in ruins; and has been so for centuries. In fact, it was recorded as being derelict as long ago as 1633. Several walls of the church still stand and built into one, as a lintel above a doorway, is an ancient grave-slab. As it forms part of the wall, it must, therefore, be extremely old. Its style appears to be of fourteenth century provenance. This grave-slab bears a floreate cross down its centre. Above this cross is a Master Builder's standard measure, his 'yard' or 'Ell' - one end of which forms a square. Below the cross is his sword. Experts feel that in the carving of this type of grave-slab, the actual sword or other artefact would be laid along the bare stone, marked out with chalk, and then carved, life-size.

The Curiosity of Measurement

If this carved mason's measure is indeed lifesize, then a curiosity is raised. Its length is 42.75 inches : the normal Scottish 'Ell' is considerably shorter, being 37.06 inches. Where then did this master's measure come from?

The medieval Hanseatic yard is identical to the Scottish Ell. The English yard is shorter. Three measures of the Scandinavian 'foot' are shorter still. The standard measures of Ireland, Spain, the Basque country, Holland, Italy, and Portugal do not reveal anything matching the length of the carving. The closest, the Portugese *Vara*, is about one inch shorter. However, there is a measure from France which fits exactly :

the carved Master's 'yard' equals forty French *pounce* - with an error of just one tenth of an inch, an error which could easily be explained by the worn nature of the carving.

Have we here, then, the grave of a Scottish Master Builder who had been trained in France? Could this have some connection with the nearby, but ruinous, Culross Abbey, a former Cistercian foundation? The Cistercians, quite apart from their connections with the Knights Templar (they shared the same Rule), employed professional building teams often recruited from outside the Order.

Scotland and France have long had a close connection. The two countries were often allies. Following the signing of a Franco-Scottish alliance in 1326, many Scots fought in the French army opposing Edward III and the Black Prince. In the next century, the bishop of Orleans, who served Joan of Arc, was himself a Scot. From 1425, the personal guard of the king of France was composed of Scottish men-at-arms and archers; they were formally organized into the famous Scots Guard in 1445. One of the last commanders of this Élite regiment was Sir Robert Moray who was at the time a member of a Scottish operative lodge.

Later, in the eighteenth century, it was a Scotsman, the Chevalier Ramsay, also in France, who made the first explicit link between Freemasonry and chivalric service. Twice, in 1736 and 1737, he delivered his famous 'Oration' to Freemasons in Paris. In it, he stated that during the Crusades "our Order formed an intimate union with the Knights of S.John" following after the example of the builders of the Temple in Jerusalem; holding the trowl in one hand and the sword in the other. While historians have accorded little truth to this statement, their reaction may have been too hasty. There has always been a penumbra of mystery surrounding Ramsay and his exiled Scottish Jacobite colleagues, whose Freemasonry showed distinct chivalric tendencies. It is legitimate to ask, did they invent their particular style of Freemasonry? Or did they draw from something far older, from some tradition long forgotten by their English Brethren?

Does this grave-slab at Culross, with its square, cross and sword reveal an ancient link between chivalry and Freemasonry? And was this link known to Chevalier Ramsay?

At the very least, this stone presents certain proof that one Master Mason was renowned for his expertise with both the square and the sword. And it is unlikely that he was alone.

Photographs and text © Michael Baigent, 1997.

THE GREEN MAN

CLIVE HICKS EXPLAINS THIS FRIEND OF THE MEDIEVAL STONEMASON

Early fifteenth century Green Man on a cloister vault boss at Norwich Cathedral. This is one of several in the Passion cycle portrayed in the Eastern range of the cloister.

pattern, shared by all, expressed through varying symbolic forms, is termed by psychologists an *archetype*. In this case the Green Man represents the *archetype* which channels and reinforces a mental attitude of sympathy for, and with, nature.

The modern concept of the Green Man associates it with a number of strands: a group of ancient tree myths; the idea of the Tree of Life; related foliage folk customs found all over Europe; folk tales such as those of Robin Hood, Gawain and the Green Knight and others; the idea of the Wild Man or Woodwose; and the old English inn name, "The Green Man", which has given the symbol its current title.

These strands are not directly linked by historical circumstances but by archetypal association within human consciousness. The Green Man *archetype* is seen as coming into manifestation in popular consciousness, periodically encouraged, in response to the circumstances of the time. Its current emergence is seen to derive from a widespread instinctive communal awareness of the ecological crisis being caused by our increasingly unbalanced way of life.

Thirteenth century Green Man corbel at Bamberg Cathedral, Germany. The corbel supports the pedestal beneath the famous statue of the Rider of Bamberg. This is a fine example of the leaf mask form.

An enigmatic figure is to be found in thousands of images carved in stone in the Medieval churches of Europe. It appears normally as just a face, usually male, sprouting foliage, becoming foliage, or growing from foliage. It has been suggested that this figure, now known as the Green Man, was a special sign for the stonemasons but there are probably just as many in wood as in stone. He is, though, almost confined to the building trades being uncommon in painting, manuscript, or stained glass. Furthermore, and mysteriously, no known Medieval account explains the reason for the Green Man.

The expression "Green Man" today embraces far more than just the carved figure of the Middle Ages. About sixty years ago connections were first conceived between a number of separate historical strands and these connections have been developed more recently: a number of separate traditions linking humanity with nature have now become seen as differing manifestations of a very fundamental and basic pattern lying deep within the human mind. Such a universal

Folk Customs

Ancient mythology tells, in many forms, of the Mother Goddess bearing a son without a father; a son who is put on the earth in order to help humanity with what it needs. But while this son is of divine origin he is not immortal and must therefore die.

In some of the myths he is associated with a tree and this connection extends into Egyptian and Classical times. His death and renewal were associated with Spring-time regeneration, the miracle essential to all communities. Furthermore, the essential mythological basis depicts the divine originator of this son as being feminine: the Mother of all. Her human-divine offspring are revealed as masculine in a mythological weaving of the traditional understanding of the origin and role of the feminine and masculine.

Springing from this mythology are folk customs which, in Europe and elsewhere, celebrate the regeneration of life in the Spring and the regeneration of the community with new birth. Michael Dames has written convincingly of the megalithic alignments at Avebury being used for this purpose in the Bronze Age.[1] Customs of this type, although forbidden in Britain during the Puritan periods, continue in this country in many places and survive all over Europe. Their antiquity is never on record and they are first mentioned in print only about three hundred years ago but their origin must be much earlier since it is implausible to envisage folk customs of this nature being inaugurated so recently.

The common factor in these customs is a character, always male and covered in foliage, known in many places as "Jack in the Green" and usually associated with the May Queen who herself represents the Goddess as Virgin. In some of the historic customs "Jack in the Green" is symbolically executed to allow in the spirit of Summer. In Britain probably the best of these folk customs are to be found in Hastings and Rochester on the early May Bank Holiday, and in Castleton, Derbyshire on Garland Day, 29th May,

The Wild Man

One of the Medieval sources of the Green Man may have been the sense of spirits in nature and the idea of the Wild Man, or Woodwose, a legendary natural man living in the wild. The ancient belief that primitive men were living wild in the forests was reinforced by actual alienated individuals and outlaws living in that way and naturally connects with stories such as that of Robin Hood; a connection

Circa 400 AD, tomb of St. Arbre, Church of St. Hillaire, Poitiers. This is the earliest known Green Man in a Christian context and is also the earliest known example where the foliage grows directly out of the face. Earlier (Roman) examples form the face directly from foliage.

Early fifteenth century Green Man, Church of St. Swithin, Woodbury, Devon. This capital contains four green men and has an instructive purpose. This figure faces into the Church and is hearing holy wisdom – and the "voice of Nature" as our 3rd Degree has it.

Early fourteenth century Green Man, Church of All Saints, Sutton Benger, Wiltshire. One of the finest in England.

supported by the traditional image used on signs of a "Green Man" inn - Robin Hood, or a forester, or a wild figure covered in hair and brandishing a club.

The Wild Man also has a psychological significance: it represents the natural person within each of us; our tastes and our talents which we have to direct to act well in the world. The Wild Man is by no means a negative image. One set of figures in York Minster shows a Wild Man protecting a Green Man from a demon – the Green Man, as we shall see, representing divine consciousness in the world being guarded by the natural forces within us. The Green Man is a worldly angel, acting not "from above" but from within the world itself. The Wild Man does not need to be subdued but his potential has to be made real, has to be tamed or smoothed – like the rough ashlar, another symbol of completion familiar to Freemasons. We have to bring together both the angel, and the Wild Man, within us.

The Carved Image

The principal incarnation of the Green Man is as a carved image, a face integrated with the foliage spilling out of it. The image is international but the different traditions appear to be separate which reinforces the concept of the image as a variation of a single *archetype*. Although many are inclined to seek a Celtic origin for the figure, in the European tradition its origin appears to be Roman as revealed in carved foliate heads dating from the second century AD together with some mosaic images in several places. The earliest known Green Man in a Christian context is found on a slightly later tomb in Poitiers but the figures remain uncommon in Christian iconography until the twelfth century, reaching their heyday perhaps in the fourteenth. After the Renaissance (fifteenth century) and the Reformation (sixteenth century), the Green Man continued as a decorative image in architecture until its use faded in the early twentieth century – until the current revival which began around 1990. At present, Green Man images are occurring widely; in the restoration of Windsor Castle, for example.

The most significant period in the life of the carved image was the Middle Ages when thousands of green men were included in church iconography. And, in spite of a complete lack of any contemporary account of the image, or the reasons for including it amongst the saints and sinners, there is a powerful sense that the green men in churches convey a profound meaning, a meaning most probably not explicitly expressed at the time – otherwise surely someone would have written of it?. They are more than conventional decoration and are found in conspicuous and important locations.

Of course, not every building was composed with a symbolism fully appreciated and many decorative features must have merely followed local precedent. Nevertheless, many of the images, especially in parish churches, were instructive. They aimed to keep us on the straight and narrow path. The Green Man is here to help in this – but to help with what we need, not with what we want; to achieve this, he is quite often fierce. There is a four-part Green Man capital at Woodbury in Devon that is clearly didactic: it points to the consequences of ignoring divine wisdom.

Consciousness and Wholeness

Many green men though look out at us through the foliage without expression, as if just seeing. In this they may be considered the consciousness of nature, the Divine consciousness, which is also to say, *our* consciousness, for we are all part of the Divine. In this, the Green Man is the witness of the holy drama of life enacted before him.

The importance of the Green Man is demonstrated by the fact that he is depicted in one church or another observing all the central events enacted by Christ and that he occurs in every conceivable location in the church. Yet the Green Man is never part of the action. He is confined to observation; to consciousness rather than action. The Green Man, consciousness in Nature, acts as the eyes of God, and of course he is us – for we are the eyes of God in creation.

The Green Man has an active, masculine role in the world but springs from a concept of the divine being feminine. Both aspects are within us. We have the task of reunifying the masculine and feminine, making that which has been separated whole again - the Sacred Marriage of the Mysteries. Following, in fact, the meaning of the word "religion", the root of which is the Latin *re-ligare*, to rebind that which has been separated.

The Green Man has a wonderful breadth, reaching the most profound meaning but also touching upon lightness and fun; the fun of finding new green men in almost any church you explore, and the fun of enjoying the sparkling gaiety of the Spring festivals.

[1] *Michael Dames,* The Avebury Cycle, London, 1977.

All photographs by Clive Hicks.

Clive Hicks was born in South Africa. He is an architect and photographer: these two specialities have united in his interest in the architecture of the medieval churches. These introduced him to the Green Man and he collaborated with William Anderson on Green Man The Archetype of Our Oneness with the Earth. *He is also the author of,* The Green Man – A Field Guide.

Green Man festival, Hastings, Sussex. "Jack in the Green" is taken in procession through the town accompanied by green men and Morris dancers to Hastings Castle where he is killed "to bring in the Spirit of Summer".

Garland Day, Castleton, Derbyshire: the Garland King and his consort in procession.

AN EGYPTIAN MYSTERY

MICHAEL BAIGENT REVEALS THE USE OF A FAMILIAR SYMBOL IN ANCIENT EGYPT

The Sphinx and Great Pyramid of Khufu at sunrise.

There are three chambers within the Great Pyramid of the Pharaoh Khufu: the upper, placed in the centre of the pyramid, is called the King's Chamber, and is entered by a passage-way leading off the end of the huge interior 'Grand Gallery'. This Chamber is around 34 feet long, east to west, a little over 17 feet wide and 19 feet high. It is lined with well finished granite brought down river from Aswan, 500 miles to the south. Within the chamber stands a stone sarcophagus – also of Aswan granite - but whether Khufu, or anyone else, was ever interred in it remains a mystery.

Nevertheless, all seems conventional enough until we study the sarcophagus: for a start it is too large – by one inch - to be carried up the initial internal passage of the Pyramid. It must, therefore, have been placed in position during the building of the pyramid, before the chamber itself was finished. And in an additional curiosity, the sarcophagus itself is unfinished: the top is still rough with visible saw and chisel marks. In this, it stands in stark contrast to the finely smoothed walls of the chamber itself.

Naturally an explanation has been advanced: that the original smoothed sarcophagus was dropped in the Nile or broken. In the subsequent panic to supply a replacement before the chamber was finished another was hurriedly prepared and placed inside, unfinished! As an explanation, it is rather weak. The interior of the King's Chamber is well smoothed and finished. The sarcophagus too could easily have been finished while inside the chamber. There is no structural or logistical necessity for it to have been

The naos in the inner sanctuary of the Temple of Edfu.

The so-called 'Kiosk' of Trajan on the island with the temple of Philae.

delivered completed. In addition, such was the skill and precision of the ancient Egyptians that had they wished to finish the sarcophagus, they most certainly would have managed it, especially since the Pharaoh was undoubtedly still alive at the time and keen that his work should be completed to the highest standard. We are left facing the possibility that the sarcophagus' rough and unfinished state is deliberate.

Could this indeed be the case? And if so, what might that mean? But first, what other examples of the rough and the smooth, juxtaposed, can be found in Egypt?

The Temple of Edfu

The best preserved of all the ancient Egyptian Temples is that at Edfu, dedicated to Horus in his role as warrior and avenger of his father, Osiris. Work on the temple began in 237 BC by Ptolemy III but it replaced and included parts of an earlier one on the same site which may have dated back to 1500 BC.

As is common with Egyptian temples, in the innermost third section, stands the sanctum sanctorum. Within this is a large, exquisitely carved and polished granite *naos*. This is an ornate stone shrine in which was held a statue of the god behind small doors which were opened each morning by the high priest. Its carvings express the very beginning of the creation of Egypt.

This stands about two feet out from the back wall of the chamber. A quick investigation reveals that while the front and sides are ornately carved and highly polished, the back of it has been left rough and unformed, but interestingly, left in this state while at the same time

allowing access to it. Of relevance is that this *naos* is older than the present temple. It is a remnant from the earlier temple, undoubtedly preserved in order to ensure continuity between the old and new constructions.

Again, the conventional explanation is that this edifice was left unfinished because the rear was not seen, in other words, for reasons of expediency. But the Egyptians undertook the most extraordinary feats of labour without resorting to any short-cuts or omissions. And given that it stands in the inner sanctum of the god to whom the entire

temple was dedicated it would seem unlikely that here, of all places, expediency would rule – over the several hundred years that this temple was in use. Again we are drawn inexorably to the possibility that the rear of the *naos* was deliberately left rough. Perhaps to show the beauty of creation having emerged from original chaos?

Given that the temple at Edfu has, carved on its walls, one of the original creation myths of the Egyptians describing how the first temple came into existence at the beginning of the world, this explanation is not so far-fetched. However, what is important to us is this distinction between the rough and the smooth and the use of it as a dynamic and spiritually instructive symbol.

The Valley of the Kings

Among the eighty or so known tombs carved deep down into the rock in the Valley of the Kings, and one of a small group at the very head of the valley, is a tomb which is little visited and little known outside archaeological circles: that of Sa Ptah (Siptar) who reigned around 1200 BC. This construction is very curious indeed.

Like all the tombs in the Valley it begins with a large open doorway. The great funerary ramp plunges down into the rock at a steep angle. The walls of this shaft are brightly, extensively and skilfully decorated with scenes and passages from sacred literature. After

The 'Kiosk' of Trajan showing, left, the smooth ashlars, and right, the rough.

The interior of the 'Kiosk' of Trajan showing the same division of rough and smooth stonework.

some way, the decline of the shaft ceases and the passage becomes horizontal. Simultaneously both the decoration and the finishing of the passage walls also ceases and the tomb appears almost primeval. A rough and unfinished passage leads into a huge rough and undecorated burial chamber. Here stands a vast stone sarcophagus with finely finished and decorated sides. The contrast is striking.

Leaving this burial chamber is a very interesting experience: one first travels along the level but very rough passage until the beginning of the burial shaft is reached. Then, one looks upwards to see light pouring in from the top of the shaft far above making the brightly coloured walls glisten. We are suddenly in the world of mankind and the need for the ascent to the Light. Certainly the transition from rough to smooth at this point is dramatic. Was this supposed to remind the dead king's spirit of its other-world destiny in accordance with the texts of the Book of the Dead? Was the transition from rough to smooth an important symbol in this ascent to the light? For those who have walked the passage with this in mind such conclusions seem plausible.

Nevertheless, we could still be influenced by wishful thinking. We still lack proof that the contrast between the rough and the smooth stone-work was a definite symbol, deliberately used. But that will come: we must move to the great temple of Philae.

Aswan and the Temple of Philae

The temple of Philae, dedicated to the goddess Isis, sits on its own island in Lake Nasser, just south of Aswan. At the east end of the island stands a construction built in Roman times, the so-called 'Kiosk' of Trajan. This is rectangular, with fourteen columns linked by walls. Its roof has long disappeared. It is thought that it formed a formal gate into the main temple, but there is something very curious about its construction: one half of the outside walls are built of smooth ashlars, the other half of rough. This pattern is repeated inside the

building as well as outside; it is an integral and deliberate part of its design. No one knows why.

Egyptologists confess to being mystified by the deliberate contrast. Here is proof that in ancient Egypt the contrast between rough and smooth stonework was deliberate and part of their spiritual symbolism. But there are no texts which elucidate the meaning of this pattern. Perhaps Freemasonry, containing, as it does, many residues of ancient symbolic thought, can help the Egyptologists? What, according to the teaching of Freemasonry, might these mean?

The Rough and Smooth Ashlars in Freemasonry

Every masonic Lodge contains a pair of cubic stones: one rough and unformed, one smooth and well finished. To every Freemason, these rough and smooth ashlars are a simple and well understood symbol. They symbolise the masonic journey; beyond this, they are symbolic of any spiritual journey: from the rough, rude, ignorant, state of being, to that which is complete, which has gained knowledge and wisdom. And, in the masonic context, towards that which can help shoulder the burden of society as a well formed ashlar helps support the weight of a building.

In Freemasonry, the rough and smooth ashlars symbolise a journey towards completion, towards knowledge, towards wisdom and ultimately, towards the Creator and Sustainer of all life. I think it not unreasonable to suppose that this was at least a part of the ancient Egyptian's understanding of this symbol as well.

All photographs by Michael Baigent.

Details of the interior walls of the 'Kiosk': left, the smooth stonework; right, the rough.

SOUNDTRACKS OF THE ANCIENTS

PAUL DEVEREAUX EXPLAINS AN EXTRAORDINARY DISCOVERY

From left, David Keating and Aaron Watson setting up their acoustic equipment at Stonehenge.

Many of us like to visit the ruins of ancient monuments and temples, trying to picture what went on at these places. But it tends to be a silent movie running in our minds, one that does not tell us what these ancient sacred places *sounded* like. Fortunately, archaeologists are at last beginning to realise that sound was vital to the religious practices of ancient peoples and so, gradually, the various soundtracks of antiquity are beginning to be investigated.

Above all others, Freemasons will appreciate that the ancient Egyptians knew many secret arts, and we can safely assume that the secrets of sound were among them. For instance, there is a fallen obelisk in the great temple complex of Karnak in Luxor. If the ear is placed close to the pyramidal point and the block struck with the hand, the whole piece of granite can be heard to resonate. Goethe referred to architecture as "frozen music" and so it seems to have been in ancient Egypt. Did the temples of the Nile have their own notes, their own frequencies?

Vision and Sound

We now know that acoustics were important in other and often much older cultures even than that of ancient Egypt. Take the Palaeolithic painted caves of France and Spain, dating back tens of thousands of years. It has been found that some of the stalactites and stalagmites in them are musical, in that they will issue pure bell-like or gong-like notes when struck. Some archaeologists refer to these musical calcite formations as 'lithophones'. Most if not all of these relatively rare features had been painted with geometric signs and animal figures in Stone Age times, and they also display ancient percussion marks. It has been found that echoes from the lithophones or human voices tend to be strongest from rock wall surfaces which contain the famous rock paintings. More recent work by the American acoustic researcher, Steven Waller, indicates that some rock art panels produce echoes that act like 'soundtracks' to paintings of animals, simulating the rumble of depicted animal herds, for instance, or the roar of a lion or sabre-toothed tiger.

Association between rock art and acoustics have been noted elsewhere. Bronze Age petroglyphs at the edges of lakes near Helsinki have been found to be carved on rock surfaces that produce distinctly more complex echoes than other surfaces when the initiating sound is delivered from boats on the lakes. Currently, Russian and Finnish researchers are studying 'palaeoacoustic' sites on the shores of Lake Onega in Russia. The surface of the lake has been found to amplify the sound these natural stone 'drums' make when struck causing it to carry over kilometres. The features are surrounded by concentrations of rock art. Similarly, archaeologists in the United

A member of the ICRL team conducting acoustic investigations at the Neolithic Chun Quoit dolmen in Cornwall.

The Neolithic passage grave of Waylands Smithy, Oxfordshire.

States have identified "ringing rocks" – boulders that emit bell- or gong-like sounds when struck – that are marked with rock carvings.

This association between rock art and sound is perhaps not surprising – information is beginning to be uncovered by experts indicating that rock art inspired by the ancient and almost universal trance-based religion of shamanism derived from the idea that a spirit world existed behind the rock face, which was conceived of as acting like a 'membrane' between that world and this. In trance, shamans felt they could penetrate through cracks and crevices in the rock-face, and also that spirits could pass through from behind it into the human world. It is not hard to appreciate that echoes would have been considered a part of such traffic.

Archaeologists have now started to use acoustic instrumentation to probe the secrets of ancient monuments. Two teams have been making the early running in the

Professor Robert Jahn of the ICRL team setting up sound equipment inside the stone chambers of Waylands Smithy.

acoustic investigation of Stone Age sites in Britain and Ireland: Aaron Watson and David Keating of Reading University, and Robert Jahn and the present writer, of the Princeton-based International Consciousness Research Laboratories (ICRL) group. The two teams have worked independently of one another.

Making the Old Stones Speak

The Reading team deployed an amplifier and a digital audio-recorder with omni-directional microphone at a range of megalithic sites. The amplifier issued pink noise – that is, sound with a wide frequency spectrum. They observed the behaviour of the sound at recumbent stone circles like Easter Aquorthies, Aberdeenshire, and found the recumbent stone to act like a stage. An officiant singing, uttering or playing music in front of it would project sounds into the centre of the circle, with returning echoes from the perimeter standing stones, which increase in size and thus reflective effectiveness towards the recumbent block. The distribution of stronger sound was contained almost exclusively within the circumference of the stone circle. In a sense, the Reading pair conjured up the ghosts of Stone Age ritualists standing at specific spots.

Elsewhere in Scotland, the Reading duo performed drumming inside the chambered Neolithic mound of Camster Round, Caithness. Although the drumming could not be heard more than a hundred yards away in the open air outside the cairn, the sound faintly but seemingly magically reappeared inside a

The entrance to Newgrange, the great Irish Neolithic passage grave. The passage entrance is behind the carved entrance stone and the roof box above that admits the beams of the mid-winter sunrise.

companion mound, Camster Long, at least twice as far away.

In Orkney, at the massive stone block of the Dwarfie Stane, which has chambers and passages that were hewn out of the solid rock in Neolithic times, they encountered another odd phenomenon: when they set up a resonant frequency inside the chamber using their voices, they found that the massive stone block and the air within it appeared to shake vigorously. The vibration was also evident to people standing outside on top of the tomb, so that the sensation of moving stone blocks could be achieved by the use of sound.

The ICRL team used an omni-directional loudspeaker as a sound source driven by a variable frequency sine-wave oscillator, and a 20-watt amplifier. This was linked to a digital multimeter to verify frequencies, and the amplitude of generated sound waves were plotted using portable sound-level meters. An effectively random selection of megalithic chambered sites in England and Ireland were tested for their natural (primary) resonant frequencies, with only the great chambered passage-mound of Newgrange in Ireland being pre-selected due to the need for special permission.

The findings surprised the ICRL researchers: all the investigated chambers were found to have a natural resonance frequency in the 95-120 Hertz band, with most at 110-112 Hz – this despite variations in sizes and shapes of the chambers. There was even some evidence of 'retro-fitting', as if internal features within the chambers had been placed to 'tune' the natural resonance to the required frequency. The great chamber of Newgrange resonates effectively at 110 Hz, and the 19m (62-foot) passage behaves like a wind instrument, with sound waves generated within the chamber filling it, their amplitude decreasing towards the entrance.

The 110 Hz frequency is in the baritone range – the second lowest level of the male singing voice. The simplest indication to be taken from these findings is that male voices were used in these supposed tombs for the silent dead. This could have been on ritual occasions, or for oracular purposes, in either case most probably at those times of year marked by the entrance of sunbeams into the chambers, for these sites are astronomically aligned – at the 5000-year-old Newgrange, for instance, the beams of the rising winter solstice sun shine through a special roof box above the passage entrance, down the long passage and into the central chamber, making the stones there glow like living gold.

Mind and Body

Both research teams have considered the physiological and mental effects of sound, on the assumption that one of its ritual functions was to generate altered mind states to aid visionary experience. In

Fused stalactite-stalagmites in the ancient Mayan ritual cave of Loltun, Yucatan. They emit deep resonant sounds when struck.

one acoustic experiment at the Orkney chambered mound of Maes Howe, Keating reported being put into a state in which his body became relaxed but his mind alert, an initial stage of deep trance. Other bodily sensations were felt during on-site experimentation, including the illusion that the sound was being generated inside the participant's head. The role of infrasound has also been considered. This is sound beneath the threshold of human hearing – a little below 20 kHz. It can't be heard but it can be felt. Drumming and the sounds of certain other musical instruments can contain infrasonic components, and these would be enhanced inside the cavities of megalithic chambers and passages.

Meanwhile, the ICRL team appear to be on the brink of scientifically linking the 110 Hz primary resonance band with effects on the brain: current experiments are showing that the specific frequency range around 110 Hz tends to stimulate a certain electrical brain rhythm associated with particular trance-like states.

Although archaeological acoustic research is still in its infancy, and much more has yet to be learnt, the old knowledge is slowly being unveiled. Soon, perhaps, the old stones will be able to tell us more of their secrets.

Paul Devereux is a prolific author and lecturer specialising in ancient sacred sites and traditional lifeways.

All photographs by Paul Devereux.

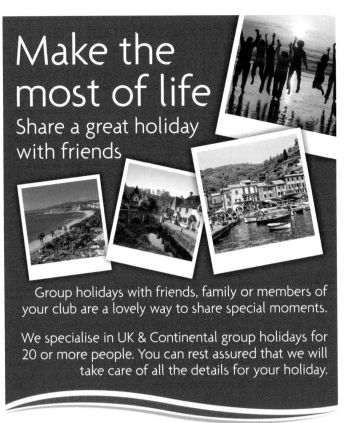

Symbolism and guilds

The strong link between the old craft guilds and Freemasonry is examined

by Michael Baigent

Culross, a small Scottish town on the Firth of Forth, is unusual in possessing two graveyards where almost every tombstone bears the symbol of a craft guild.

The more recent of these two graveyards is that of Culross Abbey, on the eastern edge of the town, which holds many graves from the 18th century. The other surrounds the older, and ruined "West Kirk", which lies across fields to the north-west. Here, the graves date mostly from the 17th century.

While trade guilds were common in ancient Greece and Rome, in medieval England the first evidence of their existence is found in the early 12th century. In Scotland, the first documented evidence dates from Perth, 1209, but no one pretends that organised guilds had not already existed for some time.

The guilds were set up to regulate their own activities, to protect the standard of workmanship, the wages obtained, the rights to practice or trade and, revealing a charitable concern, to aid those members who were too elderly to work or visited by difficult circumstances.

Their members would aspire to becoming not only masters of their craft, but also burgesses of their town, which would give them a civic as well as a trade role. Records in Edinburgh reveal that in the late 17th century it had 2,200 burgesses, of whom 57% were guild members – but only 1% were masons.

The guilds grew in wealth and influence, and in their heyday owned substantial halls, which served as administrative headquarters as well as the home for their regular great feasts. Their power and influence was maintained until the Reformation in the 16th century.

In Scotland it can be shown that operative lodges gradually converted into non-operative, or speculative, lodges. The Lodge of Edinburgh, Mary's Chapel, has minute books surviving from July 1599, when it was an operative mason's lodge. The first non-operative member is recorded in 1633. This

Above: Grave at Culross "West Kirk", showing a wood-working plane, the symbol of the Carpenter's Guild.

Left: The Mason's Guild, Culross Abbey showing the square and compasses, the position of the arms indicating a Fellow of the Craft. These symbols are surrounded by a cable-tow and are contained between the two pillars of Solomon's Temple.

Right: Culross West Kirk: The hammer and crown, symbols of the powerful Guild of Hammermen, the metal workers (blacksmiths) together with the skull and crossbones.

the

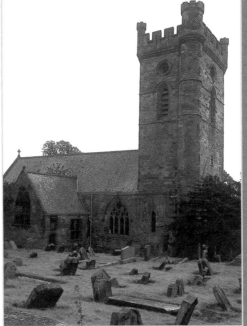

Above: View of Culross Abbey church, looking south.

Left: Culross "West Kirk" grave bearing a prominent mason's mark between two pillars.

Right: Culross Abbey: grave of a shipwright showing a ship, a wood-working plane and crossbones.

was John Mylne (the younger), whose father was master mason to the king.

In 1636, John Mylne himself was promoted to that office. By 1721-1730 the non-operative masons outnumbered operative; by 1740 they predominated, the lodge held nine operative members and 64 non-operative.

The argument over whether modern English Freemasonry arose directly out of the mason's guild has not yet been resolved. Nevertheless, it is clear that the Craft has inherited – or absorbed – much guild symbolism.

But the fact remains that none of the "Old Charges" – manuscripts detailing the legends, rules and regulations of operative masons – which were composed prior to the 18th century, mention the story of Hiram Abiff, whose tragic end is so fundamental to modern speculative masonic symbolism.

The earliest hint that the story was in circulation comes from an advertisement in 1726, which referred to the widow's son being killed by a blow; the earliest full version of the story appears in the famous exposure of Samuel Pritchard, *Masonry Dissected*, in 1730. The mystery confronting any researcher is why – and how – did the organisation of operative Free-masons become the vehicle for the highly tuned moral and spiritual system we know today?

Why, for example, were there no speculative shipwrights or speculative wheelwrights?

For the ship or the wheel could both readily lend themselves as symbols from which moral and spiritual allegories could be drawn: the ship guided by its pilot over unpredictable seas; the wheel's strong rim drawing strength from spokes radiating from the centre.

History does record that other guilds, apart from the masons, did moralise by means of allegories illustrated by their craft symbols. Prior to the Reformation, each year during Whitsun week, or on the feast of Corpus Christi in early summer, all the guilds performed plays – their pageants – on specially constructed wagons which could be driven on a circuit of prearranged performance sites in the town.

The audience would remain in position, while all through the day the guilds would, one after another, arrive, perform and move off to the next site.

Each guild presented a drama drawing from Biblical figures and events that were often symbolic to their craft. Examples abound: the Norwich Grocer's company, for example, presented a play about the creation of Eve and the expulsion from the garden of Eden. Elsewhere, the Shipwrights and the Master Mariners both performed plays about Noah and his Ark, and the Vintners, somewhat inevitably, dramatised the wedding of Cana.

In Chester, it was the water-leaders and drawers who performed the drama on Noah's flood, while the cooks chose one called the "Harrowing of Hell".

Coventry's Shearmen and Tailors performed the Annunciation and the Nativity. In York, the Tanners performed "The Creation and the Fall of Lucifer", the Coopers played "The Fall of Man", the Pinmakers chose "The Crucifixion" and the Mercers and Weavers "The Last Judgement".

Despite this evidence of a general use of symbolism in the trade guilds to teach morality, only the Freemasons were to give rise to a worldwide brotherhood founded upon a morality veiled in allegory and illustrated by symbols.

This is strong evidence that there was always something special and mysterious about the trade of Freemason and the secrets it preserved; something which was evidently not shared by the other craft guilds.

THE WAY OF THE LABYRINTH

CLIVE HICKS ENCOURAGES A MEDIEVAL PILGRIM'S RITUAL

Walking the labyrinth in the nave of Amiens Cathedral.

There is today a renewal of interest in an ancient pattern which represents the inner path at the heart of all traditions. For millennia people have laid out on the ground the pattern of a labyrinth, or elsewhere marked out labyrinth images. The earliest are prehistoric, but the most prominent are in medieval cathedrals and churches. It is almost undeniable that these had a ritual significance arising in prehistory and brought into Christian service during the middle ages.

Most follow a common design: a unicursal labyrinth, in which a single path leads, without any alternative, to the centre. It is usually circular and formed on concentric rings, often seven or eleven.

Labyrinths are set out in stones on prehistoric sites, they are found cut as gravel paths in turf and, most conspicuously, they are found set in the paving of some great medieval churches. All of these are large enough to walk in comfort, most taking five to ten minutes. Such a labyrinth is different from the puzzle-maze, as at Hampton Court, a confusing mass of dividing paths which makes the journey to the centre a considerable challenge.

No contemporary explanation exists for the ancient labyrinths. They are just there, without reason or commentary. However, anyone who walks such a labyrinth will appreciate that this action inescapably becomes a ritual that is at least subtly calming, and at best may evoke a profound inner stillness; in this it participates in the true function of all ritual. Walking a labyrinth can become a meditation. The natural pace is stately; one has to be intensely alert because every few paces produces a sharp turn or complete half turn. Paying attention diverts the mind from its usual petty concerns, and restores something of its true condition – the real function of prayer, for true prayer should be more an appeal for help in reforming one's state of mind than a request for advantage.

Walking the Labyrinth includes the three essential elements of a way of inward spiritual growth: a world view, rules of life, and a method of awakening. The world view is contained in the certainty of the destination and the purpose. The rules of life are contained in the necessity of following the one path which leads to the centre. The method of awakening is in the necessity to pay attention, and that within the rhythmic pulse of the steps along the path so that the renewal of attention flows into a mantra-like repetition. Any route to inward enlightenment needs these three elements.

Walking the labyrinth in company can produce further insights. The walkers should avoid being too close, so that each can walk at a personal pace, and they should shun the social nicety of acknowledging one another when passing. The walkers will pass and re-pass each other, sometimes in a line of three or more moving in contrary directions. This can produce a more profound sense of rapport than social eye contact, as if larger selves are meeting. In the ancient idea that each of us is body, soul and spirit, it is not the soul that is in the body, but the body that is in the soul; and both within the spirit. The silent meeting on the labyrinth can evoke a sense of an encounter at a deeper level.

Medieval Labyrinths

Medieval examples can be found in France at Chartres, Saint-Omer, Saint-Quentin and in Belgium at Maastricht. Some were removed after the Middle Ages, but others have been restored, as in Amiens Cathedral. In these, the labyrinth usually occupies the full width of the nave, often with eleven circles. It appears, at first, a strange intrusion but the effect of walking a labyrinth can evoke such an inner peace that it is less strange than other aspects of the medieval church. After the Middle Ages, the labyrinth degenerated into a garden ornament but perhaps with some element of the ritual mystery remaining.

Pre-medieval labyrinths usually follow a pattern simpler than the rich design developed in the cathedrals. Many turf labyrinths have been recorded all over England, but they require regular maintenance and have suffered varying fortunes. Many were allowed to degenerate and may not have been correctly restored. The Winchester labyrinth on St Catherine's Hill is one example, and is probably now not exactly in its original form. Others, such as the Wing Maze in Rutland, conform to the traditional pattern more exactly.

Miniature examples are found in various settings. Labyrinth images from the Bronze Age are incised on a rock face in Cornwall, moulded on a Cretan coin, and carved on a medieval vault boss in St Mary Redcliffe church in Bristol. The form is mainly European: Asian and Central American examples have been mentioned, but the latter may be of Spanish origin.

The contemporary assessment of the traditional labyrinth is that it represents symbolically a ritual path to the spiritual centre, the Holy of Holies. There is one place where it has been suggested that there was a real path to a sacred centre, a path of which signs can still be seen: Glastonbury Tor. This is an evocative site

The labyrinth marked out in the nave of St. Quentin Basilica.

and has clearly been formed into artificial terraces, sloping steps up the side of the hill. These have eroded over the centuries since the Bronze Age and are far from clear, but they have been interpreted as a ramped labyrinth, or sacred path, of the traditional form.

Walking the Labyrinth

Reading the labyrinth as a ritual path to a spiritual centre is reinforced by the traditional layout, best seen in Chartres Cathedral, the greatest temple of the Middle Ages, where it is set in the nave just where the western rose window would lie if the façade were folded down into the church. But the nave floor is covered in chairs, so the labyrinth is more practically walked in Amiens or Saint-Quentin. Entry is from the west, on the cathedral axis, towards the high altar. The path begins eastward, but halfway to the centre diverts left (north: winter and spiritual darkness) for quarter of the circle, then back to the central axis, and then again inwards, as it began. The path goes to the circle beside the centre, and then the walker is kept within the inner circles for some time, turning back and

A labyrinth marked on a Aisle Boss, St Mary Redcliffe Church, Bristol.

The nave labyrinth pattern in Chartres Cathedral.

Turf labyrinth on the top of St. Catherine's Hill, Winchester.

forth, but always near the centre.

It is as if the "novice" is, at the beginning of the pilgrimage, given a strong display of the spiritual light, and is then kept near the light for some time. Then the path starts to move out to the much longer trek through the outer circles far from the light. The "novice" is now reliant upon personal resources, not sustained by glimpses of the light. Then, after a final semicircle along the outermost path, the journey returns towards the centre, moving eastward, next to the initial path.

At the point where the first path diverted left, this path diverts right (south: summer and spiritual light) and after a quarter of a circle turns back to the axial path and the seeker takes the last few steps to the centre. When one stops, and in the peace that can be the grace arising from the effort, looks down the length of the cathedral, it may perhaps be seen clearly and innocently as if for the first time.

This is the whole purpose of any spiritual Way: to see clearly and innocently as if for the first time. This pattern of pilgrimage has been felt in many ways, in undertaking meditation, in following almost any path of self-discovery. We start with energy and are given early rewards which impel us onward, but then we have to learn that the rewards are not the purpose of the Way and we are left to find perseverance, apparently (but not truly) without help, until the effort bears fruit and we are lifted to the next step.

The labyrinth is usually seen as symbolising the journey towards the light but in the Middle Ages there was another understanding. In the labyrinth of Chartres, until the French Revolution, there was in the centre a bronze plate bearing three images: Ariadne, Theseus and the Minotaur; why such a reference to classical mythology in a Christian cathedral?

Theseus was a career hero; when he returned to Athens, he found it subject to King Minos of Crete and required to send, every seven years, seven young women and seven young men to feed the Minotaur, a monster, the offspring of one of the gods and kept in a labyrinth. Theseus, outraged, demanded to be included. Fortunately for him, Ariadne, daughter of King Minos, immediately fell in love with him. She gave Theseus a ball of thread which would lead him to the Minotaur, enable him to surprise and kill it, and help him escape. Theseus accomplished this but sadly for Ariadne, the gods, angry at the killing of the Minotaur, made Theseus forget his love and Ariadne died with her love unrequited.

This myth had real significance in the Middle Ages. Theseus survived his ordeal in the darkness through the gift of a virgin; one who died a virgin. To medieval thinking, all are helped in their journey through the darkness of life through the grace which is the gift of the Virgin Mary; the gift of Ariadne in the myth was considered prescient of the gift of Mary, an idea demonstrating the continuity of valid mythology.

The labyrinth symbolises both a journey towards the light and into the darkness. T.S. Eliot, in his Four Quartets, quotes a passage from the Greek philosopher Heraclitus: that the journey into the darkness and the journey into the light are the same. A similar truth is expressed in Eastern tradition, that Nirvana (enlightenment) and Samsara (everyday life) are one. Enlightenment comes with seeing the full significance of what is happening right now. Eliot himself says that within the dance of life there is a still point, and but for the still point, there would be no dance; and yet there is only the dance. A Buddhist Master said that all the scriptures are mere commentaries on the single exclamation, "Ah, This!", the experience of complete consciousness in this moment. Complete consciousness, and God, can be reached only in the present moment.

Walking the labyrinth in a cathedral, risking being thought silly but persevering in silence, attending to the rhythm of the steps, and responding to the Way, might bring some taste of this enlightenment, a new vision, a hint of sublime consciousness, a dazzling darkness, a resurrection.

An incised labyrinth on a rock face, Rocky Valley, near Tintagel, Cornwall.

All photographs by Clive Hicks

Clive Hicks, B.Arch., RIBA, is a photographer and an architect with special expertise in designing for the Hospice movement. He is co-author of numerous books including, The Green Man *(1990).*

PILOTING THE SHIP OF LIFE

MICHAEL BAIGENT INTERVIEWS DR. PETER KINGSLEY

Dr. Peter Kingsley, New Mexico, January 2004.

Dr. Peter Kingsley lives in New Mexico, a land of magical sunsets and endless blue skies. But I had to drive through a snow-storm to reach him: it was worth it. For while he is not a Freemason, he is sympathetic to all systems which are founded upon spirituality and initiation. His speciality is the Pre-Socratic Greek philosophers: those enigmatic teachers such as Pythagoras and Parmenides who lived before the time of Plato and Aristotle.

His *Ancient Philosophy, Mystery, and Magic*, published by Oxford University Press in 1995, expounds a radically new approach: he demonstrates that the heart of the message expressed by the ancient Greek philosophers was experiential. It was not merely a system of argument and discussion - that came later, especially in the hands of Aristotle – but was a far richer system which through meditation, contemplation, music, chant, and ritual aimed at bringing the seeker to the very deepest

and Divine levels of our reality. It encouraged entry into darkness and silence where one could 'incubate' and receive dreams and visions from the Divine source – and ground – of all Being. Furthermore, Dr. Kingsley pointed out that there was much in common with shamanism: ancient philosophy was influenced by such teachings coming through Persia and Asia Minor to Greece and Italy.

Dr. Kingsley subsequently wrote a host of academic papers and then two

books aimed at the popular market. Reading his work I was constantly struck by the parallels which modern Freemasonry has with these ancient philosophers, with their symbolic expression and their spiritual teachings. I wished to explore their works and the parallels further.

The Journey of Freemasonry

I explained to him that Freemasonry, behind all the symbols, rituals and conventions, was a journey, a personal journey towards insight and wisdom. Freemasonry is designed to be lived, I explained, not just talked about or played with and I read him a quote from the explanation of the Working Tools of the Second Degree:

To steer the bark of this life over the rough seas of passion without quitting the helm of rectitude is the highest perfection to which human nature can attain ... and in all his pursuits to have eternity in view.

He recognised the imagery immediately.

'This body is nothing but a vehicle for steering us through life. This physical world is difficult to navigate in but we must, as best we can. We are on a journey: the ancient Philosophers used the image of a ship at sea. What does this mean? The ancient Greeks were in awe of the sea, they were scared of it. You cannot control it. The weather affects you intimately. You have to use skill and alertness to navigate. The Greeks called this skill *mêtis* and it was a very important spiritual concept to them.'

Stone base discovered at Velia in 1958: "Oulis son of Ariston Iatros (healer) Pholarchos (Lord of the Lair) in the 280th year.

Two busts found at Velia and now in storage at the site. Left, that of Parmenides, right, one of the successor Oulis priests.

'It means to be tricky, cunning, skilful, attentive, to be alert to everything around you, aware of the depth of every moment of time. The sailors needed to be attentive to the stars, to the winds, to the taste and smell of the winds.'

He explained that to philosophers such as Parmenides and Empedocles such steering successfully through life always involved *mêtis*. Furthermore, it was considered that this ability came from the gods themselves.

'We can see the body as a ship on a journey into the unknown. With the sea there are no patterns, nothing ever stays the same, all things change. On the sea of life even though things may seem familiar they are in fact always different. The Divine can sweep through. You need to have a solid sense of yourself.'

'And what is rectitude? Steering with rectitude? The etymology of the word

links it with right-angles – Latin, *rectus* means upright, straight, correct, thus rectitude here suggests taking your bearings with compasses and this is an esoteric meaning behind the moral dimension of rectitude. We have a very limited idea today of its meaning for the word has lost its idea of intelligent cunning and craftiness. These qualities have now become degraded, linked more with dishonesty. Originally cunning was considered part of the spiritual path; there are deep currents always shaping our lives and we need this alertness, this sensitivity, and we need to acknowledge that any such journey is dangerous.'

I asked whether a journey without some danger is perhaps not a journey worth taking?

'We need to be able to deal with the dangers; we need some guidelines. But with all the guidelines we still need, at

crucial moments, to use our *mêtis*. We need to know when and how to embed this wisdom into our lives, into the moment.'

> *The mares that carry me as far as longing can reach rode on, once they had come and fetched me onto the legendary road of the divinity that carries the man who knows through the vast and dark unknown...*
> – *the opening of Parmenides' mystical poem. Trans. by Peter Kingsley in* Reality

'Making a journey involves a point of focus, a direction, if you are not to get distracted at every turn. The ancient philosophers were helping people to cultivate their longing, to focus their longing, for otherwise it gets scattered. General activity often contains a part of this longing, but it does not embody the essence of it and so the true journey never has a chance to begin.'

'We always scatter ourselves. We need to gather our longing, to nurture it, focus it, for only then can it take us somewhere. We need to remember that this world is set up to keep us scattered and diverted. Of course, this brings us back to *mêtis* – the focus, the 360 degree awareness which we need on our journey.'

Interestingly for Freemasons, one of the ancient symbols for *mêtis* is a circle - for it is 'the encircler ... the awareness that allows us at any moment ... to connect the beginning to the end.'[1]

Discoveries in Southern Italy

In 1958, in Italy a little to the south of Naples, at an ancient site called Velia, archaeologists made the first of a series of astonishing discoveries. In the ruins of an ancient building's hidden gallery the

Fragment found at Velia in 1960: Ouliades Iatromantis Apollo. An Iatromantis is a healer who heals through acting as a mouthpiece for the Divine.

stone bases of three statues were found. The statues had long disappeared but the bases carried inscriptions. They marked a succession of healer-priests surviving after the death of the founder of their tradition – or, more accurately, the death of the priest who first established this ancient tradition in Velia. This first priest turned out to be the ancient Philosopher Parmenides (*5th century BC*). Yet the latest date marked on a stone base for his successors was an astonishing 446 years after his death! That is, probably reaching into early Christian times.

Further information carried by these inscriptions revealed that the priests they commemorated were all *OULIS* that is, priests of Apollo, and were further called *IATROS* (healer) and *PHOLARCHOS* (Lord of the Lair). This latter title is particularly revealing: these priests were using a special technique once widespread in the ancient world, a technique which used 'suspended animation' or 'incubation'. The patient or candidate would lie down in silence and darkness in an enclosed space, an underground room or a cave. They would either sleep and have a powerful, perhaps prophetic, dream or they would enter a state which was described as something other than waking or sleeping and, in this state, they would have a Divine vision.

The *Pholarchos* priests were masters of this technique; they supervised the dark spaces and watched over those incubating within. Dr. Kingsley described this process at length in his book *In the Dark Places of Wisdom* (1999) and it is by means of such techniques that the early philosophers like Parmenides travelled to the 'Otherworld' and encouraged others to do the same.

In September 1962 another marble

The ruins of Velia: an ancient city gate, the 'Porta Rosa'.

Velia: ruins of the underground room where the artifacts were discovered.

inscription was found in the same building. It read *Parmeneides son of Pyres Ouliades Physikos*: Parmenides, a healing priest of Apollo concerned with incubation, with dreams, oracles, riddles and ecstasy and who, as Kingsley writes, 'used incantations to enter other states of consciousness'.[2] For these men and their students – men and women - philosophy was a way of life, not an expertise with intellectual argument. That was to come later.

Freemasonry and the Mysteries

I explained that an integral theme in Freemasonry is the idea of knowing how to die. As the ritual for the Third Degree states:

> Nature... prepares you, by contemplation, for the closing hour of existence... she finally instructs you how to die.

I asked whether he saw this as in any way paralleling the ancient Mystery traditions, a suggestion which has often been made by masonic writers?

'Absolutely. In Parmenides' writings it is clear that he is given the wisdom he has by going into the world of the dead. He can only do this by dying before he dies, driven by his own longing. It is a very lonely affair. Just you, face to face with death. At that moment you are on your own. Plato, in his *Phaedo*, states quite specifically that 'the practice of philosophy is the practice of dying'. Reason cannot help us here.'

Dr. Kingsley stresses the importance of the practice of stillness; 'through stillness we come to experience a reality that exists beyond this world of the senses,' and 'the greatest achievement is to listen.' He would find support in our masonic ritual which teaches us to 'Continue to listen to the voice of Nature...' by which, it explains, we can know our own immortality. He added,

'The journey is carried out in stillness. That's the paradox.'

1 Kingsley, Reality, Inverness (Calif), 2003, p.187.
2 Kingsley, In the Dark Places of Wisdom, London, 1999, p.159

Dr. Peter Kingsley's latest book, Reality, was reviewed in the last issue of Freemasonry Today. See his website www.peterkingsley.org or contact his publishers, info@goldensufi.org

Photograph of Peter Kingsley by Michael Baigent. All other photographs by Peter Kingsley.

THE WHOLE MAN

MICHAEL BAIGENT ASKS JOHN CHAPMAN ABOUT FREEMASONRY AND ALTERNATIVE MEDICINE

Expert in Alternative Medicine, and Freemason, John Chapman.

There is not much difference between the philosophy of Alternative Medicine and the philosophy of Freemasonry.' John Chapman quickly drew me into his train of thought. 'How so?' I asked.

'Both look at the whole person. Alternative Medicine considers the whole person rather than individual symptoms; Freemasonry too concerns the whole person – viewing us as both a physical body and a spiritual being. Furthermore, Alternative Medicine aims to restore personal harmony; masonry seeks to do the same thing.'

I was talking with John Chapman during a walk with his dogs across a cold wooded common north of Winchester. While his three dogs rushed to and fro picking up the scent of squirrels or deer, we moved at a more leisurely pace, musing upon the links between Freemasonry and alternative approaches to health. John is well versed in both: since 1973, John and his wife – an Osteopath – have run a clinic for Alternative Medicine in Winchester. He has also been a Freemason for many years.

One of the basic principles of Alternative Medicine, John explained, is that a person cannot be fully healthy unless he or she maintains a state of complete harmony, that is, a harmony derived from all the interconnected vital processes of the body and spirit flowing together easily and naturally. The practitioner of Alternative Medicine learns to recognise and treat all which disrupts or blocks this dynamic exchange. Professionally, this

is John's task: in order to achieve the significant healing results that he does he has trained in Homeopathy, Osteopathy. Hypnotherapy and Herbal Medicine.

These four disciplines have a different approach to the whole person: Herbal medicine involves him in preparing medicines from plant extracts although the primary ingredients which he uses are now purchased from specialist suppliers. This approach differs from Homeopathy in that the latter tends to dilute the medicines to a point beyond any ability to measure the concentrations. This diluted medicine then acts as a trigger for the body's own healing mechanisms so that one can say that it has stimulated the innate healing power of the body itself in order to produce a cure. Osteopathy deals with the physical manipulation of bones since the

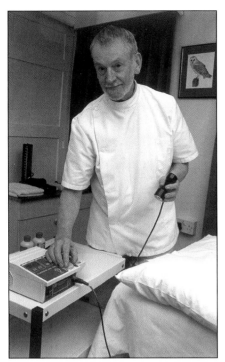

John Chapman demonstrating the ultra-sound equipment which he often uses in treatment.

displacement of even a minor part of the skeletal structure can prevent the harmonious functioning of the body through impeding the natural flow. And finally, Hypnotherapy can be used to seek out the cause of some blockage preventing the progress of healing. These represent four different but complementary paths to health each addressing particular problems.

I mentioned that Freemasonry, with its rituals, its Degree structure, and its progressive offices, is a journey, one which aids that important spiritual journey which we all – to a greater or lesser degree – follow. It struck me that John's approach to Alternative Medicine could also be seen in this way. I asked whether he ever saw it like this, as an aid on a journey?

'Oh yes. People will encounter obstacles on their way that they cannot overcome. Alternative Medicine helps them deal with these. If someone is suffering from physical symptoms it is often good to remind them that they don't have the malady, their body does. Though, of course, sometimes the reverse occurs – they have the malady but the body doesn't! We find that spiritual blocks can cause physical symptoms'.

Masonic charity

John was initiated in London, into Covenant Lodge, No. 4344, and his main charity during this time had been the Masonic Hospital. Indeed, he raised sufficient funds for them to be accorded a 'Patron's' status.

During his masonic career he has had personal experience of the charitable side of Freemasonry. Not long after he joined he experienced family difficulties and had custody of his three young children. He was struggling to cope. Freemasonry came to his aid and enabled two of his children to attend masonic boarding schools.

More recently he suffered from a serious heart condition and doubted whether he could wait for hospital treatment. Alerted by his Lodge Almoner, the New Masonic Samaritan Fund stepped in and in just over a week offered to fund half the cost of a private operation. In one further week the treatment was concluded; within three months he was able to return to his work. He and his wife have every reason to be grateful.

Freemasonry's promise

'Why did you join Freemasonry?'

'I was about thirty. I was asked to join and I agreed; I was ready for it. I had been looking into the deeper side of life for several years – I wanted to know who I was. Was I the physical being, or something more?'

'And did Freemasonry fulfil its promise?'

'It added another dimension; it was a natural progression for me. And this has continued. You join Freemasonry, first you sit on the side-line, then you take office and go through the Chair. Gradually masonry builds itself around you.'

With the result that, for a decade or more, John has served as Director of Ceremonies for his Winchester Lodge!

'Why would anyone join Freemasonry now?', I asked.

Because it gives another dimension to life. Nothing else can do that. It concerns Self-building of both the social and deeper aspects. This is an important dimension to life which many don't have today. It forms a more solid basis for living; it teaches charity, guides you to looking inwards while at the same time presenting you with an outward aspect. Life today is centred too much upon simply surviving, upon existing, Freemasonry gives a more rounded view of life.'

And Gill, his wife, added, 'Masonry is a good thing. It makes all men equal if you follow it.'

A question nagged at me: 'If Freemasonry is founded upon the most profound principles. Why then do you think that there has been such a drop in membership? Are its principles irrelevant in the modern world where there are so many alternative ways of spending time?'

'There is an ancient saying,' said John, 'that when the pupil is ready, the teacher will appear. I see this relating to Freemasonry. What masonry is going through now it has been through before. There is a time of great richness and then a period when men are less receptive to its message; their minds are elsewhere. We are going through that time when men's minds are not on spiritual things even though the teacher – Freemasonry – is there.

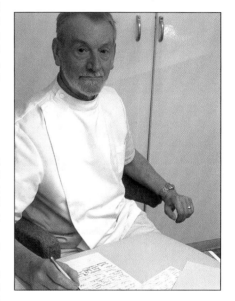

So I don't see the present time as a crisis but simply as a reflection of man's needs - needs which are not centred upon spiritual things. We are all living high at the moment, money is good, and spiritual values take the back seat. But at a period of hardship or crisis people cry out for spiritual values again. Such periods ebb and flow like the sea.'

'So,' I interjected, 'it is vital that the custodians of Freemasonry understand its spiritual heart.'

'Absolutely. They must keep it as a solemn trust. The quality of Freemasonry must be kept - and it must wait for the pupils to appear.'

John Chapman is Director of Ceremonies of the Lodge of Economy, No. 76, Winchester. He is also in the Royal Arch and the Ancient and Accepted Rite. His book, The Asthma Action Plan *appeared in its third edition in 1995.*

Photographs by Michael Baigent.

THE INNER VOICE OF FREEMASONRY

NJÖRDUR P. NJARDVIK ON THE DEEPER MEANING OF FREEMASONRY

The Meditation Room, a room of silence, in the United Nations building in New York.

The idea was to create a sanctuary for men and women to meditate, to seek some form of inner peace, where there was nothing to divide them, nothing which was connected to a particular religion, yet still giving a feeling of sacredness.

When I first entered this room as a young Freemason I immediately sensed a sacrosanct atmosphere and thought of the similarities with Freemasonry. Here I was in the headquarters of one of the biggest organisations of the world, where delegates from all continents are dealing with serious problems of humanity, and yet one can go into this small room like an inner core with peace and silence, as if entering the inner reality of humanity itself, and of yourself. All this, the effect of a polished rectangular black stone, a shaft of light, and absolute silence, was for me a symbol of the creative force of the universe.

> *One can go into this small room like an inner core with peace and silence, as if entering the inner reality of humanity itself, and of yourself*

At the opening of a Lodge with the Continental Ritual (used in the United States), the Master says: 'We are no longer in the profane world; we have left our metals outside the door of the Lodge'. We have stepped from the outside world with its conflicts into the sanctuary of the masonic realm where we seek knowledge of our own inner reality and inner peace, seek to touch our inner core with understanding; from here we can contribute to the unification of humanity. It is essential that there be nothing divisive, nothing calling attention to any special form of religion or dogma, only

In the huge headquarters of the United Nations in New York, there is a small room arranged by its former Secretary General, Dag Hammarskjöld. This small room, which has only eleven chairs, is called the room of silence. In the center there is a polished dark stone illuminated by a single shaft of light, and on the wall facing the entrance, an abstract painting in soft colours. That is all.

the the symbolic masonic furniture with its unspoken meaning.

When we enter the Lodge at our initiation we undertake a symbolic journey into ourselves which offers the opportunity of a real transformation of realising who we really are. The key to this is *change*. If our initiation and our masonic progress through the degrees does not change us then the whole masonic undertaking is in vain. We have not been able to hear the silent inner voice of Freemasonry, or hearing it, have not heeded its message.

The symbolic furniture in the Lodge act like landmarks in the unfamiliar masonic landscape; the ritual is our guidebook for finding our way through the mysterious labyrinth of inner reality to our innermost core, to the inner voice which is innate in every human being.

This journey is not one of movement

The aim of our masonic quest is to realise on earth the moral, intellectual and spiritual development for all people.

in the usual meaning of the word, therefore we are symbolised by a stone which must fit into the walls of the Temple of Humanity. We use the gavel and chisel on ourselves; we are never told to use them on others. And it is painful to use them on ourselves: we must not act too brutally as the stone might shatter; it must be a careful process. But only by hammering and chiseling away our faults can we progress to become a supporting stone in the Temple, always remembering that we can lose our carefully chiseled shape if we are not constantly vigilant.

The movement of our masonic journey is an inward movement through conduct, feelings and thinking. We are guided by the three lights on the pillars of Beauty, Strength and Wisdom to achieve beauty of conduct, strength of controlled emotions, and wisdom of thought. It may seem unattainable but this is the direction of our symbolic journey. In time we move inwards through our thinking: from where do our thoughts come? The brain is an instrument for thinking but what is this mysterious phenomenon called mind? What is its true nature? Through contemplation we come closer to our innermost core.

This is an arduous and difficult journey and even if we succeed in

reaching this far, it is neither the aim nor the end of our masonic quest. It is only one side of it, the personal, interior part, where we explore what Teresa of Avila called the Interior Castle, following the command of the Oracle of Delphi: know thyself.

The aim of our masonic quest is to realise on earth the moral, intellectual and spiritual development for all people. Simply, we can say that the First Degree deals with moral development, the Second with intellectual and the Third with spiritual but in reality we are required to consider all three aspects simultaneously in everything we deal with.

Our final aim is not only for ourselves or our masonic Brothers but for humanity as a whole. The Light we have received in Freemasonry, the Inner Voice that has spoken to us through the rituals, is not for us to keep for ourselves (although we guard its ancient secrets), but to spread so that this light can eventually illuminate all human beings.

'No man, when he hath lighted a candle, covereth it with a vessel, or putteth it under a bed; but setteth it on a candlestick, that they which enter in may see the light. For nothing is secret, that shall not be made manifest.' (Luke 8:16-17).

The inner light when once discovered will shine out from its source in a limitless manner revealing that there are no boundaries between interior and exterior reality; that one is an integral part of everything; that everything in the universe is interconnected, from the tiniest parts of an atom to the galaxies and the clusters of galaxies – and beyond.

No one owns his or her life. All lives and living beings are interconnected. Similarly, every thought, every feeling, every action, has cause and consequence.

Njördur Njardvík, Grand Master of The International Order of Co-Freemasonry Le Droit Humain.

Kindness echoes and reverberates – as does evil action.

My personal perception of Freemasonry is to explore the interior castle to find the essence of my own being, to be able to contribute in a humble way; to dip one finger into the ocean of human life in the hope that a kind action will lead to other kind actions, remembering the words of the Talmud: 'He who saves one life saves humanity'; to consider in all things the moral, intellectual and spiritual aspects; to face the immense difficulties in reconciling the perfection of our ideals with the imperfection of ourselves as human beings.

I believe that the key to this is compassion, kindness of heart. In the words of Antoine Saint-Exupéry in *The Little Prince*: "It is only with the heart that one can see rightly; what is essential is invisible to the eye".

These words could be the whisper of the inner voice of Freemasonry. ∎

Prof. Dr. Njördur P. Njardvík 33° is the Grand Master of The International Order of Co-Freemasonry Le Droit Humain, an Order of Freemasonry accepting both men and women. This Order is not recognised by the United Grand Lodge of England

SACRED SLEEP

PAUL DEVEREUX LOOKS AT THE ANCIENT INITIATORY PRACTICE OF INCUBATION

A Romano-British depiction of healing god, Aesculapius, lodged in the wall of a church at Frome, Somerset. The God's symbol, the caduceus, a serpent entwined about a rod, is clearly visible.

The practice of 'temple sleep' involved sleeping at a special temple or a venerated natural site with the aim of having dreams for initiation, divination or healing purposes. Certain ritual actions collectively known as 'incubation' would be conducted prior to sleep to help direct the dreaming mind. Such dream-seeking procedures go back to the dawn of history.

Jewish seers in antiquity would resort to a grave or sepulchral vault and spend the night there in order that the spirit of the deceased would appear in a dream and offer information or guidance. Indeed, the Jews were considered to be potent dream interpreters by the Babylonians, and this is encapsulated in the Biblical story of Daniel who was called on to interpret the dreams of King Nebuchadnezzar. Dynastic Egypt also had special temples for incubatory rituals where supplicants would fast and recite specific prayers. Immediately before going to sleep, the dream candidate might also invoke the help of suitable deities by writing their names on a piece of clean linen, then burning it.

A classic example of an Ancient Egyptian divinatory dream is that of the pharaoh, Thutmosis IV (c.1419 – 1386 B.C.). Before Thutmose ascended to the kingship of Egypt the god *Hor-em-akhet* (Horus in the horizon) appeared to him in a dream, foretelling riches and a united kingdom when he came to power. All this came to pass, and the pharaoh recorded the dream on a stela, a pillar of stone, that still stands before the Sphinx to this day.

China, too, had incubation temples and they were active up until the sixteenth century. The incubated dreams were used mainly as aids to political decision-making and state officials would spend a night at such a temple before important meetings. In Japan the emperor possessed a dream hall in his palace where he would sleep on a polished stone bed called a *kamudoko* when he wanted help in resolving a matter of state.

The Dawn of Therapy

It is from ancient Greece that we have the clearest information regarding this practice. Temple sleep there was known as *psychomanteia* and was primarily aimed at finding cures for disease. It accompanied the rise in popularity of the healing god, Aesculapius, son of Apollo. Over 300 dream temples dedicated to Aesculapius were built throughout Greece; the first such Aesculapion (or Asklepion) was in Athens, but the most important was at Epidaurus.

Founded in the 4th century B.C., this was both a religious centre and a fashionable spa. Its site nestles beneath

Mount Velanidhia (the ancient Mount Tittthion) where Aesculapius was said to have been suckled. As the ruins of Epidaurus today still indicate, it was a large complex comprised of a Doric temple, baths, a theatre and stadium, a mysterious circular structure known as the *Tholos*, hotel-like buildings, and the Enkoimeterion, the hall where the temple sleep actually took place. This was built over a well that was sacred long before Epidaurus was built.

Anyone seeking healing dreams at Epidaurus, or at any Aesculapion, would undergo a variety of spiritual and physical purifications in which water figured prominently. At the Corinth Aesculapion, for example, water was brought from a special source over 14 miles distant even though there were other springs at hand which were also used. It is interesting to note that this imported water at Corinth has been found to be radioactive, as is sometimes the case at other ancient sacred spas, that at Bath being a prime example.

The temple would contain many statues depicting Aesculapius along with displays of terracotta models of body parts accompanying testimonial plaques left by previous visitors who had experienced successful cures. Harmless snakes were allowed free rein within an Aesculapion, symbolically relating to the god's emblem of a snake entwined around a staff – the caduceus. Eventually, the person seeking the healing dream would enter a dream cell *(abaton)* and sleep on a special bed, hoping Aesculapius would appear in a dream. Temple assistants known as *therapeutes* would later interpret supplicants' dreams for them, advising on the course of treatment indicated by the dream imagery. There is evidence that the floors of *abatons* were sometimes covered in blood, suggesting that actual surgery may have been performed. The *therapeutes* also sometimes applied ointments to a supplicant's afflicted parts, or else allowed a temple snake to lick them.

Contemporary records from the Greek dream temples tell of a range of cures, some seemingly miraculous. One fellow, Heraieus, was described as not having a hair on his head, 'but a great deal on his chin'. Tired of being the butt of humour, he slept in the temple; an inscription states: 'And the god, anointing his head with a drug, made him grow hair.' Another inscription says: 'There came as a suppliant to the god a man who was so one-eyed that the other had only lids in which there was nothing. Then a vision appeared to him as he slept; the god seemed to boil some medicine and,

Epidaurus: above, the amphitheatre. Below, general view of the ruined dream temple site which was probably the leading Aesculapion of ancient Greece.

drawing apart the lids, to pour it in. When day came, he went out seeing with both eyes.'

Dreaming On

The Romans adopted and adapted the idea of dream temples, so it is not surprising that they have been found throughout the Roman Empire. One of the most far-flung was the Temple of Nodens, located over a powerful spring in Lydney Park, Gloucestershire, and overlooking the River Severn. Nodens was a native British god, patron of hunting and healing, who also had water associations. The sacred animals of this precinct were dogs, judging by the number of votive canine figurines that have been unearthed there. Like the

snakes of Aesculapius, they would have been used to lick patients' afflicted parts.

Temple sleep continues in some countries to this day. This is exemplified by the Shiva shrine at Tarakeswar, north of Calcutta in India. Pilgrims suffering chronic or incurable diseases undertake dream incubation at the site, a procedure known as dharna in Bengali. Under the guidance of a priest, the sick person fasts for a period then sleeps in a specified area within the temple.

Haunted by Dreams

Was there a psychic dimension to the spots selected for dream temples? It sounds unlikely, but the novelist and poet, Lawrence Durrell, made some astounding, if now long-forgotten, observations to this effect in *The Listener*, 25 September, 1947. On his first visit to Epidaurus in 1939, his sense was that the whole area held an aura of sanctity – there was 'something at once intimate and healing about it'. But his Greek guide at the complex let it slip that he had managed to finagle a transfer to Mycenae. Durrell wanted to know why the man should want to leave this green and peaceful place in favour of the craggy citadel. 'I can't bear the dreams we have in this valley,' the guide explained. 'What dreams?' Durrell queried. 'Everybody in this valley has dreams,' the man replied. 'Some people don't mind, but as for me, I'm off.'

He went on to comment that the dreams frequently contained the figure of a man with an Assyrian-looking visage, with dense ringlets falling down onto his shoulders. He looked like a figure depicted in a fresco in the Epidaurus museum – an image of old Aesculapius himself, Durrell suspected. But surely that was to be expected, considering that the guide spent his days in Epidaurus? 'Why should my two kids dream about him when they have never set foot in the museum?' the Greek retorted. 'If you don't believe me, ask any of the peasants who live in this valley. They all have dreams. The valley is full of dreams.' Durrell wondered if the thousands of dreams countless suppliants had experienced at Epidaurus over its centuries of activity had somehow lingered on.

In 1945, immediately after the Second World War, Durrell had reason to revisit this train of thought. While visiting the island of Cos, he encountered two British soldiers who were clearing up scattered German and Italian ordnance; they were camped near the archaeologically-

Corinth Aesculapion: entrances to the underground water reservoirs.

One of the special stone beds once used in the temple sleep chamber at the Corinth Aesculapion.

excavated site of an Aesculapion. Durrell chatted with the soldiers who asked him if he knew anything about the temple. He told them about the Aesculapian cult, and casually asked them if they had noticed

anything unusual about their dreams. This startled them. It transpired that they had moved their tent out of their initial camping spot within the temple precinct precisely because they had experienced profoundly odd and disturbing dreams. 'Was it possible, I found myself wondering again, that dreams do not disappear?' Durrell wrote. 'And especially in a place like this which must have been charged with hundreds of thousands of dreams?'

Durrell decided to conduct his own experiment by undertaking a series of sleep sessions in the Cos temple, recording his dreams in a notebook. Unfortunately, it seems he did not publish these because he felt the experiment was not complete. However, in his 1947 article he added: 'It may be years before I have time to visit Greece again and do some more work … But the material I have to date is interesting enough to suggest that dreams do perhaps live on in these ancient centres of healing, and can tell one things of great esoteric significance.' It appears he probably did not return to complete his dreaming sessions, but half a century later a loosely similar and more extensive experiment was carried out by other investigators. That is another story – one that will be told in the next issue of *Freemasonry Today*.

Paul Devereux lectures widely, broadcasts occasionally, and has written many articles, academic papers and some twenty-six books. Recent titles include, The Sacred Place (Cassell), Stone Age Soundtracks (Vega), Living Ancient Wisdom (Rider) and Mysterious Ancient America (Vega).

The remaining foundations of the dream temple of Nodens, Lydney Park, Gloucestershire.

All photographs, Paul Devereux

BUILT BY FREEMASONS

MICHAEL BAIGENT DISCOVERS THE MASONIC INFLUENCE
ON THE TOWN PLANNING OF PARATY, BRAZIL

Crossroads in Paraty revealing the symbolic stone columns on three corners while the fourth is left plain. The house on the far left, by its blue and white tiled column, reveals that it was once owned by a mason.

There are few towns which can boast of being planned by a resident masonic lodge but Paraty, on the Brazilian coast south of Rio de Janiero, is one. This profound philosophical and spiritual heritage is publicly proclaimed at the road junction leading to the main access route: in the roundabout stands a large masonic Square and Compasses.

Paraty (pronounced *Para-chi*) is one of the oldest towns in Brazil. It was an important harbour at the end of the stone-paved 'Caminho do Ouro', the 'Gold Road' which reached over 1,200 kilometers into the interior of Brazil. While a handful of houses in Paraty remain from the early eighteenth century most of the town was rebuilt in the nineteenth century and Freemasonry put its stamp on this construction. Through their influence over the town council, Freemasons had the deciding power over the future of the town.

While Freemasonry only came officially to Brazil in 1801 when the first lodge was founded under the Grand Orient of France, there had been Freemasons in Paraty before that date. The movement for the independence of Brazil from Portugal was fostered in the

lodges. Freemasonry was suppressed in 1806, briefly permitted 1815-18 and then forbidden again. The Grand Orient of Brazil was formed in 1822 but forced to remain dormant until 1832 when Freemasonry was finally allowed to be public and official. That year the first Supreme Council 33° had been established in Brazil and it is certain that the masonic rebuilding in Paraty took place after this date.

In 1833, the first - and only - officially sanctioned masonic lodge in Paraty was "União e Beleza" (Union and Beauty) was founded. Meetings were held in a single story house on the corners of the streets Comércio and Cadeia in the heart of the town.

The new town was organised into thirty-three blocks and in the local administration thirty-three officials held

responsibility, one for each sector of the town. The dominant colour of the houses was white and blue, the colours of 'Symbolic' Freemasonry' - 'Speculative' as we would term it in England. The plans of the houses in these thirty-three blocks were drawn up on a scale of 1:33.33. The houses were further distinguished: the home of a Freemason, for example, would have a symbolic column made of tiles beside the door leading to the street.

But the most amazing example of Masonic symbolism, seen by all, but recognised by few, is that at every crossroads a stone-built pillar stands at the corner of three of the houses - forming a triangle - while the fourth is left plain. This arrangement of stonework not only depicts the triangle, such an important symbol for Freemasonry, but also represents the three columns which support a Masonic lodge, those of wisdom, strength and beauty in the east, west and south: wisdom to contrive the building, strength to support it, and beauty to adorn it.

To know that these were placed there

Masonic symbols on the junction of the main road leading into Paraty.

by Freemasons, and to know that few, if any, of the many visitors to Paraty have any idea about this, is to be in possession of a secret but one which is on open display, for all to see. Yet, without the key, these stone pillars mean nothing; they are not seen. It is symbolic of masonic secrets: without the key they too cannot be seen.

The Black Glove Club

A strong local oral tradition speaks of an early tradition of a secretive 'Black Glove Club.' This was a group of Freemasons who met secretly to punish those who had left the masonic lodge or who were considered to be enemies of masonic ritual. It is considered to have operated in a very similar manner to the tradition of *omerta* seen in the Italian mafia. Meetings were usually held in a cemetery because, as it was said, 'the dead could not listen'.

In 1920, in a garret of a house across the street from the Masonic Temple, some black gloves, a black hood and several masonic aprons were discovered. This house had been owned by a judge who died in 1870 and was believed to have been both a Freemason and a member of the Black Glove Club.

Freemasonry in Paraty today

Paraty is host to an International Literary festival each July and while staying with my stepson, David Milne-Watson, who has a small organic farm and is involved in the sustainable agriculture movement in Brazil, I visited Paraty for a few days to hear some of the writers speaking about their work. Intrigued by the legends of masonic influence on the town I contacted the local Freemasons, all members of the Paraty Lodge União e Beleza, No. 88 in the Grand Lodge of the State of Rio de Janiero. They could not have been more friendly. My stepson, who speaks good Portuguese, provided important translations.

As it happened, the next day a new Fire Brigade Headquarters was being opened with considerable ceremony and as members of the Brigade were also Freemasons, lodge members were officially invited to the function. I and my stepson were invited along with them.

Editor of Freemasonry Today with members of the Lodge União e Beleza in Paraty at the opening of the new Fire Brigade Headquarters.

The band played music with a samba rhythm, politicians spoke at length, chief officers praised their men and The afternoon proved to be very pleasant. I felt privileged to be able to experience something of local importance; had I not been part of the international Brotherhood of Freemasonry, this would have passed me by and I should have been the poorer for it. I look forward to returning to Paraty and continuing this new friendship.

With thanks to members of Lodge União e Beleza in Paraty.

ETERNITY IN VIEW

PAUL DEVEREUX LOOKS AT RESEARCH INTO NEAR DEATH EXPERIENCES

Detail from the painting Ascent of the Blessed *by Hieronymous Bosch, now in the Doge's Palace, Venice, showing the dead moving up a long tunnel towards the Light.*

photo: akg images

While most people who nearly die from some accident or medical emergency recall nothing when they are resuscitated, some do, and their reports tend to contain common features. Typically, the person's consciousness seemingly leaves the body and floats a few feet overhead. Everything that is going on is seen and heard, even though the physical body is unconscious. The person can then feel as if being rapidly drawn away elsewhere, often with the sensation of flying through a long tunnel.

He or she usually emerges into a brilliantly lit landscape or garden of otherworldly beauty. Then a being appears – a deceased relative, a religious figure, or a 'being of light' – saying it is not yet time to die, and the person returns to the physical body in the throes of being resuscitated.

On recovery, the person often discovers that the fear of death has disappeared and may even seemingly have acquired novel healing or creative powers.

This is only a prototypical description, and there are many individual variations to this basic blueprint.

Psychiatrist and philosopher Dr. Raymond Moody, coined the term 'near death experience' (NDE) in his 1975 bestseller *Life After Life*, but the actual area of research was instigated by Elisabeth Kubler-Ross who from the 1950s had been drawing attention to the recurrence of near-death visionary narratives in terminally ill patients.

Whether there is life after death is one of the primary philosophical conundrums we face as human beings, and believers have seized on the NDE as evidence of survival.

Most scientists dismiss this - while there is no doubt about the occurrence of NDEs - the explanation they give for them is that as the brain dies electrochemical changes occur within it that trigger hallucinatory states containing imagery one would associate with the situation, such as glimpses of paradise, spiritually powerful beings, and deceased relatives.

It has even been suggested that our brains contain a final 'program' of appropriate signals, which are released into consciousness when death seems imminent. But the whole matter might not be so black-and-white.

Neutral researchers look for two types of evidence that might indicate that there is an objective aspect to the NDE - verifiable information in the near-death visions or hallucinations that seems to have been obtained by extra-sensory means, and whether the experience occurs when the brain has ceased functioning.

AT THE HOUR OF DEATH

There is some tantalising evidence concerning near-death information. I recall the case of a friend who lay close to death in hospital. At one point she nearly died and felt her consciousness leave her body and float around the hospital ward. It was an L-shaped ward and my friend had been placed at the end of it throughout her crisis. As she 'floated' around she noticed a patient with very distinctive red hair in one of the beds that was permanently out of sight of her own bed. It later transpired that the redheaded patient had been brought into the ward after my friend had been admitted, and had never passed in sight of her.

In their book, *At the Hour of Death* (1977), Karlis Osis and Erlendur Haraldsson cite a number of reports. For example, one man died in Connecticut the day after his sister's passing in Ohio; prior to expiring, the patient mentioned seeing his sister in the hospital, yet he had not been informed of her death.

This type of case can work in reverse as well, in that people around the time of death can seemingly 'call out' to a distant friend or relative resulting in the distant recipient seeing an apparition or otherwise gaining a sense of the dying person's presence.

Another friend of mine had an uncanny experience of this kind. He received a phone call from a colleague who did not give his name but who had a very individual type of humour that my friend immediately recognised. It turned out that this had happened ten minutes after the caller's death. Had the incident been a hallucination triggered by an extra-sensory impression of the deceased person's presence?

BEYOND THE BRAIN

There are many such reports of inexplicable near-death information, but the trouble is they make up a body of evidence that is only *anecdotal*, which science finds hard to accept. To make mainstream science take NDEs more seriously a harder type of evidence will be required. This is where a current NDE researcher, neurophysiological consultant Dr. Peter Fenwick, is focusing his efforts. Much of his research is presented in his book *The Truth in the Light* (1996).

Dr. Fenwick points out that an NDE has great clarity - it seems fully 'real' - and the subject is completely engaged

ORACLE OF THE DEAD, Baia, Italy.
Left: *the six-hundred-foot long tunnel into the cliff leading to the underground waterway and sanctuary.* **Above:** *two of the tunnels in the underground complex showing how the rubble fill has settled over two thousand years.* **Below:** *the walled-up sanctuary with a fresh sprig of myrtle in the small offering niche to the right of the entrance. The Romans were so concerned about this underground site that they sealed the sanctuary and filled most of the tunnels with rubble. It seems likely that the 'Near Death Experiences' were induced in this complex.* Photos: Michael Baigent

in it, perhaps communicating with otherworldly beings, seeing fabulous landscapes and other effects. Because electrical activity in the brain ceases a number of seconds after the heart stops, this cannot be a neurophysiological effect if it occurs during this period.

During resuscitation from that state a person is confused and recovers consciousness only slowly. Significantly, NDEs are too lucid and structured to be happening in such a mental state so if the NDE can be proven to occur during either of these conditions a new scientific model will be required to account for it. So far, it seems there has been just one recorded case of an NDE occurring when monitoring equipment showed the patient's brain had become electrically inert.

Knowing that there will have to be several rigorously monitored cases of this kind for science to be obliged to reassess its ideas about the NDE, Fenwick is alerting doctors to help test for this. He has also proposed that emergency rooms in a large number of hospitals be fitted with special signs in places like the tops of ceiling lampshades or wall cupboards that would be visible only to a patient experiencing an NDE out-of-body episode. If consciousness does actually become independent of the brain in such experiences then over time the signs will be noticed in a number of cases, but not at all if the out-of-body sensation is just a neuropsychological effect. This nationwide experiment has not yet been set up.

SWAN SONG

Dr. Raymond Moody, who currently holds the Bigelow Chair of Consciousness Studies at the University of Nevada, is taking more unusual approaches to the study of the NDE. One involves what he calls the 'swan song', when a person shortly to die starts to recite or even to sing. Moody has collected hundreds of examples of this phenomenon, and points out that in Japan there is even a tradition of death poetry. The Pythagoreans of ancient Greece also recited as they 'passed over', and these included some deliberate nonsense words. The Gnostics, too, had a similar practice.

Moody likens the swan song to the 'shaman's song' which is used to help carry the shaman into trance on his journey to the spirit world. Such songs contain 'an integrated intelligible language of nonsense words' Moody informs us, much like the babbling involved in 'speaking in tongues' (*glossolalia*) which is also associated with trance states.

He argues that the use of the swan song phenomenon could give the dying and those caring for them a language to cope with the ineffable quality so often reported by those who have had an NDE. He reckons we will only be able to understand what is involved in crossing the threshold of death by creating 'an alternative form of logic'.

EVOKING THE DEAD

Another of Moody's highly original approaches to researching the near-death state involves his invention of the 'psychomanteum'. This is a dark-walled, dimly-lit small room or cubicle which is empty save for a comfortable chair and a reflective surface, such as a glass or crystal object, a bowl of liquid, or a mirror. The reflective surface has to be so placed that the user of the psychomanteum is able to see it from the chair without looking directly into it.

Moody got the idea for this arrangement from his visits to ancient Greek sites dedicated to necromancy

Entrance to the Oracle of the Sibyl at Cuma, Italy. Photo: Michael Baigent

(*necromantions*), such as the Oracle of Poseidon associated with the Diros Cave at the southern tip of Peloponnessos near Sparta. It contains a hole now covered with slabs that was said to lead to the kingdom of the dead. Such sites typically feature caves or labyrinthine subterranean passages. Moody had

noticed a stone bowl in the site he investigated and figured that it had been used to hold a liquid to provide a reflective surface for gazing into.

Moody claims that if a person enters a meditative state in the conducive environment created by the psychomanteum and then gazes at the reflective surface, the face of a deceased friend or relative may appear in it. In one experiment, 153 out of 155 subjects experienced 'a re-union with a departed loved one'. Auditory hallucinations occurred in about thirty percent of the cases. Moody himself claims to have seen a vision of a dead grandparent under these conditions.

It is said that space is humanity's last frontier, but in actuality it is the nature of human consciousness that challenges us. We still do not know what lies beyond the threshold of death's door, but our curiosity and ingenuity continues to make us strain to see. One day, the living may be able to understand what only the dead now know.

Further reading: Otherworld Journeys, *C Zaleski, 1987;* The Near-Death Experience, *L. W. Bailey and J Yates (eds), 1996.*

Paul Devereux is not a Freemason but has a strong interest in the spiritual and its links with science. He has written some twenty-six books, the latest Fairy Paths & Spirit Roads *is available from Amazon or www.pauldevereux.co.uk.*

The Chamber of the Sibyl, Cuma. She would give prophecies and direct those with the desire and funds to the Oracle of the Dead at Baia which was nearby. Photo: Michael Baigent

TO DWELL TOGETHER IN UNITY

The melting voice through mazes running
Untwisting all the chains that tie
The hidden soul of harmony.

John Milton

We are divided by much in the modern world. We are divided by language, and all the attempts to make the English language international won't put that right. We are divided by cultural imprints, and no single one is superior to any other. We are divided by race, and we are only overcoming that division slowly and painfully. We are divided by religion, or we seem to think we are. We are divided by ideology and politics, often through our own blindness to see some truths parallel to the one we hold to. It seems impossible sometimes to have a view of unity, of one-ness, of those things which bring us together rather than those which cast us asunder. Even Freemasonry has its different, mutually unacceptable traditions.

Diversity can of course unite. God forbid that we should assume that dull and faceless uniformity which totalitarian regimes have sought to impose on us. Diversity ensures that we imbibe the richness of other ideas, of other cultures, a richness that comes to birth when we achieve a fusion of art, music, poetry or social harmony from elsewhere, and use it to enhance our own culture, our own lives, to give us other perspectives.

But too often we have perceived diversity in thought, conduct and belief as being divisive, perceived it as a threat. Out of divisiveness can come confrontation. When confrontation looms, the animal instinct is to hit back rather than to stop, think, analyse. Civilised man learns slowly, to assess, to evaluate, to interpret, to weigh up and to appraise. It does not always come easily to him to make a measured response, a response we might say which is called for by the symbolism of the twenty-four inch gauge, in assisting him to measure and to mete out appropriately. It has been man's failure to respond in this way that has so often in the past led to bloody conflict, and still does today.

And in such conflict, even attempts at conciliatory behaviour can be overlooked, diminished and decried. Many are the stories, now told with pride, of Freemasons on both sides in the American civil war cooperating to bring aid and relief to those supposed to be their enemies. Ireland too is proud to count Freemasons from both sides of the sectarian divide. I have also heard of Freemasons on both sides in the Arab-Israeli conflict who maintained bonds of brotherhood despite the hostilities. But when I was a child, nobody recounted the stories, told later, of troops from both sides in the first World War celebrating Christmas together across the trenches. In my childhood, there was yet another war going on, and it didn't seem right then to throw light on enemies actually getting on well together.

Recently, eighty-eight years after the end of that terrible war, we have witnessed two brave men, brave in more than one sense, imprinting the stamp of unity on a divided world, and doing it together, a man joining with his former foe to honour lives so tragically and needlessly lost. Last autumn, Henry Allingham, at 110 years old Britain's oldest First World War veteran, travelled to Germany to lay a wreath of poppies at the foot of the war memorial in the town of Witten near Dortmund. A British veteran laying a wreath at a German war memorial? This would have been amazing and heart-warming enough, but he did not do it alone. He was joined in this sublime act by the 109 year-old German veteran Robert Meier, and together they laid the wreath.

There was no superfluous question of whom they were honouring. There were no issues of the nationality of the fallen. No points were scored. No recriminations or reservations. No history lessons were given. Certainly, they were honouring by this simple act, all those who gave their lives, but there was another dimension, another horizon. These two men did not speak each other's language, and they hardly needed to. Once they had clasped hands, they could not let go, so great was the energy flowing between them. The unspoken words of Wilfred Owen hung over the encounter – 'I am the enemy you killed, my friend' – but these were those who had survived, and the reason for their survival, it seemed, was to redeem their former enmity and to do honour to all their comrades, and to do honour to the new-found bond of friendship forged in this remarkable way.

Yes, unity is precious. Unity should be highly prized. But unity is a delicate plant and needs to be nurtured. And this is the first and best reason why the words of Anderson's Constitutions are appropriate:

> But though in ancient Times Masons were charg'd in every Country to be of the Religion of that Country or Nation, whatever it was, yet 'tis now thought more expedient only to oblige them to that Religion in which all Men agree, leaving their particular Opinions to themselves; that is, to be *good* Men *and true*, or Men of Honour and Honesty, by whatever Denominations or Persuasions they may be distinguish'd; whereby Masonry becomes the *Centre* of *Union,* and the Means of conciliating true Friendship among Persons that must have remain'd at a perpetual Distance.

jrees@aol.com

You can help our operation be a success

The Royal College *of* Surgeons *of* England

Registered charity number 212808

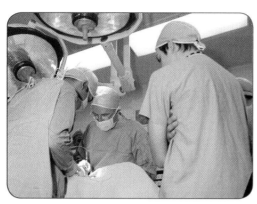

Every year, over 6 million people place their lives in the hands of surgeons – you may have benefited personally from surgery or know someone who has. A registered charity, The Royal College of Surgeons of England exists to drive forward standards in patient care.

Saving lives, the relief of pain and improved quality of life through surgery is the result of research, education and training into new techniques, technology and the understanding of disease. To fund these vitally important programmes the College relies heavily on legacies and personal gifts from friends and supporters who share our aims.

Please support The Royal College of Surgeons of England with a legacy gift in your Will and help us train and equip the surgeons of the future.

The College is very proud of our relationship with Freemasonry and is delighted to provide speakers at local and national events to talk about present advances in surgery, the history of surgery or topics of particular interest or concern.

For further information on presentations or making a legacy gift please contact:
Louise Jary, The Royal College of Surgeons of England, 35–43 Lincoln's Inn Fields, London, WC2A 3PE
Tel: 020 7869 6083
Web: www.rcseng.ac.uk/about/fundraising

THE DEGREES

The truths of the masonic system are communicated by allegorical two-part plays, much the same as the medieval mystery plays. These two-part plays are three in number, each one referred to as a 'degree', or in other words a grade of achievement. Each degree is conferred on an aspirant, or candidate, by means of a ritual form of words, actions, movements, much as any stage play is conducted. The aspirant has the degree conferred on him in the body of a lodge, and the actual conferral is made by the Master of the lodge.

Since Freemasonry works according to allegory, the first degree is concerned with birth – birth of the spirit, the emergence out of darkness, or unknowing, into light, the light of knowledge, the knowledge of the Self. The second degree is concerned with light and life and, most importantly, the intellectual and moral growth each individual experiences on his

journey. The third degree explores the transfiguration possible at the end of life, and suggests the death of the old, unregenerated person, to give way to the spirit seeking perfection and wholeness.

Initiation into mysteries has followed many different paths throughout history, and indeed from prehistoric times. In the first degree, that of initiation, the aspirant is first tested to see that he is free, or seeks to be free, of the attachments of the material world – wealth, power, doctrine and dogma, political or ideological considerations. After this, the Master questions him as to his motives for wishing to be initiated – are his motives free of selfish or self-centred notions? Does he sincerely wish to work for the betterment of himself and the society of which he forms a part? The aspirant undertakes three symbolic pilgrimages in the lodge during his testing. The allegorical light which he is then able to attain becomes, he learns,

the light of knowledge and truth.

In the second degree, the aspirant learns of his responsibility to his fellow-men. He symbolically follows the path of those in King Solomon's Temple who ascended to the Middle Chamber of that Temple. They went there to make restitution for past transgressions and to receive their spiritual wages as a reward for making moral progress in themselves. In the process, the aspirant's intellect, the intellect of the heart, is engaged.

In the third and sublime degree, the aspirant learns that he must now renounce his former unregenerated self and seek perfection. Now he understands that the light of the first degree, and the understanding or intellect of the second degree, have been calling him to a pursuit of the path leading to perfection of his character, of his being.

At the end of the masonic ritual journey, the true journey has only just begun.

THE JOURNEY OF THE INITIATE

MICHAEL BAIGENT EXPLORES THE QUEST FROM DARKNESS TO LIGHT

The Temple of Eleusis

(Photo: Ancient Art & Architecture Collection)

Freemasonry is a journey of initiation and that remains the basic reason for its being. But what inspires anyone to seek initiation? The answer is put by the Sufi poet, Rumi:

> **"Jars of spring-water are not enough anymore.**
> **Take us down to the river".**

And we must swim in this river. To be initiated, we need to be part of the process itself, for initiatory ritual needs our involvement. The ancients knew this path very well, Seneca wrote of:

"...initiatory rites, by means of which are revealed, not the mysteries of a municipal temple, but of the world itself, the vast temple of all the gods."[1]

So, let us be clear: initiation involves an encounter with the sacred. And here we touch upon something which is integral with our very humanness.

Deliberate burials of early *Homo sapiens*, date to 120,000 years ago. From around 70,000 years ago, Neanderthal burials are found. This practice then, existed across species and across cultures and remained consistent from that time on. Furthermore, a number of the Neanderthal graves reveal ritualistic associations, one, for example, has animal horns arranged beside the interred corpse. Such a respect for the dead indicates that ancient peoples knew of the simultaneous existence of two worlds; that physical world of existence where we are born and die; and that non-physical world into which death leads us. With these burials they marked the transition from one to the other.

Tens of thousands of years later, writing developed. By the 3rd millenium BC a complex language had evolved. And with this new means of expression what stories were told of humanity and its destiny? That of Gilgamesh who travelled from this world into the next.

Gilgamesh was a king of ancient Uruk. But, gripped by a fear of death, he wished to find the secret of eternal life. He abandoned his throne and began a life of wandering, seeking entrance into the other world, in order, he said, to "Let my eyes see the sun and be sated with light".[2] Entering this world, he journeyed through the vast regions of darkness to the garden of light. But, by failing to stay awake, he was not granted immortality and was required to return to this world; he had the vision, but afterwards had to return to his earthly task until death should finally call him. Gilgamesh was, by any definition, an initiate.

Initiation was, and is, the entrance into direct knowledge of that eternal other world, one suffused by omnipresent

Hermes bringing light but advising silence and stillness for the inner path of initiation.

(From Achille Bocchi, Symbolicarum quaestionum, 1560

Divinity, perceived, to this very day, in the form of an endless clear and living light. Research currently progressing at the University of Wales has revealed – contrary to the endless sceptical arguments of philosophers of religion – the existence of a "common core" to religious experiences which cuts across the differences of faith and culture. 1000 members of Christianity, Islam and Judaism have all described having religious experiences of "intense light and a sense of encompassing love". The researchers suggest that humans "share a common spirituality regardless of religious affiliations".

We are not here speaking symbolically; we are speaking literally. The Divine world exists, of this, there is no doubt, however much we may be forced, by the limitations of language, to express it symbolically. Furthermore, it is possible for us to cross over to this other world, to glimpse – like Gilgamesh - its splendour, before returning to our allotted tasks here. *This* is initiation – standing for a moment, on the threshold of this eternal world. It can never go away; it can only be forgotten, the maps to its entrance mislaid. And here lies the importance of ritual: for part of the process involves being reminded where that door is and what lies beyond.

Initiation takes place in the eternal here and now; it is a spiritual transformation aided by ritual which raises one's consciousness so that profound, rather than mundane, events might be given the chance to occur. But first the foundations of personality and social conditioning must be shaken, even shattered, for the candidate must move beyond the safety and comfort of his ordinary world. For this, he must have courage.

This knowledge can be found embedded in our rituals: it is this upon which Freemasonry is built, the journey

The Egyptian Temple of Philae, near Aswan, where the sacred mysteries of Isis were celebrated (Photo: Michael Baigent)

towards knowledge of the Divine world. And along the way, we learn our responsibilities to *this* world.

The Third Degree speaks of the grave and of knowledge of yourself. The Second Degree speaks of the hidden mysteries of nature and science. The First Degree speaks of the initial step which becomes the foundation stone both of Freemasonry itself and of that inner temple which each man must laboriously construct.

At the very beginning of the First Degree ceremony, the candidate for initiation is blindfolded, put into a state of darkness, symbolising the unenlightened state of man. A masonic ritual from 1751 explains that the blindfold and the subsequent perambulation around the Lodge is to remind the candidate, "that a man, who is in darkness, should advance towards the

light and seek it."[3]

The candidate is led, blindfolded, to the east, where, upon a sacred book, he takes his obligation. Only then is he restored to light. With this, he comes to the end of his first journey in Freemasonry; yet, it immediately proves to be the beginning of another. And this is the way of Freemasonry. Each apparent ending stands one upon the threshold of another journey.

Ritual is at the heart of Freemasonry; the festive board is the later celebration of its fruits. Without the ritual, there would be nothing to celebrate. Ritual is a sharing in the timeless; its unchanging form helps free it from mundane time. There are moments when a stillness and a silence precipitates out of the words and the movement. And, sitting in the lodge, one is aware of the soft embrace of the eternal.

Freemasonry will always remain a journey: from ignorance to knowledge; from selfishness to compassion and charity. When we enter masonry, with our first words to the Master of the lodge, we attest to our freedom. It is that freedom which allows us to move ahead on our own journey from darkness to light; from sipping at the jars of spring-water to drinking from the great river itself.

[1] *Epistulae Morales, xc, 29.*

[2] *The Epic of Gilgamesh,* A George, London, 1999, p.71.

[3] *Le Maçon Dèmasqué,* in *The Early French Exposures,* H. Carr, London, 1971, p.427.

A masonic initiation; the candidate enters blindfolded. (Illustration: Library and Museum of Freemasonry)

THE GREAT AND LESSER LIGHTS

JOHN ACASTER ARRIVES AT THE FASCINATION OF LIGHT

Frontispiece to Ars Magna Lucis by Athanasius Kircher 1671, engraved by Pierre Miotte. Apart from the imagery of Apollo (sun) and Diana (moon) the plate defines four sources of knowledge: Sacred Authority, embodied in the Bible, is shown as a ray direct from God; Reason is close to God, but filtered through the inner eye; Knowledge of the Sensible is supplied not by God's intellectual light but by that of the sun, here shown enhanced by a telescope; Worldly Authority, by comparison with the others, is a mere candle, shining among clouds of unknowing. Acknowledgement: Michael Powell, Chethams Library, Manchester

The three great, though emblematical, lights of masonry are revealed immediately after an initiate has been 'restored to the blessing of material light'. Blinking, and for the first time conscious of his curious situation, the newcomer has a moment to glimpse the objects before him as each is briefly explained. A moment later, now standing, he is turned round. He sees for the first time the room in which he is situated, and the Brethren all observing him, for they are interested to see his reactions. And then he has pointed out to him, by a sweep of the Master's arm, the three lesser lights in masonry, oddly said to represent the Sun, Moon and Master of the Lodge.

There is then, or thereafter, no further explanation. He has arrived in the masonic universe and is left, if and when he is so inclined, to explore it for himself. No wonder that new Brethren feel the need for masonic education. No wonder there is a groundswell for lodges of instruction and research to come to the rescue, to change their habits of a lifetime grinding out their own brand of instruction, and to impart instead 'genuine knowledge', directed towards helpful and immediate understanding of their environment, to all masonic journeymen.

There is no better place to start than with the lights of masonry. After all, Freemasonry prides itself on affording light of a special sort to its Brethren. What is the nature of this light? How do we know when we have it? Can others see it? What evidence is there for its existence? If we start in the dark, how do we hope to find it? These are questions to ponder, for the ritual answers are Delphic.

Unfortunately repetition and familiarity dull the sharpness of our senses. Ideally we ought to enter each moment with the freshness of a three-year old, or do I mean the heightened

The lesser lights in a modern-day German lodge.

every uneducated person would have known this. Before the introduction of gas and electric light the rising of the sun in a very real way meant the start of the day. It meant natural warmth, and growth. And when that great light eventually sank down towards the brink of the horizon, only the well-off could light their private domestic candles. The poor, unless enjoying the warmth and light of a tavern fire, would settle down to sleep. The moon, as it silently waxed great and waned small, truly governed the night. Its effluxions ruled men's possibilities for travel and for harvesting. It was the mysterious power which drew up, and then released, the mighty sea. And, by the mere motion of its rhythms, who knows what else?

These are the works of the fourth day in the first chapter of the Book of Genesis:

And God said, Let there be lights in the firmament of the heaven to divide the day from the night; and let them be for signs, and for seasons, and for days, and years:

And let them be for lights in the firmament of heaven to give light upon the earth: and it was so.

And God made two great lights; the greater light to rule the day, and the lesser light to rule the night; he made the stars also.

And God set them in the firmament of the heaven to give light upon the earth,

And to rule over the day and over the night, and to divide the light from the darkness: and God saw that it was good.

sensations of one who has returned from a near-death experience? Surprise and delight ought to be bubbling near the surface. Freemasonry can offer, despite all appearances, the stimulus to renew this.

THE THREE GREAT LIGHTS

Let us approach the three great lights. They are a stroke of genius. They are little short of revolutionary. They declare. We are their children. To remind ourselves, they consist of the Volume of the Sacred Law, the Square, and the Compasses. The Sacred Writings are to govern our faith; the Square to regulate our actions; and the Compasses to keep us in due bounds with all mankind, particularly our Brethren in Freemasonry.

You will recall that the first action after the opening of the Lodge is an assembling of the three great lights in front of the Master. Separately they each have their significances; together they gather a collective meaning and authority. At the very conclusion of the Lodge meeting these fissile elements are dispersed, closed and put away, and Brethren return to the material world, their masonic secrets locked away in a certain safe repository.

The fact is that in the natural world, both by biblical authority and by our unvarnished senses, there are only two great lights. In previous centuries, when the ritual was created, every educated person would have known this; indeed,

The frontispiece for the Moderns Book of Constitutions of 1784. The explanation of the symbols published by Grand Lodge reads: 'The uppermost figure represents Truth holding a mirrour, which reflects its rays on divers ornaments and also on the Globes and other Masonic Furniture and Implements of the Lodge. Truth is attended by the three Theological Virtues, Faith, Hope and Charity: under these the Genius of Masonry, commissioned by Truth and her Attendants, is descending into the Hall, bearing a lighted Torch.'

Acknowledgement: The Library and Museum of Freemasonry, London

First part of Chapter 1 of the Book of Genesis of the Bible.

This is a clear statement. God created the natural lights by which we see. Of these there are two great ones, one of which is lesser. Later biblical traditions produce other lights including, symbolically, one of special importance, the 'Light of the World'. Freemasonry, however, is so bold as to claim not one, not two, but three great lights. That statement is meant to startle us. It is no commonplace to be muttered. It is a highpoint, indeed the first highpoint, of our masonic experience.

SUN, MOON AND MASTER

Now consider the context in which this formula is stated. The initiate is quickly drawn to discover the three lesser lights in masonry. Situated in the east, south and west, they are said to represent the Sun, the Moon, and the Master of the Lodge. In other words, God's two great lights of creation are relegated to a distinctly lesser status than the three great lights of masonry! You will now appreciate why the elevation of masonry's three great lights can be viewed as revolutionary.

It is for each of us to consider and judge whether this extraordinary, unorthodox, conception is justified. For it is a bold claim, is it not? It is indeed a brilliant construct. Out of an original twelve lights in masonry – and if you

know what these were, write to the Editor of *Freemasonry Today* – some ritual craftsman has cut and polished them to three. They can be comprehended as a whole and sparkle the more powerfully.

The first light is the Volume of the Sacred Law. There are many wise words about this in the ritual. Whatever else the Sacred Volume might be, it is the guide to our personal faith, and an inspiration to many. It speaks to the individual and his conscience in the context of eternity. The concept of the masonic Sacred Volume comprehends the whole of religious scripture, and is inclusive across the world. That light floods and, at its profoundest, binds the best.

The second great light, the Square, is the peculiar inspiration for spiritual Freemasonry ('All our signs is taken from the square, according to every subject in handling'). The Square is rich in connotations. It is an earthly object of truth.

The third great light, the Compasses, also connect universal symbols across a wide range. We may think that they inextricably indicate action, creativity, beauty, balance, harmony, wisdom and justice. Compasses are said to belong to the Grand Master, and we can accept that, if our Grand Master is God. Overall, what a grand concordance! What spiritual power can flow by, and from, this happy conjunction of great masonic lights! May our works, Brother to Brother and within society as a whole, ever reflect our ideals and our three-in-one claim.

But what of our lesser lights, those confusingly indicated by the broad sweep of the Master's arm, those that most people find difficult to understand? How can the Sun, the Moon, and the Master, be linked together? Is it the Junior Warden who represents the Sun, who rules the day, and the Senior Warden who represents the Moon, who rules the night? What curious nonsense is being offered here? To understand

what has become an unfortunate compression of words and ideas we need to go back to source, the ritual of the Antients. Jachin and Boaz, of 1762, says:

> Mas. What were the next Things
> that were shewn to you?
> Ans. Three Candles, which I was
> told were the three lesser
> Lights in Masonry.
> Mas. What do they represent?
> Ans. The Sun, Moon and Master-
> Mason.
> Mas. Why so, Brother?
> Ans. There is the Sun to rule the
> Day, the Moon to rule the
> Night and the Master-Mason
> his Lodge, or at least ought
> so to do.

We now can surely appreciate that the three candles represent the realm of the lesser, tangible, lights. Each Warden, by his light, is expected to have control over the masonic activities of members, at work by day, or at leisure by night. The duty of the Master is, in some manner, to act as understudy for the Great Architect, to oversee both, which great ambition can, in fact, be seen as the ultimate aspiration of every Freemason.

The badge for the Collegiate Church of Manchester, dating from around 1650. It may well have been instigated by the brother of the poet Robert Herrick, who was from 1635 to 1665 in charge of that church. The Bible is open at Psalm 119, v.105 'Thy word is a lamp to my feet and a light to my path'. Beneath the Bible is a sprig of what may be acacia.

Acknowledgement: Michael Powell, Chethams Library, Manchester

THE HEART OF FREEMASONRY

The Pro Grand Master in conversation with Michael Baigent

The Pro Grand Master, Lord Northampton on his estate, Compton Wynyates, Warwickshire.   Photo: Michael Baigent.

"**Freemasonry is a system of becoming; becoming something better than you are now". Lord Northampton spoke with great enthusiasm. "And above all, Freemasonry is a system which teaches us to be openhearted".**

Rather than rush through an interview in the midst of a frenetic day at Freemason's Hall, the Marquess and Marchioness of Northampton invited me to stay at their home in southern Warwickshire, Compton Wynyates, in order that we might be able to discuss Freemasonry in a relaxed and congenial manner. I welcomed the opportunity to see them in the home they love, amongst the countryside where twenty-eight generations of Lord Northampton's family – the Comptons - in direct male descent, have lived since at least 1204.

Compton Wynyates is settled – or, more accurately, *centred* – in an artificially levelled and terraced bowl below wooded ridges. From the road, through large gates, the house is visible at the end of a long curving drive. It is a large Tudor country house of pink brick, with steep gables, towers, and a forest of extraordinary slender chimneys, each apparently different with their ornate twists and curves; around the house climbing roses creep up much of the brickwork. An ancient wooden door gives access to a large inner courtyard gazed upon by tall windows; a flagstone path crosses through a lawn and garden. From here the basic house design can be seen; it is built around the sides of a square. Very fitting, I thought, for the Pro Grand Master of Freemasonry. But, as I was to discover, there is much more about this house which reveals that the Compton who built it and his immediate descendants were deeply immersed in something very interesting; even, perhaps, an early form of Freemasonry.

Lord Northampton took me around the outside of his house to show me something curious: a tower stands at the middle of the western face of the house, another stands at the north-east corner and yet another at the south-east corner. We began at the latter: embedded in its Tudor brickwork is a design picked out by much darker bricks. It depicts a key with two bits at the end of its shaft.

The design of a key picked out by bricks in the wall of the south-east tower of Compton Wynyates; one of three in the external wall of the house.   Photo: Michael Baigent

We then looked at the west tower: it too had a key picked out in darker bricks, but this key had three bits at the end of its shaft. And at the north-eastern tower there was yet another key but, due to reconstruction in the past, only the shaft was visible. But it would seem logical that this key's shaft would have held one bit. Were we seeing connections with masonic ritual? The First Degree being marked by the key in the north-east, where today a candidate is placed in the lodge after initiation;

the Second Degree marked by the key with two bits in the south-east, exactly where the candidate is placed after having passed through his Second Degree ceremony; and the Third Degree marked by the key in the west with three bits. But why should this be placed in the west rather than in the east where the Master is placed in the lodge? Well, perhaps, as the opening of the Third Degree states, a mason goes to the west to seek the genuine secrets of a Master Mason. Does our ritual preserve some ancient residue, one which gave rise to this curious feature embedded in the walls of Compton Wynyates?

Within the house, a first floor drawing room holds an elaborately carved chimney-piece. By the irregular nature of the curious symbolism it is clear that a message is being conveyed but without the key to the symbols and their meaning, its full extent cannot be established. But this panelling is known to have come from Canonbury House, Islington, the remaining tower of which now houses much symbolic carved panelling and is the site of the Canonbury Masonic Research Centre.

There is something else which also seems to have come from Canonbury: a pair of carved chairs, the first dated 1595, with a design on the seat back showing, through two pillars, a chequerboard floor and an archway entrance veiled by partially drawn curtains. One is encouraged to seek entrance. The second chair, dated 1597, also shows the chequerboard floor but visible through the archway is a Christian cross: curiously, the vertical post is black, the cross-bar is white and there is no figure of Christ on it. In addition, the theme of black and white is repeated in the design. Put these two chairs together and they reveal a progression, a symbolic journey into a veiled mystery. Every indication is that these two chairs were used as part of an Order working a ritual involving a symbolic journey into the Sanctum Sanctorum of the Temple wherein resides the key to the mystery of Golgotha.

I was immediately curious about the owner of Compton Wynyates at the time; what might he have been involved in. Could it have been some sort of proto-Freemasonry? The house had been completed by Sir William Compton in the time of King Henry VIII and Catherine of Aragon, both of whose arms appear above the main door. His great-grandson, William, 2nd Lord Compton, later created 1st Earl of Northampton, married the daughter of Sir John Spencer, Lord Mayor of London and owner of Canonbury. Lord Compton had been a friend of Sir Francis

Compton Wynyates, completed during the reign of King Henry VIII and Catherine of Aragon.
Photo: Michael Baigent

Bacon to whom he let rooms in Canonbury for a time. Lord Compton must have been a man of great depth.

"What papers remain from that time?"

"Unfortunately, none relating to the building of this house. They may have been destroyed in the civil war when the house was attacked, bombarded by cannon, and the family expelled. They fled to join the Royalist forces in Oxford."

But the family regiment still survives – now as part of the Sealed Knot society, which re-enacts civil war battles. Lord Northampton, as Honorary Colonel, three years ago led his troops with their black-powder weapons in a smoky re-enactment of the battle for Compton Wynyates.

A Vision for Freemasonry

I broached the subject of the role of the Pro Grand Master: I confessed rather sheepishly that I had little idea of what task this office demanded. Lord Northampton explained: the Pro Grand Master acts on behalf of the Grand Master. The rulers of the Craft, provide the vision, and direction in which Freemasonry moves forward.

"And we have the possibility to create an inspiring future for our Order." He spoke with certitude. "We must look *forward* with a vision which will re-enchant the Craft. The key of course, is how to get there. The ritual describes the key as the tongue of good report and the future depends on the quality of our candidates!"

He explained though that we cannot ignore our history, "We must look back and see what was in the minds of the people who created this system but we

A carved chair dated 1595 depicting a scene using symbolism now found in Freemasonry.
Photo: Property of Lord Northampton

A second chair, dated 1597. Together these chairs depict a symbolic journey through the veil.
Photo: Property of Lord Northampton

need not become stuck in this investigation. We cannot enthuse people with historical facts alone, people are inspired by experiencing what Freemasonry has to offer them. It is only through participating in the ceremonies that we can turn knowledge into a felt experience."

Of course, Freemasonry is also a large and complicated organisation with an extensive internal hierarchy. Its executive structure is represented by the Board of General Purposes which runs the Craft on a daily basis. But Freemasonry is not like a public company, rather, it is like a shareholders cooperative with the Grand Master representing the interests of the shareholders.

"We need to use best business practices to run the organisation which is there to provide the framework in which the ceremonies can take place. For it is here that the meaning of Freemasonry resides." Our First Degree teaches morality and an understanding of how to act within society. Our Second Degree concerns the importance of knowledge, and our Third Degree leads us to contemplate our own mortality.

This brought us to a consideration of the difference between the form of Freemasonry and its content: "The form", explained Lord Northampton, "is the structure within which the rituals take place. The content is in the rituals themselves." And in these resides the mystery of Freemasonry. A *mystery* which must be *experienced*.

It is quite possible for a non-mason to buy a book of ritual and read the words and directions but such a person learns little of value. "The mystery is protected from the uninitiated. We have to take part in the ritual to understand it by experiencing it."

Spiritual Values

"Freemasonry has an important spiritual significance; even though the rituals have been clouded by later additions, enough remains for us to see what our forefathers were trying to do. What I like is that there is no dogma in Freemasonry – it is not a religion – it says only that if you practice its tenets and principles you will become wiser. Its final goal is the Wisdom and Truth to which we dedicate our hearts. It is a system with philosophical principles which has psychological effects on those who practice it." Lord Northampton pointed out that our three Grand Principles, as stated in the ritual are Brotherly Love, Relief and Truth. You cannot be openhearted unless in a trusting environment but once you are, compassion is a natural consequence and the pursuit of Truth becomes the quest.

As one of many examples of precisely phrased wisdom in our rituals he pointed to the `long' explanation of the Working Tools of the Second Degree – that dedicated to "the hidden mysteries of nature and science". This explains to the candidate that,

"To steer the bark of this life over the seas of passion without quitting the helm of rectitude is the highest perfection to which human nature can attain…"

As advice on how to live a fruitful life in an imperfect world, it is all there.

Lord Northampton added, "The point of Freemasonry is to change people; to encourage a transformation through a better understanding of themselves and a better understanding of their place in the Great Architect's grand design." As the address to the new Master of a Lodge upon his installation explains, a Freemason is one,

"…whose hand is guided by justice, and whose heart is expanded by benevolence".

"Freemasonry has a way of steering you to find the answers. It doesn't say, do this, or do that; it says, if you do this, then that will happen. You can treat it as a congenial social bonding; you can enjoy it without going into anything deeper for Freemasonry provides a strong support network in an unstable world. But if you want to go further it can point you in the right direction. But your progress is up to you, for within Freemasonry you can only move to a better understanding through your own efforts. This involves sharing your experience with others. There are those who have had deeper insights and can point the way; we must help each other along the path to Self Knowledge."

Lord Northampton; in the background, the family church where many of his ancestors are interred

Photo: Michael Baigent

He described a carving on the outside of Bath Abbey which depicts a ladder upon which angels are climbing upwards. The angels above are reaching down to help those below climb higher.

"Freemasonry is a journey: it begins in the First Degree the moment your blindfold comes off. It ends when you discover Truth. The words over the doorway to the oracle 'Man know thyself' could equally apply to Freemasonry.

Service to Freemasonry

In his late twenties Lord Northampton used to have interesting philosophical conversations over a pub lunch with his forestry consultant, Bro. Charles Bloor, at Castle Ashby, and it was through the latter's influence that he was initiated into Ceres Lodge, No. 6977, Northampton, in 1976. And what has been the result?

"Freemasonry has affected my life in many ways but principally it has given me a standard to try and live up to in my every day dealings with others. It has taught me much about human relationships and has developed psychological changes in my character, which have made me more tolerant and compassionate".

"I have had tremendous support from my wife, Pamela, over the last thirteen years. She is as committed as I am to the

The Chapel Tower, Compton Wynyates, showing above, a curious design of three chimneys
Photo: Michael Baigent

principles of Freemasonry and the potential it has to help men gain self-confidence and discover more of their true nature."

He has often put his own resources into the service of Freemasonry. He stresses the importance of the Centre for Research into Freemasonry at the University of Sheffield to enable scholars to see the social and cultural importance

that Freemasonry has had on society. Twenty-five percent of the funds needed to run the Sheffield Centre for three years were donated by Lord Northampton. He also supports the important Cornerstone Society, which focuses upon the spiritual values and philosophical meaning of Freemasonry. Lord and Lady Northampton jointly sponsor the Canonbury Masonic Research Centre, based in Canonbury Tower. This encourages both the study of wisdom traditions and, through its international conferences, the dialogue between academics and academic Freemasons from many different Grand Lodges. This can only be of great benefit to Freemasonry as a whole, as the body of knowledge will be used to inform and inspire the Craft by creating awareness of the potential of this great Order.

Lord Northampton is a man of great generosity of spirit, with an expansive vision. He cares deeply about Freemasonry and, as many who have met him during his frequent visits to Lodges can attest, he knows that the strength and future of the Craft resides in every individual Freemason. We are fortunate to have him in such an important position in the Order. His influence will be far-reaching and beneficial to new generations of Freemasons who are, even now, entering the Craft in order to learn of that mystery which lies at its heart.

SYMBOLS OF HIGH RESONANCE

*I am the eye with which the Universe
Beholds itself and knows itself divine;
All harmony of instrument or verse,
All prophecy, all medicine is mine,
All light of art or nature; – to my song
Victory and praise in its own right belong.*

Percy Bysshe Shelley, 1792-1822

It has been pointed out to me twice recently that we more often use the word 'compasses' in Freemasonry, than 'compass'. The compasses, of course, are a draughtsman's, architect's and mathematician's implement for describing circular figures and for delimiting objects. Compass, on the other hand, has two principal meanings – in the concrete sense it is a device for determining the magnetic meridian or the relation to it, and in the figurative sense it is used to denote range or extent of something ('within the compass of ability'). It got me thinking about symbols and allegories in the wider sense, those implements we, as Freemasons, would be lost without. Our Craft is full of them, and of course no masonic work is possible if symbols are not there to work on.

But so often, perhaps always, they go hand in hand with allegory, defined as a 'description of a subject under the guise of some other subject, of aptly suggestive resemblance'. Allegory at once stands in for the symbol, and helps us to decode it. We start, at the beginning of our initiatic quest, with the blindfold, an object certainly not provided to prevent us looking outwards, but rather to remove distractions so that we may look inward. This is our first, but not our last, experience of darkness, another allegory, but note that it is personal darkness, not general – the aspirant is the only one in the lodge to be subjected to it. This is in contrast to the darkness we meet with later on our journey, which is by contrast a general darkness, and the two have very different connotations.

As symbols, the working tools are possibly more rich in meaning than is apparent on the superficial level when they are presented to us. Kirk MacNulty has a good deal to say about this in his book *The Way of the Craftsman*. He points out that the working tools of the first degree are not used in actual building: they are more tools of preparation. With the first tool we measure the work; with the second and third we prepare the stone and 'render it fit for the hands of the more expert workman'. He also refers to the application of the Rule of Three, in which one agency may be regarded as the active principle, the second the passive, and the third agency mediates between, and coordinates, the first two. In this case, the gavel is the active principle, representing the passionate, driving side of our nature. The chisel is the passive principle, receiving the blows of the gavel passively, but in its own nature capable of fine, analytical work. The twenty-four inch gauge mediates, acting to temper the forceful gavel and to stimulate the chisel, our finer feelings, and to coordinate them to achieve a *measured* course of action, measured therefore in more than one sense of the word.

Kirk refers to the second degree working tools as tools of testing, a sort of quality control. By now the stones have been prepared by the tools of the first degree, they are beginning to fit together, and the building has commenced. We need to test what is being done so that, in the words of the lecture, we may 'carry on the intended structure with regularity and propriety'. I hardly need to point out the functions of the level and plumb rule in building, but the square, apart from proving square corners, is actually a combination of level and plumb rule, having one arm horizontal and one vertical. You can easily work out now which is the active, which the passive and which the mediating or coordinating principle.

The tools of the third degree Kirk refers to as tools of creativity, and space won't permit me to go into them now. There is however another allegory, namely that the third of the three pillars supporting a Freemason's lodge is that of beauty, the beauty of the creation, so we can see it is no accident that the tools of the third degree should be tools of creativity.

I would maintain that, since Freemasonry is a path to enlightenment, light remains the greatest allegory of them all, so here we are back with the removal of the blindfold. When, in this way, the allegory of light is made plain to us, we are able fully to appreciate its value, symbolic as well as physical. It is possible that a blind aspirant will have a yet more powerful appreciation of this than a sighted aspirant and if, as sometimes happens in that situation, the Master then takes his hand and places it on the square, compasses and bible so that he can feel what is being described to him, he may quite possibly be seeing with his heart what you and I will see with our eyes. We may perhaps aspire to that insight ourselves, by closing our eyes for a moment and experiencing the eloquence of those symbols by the sense of touch, and by opening our heart. We may surprise ourselves.

jrees@aol.com

ADVERTISEMENT FEATURE
REPRODUCED FROM FREEMASONRY TODAY ISSUE 21

FROM THE ROUGH TO THE SMOOTH

MICHAEL BAIGENT LOOKS AT HOW OUR REGALIA IS MANUFACTURED

David Boston and Frederick Trowman of Light & Boston, Regalia manufacturers in Birmingham.

A selection of the dies used in the stamping of jewels and medals.

Cast masonic collar jewels, including rings from a Provincial Grand Master's chain, prior to the despruing and fettling processes.

Located on the edge of Birmingham's Jewellery Quarter is the Masonic regalia manufacturer, Light & Boston. At their base, they have a showroom and a factory, where not only are aprons and collars sewn but also metal work is made on the company's own presses and computer controlled milling machines.

This gives Light & Boston the freedom to give the individual touch to all its regalia: producing long runs for stock of standard items, stamping each year's supply of individual past-master's jewels and designing and manufacturing one-off and short runs. The minimum quantity for an order is one.

Whilst traditional techniques are honoured, they are modified or replaced with state of the art solutions, which do not sacrifice quality but adapt old-fashioned processes to modern manufacture, enabling the best price and finish to be achieved for their customers.

Also, by using new technology, customers' thoughts and ideas can easily be incorporated into designs for jewels and banners – with the facility of the customer to supervise minor changes and additions without the need to make costly proofs.

The use of new enamels, used alongside traditional ones, allows in many cases a wider range of vibrant colours to be used to embellish founders' and past-masters' jewels.

Further development of new techniques has led to the launch of short runs of cufflinks and jewels which will emulate the hand-painted jewels of old – at a price which modern budgets, especially those dictated by the reduction in the size of lodge membership, can appreciate.

All photographs by Michael Baigent.

Contact Light & Boston Ltd.
Tel 0121 359 1500,
www.lightboston.co.uk,
email: sales@lightboston.co.uk

While each masonic apron is individually constructed, the elements of the design are machine cut together with alignment markings in order that a uniform standard can be maintained.

The rituals of Craft Freemasonry involve a symbolic journey over three symbolic days; in other words, a pilgrimage, a quest. The work for the initiate is his own quest, one revealed as the search for the Lost Word. It is not fully resolved until the 3rd Degree is completed in the Royal Arch.

The peak moment of this mysterious journey comes in the Third Degree with the Charge. I would like now to take a closer look at it and try to seek its meaning. What vision is seeking expression in the words?

We can divide this charge into 3 sections:

The first speaks of the "mysterious veil which the eye of reason cannot penetrate"; it expresses the relative darkness within which our lives are conducted, a relative darkness which cannot be relieved by means of our use of reason. Something more is needed.

Now most masons uttering this are not aware that it is a thoroughly revolutionary statement; one which grows out of an argument at least 2500 years old.

Let me explain. Our philosophical heritage has a strong link with ancient Greece. The earliest philosophers, the so-called Pre-Socratics such as Parmenides, Empedocles and Pythagoras, were all healers, doctors, shamans as well as philosophers. They experienced Divinity.

They had, as both scholarship and archaeology has proved, very close links with the teachings of ancient Egypt. Early Greek tombs have revealed thin gold plates bearing ascension texts from the Egyptian 'Book of the Dead'. This is a modern title. To the ancients it was "The Book of coming forth by day" – or, *of coming forth into the Light*. We can see the connection.

Plato, however, sliced off the experiential side and developed what we now call philosophy, that is, a search for the heart of reality based upon argument, intellectual display. Great as he was, in this he did us all something of a disservice. He began the process of cutting philosophy off from its mystical roots.

Plato's student, Aristotle, completed the emasculation: he had no room for anything beyond that which could be apprehended by means of human reason. Reason, in his opinion, was the only way to truth. It was not until some 800 years later that a Platonist, Plotinus, again brought philosophy back to its mystical roots. And his younger

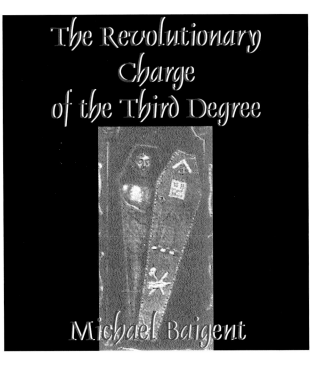

The Revolutionary Charge of the Third Degree

Michael Baigent

contemporary, Iamblichus, reintroduced both ritual and elements from the Egyptian temples. This approach is now called Neo-Platonism but this word is a modern nonsense. For these two philosophers simply returned philosophy to its experiential pre-Socratic origins.

Reason is all very well, it is certainly rather useful and it underpins our scientific and technological culture; also, via Descartes and Kant especially, our philosophy. But it deals only with the phenomenal world and our reality is much greater than that. Reason alone cannot comprehend the irrational, the metaphysical, the spiritual. Reason alone cannot penetrate that mysterious veil which shields all of us from 'the prospect' that is the vista – "of futurity", meaning eternity.

It cannot do so - and here is the point - unless assisted. Assisted by what? By that "Light which is from above". By the influx of true knowledge that is experienced as a blinding Divine Light. This is pure mysticism. This is the Sun rising in the middle of the night.

The second section of the charge insists, in no uncertain manner, the importance of 'knowledge of yourself'. This echoes the preoccupation of the ancient Mysteries: above the door of the entrance to the Greek Eleusinian Mysteries was carved, "Man, Know Thyself".

What does this mean? It means not just to know your own likes and dislikes, it means much more than this. It means to know, that is, to experience, what the true self is. Here we are again moving beyond the external world in search of something much deeper, much more profound. It is asking, *who are you truly? Why*

are you here? What is required of you? These implicit questions are then immediately answered in the third section of the Charge.

The third begins, "Be careful to perform your allotted task while it is yet day". And how can we be sure to do this task correctly? By listening to the 'Voice of Nature'. It is asking that we act in harmony with ourselves and our world. To do so we need to seek those still moments when the 'Voice of Nature' is not drowned out by the rough and tumble of modern life. We need to seek these moments out, put time aside for them, and to trust them. The intense darkened moments during which this Charge is given in the Third Degree allows the opportunity for such moments. When this Charge is delivered, take it slowly, allow time for these spaces to communicate to the candidate.

We see, expressed concisely and dramatically, in this Charge, important instructions for building our lives in accordance with our destiny.

And what is our destiny? As the charge states, using the most ancient symbolism, it is to "lift our eyes to that bright Morning Star, whose rising brings peace and salvation..." This serves to both humble us and inspire us. For there is none too great or too powerful to whom this is not directly addressed.

The Morning Star - it could be Sirius of the ancient Egyptians or Venus of the ancient Babylonians - is not to be taken literally, although it is a beautiful and refreshing symbol, a symbol of a new light following the darkness.

This morning star arises within; it is the first vision of the Light from above. The New Testament (II Peter 19) advises,

"...take heed...until the day dawn, and the day star arise in your hearts."

And the experience of this Light brings peace, and brings salvation. By knowing this Light - whenever in life it may come - you have passed through the veil which has previously shielded eternity from your grasp. You have reached the end of your journey; you have discovered the "vital and immortal principle" within. You have discovered the word which was lost. This, in truth, is our destiny.

It is this secret, open to all but recognised by few, which lies at the heart of Freemasonry. A secret that needs to be experienced, not simply recited. It is this that is the prime concern of the charge to the newly obligated Master Mason. And may it ever remain thus. ∎

THE THREE DEGREES

JULIAN REES LISTENS TO RESONANCE

The Blazing Star, emblematic of divinity and paradise, reached by Jacob's Ladder; the tracing board also depicts the 'messengers of God's will', the sun and moon.

Photo: Library and Museum of Freemasonry

The temptation to see the three degrees as separate ceremonies in themselves is almost unavoidable; yet these three stages are in reality parts of a whole. There are many correspondences between the three degrees, and these need to be examined for what they can teach us.

The first degree, we are told, deals with the emergence out of darkness into light. This is the journey from unknowing to knowing; the first stage on the path to self-knowledge. The second degree encompasses, in more senses than one, the journey through life, and the Fellow Craft for this reason is sometimes known in other jurisdictions as the 'Journeyman', the man journeying to acquire knowledge in order to free himself from his apprenticeship. The third degree deals with the transition from earthly life to the eternal.

We enter the temple as an aspirant in darkness, but this darkness is ours alone, because the journey from darkness to light is an individual, personal journey. The Brethren in the Temple are with us

Michaelangelo's The Creation of Adam. *Fresco detail from the Sistine Chapel ceiling in Rome.*

The hexalpha, an allegory of the union of heaven and earth, God and Man.

photo: Library and Museum of Freemasonry

contrast; now all is darkness, not only for us as aspirants, but for all those present. The Brethren are now able to share with us the deprivation of all but the faintest light in the east. The near-total darkness is a bleak reminder for all present that the quest for our Self, newly-purged of all material concerns and obsessions, is a serious one, and that the goal is one we all ultimately aspire to: first a glimpse of, and then an experience of oneness with eternity, should we be so fortunate. It has a resonance with the first degree lecture:

So ought every mason to conduct himself towards this world; to observe a due balance between avarice and profusion; to hold the scales of justice with equal poise; to make his passions and prejudices coincide with the just line of his conduct; and in all his pursuits to have eternity in view.

THE JOURNEY

But the resonance between the degrees is not restricted to their beginnings. If we view the whole of Freemasonry as an allegory of a journey, leading from birth, through life, to death and perfection, then within each of those degrees we find pilgrimages within the overall journey. In the first degree we first progress round the temple to show that we are deserving of Freemasonry; our second such journey is to prove what we have learned. In the second degree we first prove ourselves as

his journey. The whole feeling of this degree is one of light, happiness and peace. Where in the first degree, disabled physically and disoriented mentally, we had stumbled and faltered, here we are able to journey, freely appreciating the beauties and the joy of nature, an allegory of our own nature that we are in the process of discovering.

Our admission to the Temple in the third degree can only offer a yet starker

in a spirit of brotherhood, first to ensure that we meet no harm, physical or spiritual. Secondly, they are there to ensure that our initiation is regularly and properly conducted. Thirdly, and importantly, they are there to re-visit the experience of their own initiation and to contemplate the lessons they have themselves learned.

When we enter the Temple for our second degree, the contrast could not be more stark. Where before there was no light – except for the light we might have found within ourselves – now all is light, the light of day that any journeyman might need to progress on

The winding staircase, turning through 90°; an allegory of the need for a shift of perspective on our way to the middle chamber.   photo: Library and Museum of Freemasonry

masons, secondly to prove that we have completed the necessary work to be advanced and then, after advancement, the examination to test us once again.

Crucially the third degree is different. We undertake three pilgrimages. The first two are related to the first two degrees, and the third to prove that we are qualified to advance. What is missing here is the final pilgrimage, the one with which we are examined for proficiency and prove our knowledge. But the secrets demonstrated by the Wardens in the third degree closing are but the substituted secrets. The true secret, the one in our hearts, is so private as to be incommunicable to another, and that is as it should be, for this secret concerns eternity; and that we must discover for ourselves.

ADVANCING TO THE EAST

Consider also the means of advancing to the light in the east in the three degrees. In the first degree, we are in total darkness. The steps we take are necessarily faltering and are achieved only by the guidance of the Deacon at our side. Each step is a little more sure than the previous one, since we gain in confidence as we progress. But all steps in the first degree are in a straight line, and all of them on the same level.

In the second degree, not only do we stray from the straight line, we also ascend; a powerful allegory of the ascent from material pursuits to the union hoped for in the middle chamber. These steps are assured and purposeful and reflect the new-found confidence that the second degree permits.

In the third degree, the difficulties are far greater than we encountered in the first. True, we can see the way ahead for the steps we are to take, but that way is blocked by an obstacle, and the very object over which we have to pass is the negation of life. By these steps we allegorically bury our old materialist self in order to approach perfection.

WORKING TOOLS

The working tools in the three degrees afford another interesting insight into the correlation of the whole. Kirk MacNulty, in *The Way of the Craftsman*, points out that the only tools of true construction are those of the second degree. Those of the first degree are tools of preparation – with them we prepare, cut to size and embellish the different stones using gavel, chisel and rule. Those of the third degree are tools of creativity, in laying out the ground properly

The light of the Blazing Star floods in through the dormer window, illuminating the Holy of Holies. At the summit of the initiatic quest this light ensures that all is enlightenment, even the dark squares of the pavement. photo: Library and Museum of Freemasonry

surveyed, determining the proportions and design of the building, and then committing that to the drawing-board.

But in a real sense it is the tools of the second degree that are the most telling. We have the stones, properly prepared and ready to be set, to form the integrity of the building. We have the newly-created plans and the ground-work on which to commence. The square, level and plumb rule will enable us to place the stones, and so they are tools of quality control, enabling us to be assured that our building has a level basis; that the stones, proved by the square to have been truly formed, will fit together, and set in an upright way, as will be proved by the plumb rule.

DARKNESS AND LIGHT

One of the first things we notice after being restored to material light in the first degree is the chequered floor on which we stand. The white and black remind us, intentionally, of the contrasts of joy and sorrow, light and dark. So although material light is restored, fortune and adversity may always be present through our lives. The Fellow Craft will therefore travel, in the second degree, through his new landscape of joy and fruitfulness, but constantly reminded that darkness is an ever-present contrast. In one sense it proves to be a forewarning since when he comes to the third degree he finds a darkness far more

bleak than he experienced in the first degree; it is to be hoped that the sustenance of the second degree, the corn, wine, and oil, will be sufficient to support him in this last and greatest trial.

THE DESTINATION

Although the whole of Freemasonry is depicted as a series of journeys, there are important differences as regards the destination in each of them. The first degree takes us, by level steps, to that place where, by means of the vow of fidelity, we may receive light, material and symbolic. But for the moment it goes no further than that. In the second degree our steps are no longer level; having passed the altar, the point at which we attained light, we have the right to ascend, as proved by our use of the password, to another level, one on which we gain admittance to the middle chamber, there to pay our dues and to show we are worthy to receive our wages, wages symbolising a spiritual value.

In the third degree, we remain on that higher level but pass through the veil separating us from the hope of eternal life into the Holy of Holies. This is why the third degree is referred to as sublime since it is here that we come face to face with the Great Architect and learn to know and to own the divine spark within ourselves, which may rightly be regarded as the summit of our journey and the object of our true aspiration.

THE SEVEN LIBERAL ARTS

CLEMENT SALAMAN REVEALS HOW THEY WERE DEVISED AS A PATH TO TRUTH

Geometry, as depicted in the Board Room, Freemasons' Hall, London.

United Grand Lodge of England/Photo: David Peabody

Clement Salaman.   Photo: Michael Baigent

adhering to reason, the human being could attain the virtue of wisdom, and where wisdom prevailed, just actions would inevitably follow.

When the passions of the soul came under the control of reason, a man would know what to fear and what not to fear. Plato had no doubt that one need not fear any harm to, or death of , the temporary and shadowy body; but one should fear harm to the real and immortal soul. And with the mind and the passionate part of the soul in accord, the appetites of the senses would be controlled; the individual would then be close to the joy of the Supreme Good.

L iberal Arts was a term coined in the Middle Ages: 'liberal' from the Latin *liber*, meaning 'free'. The name is apt; these arts are intended to bring freedom to the mind. We need to be reminded of the source of freedom now, with the world threatened by the grossest forms of mental oppression and spiritual intolerance.

The Liberal Arts go back over 2,500 years, to classical times. They were practised over Europe, North Africa and the Middle East, being disseminated through the empires of Alexander and Rome; they are part of our heritage.

The most important influence on education in classical times was that of Plato (427-347 BC). His concept of education – which he attributes to the earlier philosopher Socrates – was based on 'excellence': every individual had his own particular excellence, but the excellence of the human being, in general, resided in the soul; the excellence of the soul being expressed by justice. Thus, the main aim of education was the cultivation of justice.

For Plato, the source of creation is the "Good", the Light of pure spirit; all physical creation being just a shadow or reflection of this. He refers to the "Good" also as the "One" or as "God": for him, all education must be designed to bring about a recognition of this "One", a recognition not just in theory, but in *experience*. For once experienced, he believed, the pure Light of the Good would become the basis for every decision and action that a man or woman might take. And where the principle of justice guided the rulers, there one would find a happy state.

Instruction in the Virtues

To Plato, reason meant far more that it does today, it meant the knowledge of what is truly good for man. Through

To use the medieval terms, the Liberal Arts consisted of the *trivium* (grammar, rhetoric and logic) and the *quadrivium* (geometry, arithmetic, music and astronomy). To the extent that they represent a twofold approach, the first based on language and the second on maths, they still form the basis of education today.

Learning of Divine Things

Even before Plato, many of the basics of education had already been established among the ancient Greeks. It was the practice for children, before the age of seven, to be given music to develop their soul and gymnastics to develop their body. Much more of Plato's programme – particularly that designed for ages ten to seventeen – had been accepted from at least the time of Pythagoras (6th century BC). But we have only Plato's explanations as to why these subjects were so important.

Plato argues that geometry and arithmetic have their origins in realities which are the abode of the Good itself. Through contemplating the importance of geometrical figures and arithmetical mysteries, the soul is easily led back to this Divine realm which it once knew before being locked into a body on earth. Plato writes in his Republic:

"the knowledge at which geometry aims is knowledge of the eternal, and not of anything perishing and transient".

FREEMASONRY AND THE SEVEN LIBERAL ARTS

During the explanation of the Second Degree Tracing Board, it is explained to the candidate that the seven steps of the winding staircase leading to the middle chamber of King Solomon's Temple symbolise (among other things) the seven liberal arts and sciences. They are, then, an important part of the journey which every Freemason must make on his way to wisdom. This well reflects Plato's concept that the arts bring about a recognition of the "One".

Creation and the Mean

Of all the aspects of arithmetic, Plato was particularly interested in the concept of the 'mean' because it connected directly with the central tenet of his philosophy, that the universe was One.

Plato states that creation proceeded in accordance with the 'mean'. He gives three kinds of mean: the first and most simple is represented by the series 2,4,8 – four being the mean. The second is the series 1,2,3 – two being the mean. The third is a series 3,4,6 – four being the mean since it is a third more than three, and a third less than six. In each case the first term bears the same relationship to the middle term, as the middle term does to the last.

This *equality of proportion* was how Plato considered that the unity of the One is carried into the multiplicity of Creation. In other words, the multiplicity of Creation is harmonised by an equality of proportion.

These proportions are also those of the musical scale and hence the importance of music: the soul recognises the beauty of music because the soul and music resonate to the same proportion. And astronomy was directly linked to music

The memorial of mathematician, John Blagrave (d.1611), in the Church of St Laurence, Reading. Note the pyramid, cubic stone and square.   Photo: Michael Baigent

and mathematics, thus also to the One. However, according to Plato music in the educational curriculum must only be such as to inspire courage or temperance.

Astronomy was all important because Plato associated the heavenly bodies with the 'World Soul' – he did not mean that their physical characteristics were substance of soul but that this was the inner intelligence which moved them.

It would be wrong to believe that Plato did not attach any value to the study of literature. He is certainly severe on occasion: in his *Republic* he bans poets and playwrights on the grounds that they reflect that worldly life which is only a *reflection* of reality. But elsewhere, after remarking that poets and storytellers were wrong to present unjust men as happy, and just men as wretched, he adds that we should "require their poems and stories to have quite the opposite moral".

Astronomy

United Grand Lodge of England/Photo: David Peabody

The inclusion of grammar, rhetoric and logic in the ancient curriculum was mainly due to the work of Isocrates, who had founded his academy in Athens in 393 BC, six years before Plato founded his which uniquely, for the times, was open to both men and women.

These two masters, Plato and Isocrates, shaped the course of education for millennia. In Roman times the study of Rhetoric and Grammar continued, and in the Middle Ages, while education became Christianised, the subjects remained.

The Italian Renaissance reintroduced the ancient concept that education concerned the whole man – body, mind and spirit – and this idea passed into the English educational system through the early Public Schools

The Liberal Arts need to be reconnected with their origins. The *quadrivium* is essentially the search for abstract truth and the *trivium* the rediscovery of the essential being of every man and woman which has been reflected in literature through the great writings of the past. The main purpose of the latter was to present noble characters (or heroes) as models whose virtues men and women could imitate thus fulfilling their full, and true, potential.

Clement Salaman is a translator, writer and lecturer on Renaissance subjects, particularly the Neoplatonic and Hermetic ideas which found expression at that time. He is the leader of the team which has translated the five volumes of letters of Marsilio Ficino and also the Hermetic Texts (reviewed in Freemasonry Today, *Issue No. 17).*

Square Events Management Ltd
E: info@squareeventsmanagement.com
W: www.squareeventsmanagement.com

Organisers of Masonic Ladies Festivals.
City Breaks, Country Retreats
& Coastal Resorts.

Ladies Festivals Ltd
E: info@ladiesfestivals.net
W: www.ladiesfestivals.net

The one-stop-shop for all
you need to organise your
own Ladies Festival.

Are proud to present the

New Year's Eve Grand Masonic Ball

Monday 31st December 2007 at Latimer Place, Latimer, Chesham, Buckinghamshire (near J18 M25).

See in the New Year in opulent style with your family and friends at this stunning De Vere Venues' Spa location. Enjoy a drinks reception in the elegant library, partake in a 5-course banquet in the dining hall whilst enjoying table entertainment. After dinner try your hand in our casino room (just for fun) or dance the night away in the Ballroom to a live band. At the end of the evening stroll back to your room rather than worry about how to get home and after breakfast why not indulge yourself at the Spa facilities to relax and unwind after the celebrations of the night before.

Tickets £169 (normally £189) when quoting this advertisement.   **Call 01932 783 877 for more details of the Ball or Ladies Festivals.**

ProstateResearch
PROSTATE CANCER RESEARCH FOUNDATION

www.thepcrf.org
www.giveafewbob.org

The legendary British comedian Bob Monkhouse died of prostate cancer and has recently starred in a television commercial to promote the activities of the charity The Prostate Cancer Research Foundation. Bob was a member of Chelsea Lodge No. 3098.
All charity money raised on the evening will go to this appeal.

2008 EVENTS: St Geroge's Day Grand Masonic Banquet; Grand Masonic Summer Ball and Grand Masonic Casino & Cocktail Party. See website for details.

masonic
ladies
festival weekend

The Best Western Brighton Hotel is a Regency Grade II listed building located directly on the seafront. The hotel has 52 well-appointed rooms many of which have panoramic sea-views. We understand the importance required to make each Ladies Festival weekend a great success.

A perfect venue for exclusive use - On the seafront!

BOOKINGS
Please contact our dedicated conference & banqueting sales manager on
T: 01273 820 555 E: sales@thebrightonhotel.com
W: www.thebrightonhotel.com

THE BRIGHTON HOTEL
143 - 145 Kings Road, Brighton, East Sussex, BN1 2PQ

Best Western

THE ART AND ANTIQUITIES

Freemasonry is a system of morality and insight which is deeply embedded in society, art, culture, poetry, music and legend, and so it is natural that the fraternity and its practices form an integral part of the world in which it exists, a world which contributes to Freemasonry and its development, and a world which, in its turn, has been much influenced by the Craft. Freemasons practise their art in a building or room called a Temple, and so it is natural that Freemasons should, throughout history, have drawn their inspiration from temple-like structures, be they natural phenomena such as mountains or caves, or buildings of great antiquity and import, such as Egyptian temples, gothic cathedrals and many places of sacred significance.

We find evidence of religious and spiritual observance in prehistoric caves, in eighteenth-century gardens, in stone-carvings and wood-carvings of all ages, in the making of artefacts of all kinds right up to the present day. And while the symbols and symbolism of Freemasonry have contributed much to the art and architecture of the world we live in, so also have individual Freemasons, drawing on the inspiration that their Craft gives them, contributed much to the profane and secular world in the form of painting, sculpture, architecture, poetry and music.

It is no accident that wherever Freemasons are organised into Grand Lodges, or Provinces or Districts around the world, they almost always have their own masonic museum. So closely entwined are symbolism, imagery and allegory with art, architecture and anquities, that wherever the opportunity presents itself, Freemasons will establish a museum and library in order to preserve their rich heritage, and in order to draw on that heritage, the riches of the past, to ennoble their present-day aspirations.

But it would be a mistake to think that all masonic interest in art and culture was rooted in the past. In the following pages, we have inspirational poetry, written very recently, and animated by masonic symbology. We have one of the stories of how the effects of Freemasonry came to bear on art nouveau architecture and design. We read of the pride of Freemasons in their own local museums, caretakers of local cultural heritage. We also read of masonic artefacts created by men on active service and in prisoner-of-war camps under the most extreme circumstances, ample evidence of bonding between men on the field of battle or in imprisonment.

Works of art and artefacts of all kinds serve not only to adorn the masonic profession, but also to act in themselves as allegories, often illustrating by skill and ingenuity that which words can never communicate.

THE ORIGINS OF TEMPLES

PAUL DEVEREUX ASKS US TO CONSIDER WHY SOME PLACES ARE SACRED

Caves were the first cathedrals. Here, sunlight streams into a cavern within the Mayan ritual cave complex of Loltun, Yucatan, Mexico.

The concept of the temple is a particularly familiar one to Freemasons because of the legendary associations of masonry with the Temple of Solomon. Less familiar is how the very notion of temples, or sacred places of worship in general, originated. The answer emerges if we look at examples of temples from three ancient cultural periods, namely ancient Egypt, Minoan Crete, and the pre-Columbian Americas.

While engaged in fieldwork in the Valley of the Kings in 1991, Egyptologist V. A. Donohue suddenly noticed that in the cliff face behind Hatshepsut's temple there is a natural, highly eroded configuration of rocks hundreds of feet high resembling a pharaoh with a cobra rearing up behind, a major symbol of royal power in dynastic Egypt. It is so big and so eroded that nobody had noticed it before. Although the likenesses were essentially natural and accidental, Donohue suspects that the configuration may have been subtly enhanced by human art.

Directly across the Nile in the Temple of Karnak at Luxor (the ancient Thebes), a sculpture was uncovered that showed a pharaoh beneath a towering cobra, the precise arrangement in the cliff-face behind Hatshepsut's temple. Wondering if the locations of other temples along the Nile could have been determined by such simulacra in natural rock formations, Donohue went on to discover several other instances.

One example is a pre-dynastic rock-hewn temple dedicated to Min (later the Roman god, Pan) carved into a massive rock outcrop which bears the startling natural appearance of the profile of an aged man – old Min himself? In another example, a pre-dynastic temple was hewn out of a rocky hillock that had an enhanced form looking suspiciously like a proto-sphinx. Whether landscape configuration informed the religious iconography of ancient Egypt, or whether iconographic symbols were seen in the natural forms of the landscape remains an unanswered question.

Cretan mountains that have cleft or twin peaks were venerated from Stone Age times on the island, and the Bronze Age Minoans built shrines on them and had their temples refer to them. Take the famous palace-temple of Knossos, for example. Atop Mount Juktas, the cleft peak overlooking the site, the ruined walls of a Minoan peak shrine are still visible, enclosing a natural fissure into which offerings were cast. Various other Minoan palace-temples, like Phaistos, for example, orient on similarly distinctive mountains.

The Yale professor emeritus, Vincent Scully, is convinced that this cleft-peak shape was originally seen as representing the breasts or vulvic area of a landscape goddess, and triggered the sacred iconography of the Minoans, visible in such artefacts as their "Horns of Consecration", the ubiquitous double-axe or labrys, as well as the upraised arms salute shown time and again in Minoan figurines. As with ancient Egypt, it is the same open question as to whether land configurations informed religious imagery, or vice versa. Whichever was the case, the relationships of temples with cleft-peak mountains found its way onto mainland Greece during the later Mycenaean period.

In the New World, the Olmec of La Venta on Mexico's Gulf Coast built a giant clay model of the mighty volcano San Martin Pajapan, and this was the forerunner of the later stepped pyramid temples of the Maya and Aztecs which were also in effect models of sacred mountains. Similarly, in the Andes 2,000 years ago the people of Tiahuanaco built a great pyramid, the Akapana, containing materials from distant sacred peaks.

Ancient peoples almost everywhere saw their gods and sacred symbols in the natural forms around them. The landscape acted as a kind of giant sacred text.

Sanctity in the Landscape

As well as sacred mountains, caves were considered places of natural sanctity in prehistory. Twenty thousand years ago

The stepped pyramid platform known as the Castillo at Chitchen Itza, Yucatan. Like other Mayan pyramids it represented the Mount of Creation arising from the primordial sea of creation which was symbolised by the surrounding plaza.

the underworld. In some cases Mayan priests carved stalactites in order to enhance the faces and forms glimpsed in their natural folds.

Trees were undoubtedly also a focus of natural sanctity in ancient times, and tangible proof of this came in 1998 with the discovery of 'Sea Henge', a feature that emerged out of the sands on the Norfolk coast. This was a timber circle surrounding a tree bole, inverted so its

the tree's own annual rings showed very precisely that it had been felled in the year 2050 BC. In addition, Stone Age Europeans built great timber temples as well as megalithic sites.

Water, too, was revered in ancient times, as remembered still in Christian baptism and the sacred bathing of Hinduism. Virtually all peoples worshipped lakes and pools, rivers, springs and waterfalls. In Mexico, the ancient Maya felt that cenotes – deep natural pools of water in limestone – were inhabited by deities, and could be use for divination.

The Sacred Cenote at Chichen Itza was a major Mayan pilgrimage site, and human beings were sometimes thrown into it, as were inanimate offerings such as stone and ceramic figurines or jewellery. The Celts considered springs to be the entrance to the Underworld, and like peoples of other times and places heard the voices of spirits in the roaring sounds of waterfalls and so used them as places of divination – especially dream divination.

From Natural Place to Temple

What seems a fairly distinct sequence of how venerated natural places gradually led to constructed sacred sites has now been identified, allowing for variations at different times and locations. The unadorned natural features must have been considered holy for untold generations before that instinctive human reflex of "improving on nature" began to kick in. One of the first signs seems to

The Sacred Cenote, Chichen Itza, Yucatan. Human sacrifices were cast into the water from the temple platform at the right.

Palaeolithic shamans conducted their rituals in such places, and left their paintings on the walls. The ancient Maya similarly felt that caves were entrances to

roots stuck up in the air causing it to resemble a crude idol, exactly as the Saami of Lapland did up until recent centuries. Radiocarbon dating linked to

have been the occurrence of offerings at venerated spots. In Britain, for instance, objects like pottery or Bronze Age weaponry have been found in concentrated deposits in certain reaches of rivers: archaeologists now realise that these were not 'lost' items or hoards but votive deposits offered to water deities by many people over long periods of time.

A variation of this was the sourcing of votive deposits from the material forming specific features. Precipitous locations high within the range known as the Langdale Pikes in Cumbria, for example, have been identified as the origin points of many ceremonial, votive stone axe heads (for unknown reasons, the axe was a widespread sacred symbol in prehistoric Europe). The most likely explanation for this is that the Langdale Pikes were considered to be holy mountains, for the same type of rock was available in much more convenient and safer spots. This is but one example of what Reading University archaeologist Richard Bradley calls the traffic of "pieces of places" from one area to another: relics not of holy people as in medieval Christianity, but of holy places. This has a bearing on the debate as to how the Stonehenge bluestones were transferred from the Preseli Hills in south-west Wales to Salisbury Plain. The real question is why. The answer has to be that to the builders of Stonehenge the rocks from Preseli embodied a special, mystical charisma.

Other types of embellishment of natural places included the building of subtle walls and boundaries – often imperceptible to the untrained eye today – around venerated spots, and the inscribing of markings and symbols onto natural rock features. The study of such rock art has become a major focus of archaeological enquiry, and astounding insights are being made. It is now thought, for instance, that the geometric, abstract patterns found in virtually all rock art everywhere derive from patterns produced in the human brain during ritual trance states – especially those produced by the use of mind-altering plants. This was first deduced in Bushman rock art in southern Africa, and similar findings have subsequently been made concerning Native American rock art and carvings in Ireland. Even representational rock art is thought to as often as not relate to visionary images and scenes as to everyday sights.

The final act in the evolution of sacred

Archaeologists found bronze and pottery votive objects crammed into every nook and cranny among these stalactites inside the Psychro Cave, the birth-cave of Zeus on Mount Dikte, Crete.

temple monuments from natural places was the creation of freestanding, wholly artificial features. In Western Europe this was marked by the onset of the Neolithic era, c.4,000 B.C., when various forms of

stone-chambered structures and later stone circles appeared. Later, in other parts of the world, such as in the eastern Mediterranean region, more refined temples were constructed. As we have already seen, these latter structures still acknowledged venerated peaks by being within sight of them, or even aligning to them. This was also often true of megalithic monuments. In Preseli, for example, the stone circle of Gors Fawr is at the foot of the ridge from which the Stonehenge bluestones originated. Again, on Bodmin Moor, all the stone circles occur at the foot of natural tors, or were very accurately placed to be just at the extreme point of visibility from them.

The way early people perceived venerated spots in the landscape may hold both spiritual and ecological lessons for us today, as we increasingly lose our cultural sense of the spirit of place. ∎

Paul Devereux lectures widely, broadcasts occasionally, and has written many articles, academic papers, and some 26 books. Recent titles include: The Sacred Place *(Cassell),* Stone Age Soundtracks *(Vega),* Living Ancient Wisdom *(Rider), and* Mysterious Ancient America *(Vega). His latest title is* Fairy Paths & Spirit Roads – Exploring Otherworldly Routes in the Old and New Worlds *(Vega).*

All photographs by Paul Devereux.

The ancient Mayans quested deep into the cavern systems of the Yucatan to obtain what they called 'virgin water' - pure water from within the earth for ritual use rather than for drinking. This underground lagoon in the lowest depths of the ritual cave of Balankanche, Yucatan, had offerings placed in it.

THE MYSTERIOUS TEMPLAR CARVINGS OF CHINON CASTLE

MICHAEL BAIGENT VISITS THE CASTLE'S PRISON TOWER

The Prison Tower at the castle of Chinon on the Loire River, France, where the Templar commanders were incarcerated for interrogation by Papal representatives in 1308.

The dramatic events had begun seven years earlier when, at dawn on 13th October 1307, the king of France ordered all the Templars in his domains to be arrested on a series of charges drawn up by the Inquisition. The knights were taken, locked up, charged and for the most part, tortured. A number died as a result of this ill treatment and, over the next seven years, a hundred or so Templars were burned alive.

This sudden move against the wealthiest and most powerful military Order in the world had been carefully planned. During the summer of 1307 the king of France, Philippe le Bel, had sent a letter to his regional seneschals ordering them to secretly investigate all holdings of the Knights Templar and prepare to move against them when the command should come.

A month or two passed. The Grand Master, accompanied by a large entourage and much of his treasure, came to France from his headquarters in Cyprus and was resident in Paris. The Templars' fame was at prodigious heights and its treasure vast – just the holdings in Normandy had a greater income than that of the King of England. Suddenly, the French king's men struck. They wished to destroy the Order and confiscate their treasure and

On the evening of March 18th 1314, the Grand Master of the Knights Templar, Jacques de Molay, was cruelly burned to death on a small island in the Seine, in Paris. Sharing his pain and death was the Templar Preceptor of Normandy, Geoffroy de Charney. It was the last brutal act in an enigmatic drama.

Heads and a ship carved inside the tower by the Templars. Access to them is very restricted and photography is difficult.

The castle and town of Chinon looking across the Loire.

lands which could then be passed to a jealous and greedy French Crown.

Or so was the theory. In fact it was not quite like that. A quick look at the Inquisition records reveal that no treasure was ever found. Where it went and who ultimately benefited from it, remains a mystery to this day. One arrested Templar spoke mysteriously of a Brother leaving the Paris Temple, some days before the arrests, taking with him all the treasure held there. Certainly no money was found in any of the preceptories or castles seized. The lists of goods taken by the Inquisition are noteworthy for their tedium and lack of value.

The records reveal too that it was mostly the old and the young who were arrested. Indeed, a survey of the manpower of the Templars before the arrests, and the numbers arrested, shows a shortfall of just over a thousand militarily active members. The suspicion arises that the Templar leadership had advance warning of the cataclysm which was to befall them. The military and financial strength of the Templars seemed to have simply melted away.

The Fate of The Templars

Much has been written on the fate of the Templars and the Treasure. English records reveal that at least some English Templars fled to Scotland undoubtedly to join Robert Bruce. Others may have joined these few for there was a sea route, safe from English ships, leading from France via the west of Ireland. In France itself, Templars may have hidden in the hills – one document claims over a

thousand in the south. Others may have fled north to Germany or south to Spain, Portugal or Italy, or even over to Hungary where the Order held some castles. No

documents shed any light on this mysterious disappearance.

All those who were arrested – in France, a total of 620 knights, sergeants, priests and clerks – were imprisoned. But they were nominally under the "protection" of the Pope and seemed to have believed, initially, that they were pawns in some political shake-up which they would have to ride through before being released. However, disillusionment soon set in, especially once Templars began to be tortured; and began to die from those tortures. Suddenly it seemed as though the Order had been abandoned by the very man they thought would save them, the Pope.

In prison the pressure began to tell: Templars confessed, then withdrew those confessions. Moves were made to seek some redress from the infamy of their incarceration. In 1308 the Pope, a weak and ill man, dominated by the French king, found some personal courage and agreed to meet with a group of the Templar commanders who would present the case for their innocence. In February , he suspended the Inquisition.

In June, seventy-two Templars were

Templar graffiti including (above) a cross bearing a heart and (below) a heart with a flower growing from it. These long predate the Catholic cult of the Sacred Heart

Inscribed names together with a disembodied hand; is it raised in worship?

transported to Poitiers by the king to testify before the Pope; between 29 June and 2 July they did so. But under pressure they all confessed to the charges, horrifying the Pope. But none of the Templar leaders were amongst these men.

The Interrogations at Chinon

In August 1308 some sixty high Templar officials – all mature men and leaders - each of whom had spent a minimum of

A radiant heart beside a figure which might represent a priest.

twenty-eight years in the Order, were taken from various prisons in France and brought to the castle of Chinon, on the Loire, not far from Poitiers. They included the Grand Master himself, Jaques de Molay, the financial head of the Order, Hugues de Pairaud, and the preceptors of Cyprus, Normandy and Poitou and Aquitaine.

Finally, between 17 – 20 August 1308, they were interrogated by three Cardinals specially sent there by the Pope who was

Geometrical patterns and other graffiti of unknown significance

staying some miles away near Poitiers. Unusually, these interrogations apparently were not recorded; there is no official transcript of the proceedings - a curiosity at a time when all was meticulously noted down by scribes. All we know about the hearings comes from a letter written by the Cardinals to the King of France.

Collectively the Templar leaders all pleaded guilty to the charges. A misguided action which reveals a pathetic confidence in the power of the Pope to

save them and the Order. But at Chinon, having accepted the charges and the guilt, having abjured their heresy, they were reconciled with the Church. They must have hoped that this would be the end of their imprisonment and ill-treatment. But they were tragically mistaken. They were later to regret their confessions and to proclaim their innocence.

All these Templar leaders were locked up in the prison tower in the castle of Chinon. It is no surprise then to find that they covered some of the walls of the tower with graffiti, scratched into the stone by whatever hard implements they could obtain. But this graffiti is enigmatic. No one has provided an explanation of it. Neither do most of the images find a correspondence in the official symbolism of the Church of the time. We can see such images as geometrical grids, a heart crucified on a calvary cross, a flower growing out of a heart,the Hermetic six-pointed star of two triangles (now the Star of David) and others. Due to the confined space, they can only be photographed with great difficulty.

In the end the Pope refused to exonerate the Templars or keep them out of the control of the French king. They were returned to their prisons, some disillusioned, some still defiant. In 1310 over five hundred Templars joined together to proclaim their innocence. For a while they sensed that success could come. But on 12 May 1310, fifty-four were quickly taken and burned alive outside Paris. All died denying the charges made against them. More were soon burned; resistance finally crumbled. The end was inevitable, the Order of the Temple had been abandoned by history. It remained only to be destroyed.

It was dissolved by the Pope in 1312; the Grand Master and his Preceptor of Normandy were burned in 1314 over a slow fire on an island in the Seine; Pont Neuf now stands there, a plaque commemorating their deaths.

But the legends and mysteries of the Templars have never faded. For there seems to have been real fire beneath the great cloud of smoke which continued to billow down through the centuries however much some historians would like to wish it away.

All photographs by Michael Baigent.

The castle of Chinon is near to that of Tours where the masonic exhibition is being held this summer. Brethren travelling to France are recommended to visit both.

NEARER TO THE GREAT ARCHITECT IN A GARDEN

CHRISTOPHER MCINTOSH STUDIES SYMBOLISM AND GARDEN DESIGN

The Hierophant as depicted in the Tarot Garden of Niki de Saint Phalle in Tuscany.

A garden, like a building, can convey a deliberate message. If, for example, you visit Chartres Cathedral, you experience not just a construction of stone and mortar but a kind of 'book' in which you can read the world view and beliefs of the medieval Christian mind. Similarly to visit, say, the gardens of the Alhambra or the Generalife at Granada in Spain is to catch a glimpse of the Islamic world view, in which gardens are intended to give a foretaste of paradise. In fact, the very word 'paradise' comes from an old Persian word meaning a walled garden. The thought expressed in the saying 'nearer to God in a garden' has a long history.

The idea of the garden as an image of paradise is one that goes back some 5,000 years to ancient Mesopotamia being mentioned in the *Epic of Gilgamesh*. This was largely an arid region, where people longed for green shady places with plenty of water. It was natural to think of the gods and the privileged human beings who had become immortal as dwelling in a garden. This idea mingled with the notion of a primal garden, the Garden of Eden, in which there were four rivers, which flowed out into the wider world from a central source: 'Now a river went out of Eden to water the garden, and from there it parted and became four riverheads,' states Genesis.

In the *Koran* these become rivers of water, wine, milk and honey, and this is reflected in the typical design of Islamic gardens with four water channels. In the centre, where the channels meet, there is often a fountain representing the primal

At first sight you might not think that there is much of a connection between gardens and Freemasonry. Masonic symbolism is surely all about architecture, and gardening is about working with things that grow. Nevertheless there is a connection, in fact many connections, and if this seems far-fetched it may be because we need to widen our conception of both gardening and what a 'masonic garden' might be.

The 'snake stone' in the garden at Weimar.

source of the four rivers. In the Islamic garden these elements are part of a whole symbolic pattern in which plants, buildings and other garden features all have their special significance.

The paradise garden tradition also has its echoes outside the Islamic world. One of the features of paradise according to the ancient writings is a sacred mound or hill, which stood in the centre and was sometimes combined with a fountain or spring. At one time paradise mounds were a popular garden feature, and a few of them survive. Examples in England include those at Little Moreton Hall in Cheshire, Packwood House in Warwickshire and New College, Oxford.

Apart from the paradise garden tradition we can find many examples in different cultures of the use of gardens to convey a symbolic message. These include the gardens of China with their immortal rocks and careful balancing of earth energies, the serene Zen gardens of Japan, the gardens of Renaissance Italy with their rich mythological imagery, even the landscaped parks of England such as Stourhead, which symbolically reproduces the journey of Virgil's hero, Aeneas, around the Mediterranean. There are also quite a number of striking modern examples such as the remarkable Tarot Garden in Tuscany, created by the French sculptress Niki de Saint Phalle featuring enormous figures representing the Tarot trumps, some of them as large as a house.

A visual language

While a garden can be made to contain infinite number of different messages, the visual 'language' used convey them has basically three different elements. First there is the overall form of the garden, the shape of the perimeter and the internal divisions, the compass alignments, the degree of symmetry or asymmetry. Secondly, there are the natural or man-made features: mounds, water channels, fountains, labyrinths, statues, monuments. Third, there are the plants with their symbolic associations.

A plant has many different meanings and associations depending on the region and cultural context. In the west we can think, for example, of the laurel, sacred to Apollo and symbolising glory and poetic inspiration, the oak, sacred to Jupiter, the ivy and the vine, sacred to Bacchus, and of course the acacia, with its well-known symbolic associations in Freemasonry.

Considering that gardens have been used for so long to convey symbolic messages of one kind or another, it is natural to wonder if they have they ever

The Venus Temple in the garden at Wörlitz.

An icehouse in the form of a pyramid in the New Garden, Potsdam, created for the king of Prussia.

been used to convey a masonic message, as the architectural historian James Stevens Curl argues in his book *The Art and Architecture of Freemasonry*. We would expect the 'masonic garden' to be filled with features that point to masonic ideas, creating what I have described as a 'symbol-strewn landscape'. A landowner wishing to create such a landscape could

An orangery resembling an Egyptian Temple in the New Garden, Potsdam.

turn to the pictures often found on masonic diplomas and aprons as well as in books on Freemasonry. Many of these depict landscapes full of things alluding to masonic tradition: ruined classical

temples, pyramids, obelisks, broken columns as well as symbolic creatures such as lions, sphinxes and snakes.

Symbolic gardens

One place reminiscent of such a landscape is the Parc de Monceau in Paris, with its Roman colonnade, pyramid, stone archway, obelisk and other romantic follies. The park was originally laid out in the 18th century for the Duc de Chartres, a leading Freemason of the time, so it is tempting to see a masonic influence in its design. The same is true of another French 18th-century park, the Désert de Retz, near Marly, created by François de Monville, also a Freemason. The park featured, among other things, a grotto guarded by torch-bearing satyrs, a pyramid that served as an ice-house, and a house shaped like a gigantic broken column of the Tuscan order, in which de Monville himself lived. Several of the features found in one or other of these parks, such as the pyramid, the obelisk and the broken column, also appear in the early painted Master's aprons.

Turning to Italy, we can detect

masonic influences in the Torrigiani garden in Florence, created in the early nineteenth century by the architect Luigi Cambray Digny for the Marquess Pietro Torrigiani; both were members of the same Florentine masonic lodge. The original features of the garden, most of which have now vanished, included a statue of Osiris at the entrance, a Gothic basilica, a sepulchre, a huge statue of Saturn and a Gothic tower built on a high point of the garden.

The initiating journey

Common to the gardens just mentioned is that they are laid out so as to create an initiatory journey, a theme that features in Craft Masonry and in a number of the higher degrees, sometimes involving symbolic dangers and tests of endurance.

The motif of the initiatory journey is particularly striking in certain German gardens, notably the park of Wörlitz in the state of Sachsen-Anhalt, built around a salient of the river Elbe in the latter part of the eighteenth century by Prince Franz von Anhalt-Dessau and his architect. This park includes a Hermitage, a Mystagogue's Cell, a Temple of Venus, a series of grottoes corresponding to the elements, and a labyrinth with tunnels through rock, twisting paths, false turnings and inscriptions containing advice to the wanderer. In this park we feel close to the world of Mozart's *Magic Flute*, with its message of spiritual quest, its themes of darkness and light and its elemental initiations.

Although it is not recorded whether the Prince was a Freemason (he visited England and could have been initiated there), he was in contact with a number of prominent Masons including the poet

The entrance to the labyrinth in the garden at Wörlitz.

Early Master Mason's apron depicting a landscape with masonic symbols placed in a garden.
Eaton Lodge

Goethe, whom he visited at Weimar. Indeed, the park at Weimar, laid out along the banks of the river Ilm, was strongly influenced by Wörlitz. Goethe played an important part in the laying out of the park, and here again we find elements that suggest a masonic influence, such as a grotto with a sphinx, and a stone pillar encircled by a snake.

Even more striking in its imagery, is the New Garden at Potsdam. This was created for King Frederick William II of Prussia (reigned 1786-97), who had a strong interest in esoteric matters and belonged to the Golden and Rosy Cross Order, an exotic, high-degree masonic rite with a strong emphasis on alchemy. Charmingly laid out on the banks of a lake, the garden contains a number of objects redolent of Rosicrucian mysteries. Near the entrance is an orangery resembling an Egyptian temple, with a sphinx over the portico and two Egyptian gods in black marble guarding the doorway. Equally imposing is an ice-house (reminiscent of the one at Retz) in the form of a pyramid with a row of gilded alchemical sigils over the entrance. Other features have unfortunately disappeared, including a grotto and a hermitage with a ceiling painted with planetary images.

Further examples of masonic gardens include that of Schloss Louisenlund in Schleswig-Holstein, home of the Landgrave Carl von Hesse-Cassel (1744-1836), a leading Freemason, active in various high-degree rites and an ardent devotee of alchemy, who harboured the mysterious French alchemist, the Comte de Saint-Germain during the last year's of the latter's life. The park at Louisenlund contained an Alchemical Tower, a Grotto of Initiation and other features, now mostly vanished. In its heyday it must have been a place of potent magic.

These few examples should give an idea of what we might understand as a masonic garden or - more broadly speaking - a garden with a symbolic message. Such gardens are still being created, as the Tarot Garden shows. While not many people today have the resources available to the King of Prussia or other continental aristocrats, we can still draw inspiration from their visionary creations.

Dr. Christopher McIntosh gained a doctorate in history from Oxford University and is the author of many books including two studies of the Rosicrucian movement and, most recently, Gardens of the Gods (I.B.Tauris, London) reviewed in the last issue of Freemasonry Today. He has been a Freemason for over twenty years and since 1994, has lived in northern Germany where he enjoys contacts with a number of lodges.

Unless specified, all photographs by Christopher McIntosh.

BATH AND THE 'LOST' FURNITURE

YASHA BERESINER VISITS A HIDDEN CITY-CENTRE MASTERPIECE

The Masonic Temple at Bath, originally the Theatre Royal and then a Roman Catholic Church.

It was at a chance encounter late last year with the Assistant Grand Master, David Williamson, that the extraordinary Masonic Hall – the converted Theatre Royal - in Old Orchard Street, Bath, was pointed out to me. Bath is a University City and David Williamson's interest is in the contacts between University students throughout the country and local masonic authorities. The Masonic Hall at Bath will certainly make an exceptional venue for such meetings.

In 1866, the building in the heart of the ancient City of Bath, was converted into a Masonic Hall and consecrated by Freemason, the Rev. C.R. Davy, Master of the Royal Sussex Lodge, No. 53. It had been purchased from the Roman Catholic authorities of Prior Park and Downside Abbey who, in turn, had bought the property in 1809 from the Theatre Royal. All three stages in the history of these unusual premises are still evident and give the Masonic Hall a

unique atmosphere.

The theatre opened to the public in 1750, and in 1786 received a Royal Patent, the first outside of London. By the end of the century it had outgrown the space available and in 1805 the new Theatre Royal opened its doors in Beaufort Square. But constant reminders of those heady years as a theatre remain: the ground level is raised some five feet, the stage in the East is intact, decorated with Corinthian columns which were

The Master's Chair with the Prince of Wales' feathers.

Junior Warden's pedestal.

Senior Warden's pedestal.

The Master's pedestal.

The pedestals belonging to the Master and Wardens have paintings of the three graces, which have been optimistically attributed to the famous Swiss artist Angelica Kauffmann (1741-1807) but they are more likely to be the work of one of her pupils.

erected by the Church authorities when the building was changed from a theatre to a Church one hundred and forty years ago. The upstairs gallery has been converted into an elongated dining room. There are other vestiges of the Catholic occupation from 1809 until 1866. The Church's oak panelling now forms sidewalls to the temple allowing for storage space beyond. These walls are decorated with the coats of arms of the various Knights Templar encampments meeting there.

The most striking object as you enter the Masonic Temple is the reredos, a decorative screen placed behind the altar in a church Bro Dennis Moseley was kind to point out that this particular reredos is unique in being an extremely rare original example rescued from a `georgian Church or chapel and has been attributed to the celebrated Bath architect John Wood the younger (1728-1782). Here, at the back of the stage, it forms an impressive backdrop to the Master's seat in the East. Solid Corinthian and Doric columns divide the triptych. In the centre is King Solomon, to his left is Hiram King of Tyre, and to his right, Hiram Abif, all painted by Baker, a well-established Bath artist. At the top of the wooden structure is a crown representing orders beyond the craft and below is the square and compass.

In the centre of the room are two columns topped by 8-inch celestial and terrestrial globes, covered, as they should be, by canopies. In front of the columns three large old Harris tracing boards lie on the ground. They were painted in 1852 by Bro Charles Haseler, a Past Master of the Lodge. An unpleasant event in Bath's masonic history took place in the mid 1800s known as the the 'Bath Furniture' incident.

The Bath Furniture Dispute

Prior to moving to the present premises, three Bath Lodges, Royal York, the Lodge of Virtue, and Royal Cumberland, met at the Masonic Hall in York Street. Among the members of the Royal Cumberland Lodge was a wealthy wine merchant, Charles Geary, who was Master when the York Street premises were purchased by the Brethren of Bath. It would appear the financial burden on the Brethren was too great and Geary, in 1823, took over as sole proprietor of the premises and immediately found himself in dispute over the rent. The Brethren were unable to pay and so Geary decided to close the premises and confiscate the Lodges' valuable antique furniture and other property. The dispute lasted the best part of 20 years until in 1843 Geary decided to sell the furniture by lottery. The winning ticket, quite legitimately, was his own, and he offered everything for sale for one hundred guineas. The Brethren of the Loyal Lodge, No. 312 (now 251), of Barnstaple in North Devon moved fast and purchased the whole 'lot' except for the tracing boards which remained behind.

In 1939 the Lodge was presented with an exact replica of the original Master's chair made by the well known Bath Furniture Craftsmen Mallett and Son. The chair with the distinctive Prince of Wales feathers and red cushions decorated with embroidered emblems on the backrest is an reminder of the

The painted reredos: in the centre is Solomon; Hiram of Tyre to his left and Hiram Abif to his right.

excellence of the original furniture.

On our way up several floors to the Leslie Norman Museum we made a short stop in the Masonic Library, which is still in the process of being organised by Tony Carter, the newly appointed Librarian. His awesome task is to locate, catalogue and file into their respective shelves the hundreds of books still in the boxes in which they were delivered from the home of Edward Gaynor now in his ninetieth year and Curator and Librarian for the past 40 years. The task of Curator was passed on two years ago to our host for the day, Brian Wootton, who impressed us with his jovial and friendly enthusiasm as we entered the Museum.

The first impression was a display of numerous objects and cabinets, which, in their lack of orderly standardisation, gave the Museum a warm ambiance. The seven standing units were of varying sizes and shapes, the central one a disused water font transformed to allow the pleasing display of jewels, medals and photographs.

There were some exceptional items

The small chapel now used by the Masonic Knights Templar.

Behind the stage is a small chapel which was built in the 1820s by the Catholic authorities as a private prayer room. It is now a perfect setting for Knights Templar meetings. It is compact, its stone walls decorated with the banners and shields of the Order.

The seal of the Lodge Secretary together with other implements.

we had not come across in other masonic museums: in particular a most unusual masonic gas appliance of the mid-nineteenth century used specifically as the 'bright morning star' in the third degree ceremony.

On display too was a trinket belonging to a lodge Secretary and consisting of five miniature metal implements: a hammer and anvil, a revolving unit onto which emblems of Freemasonry had been carefully engraved, and a seal, which would have been used to imprint the melted wax on summonses and letters sent to the Brethren. Brian also showed us a pair of the Napoleonic prisoner-of-war handcrafted jewels encased in watchcases, of which several good examples are in various museums. There was too a miniature set of seven ivory working tools: a trowel and a movable 24 inch gauge, a maul, the square and

compass, plumb rule and level, all in their original velvet box.

Among the various framed prints and documents on the walls was one historic letter dated 9 November 1793 in the distinctive handwriting of Thomas Dunckerley, and signed by him, addressed to the Grand Secretary James Heseltine and requesting his own appointment as Provincial Grand Master of several Provinces, including that of Somerset.

The Museum had been set up for a Lodge of Instruction meeting and the idea of the Brethren being exposed to Masonic artefacts whilst learning the ritual and perambulations seemed

A mid-nineteenth century gas powered 'bright morning star' for use in the Third Degree.

particularly appropriate and an idea perhaps other museums could emulate.

This had already been a memorable visit but there was more to come: because the Roman Catholic Church was not allowed consecrated ground for burial until the Emancipation Relief Act of 1829 the subterranean vaults had been used to bury the bodies of the dead. When Freemasons took over the building some mortal remains had to be removed and re-interred in newly consecrated ground in the cemetery at Perrymead. Just two years ago four of the elongated vault chambers were refurbished and all but one have been cut off with wooden panels and mirrors and comfortably furnished for use as committee and Lodge of Instruction rooms. The fourth chamber runs some 200 feet and is used as a fire escape route, having been converted with all the reverence due to those who had passed beyond and buried on the site; their gravestones are displayed along the walls.

This was a true eye-opener of a private Masonic Hall and Museum, capably administered by dedicated volunteers. The present ownership of the Hall by the Bath Masonic Hall Trust Limited, is composed of representatives of the seven Bath Lodges currently presided over by Reginald Simmonds

Visits to the Museum can be arranged by telephoning Brian Wooton on 01249 720556 or e-mailing him at gbwootton@aol.com

All photographs by Michael Baigent

HIDDEN TREASURES

Museum Curator, Mark Dennis, Discovers Some Special Items

A marquetry Master's Board dated 1777 depicting the Temple with a vaulted chamber beneath. It was presented to Grand Lodge by St. Andrews Lodge, No. 231, London, in 1907.

Freemasonry has always attracted men of great skill in the crafts. Probably one of the most famous was Thomas Harper, Deputy Grand Master of the Antients Grand Lodge from 1801 to 1813, who created large pierced jewels of exquisite beauty. Any masonic museum which holds examples of his work has readily displayed them. And this is the rub: museums are always keen to show such high value and well-crafted silver, gold, or ceramic objects; the less valuable pieces representing the craft skills of amateurs or artisans are not commonly shown. In particular, wooden objects do not seem to have received the attention they deserve. Many, perhaps because of their mundane nature, remain in storerooms; others are unnoticed or unmarked as something special and remain in use in Lodge rooms around the country.

Latticework photo frame dated 1874, the year in which the Prince of Wales became Grand Master of United Grand Lodge of England. The inclusion of the motto of the Order of the Garter makes it likely that this frame originally held his portrait.

A Master's Board displaying the use of laid straw which can be used to simulate marquetry or metal, since it reflects the light in a way wood does not. It has stylistic parallels to Napoleonic period French prisoner of war work and this may well be its source. It was presented to Grand Lodge in 1870.

Cigar box formerly owned by H.R.H. The Prince of Wales (later King Edward VII). Presented to Grand Lodge in 1955 by the Guild of Freemen Lodge, No. 3525, London.

Certainly they are appreciated by those Lodge officers who use them or the Tylers who arrange them but they are rarely studied methodically. They are seen as simple masonic tools to be used, sometimes for centuries, their commercial or artistic value as antiques ignored in the face of their greater value as a part of Lodge tradition. And, perhaps as a result of their constant use in the Lodge, all too often little is remembered of their origins, of who made them or of the conditions under which they were bought by the Lodge or presented to it.

Over the years, many such objects have been given to the United Grand Lodge of England; some are displayed but space being always limited many were placed in store. It could also have been that certain of the pieces, being concerned with aspects of ritual symbolism, were considered too sensitive to be placed on open display. Happily today we are rather bolder in our desire to show the richness of masonic craftsmanship to the world and to allow these pieces to find their rightful place in the history of English art and craft.

Viewing the store room

When Mark Dennis, Curator of the Museum of Freemasonry in Freemasons' Hall, London, was first appointed, one of his early actions was to take a look in the store-room. He stepped inside and was stopped in his tracks; he commented afterwards that he felt rather like Lord Carnarvon entering Tutankamun's tomb - well, at least a little like him - for before him sat shelf after shelf of treasures all carefully preserved, placed side by side, as he said, 'with not a millimetre between them'. It was the most diverse range of objects he had ever seen in his museum career. He was particularly struck by a number of wooden objects, which displayed a skill at Marquetry, fretwork or pokerwork.

It happened that a new carpenter had also come to work at Freemasons' Hall and so Mark decided to get some of the

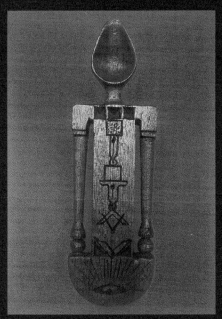

Anointing spoon for use in the Royal Arch.

Pocket watch case.

Carved picture frame dated 1900. These were ornately carved to a standard design and were used for displaying masonic certificates – something Freemasons have long been taught not to do.

pieces out, show them to the carpenter, and gain his opinion. The carpenter was impressed and immediately enthused over the level of craftsmanship which they represented. So Mark decided to bring a display together, one of 'Craftsmanship serving the Craft'. A cabinet to the right of the entrance to the Museum was cleared and a display mounted of these wooden objects drawn from the store.

The museum is now bringing more and more objects out of store in order to support the thematic displays which are now becoming a feature of the Museum. In the future we can expect to see many more artefacts which have not been on display for many years, if indeed, ever. ■

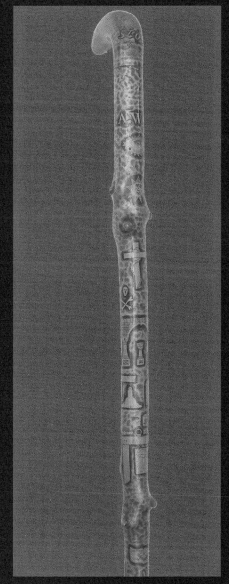

Pokerwork masonic walking stick.

Hexagonal tobacco box, lead-lined internally with a close sealing lid.

Early carved box which once contained wax seals of the masonic Knights Templar.

All photographs courtesy Library and Museum of Freemasonry, London.

TRENCH ART

NICHOLAS SAUNDERS EXPLAINS THE MAKING OF MEMORIES OF WAR,
EXHIBITED AT FREEMASONS HALL, 26 JUNE – 19 SEPTEMBER 2003

A commemorative snuff mull created from a horse's hoof.

Art is often born out of hardship, adversity and suffering, and this is nowhere more true than in the field of armed conflict. From the Spanish Armada to Vietnam, from the Boer War to Bosnia, across more than two centuries and five continents, the most amazing collection of artefacts of all kinds – much of it masonic - has come into being as a result of war.

Trench Art is the name given to objects - be they of metal, cloth, wood, bone, stone or any other material - made by soldiers, prisoners-of-war, civilians and internees alike. It takes its name, and is best known, from the Great War of 1914-18, the world's first global industrialised conflict. Trench Art is a term as evocative as it is misleading. Its astonishing variety reveals the human skills and fortitude which emerge under the pressures of combat, imprisonment and displacement. Furthermore, of the millions of pieces made over the last two hundred years, each is unique.

All Trench Art objects were once familiar to every soldier and family of the war generation which produced them. Yet until recently, most examples have been ignored by museums and historians. This is particularly true of Great War Trench Art. Only now, at the beginning of the twenty-first century, are these objects being reassessed as unique and valuable historical items, testaments to the extremes of human behaviour represented by war. The main problem with Trench Art has always been how to uncover the human stories that have lain hidden in their strange and unusual shapes, sometimes for hundreds of years. It can be very fruitful to establish the historical significance of such art by investigating the human circumstances of production: who made what, and where, and when and why?

Yet it is the items typically made by and for Freemasons which add a new dimension to the study of Trench Art. In such an art-form defined by its diversity, the imagery of masonic symbolism cuts across time, place, and raw materials.

Masonic Art

In the endeavour to recover the 'lost worlds' of Trench Art, these objects made by Freemasons offer a unique perspective. While every Trench Art object ever made is a one-off, many masonic items, particularly of the twentieth century, share a single set of shapes and a common purpose. Whatever material they are made from, they are often fashioned into the shapes of masonic ceremonial instruments, paraphernalia and symbols: the gavel and block, mauls, squares and compasses, Master's emblems, the all-seeing eye, and aprons. Of course, there exist many spectacular examples and

A boxwood snuffbox, a model of the prison hulk, made by a French Prisoner of War during the Napoleonic period.

Lucknow, the defence of which became a key imperial legend and whose commander, Sir Henry Lawrence, was feted as an imperial martyr. The earlier of the two bears a plaque stating that the wood was taken from the room in which he died. The second gavel was created in 1907 on the 50th anniversary of the event and illustrates the durability of the legend which had, by then, been joined by many others.

Across the Lines

This recurring imagery of masonic symbolism can also cut across the divides imposed by the conflict itself. Of the few examples of masonic Trench Art made under fire, the gavel of St Catherine Park Lodge, No. 2899, is a most potent example. The head was carved from the wooden parts of a German Mauser rifle found in a captured trench by the New Zealand Expeditionary Force, and the gavel itself was used in meetings held within the combat area. It passed to the United Kingdom lodge in the 1920s because of that lodge's hospitality to overseas masons during the war. Another illustration of the international dimension to masonic Trench Art is the gavel made in a British Prisoner of War camp by a Boer prisoner and presented to his captor, Lt. Colonel Cordes of Benevolent Lodge No. 303.

exceptions to this rule-of-thumb. There is the maul made from the timber of a Spanish Armada ship wrecked in Scotland in 1588, and the many marquetry boxes and carved-bone galleons made by French Freemason prisoners-of-war during Napoleonic times.

The latter are as much Trench Art as are items fashioned by soldiers in the First World War; here we have a rich seam of masonic Trench Art to explore. These items were produced during the wars with France from the early 1790s to 1815. The jewels followed the pattern of the plate and pierced jewels on sale in England for masonic wear, but in common with other prisoner-of-war work they were constructed from easily available materials such as card, bone and human hair. They varied greatly in size and can be found mounted for wear as lodge jewels or as cravat pins, rings and cufflinks. Snuffboxes carved from bone with painted illustrations in the lid are also common and follow the general pattern of commercially produced masonic snuffboxes on the continent. These usually depict a patriotic or martial scene designed to appeal to the intended market.

The siege of Lucknow during the mutiny of 1857 has left us some masonic memorabilia: two gavels exist which were made from the wood of the Residency at

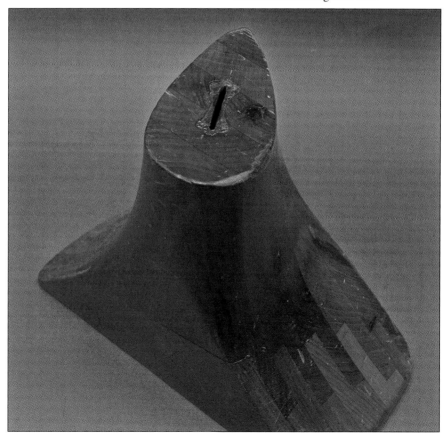

A collecting box created from a First World War SE2B propeller and used by the Ad Astra Lodge, No. 3808.

A tie-pin created from a bullet.

Other examples of masonic Trench Art from the First World War include wooden boxes made by British soldier masons who were interned in Holland from 1914 and who set up a lodge at their camp in Groningen. In Germany patriotic masonic lodges between the world wars used jewels made from recycled Iron Cross decorations; in a poignant irony these lodges were closed during the Third Reich as representing a threat to the Fatherland, and their members were ostracised and barred from many aspects of public life.

The Ad Astra Lodge, No. 3808, was formed from the Air Inspection Directorate. The work of the latter was commemorated in the lodge by the collecting box, made from the central section of a laminated wood propeller. Little was thought about this artefact until recently, when an examination of the serial marks on the wood allowed the identification of the plane as a SE2B, an experimental design with a rear-mounted propeller. This plane saw much service in the First World War.

Memorial Objects

While some examples of soldier-made Trench Art, such as aluminium finger-rings, were made in the trenches, others such as sophisticated shell-case vases were made in safer rear areas. Some of these items were produced by experienced craftsmen with professional tools, such as blacksmiths and the Royal Engineers, and others by men with little or no artistic ability. Some objects were made to order and for sale, others for barter and exchange, and some as personal mementoes or souvenirs sent home to families. In fact, objects made by civilians between 1919 and 1939 were sold to war widows on battlefield visits as poignant memorial objects. These items helped authenticate the pilgrimage experience, and enabled the bereaved to take home a tangible link with the dead.

One masonic Trench-Art object represents both the traditional concerns of its Freemason maker as well as symbolising the new kind of warfare which the 1939-45 conflict embodied. Preserved today in the Museum of the United Grand Lodge of Freemasonry, it is a beautifully carved maul, made of oak from the roof of London's Guildhall which was destroyed by the Luftwaffe on 29 December 1940: this maul was presented by the Lord Mayor of London, Frank Newson-Smith.

Each war produces its own heroes, its own histories, and its own mythologies. Those who were not present at the time can never truly understand the dramatic changes in human behaviour and attitudes that war produces. The bravery, pain, and sense of loss, the relief, boredom and endurance suffered during conflict, inevitably fade with the passing away of the war generation. At such times, words often fail, and later written accounts cannot capture that spark of immediacy. Only objects which can be touched, passed through the fingers, and pondered, evoke anything like true human emotion.

An obelisk ash-tray created from a brass shell case.

Crucially, the key element in Trench Art remains the 'context of war', a context which breathes life into the objects and conjures up human experiences of armed conflict, that most extreme cultural phenomenon.

All photographs courtesy of The Library and Museum of Freemasonry, London.

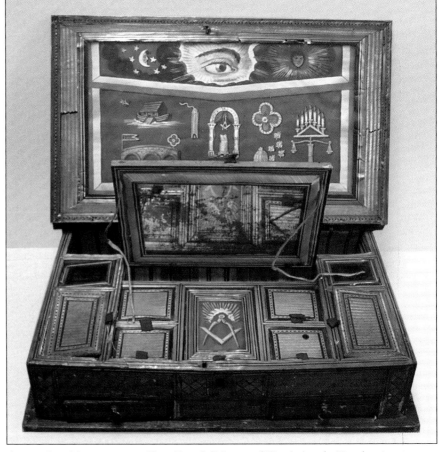

A masonic writing case created by a French Prisoner of War during the Napoleonic wars.

RAISED FROM ADVERSITY

YASHA BERESINER VISITS THE JERSEY MASONIC LIBRARY AND MUSEUM

The Masters' Chair in the Lodge Room of The Masonic Temple.

Our visit to the Jersey Masonic Library and Museum, the fifth of the joint trips Michael Baigent and I have undertaken, was to prove enjoyable and instructive. The Channel Islands have a unique history, not least because they were the only part of British Territory occupied by the Germans in the Second World War.

These traumatic events had many repercussions, in particular on the Masonic heritage of Jersey. The Temple in St Helier was appropriated by the occupying forces on 19 November 1940 and *The Secret Field Police* sealed all the rooms containing valuable Masonic artefacts and priceless items in preparation for the systematic looting and destruction of the contents of the building

two months later by special German troops, the *Einsatzstab*.

The librarian and curator at the time, George Knocker, described how he discreetly walked up and down the opposite side of the street to witness, over a two day period, the pillaging and burning of cherished books and documents, records and lodge furniture. The present Library and Museum is dedicated to his memory.

After his death in 1952 there was a hiatus until the appointment of Dennis Perrin in 1981. Since the latters' retirement, after 11 years of dedicated service, it has proven difficult to find a long-term curator: the search continues. Meanwhile Dennis remains the main contact for all matters relating to the Museum. His enthusiasm is infectious and his Masonic knowledge and standing unsurpassed not only in Jersey but throughout the UK. He was recently distinguished with the Order of Service to Masonry, the highest honour that the Grand Master bestows on any member of the Craft.

Brethren of the Province of Jersey take great pride in their splendid classical style Masonic Temple with an

Jersey Masonic Temple.

external staircase and imposing porch with four Corinthian columns rising 26 feet high which was consecrated on 25th May 1864. The greatest concern of the Brethren who established the Jersey Masonic Temple Company in November 1862 was finance. Funds were raised in many ways but new legislation on Limited Liability that same year allowed joint stock companies to be formed. These circumstances led to the creation of one of the great ephemeral curiosities unique to the Island: the 1866 issue of the Jersey Masonic One Pound Note. One example of this rare currency item survives in the Museum.

As we entered the building through the side door, Dennis directed us into the Provincial room where we enjoyed a first taste of Masonic artefacts. Several interesting prints decorate the walls, including an early 18th century edition of William Hogarth's famous 'Night'. On display on well-illuminated shelves is a range of gavels in their original decorative presentation boxes and the top shelves exhibit a few select pieces of early Masonic pottery. One large Sunderland jug struck our attention immediately. The attractive transfer decoration was that of a man-of-war, NORTHUMBERLAND 74, the number referring to the vessel's 74 guns. Although unidentified, the design suggests that Moore & Co of Southwick produced this piece, between 1789, when the company was founded and 1830. Typical also is the decorative ditty in one of the panels on the side of the jug:

> Let Masonry from Pole to Pole
> Her sacred Laws expand
> Far as the mighty waters roll
> To wash remotest land
> That virtue has not left mankind
> Her social maxims prove

For stamped upon the masons mind
Are unity and love

This is the first verse of an old song published in William Preston's 1796 edition of *Illustrations of Masonry*. There is a Jersey connection in the name and date painted on top of the glaze: *Jeane Mourant 1845* - a well-known Jersey mason. Upstairs in the Museum we found a matching jug in the identical Sunderland style and decorated with the same transfer. It appears that these were originally purchased in London and brought back to Jersey where Mourant added his name and the date. Two other pairs of 'Jersey' jugs complement a rather nice collection of Worcester, Staffordshire and Sunderland earthenwear of various

styles and periods. A rare unidentified hexagonal pair of exceedingly attractive white pottery jugs have golden Masonic emblems as decorations. The jugs were clearly intended as utilitarian implements, probably custom ordered. The logo reads, *Farmers Lodge No. 302 Jersey*, now the Yarborough Lodge No. 244. A second matching pair of jugs are attractively coloured with a dark blue line across the lip of the jug and another encircling it on either side of the coat of arms of the United Grand Lodge. The word JERSEY is stencilled below.

Dennis takes particular pride in the extensive Library he has assisted in re-building over the last few decades. It was first put together by Loge La Cesaree in 1858 and passed on to the Province some years later. The boost to the library holding, however, came with the recent bequest of the late Cosby Jackson, a Past Master of Quatuor Coronati Lodge. It now includes, among many other volumes, a first edition of Anderson's *Constitutions*, all of the major exposures of the 18th Century, and a very wide selection, appropriately, of French texts. One series of manuscript ritual books in the library is worthy of attention. It is attributed to Dr Henry Hopkins, a talented and well-known Jersey mason, who 'published' a set of rituals in his own handwriting. The quaint symbolically annotated texts incorporate the Craft degrees as well as the opening and closing of Provincial Grand Lodge.

EMERGENCY REGALIA

The recovery from the German occupation is reflected in the small collection of emergency aprons that were distributed to the Brethren at the first Lodge meetings following the war. The Germans had either looted or burnt all of the regalia and much of the furnishings stored in the Masonic Hall. The Brethren, eager to meet as soon as possible, created the aprons from various materials, ranging from linen and calico to starched paper, on which the emblems of Craft and Royal Arch were faithfully reproduced with paint, pen and ink. Provincial Stewards were presented with their own red aprons. These remained in use for a year or more, until clothes rationing ceased and regalia was again available.

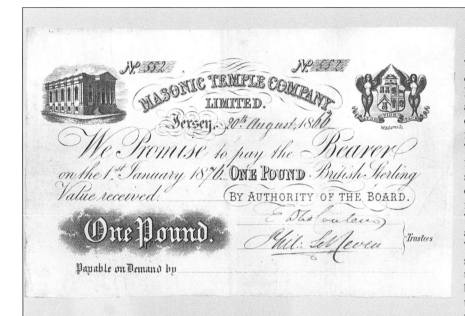

JERSEY BANKNOTE

The Jersey banknotes are unique and exceedingly rare. They are genuine Masonic banknotes, subject only to allowing a little leeway to the definition of a banknote. As the need for the financing of the newly built Masonic Temple in Jersey increased in 1866, a few masons came up with an ingenious scheme to raise funds: a circulating currency note that was effectively an interest free guaranteed ten year loan. The One Pound notes, issued by authority of the board of the Masonic Temple Company over a period of several months of the same year, had all the ingredients of a legal tender banknote. The design, which resembled the Bank of England, One Pound note, was executed by William Adams, Provincial Grand Secretary of Jersey from 1857. They were known as *'redeemable certificates'* ; perfectly legal issues at the time. The Provincial Masonic coat of arms appears on the top right of the note and an engraved view of the Temple on the opposite side. The notes, hand numbered, dated, and signed, by the trustees state: *'Payable on Demand'*, the catch lies in the printed repayment date, ten years after issue! An added clause: *Payable to the Sultan of Turkey and the Khedive of Egypt* indicates the contributory nature of the note. In October 1998 an example of the Jersey £1 note fetched £ 1,400 at a Phillips auction in London.

Dennis' adrenalin levels rose considerably when, in 1992, some colleagues making repairs to the roof of the building informed him that a number of items dating well before the occupation had been discovered in the attic. Quite a few unusual artefacts emerged. Until about 1860 the building was lit by gas fires for which special glass lamp globes, decorated with the square and compass, were used. Eight of these original globes were found and soon used as lampshades in the anteroom to the main hall, several additional ones are on display in the Museum. Also discovered were a number of local soda siphons, which caused considerable furore in Provincial Grand Lodge. Freemason, Peter P Deslandes, a Jersey merchant, had been effectively disciplined in October 1879, for claiming the square and compass design on the bottles to be his own Trade Mark!

The Museum can be visited by appointment Monday to Friday 10.00 to 4.00 by telephoning Dennis Perrin at 01534 851105 or the Provincial Grand Secretary (Bro Barry de la Mare) 01534-853084.

All photographs by Michael Baigent.

MISSING

The depleted collection of books in the Jersey Library following the war was enhanced by the return of some 250 books by the British Army, all of which have a note attached to the bookplate stating: *This book was looted by the Germans January 1941 and returned to Jersey by the British Army in March 1947.* Among these is a rare booklet which was presented to the library by a local brother in 1935, entitled *Statutes of the Royal and Exalted Religious Military Order, Grand Elected Masonic Knight Templars of St John of Jerusalem, Palestine, Rhodes of Heredom*, dated 2 June 1791 (revised edition 1809), coinciding with the election of Thomas Dunckerley as head of the Order. The title is a quaint reminder of the confusion of the degrees and orders in pre-

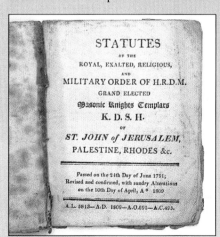

union days. It incorporates a foldout list of Knights Templar encampments between 1790 and 1810 and copies of correspondence between Jackson – who rediscovered the booklet in 1972 - and the Librarian at Grand Lodge. The letters in question mention the existence of a Charter attached to the Statutes and signed by several Knights Templar, including Johann Christian Buchurdt, and the counter signatures of Waller Rodwell Wright, Vice Chancellor and Robert Gill, Registrar. This document is now missing from the Library. The Province of Jersey would be grateful to hear from anyone who may know its whereabouts.

THE TWIN GLOBES

One of the most important and valuable items stolen by the Nazis were two fourteen-inch Terrestrial and Celestial globes created by the famed Cary family of globe makers and dated circa 1810. The Germans had photographed the lodge room to allow its recreation in an antimasonic exhibition in Belgrade, in 1942, and the globes appear in one of these photographs. They have never since been found. They have, however, been replaced by somewhat simpler globes and columns presented to the Provincial Grand Lodge by Freemason Stanley Amy, an amateur cabinet maker, who converted two of the posters of an antique bed to two decorative and handsome pillars mounted with celestial and terrestrial globes. The globes do not match, the celestial being an earlier French globe whilst the terrestrial is in a later English version, but they do handsomely decorate the lodge room and are a constant reminder of the beautiful furniture that once decorated the Temple

MASONIC PAINTINGS IN A BERKSHIRE CHURCH

DAVID SERMON REPORTS ON A REMARKABLE FIND IN ALDERMASTON

Interior of the Church of St. Mary. Aldermaston.

Charles Edward Keyser, 1853 - 1929, was a highly successful late Victorian businessman looking for a country seat when his sister, Agnes, drew his attention to Aldermaston Court which reminded her of Sandringham where she had been a guest. Offered for sale by auction at The Hind's Head in the nearby village of Aldermaston, it comprised over 2500 acres of parkland, meadows and farms, and boasted a lake as well as a splendid mansion, making it an ideal purchase. Keyser grasped the opportunity, bid £160,000 and thus became Lord of the Manor of Aldermaston and Patron of the Parish Church of St Mary the Virgin which stood just yards from his new home.

The son of a stockbroker, Keyser had progressed from Eton to Cambridge where he read Law and acquired his MA; he was initiated into Isaac Newton University Lodge, No. 859, to commence what turned out to be a truly extraordinary masonic career. Turning aside from Law, he followed his father into the City where his energy and acumen built a fortune on his own account to match the one he later inherited. This wealth enabled him to pursue and distinguish himself in his chosen field becoming a published authority on English Church Architecture specialising in mediaeval churches.

When he arrived at Aldermaston Court in 1893, Keyser, at 40, was a happily married man of benevolent disposition with a son and two daughters, moving easily and naturally into the role of the Squire. From the start he read the lessons each Sunday and later became Churchwarden, an office he held to the end of his life. Meanwhile there was much to be done. Essential structural work was put in hand at the Church and new oak seating installed for the comfort of the worshippers. Two of the village almshouses were rebuilt and a completely new Village Hall soon erected in a pleasing Tudor style but the master plan for the beautification of St Mary the Virgin would take longer to accomplish.

There had been a Church at Aldermaston from Norman times and the building Keyser took in hand retained some stained glass from the thirteenth to sixteenth centuries as well as traces of early wall paintings. To a man who ten years before had compiled a list of the buildings of Britain that contained mural paintings this constituted a challenge and an opportunity but the security of the building determined that the glass should take priority.

Philip Harry Newman, a competent and experienced artist was recruited in 1895 to begin the work and he recovered thirteenth century medallions depicting *The Annunciation* and *The Coronation of the Virgin* from the former east window and re-set them to form two new windows for the chancel. A second glassmaker, Charles

The wall painting to the left of the altar is believed to include a portrait of Mrs. Keyser but no one is now sure which figure represents her. The wall painting to the right of the altar depicts Charles Keyser (upper centre) with his Edwardian moustache. His daughter Muriel is shown below as an angel. The text beneath each painting is of relevance to Rose Croix Freemasons.

Eamer Kempe, known in his lifetime as 'The Master of Glass', came on board and in 1897 - 98 created a focus for the devotions of the congregation in the form of representations of *The Crucifixion, The Nativity* and *The Three Great Prophets*, each in sections running across the triple lancet at the east end of the sanctuary. His

other five contributions were *The Adoration of the Magi, St Michael* and *Salutation of the Virgin*, in the chancel together with St George and a splendid St Anne Instructing the Virgin in the nave.

Alongside this work, Newman reset the fine armorial of *Lords of the Manor* in the Lady Chapel and made *Abraham and*

Isaac as well as *Adam Naming the Animals* for the nave. In the choice of subjects used both men pay tribute to the historic dedication of the church while extending the scope for contemplation.

Their Patron was also busy at this time getting elected to Berkshire County Council; taking on the duties of Justice of the Peace and High Sheriff as well as President of the Berkshire Archaeological Society and publishing an article about Aldermaston Church in a national Journal.

The next year he became Founding Master of Aldermaston Lodge, No. 2760, which was consecrated at The Hind's Head. The jewel struck to commemorate this event can be seen at The Museum of Freemasonry, Freemasons' Hall, London. The lodge still meets regularly.

Altogether Keyser was a subscribing member of thirty-six lodges, Past Master of twenty-four, including six of those he founded, yet still he found time for many other orders. By the end of his life, he had completed sixty-one prodigiously active

Two explicitly masonic symbols of the square and compasses, level and plumb rule, below the painting of Solomon on the north wall.

years in Freemasonry and risen to Grand Rank in Craft, Mark and Royal Arch. He became Provincial Grand Master for Hertfordshire in both Craft and Mark and was Inspector General in Rose Croix for what was then the Southern District of England. Perhaps his greatest Masonic achievement was becoming Supreme Grand Ruler in the Order of the Secret Monitor.

Kempe having departed, it fell to Newman to complete the glazing project by putting *Christ Giving Sight to the Blind*, from Sulhampstead Church, into the vestry as well as resetting 8 *Forster Armorials* from the old east window and designing a completely new *Covenant Between Laban and Jacob* for the nave. The fabric now being watertight the way was open for phase two, the wall paintings, but a significant event took place first. Keyser proposed his trusted artist, Newman, as the second candidate in Aldermaston Lodge and his three ceremonies took place in July, August and September 1902.

Brother Newman's initiation had a profound effect on him: it stimulated a great flowering of inspiration for the seventeen paintings with which he clad the walls in various parts of the church over the next six years, by which time he was on the way to the chair of Aldermaston Lodge which he eventually occupied in 1911.

Many of these works are conventional subjects like *St Michael Warring Against the Vices, St Margaret, Allegory of Sacred Music* which, while assisting devotion and pleasing the eye, imply no masonic connotation. *Faith Hope and Charity* extolled over the vestry arch and *Let Your Light So Shine Before Men....* emblazoned on the north wall as a prompt to benevolence, might well strike a particular chord in masonic breasts. Royal Arch masons would doubtless examine the east side of the Lady chapel arch with special care when contemplating Newman's interpretation of *Moses Descending From Mt Horeb* though the uninitiated would discern no special significance.

However, *Solomon Dedicating the Temple at Jerusalem* is in a completely different category. Prominent on the north wall of the nave, it is huge,

Founder's jewel of the Aldermaston Lodge, No. 2760 presented to Charles Keyser, 1899.

Wall painting on the north wall depicting Solomon dedicating the temple in Jerusalem.

colourful and contemporary in style in contrast to the more tradition tenor of the others. Fresh from his ceremonies, Newman has shown King Solomon in glowing red robes at the moment recorded in *I Kings 8.55* where, having completed his long prayer unto the Lord, he rose from the altar with his hands spread up to heaven and he stood and blessed the congregation of Israel with a loud voice.

It is not difficult to identify the figure kneeling behind him as the Assistant High Priest who officiated at this dedication. Newman signed the painting on one of the scrolls in the lower right foreground and, pinning his heart firmly on his sleeve, added roundels beneath the painting, one showing the sacred volume complete with square and compasses, the other depicting the level and plumb-rule earlier used to villainous effect.

Even this moving representation is eclipsed by Newman's comprehensive decorations to the east wall of the sanctuary. Here above Kempe's triple lancet east window we have a vision of *Christ in Majesty*, the Saviour ringed by the four evangelists characterised by an Angel a Lion, an Ox and an Eagle with Alpha and Omega symbols above. Mary, His mother, kneels on the left as does St John, the beloved disciple, on the right.

Beneath St John is a panel containing a dozen male saints and martyrs including His earthly father Joseph, wearing a conspicuously Edwardian moustache and modelled by Charles Keyser, and his daughter, Muriel, attending in the character of an Angel. The corresponding female panel below Mary is believed to include a portrait of Mrs Keyser, but no one is sure which.

The composition is completed by a row of six castellated arches and angels bearing shields representing the implements of the Passion. That showing the Crown of Thorns and another with a ladder and *INRI*, the superscription on the cross, must draw the eyes of Rose Croix masons who will also note the ribbon quoting *Isaiah 53.5*: 'He was wounded for our transgression, He was bruised for our iniquities'.

The project at Aldermaston, conceived and funded by Brother Keyser, realised by Kempe and Brother Newman, was accomplished in just over a decade but the legacy has lost none of its former lustre, more than a century later. Keyser employed Newman again to design nine overtly masonic stained glass windows for the apse of the chapel he donated to the Royal Masonic School for Boys at Bushey. Sadly, these are no longer readily accessible to members of the Craft but any of us could gain welcome spiritual refreshment by a visit to the Church of St Mary the Virgin, Aldermaston.

David Sermon is a Past Master of the Lodge of Economy, No. 76, Winchester and holds Provincial Grand Rank. He also holds an advanced rank in the Ancient and Accepted Scottish Rite. He has contributed articles of masonic interest to Ars Quatuor Coronatorum *as well as to* Freemasonry Today.

All photographs, except the founder's jewel, by Michael Baigent.

SPECIALISTS IN FREEMASONRY

Yasha Beresiner Completes His Review Of The Library And Museum At Freemasons' Hall, Dublin

Sphinx in the Egyptian Chapter Room.

Elizabeth St Leger was born in 1693, the fourth child and only daughter of 1st Viscount Doneraile. The story reports that she was caught in the act of spying in her father's library in County Cork where a second-degree ceremony was taking place and at which her father was the Master; as a result of this, the story adds, she was initiated into Freemasonry some time around 1710-1713. She is buried in the cathedral in Cork and an apron attributed to her is today on display in the Provincial Grand Lodge of Munster, at Cork.

From the archives of Grand Lodge, with which our hostess Rebecca Hayes the Archivist is particularly familiar, she was able to retrieve for us what is believed to be Elizabeth Leger's leather bound diary with a damaged cover and clasp and entries beginning 29 July 1753. The entries are in fact a record of recipes - the first a medical recipe for a cold - payments and receipts and transcripts of bills of exchange, several for considerable sums of money. The evidence that the

A woman's apron for a charity event.

One perennial legend associated with Irish Freemasonry is that of Mrs Elizabeth (Richard) Aldworth neé St Leger, 'The Lady Freemason'. While very little of her story can be confirmed by solid documentation there is certainly evidence, according to the Grand Lodge of Ireland, of masonic activity relating to her story: she was very involved in masonic charitable work and a patron of the Craft during her lifetime.

Early hand embroidered masonic apron.

Military Lodges with a display of the regimental banner, drums and lancets and other military artefacts dated 1796, of the first Volunteer Lodge of Ireland. The importance of these displays in the historic content of the development of Freemasonry worldwide cannot be over emphasised. It was Irish military Lodges that were the first to be given ambulatory warrants in 1732, referred to as 'travelling lodge' warrants in England. The beginnings of Freemasonry in the early 18th century in New South Wales and Tasmania as well as the West Indies is directly attributed to the introduction of the Craft to those territories by Irish Military Lodges.

The two central cabinets display some exceptional jewels, many manufactured in the late eighteenth century by the Irish jeweller and Freemason, James Brush. He specialised in masonic jewellery and an excellent example of the quality of his work is to be found in the large commemorative silver encrusted jewel, set with paste stones in a framework design, inscribed:

*Presented to Charles Scales by the
Brethren of Good Intent Lodge No.387
12th December 1811*

James Brush's commercial interests in producing jewels for the Grand Lodge and its officers also extended to his considerable interest in the charitable aspects of the Craft. He was instrumental in 1792 in the foundation, with members of Royal Arch Chapter, No. 190, of the 'Society for Schooling of the Orphan

notebook is the property of Elizabeth Aldworth herself is to be found in a loose sheet of paper inserted into the diaries in which the manuscript entries of several receipts are personally signed *Eliz. Aldworth*. For the 275th anniversary celebrations of the Grand Lodge in Ireland in 2000, the Museum purchased a contemporary painting of Mrs Richard Aldworth attributed to the Irish portrait artist Garret Morphy (fl.1676 - d.1716).

Though the Grand Lodge Museum does not own Elizabeth Aldworth's original apron, it possesses a stupendous collection of early aprons made of silk, linen and pure lambskin, all of them decorated with the emblems and symbols of the Craft and other Orders. They are carefully protected and pleasingly displayed in frames on the wall and a dozen pull out trays, each carefully labelled and accurately dated.

Striking among the many examples is an intricately hand-embroidered apron with the familiar design of the allegorical figures of Charity, Truth and Prudence flanked by two columns. Interestingly the exact same design, now professionally engraved, is used as a transfer on an adjoining apron on display. The

implication of this repetitive pattern is that there must have been, in the 1830s, a common source for these apron designs.

A large cabinet is dedicated to Irish

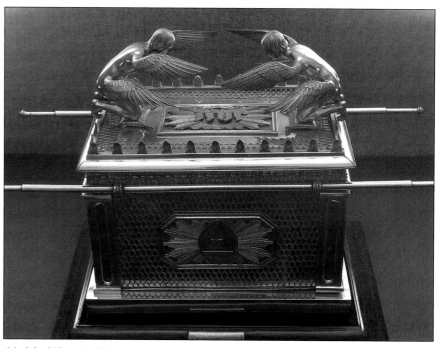

Model of The Ark of The Covenant still in use today.

Whilst out of the main Museum room, we had the opportunity to view the several Lodge rooms in the building, each decorated in its own, different architectural style and each dedicated to an Order beyond the Craft. On the first floor opposite the Grand Temple is the little corridor that leads to the colourful, if not extravagant Egyptian Chapter room, fully decorated in plush red upholstery. Hand coloured sphinxes and pharaoh-heads act as seven-branch-candelabra wall-stands; it is not called the Egyptian room for nothing. The Mark degree, totally under the wing of the Supreme Grand Chapter of Ireland, also has a dedicated room, which at first appears an anomaly as all the 'action' for the order normally takes place in Chapter. As it is, the room portraying paintings of the Grand Masters of the Order, is in use on those rare occasions when the degree is separately worked or conferred.

Female Children of Distressed Masons'. This was later to become the 'Masonic Female Orphan School', which only closed its doors in 1972, followed by the Boys school in 1981. Dedicated rooms in the lower ground floor of Freemasons' Hall pinpoint the emphasis that Grand Lodge placed on the Charities in past centuries. Here the walls are covered with photographs and illustrations that give a visual history of the activities of the orphanages and schools through the years.

One of the most popular events was the occasional open market, which culminated in a huge bazaar and 'fancy fair' over a five-day period in May 1892 to celebrate the centenary of the Orphan School Charity. It was specially organised by the Committee of Charity at the Royal Dublin Society premises to raise funds for a new building. A beautiful gold and enamel snuffbox by West & Sons, on exhibit in the Museum, was presented to Lord Justice Gerald Fitzgibbon, Chairman of the Centenary committee, to thank him for his efforts and commemorates the event. The lid depicts two children of the School dressed in the 1792 and 1892 uniforms respectively. Individual Lodges and Masons' wives and children from the school ran the Bazaar stalls. The Duke of York Lodge, No. 25, produced the quaintest masonic attire ever fashioned for the ladies manning their stalls. Aprons were made to look like elongated versions of a standard masonic apron.

Some other of the excellent Irish medals and jewels have a 'JT' mark on them, referring to the well-known Dublin jeweller of the early 1800s, John Tate. The last of the medals that drew my attention in particular is the one dedicated to Dr William Chetwode Crawly (1844-1916).

Crawley was the greatest Irish masonic historian. His imposing portrait, painted whilst he acted as Grand Treasure of the Grand Lodge of Ireland between 1903 and 1908, hangs in the anteroom to the main Temple. Crawley is the author of the standard work on Irish Freemasonry *Caementaria Hibernica*. Of greatest relevance to our visit was that he was, with Francis Crossle, Grand Secretary in 1894, the instigator of the formation of a Grand Lodge Museum. A past Master of the Quatuor Coronati Lodge 2076 (EC), Crawley spent his life writing and collecting books. He died in 1916 and Grand Lodge purchased his Library of some twenty five hundred eighteenth and nineteenth century masonic books intact, for which purpose custom-made cabinets were built. Previously the Grand Lodge had purchased the important Furnell and Crosslé libraries and this new acquisition changed the status of the Grand Lodge library collection to one of major consequence and importance. The overall library now consists of some twelve thousand books.

The Crawley collection is given place of pride and is housed in the same purpose

18th century gold and enamel snuff box depicting two children of the School for Orphans.

Portrait of Dr. William Chetwode Crawley (1844-1916), with a commemorative medal to the left.

As we approached the *Knights Templar Room*, an additional small stained glass panel has been embedded into the wall and is visible from both sides. It is the gift made to the Grand Priory by H R H Albert Edward Prince of Wales, Grand Master of the Religious and Military Orders of the Temple and is dated 7 April 1873, the sad year of the failed attempt to unite the various chivalric orders under one single roof. The purpose-built room dedicated to the Order of the Knights Templar is sombre and impressive, with heavy wooden seats and a well-equipped altar. Through the adjoining corridor we reached the *Grand Chapter of Prince Masons Room* dedicated to the Ancient and Accepted Rite and decorated in a mixture of mock Tudor and Gothic Styles. A very recent Temple in the building has been dedicated to Knight Masonry, with which we are not familiar in England. It was founded in 1923 and contains the Degrees that are worked under the jurisdiction of the *Grand Council of Knight Masons* who are headed by a Great Chief. The degrees worked are *The Knight Of The Sword, The Knight Of The East and The Knight Of The East And West*. The purpose of the Order is to give a semblance of chronological continuity to the various Orders and degrees of Freemasonry.

built cabinets in Rebecca's office. The books have now been amalgamated with the remainder of the pre-1851 volumes

Display of Knight's Templar regalia.

and are now fully catalogued with extended entries. Rebecca took great pride in showing me the collection. The books cover the spectrum of masonic literature with considerable emphasis on Irish Freemasonry and the whole range of Constitutions, Exposures, Appendant Orders, Ritual and History as well as sections dedicated to Philosophy and Ethics, Ancient Mysteries, Symbolism, Fraternal organisations amongst others. A foreign section is arranged in geographical order by country. It includes several of the classical French and German texts. They are all well bound copies in good condition. The remainder of the library is more accessible to view. Some two thousand books are displayed on several glassed and locked shelves along the walls of the lounge bar on the ground floor.

On the way to the second floor we passed the outstanding stained glass windows on the landings. The four colourful side panels represent Faith, Hope, Charity and Patience and were made by J P Clarke and Sons. These were originally installed in the Masonic Female

Orphan School between 1894 and 1902 and moved to Freemasons' Hall in 1977, when the school closed. The large central panel has the portrait of Shakespeare and is dated 1916. The Shakespeare Lodge and Chapter No.143, donated the glass pane to commemorate the tercentenary of the death of Shakespeare on 23rd April 1616. It is also in memory of those who lost their lives in the 1914-1918 war.

The Museum and Library at the Grand Lodge of Ireland in Dublin is easy to view and understand, and fascinating to study. It is in the capable hands of professionals, efficiently and conscientiously run. Rebecca showed us that you do not have to be a Freemason to show fraternal love for masonic objects and books - and your guests.

The Hall is open to the public weekdays 9.30 to 5.00pm and for guided tours for groups by prior arrangement. For details please call (353)1676 1337 and ask for Rebecca Hayes. Website www.irish-freemasons.org

Photographs by Michael Baigent.

ARCHITECT, FREEMASON AND VISIONARY

KATY HOUNSELL-ROBERT REVEALS THE ART NOUVEAU GENIUS OF VICTOR HORTA

Stairway in the Musée Horta in the Rue Américane, the house which Horta built for himself as his home and studio.
                                                                                            photo: akg images

The exit from the Gare Midi in Brussels leads straight out into the wide square named after Baron Victor Pierre Horta. Further along, in the rue Americaine, is Musée Horta and you cannot go far in Brussels without encountering places and buildings bearing his name, and sporting the romantic curves and classical proportions of Art Nouveau, with which he is associated. He was undoubtedly one of the most famous 19th century architects and skilled lecturers in architecture, but perhaps it is less well known that he initially drew much of his inspiration from his dedication to Freemasonry.

This ambitious perfectionist was born in Ghent on 6 January 1861. He was initially attracted to music as a career, but soon found he was more interested in art and design, and decided instead to study architecture. He had the good fortune to become an assistant to Alphonse Balat, Architect to the King and lecturer at L'Université Libre de Bruxelles, who led him to expect the highest standards of himself, in realising his own potential.

In the 1880s, partly in coming to terms with the reality of the new independent state of Belgium with its new boundaries, and partly because of the enormous power of the established Roman Catholic Church, Belgian architecture and artistic design became embedded in nostalgia, harking back to the days when Flanders was a wealthy power. Only Neo-Gothic or Flemish renaissance designs were used, and no reputable craftsman would think of using new materials like steel or glass. Furthermore, only the nobility and the rich were thought worthy and able to appreciate beautiful houses and gardens and to have elegant ornaments, and even they were discouraged from using anything outside the old-fashioned designs. Horta, inspired by the astounding British Crystal Palace master-minded by Queen Victoria's Consort, Prince Albert, and influenced by the French impressionists, was one of many designers who wanted to use new shapes, colours and materials, and also to give the less privileged the chance to enjoy public places that were beautiful and uplifting as well as serving their intended purpose.

ART AND FREEMASONRY

With Horta's high ideals and youthful desire to express his creative ideas, it was natural that he should join forces with other young men with similar ideals, among them Autrique, Tassel, Charbo and Lefebure. They all belonged to 'Les Amis Philanthropes', one of the most liberal and politically powerful lodges in Belgium, No. 5, in the Grand Orient. They invited him to join and his first meeting in the lodge, in rue du Persil next to Place des Martyrs, thrilled him.

He found in it a movement of like minds and uplifting ideals as he later wrote in his memoirs: 'Great returns from a small investment, especially since a meeting of Masons wasn't an architectural association!

Victor Horta's House. photo: Katy Hounsell-Robert

But it was a respite for the spirits, an excitation of one's energies . . . Just as there are those born to be in government, there are those who are moulded in the "dough" of opposition: I was one of the latter politically, aesthetically, in my sentiments. By nature, without flattering ourselves, we all were. In this closed circle, with its views about the infinity of knowledge, there could only be amicable understanding; what pleased one pleased the others.'

He was initiated on 31 December 1888 and was passed to the second degree in December 1889. His close friends in his lodge thought so highly of his skills that

they tried to persuade the Academic Council to appoint him to a vacant post as a lecturer at L'Université Libre de Bruxelles. This had been founded in 1834 by the Esperance masonic lodge, under the leadership of the famous Belgian painter and engraver Fernand Verhaegen, as an alternative to the Catholic Universities such as Louvain, and was based on masonic principles, where the curriculum supported 'freedom of conscience . . . rejecting all principles of authority in philosophical, intellectual and moral matters.'

This incensed the Catholic bishops so much that they condemned all masonic lodges in 1838, which led to them all combining to form the first Liberal Party, 'Alliance Liberale'. Article 135 decreed by the Grand Orient in 1833 forbade political and religious discussion in the lodges. From 1854 to 1866 this was repealed, and even after it was reinstated lodges got round it by regrouping outside official meetings.

As well as Horta's friends, Alphonse Balat, his teacher, also approached the president of the University, Emile de Mot, a high ranking mason. However De Mot disapproved of 'preferential treatment for Masons' and nearly rejected Horta out of hand. Horta did eventually get the job, largely because of his own talent and dedication, but it caused considerable disagreement on the Academic Council for some time.

MAISON AUTRIQUE

His friends continued to support him, and one of his first commissions in his second year after becoming a Master Mason in 1892, when he was not yet 30, was to design a house for Eugene

Autrique, now a qualified engineer. Horta was determined that although it would be a fairly small town house in an ordinary road, it would be given all the latest innovations and attention to detail that he employed in all his work.

The Maison Autrique in Chausée de Haecht has recently been restored, and with clever projection and use of audio tapes has been brought to life as it was in the late 19th century. In the semi-basement kitchen white sheets hang up to dry in the heat from the stove, while sounds of cooking are to be heard. In the bathroom there is a projection of a lady bathing and the sound of running water is heard. Every

The Dining Room in Horta's House.
photo: Katy Hounsell-Robert

room is beautifully proportioned and delightfully light and Horta has considered all the needs of the family both above and below stairs. He even used hand-painted linoleum, the latest easy-to-clean flooring and an improvement on draughty ill-fitting boards. It is on the outside of the house however that Horta, with the approval of Autrique, embellished it with the many symbols which said to the world that it was a house whose owner and architect were not afraid to proclaim their masonic affiliation.

The actual design of Maison Autrique is more medieval Tuscan than anything else, perhaps as a protest against Catholic conservative architecture. The designs on the mouldings, frames and brackets are abstract, but the wrought iron grilles on the kitchen windows contain certain symbols of triangles and shapes of hooded cobra or the uraeus on a pharaonic crown. Higher up are similar symbols on the parapet of the pseudo loggia and bel étage window, echoing the

Living Room in Horta's house.   photo: Katy Hounsell-Robert

Victor Horta at work in his studio.   photo: Horta Museum

Egyptian motifs decorating the Grand Temple in Brussels. It is interesting that the pyramid triangle identified Autrique and Horta as members of 'Les Amis Philanthropes', as this symbol appears on the reverse of the lodge medal.

EGYPTIAN SYMBOLS

By the time Horta built Emile Tassel's house, although he used a number of Egyptian symbols in his original design, the only ones to be seen are two purely decorative iron columns on either side of the staircase leading up to the main floor which probably represent the two pillars of Jachin and Boaz standing at the entrance to Solomon's Temple. Horta was never short of masonic clients, but rarely used masonic symbols on the buildings after this, as the clients often held high positions in authority and needed to be discreet about their loyalties.

The Catholic authorities were horrified with Horta's designs and Art Nouveau in general, and condemned it 'on the ground that its sinuous curves appeared to be the mark of a totally pagan lubriciousness, and forbade its teaching in the [Catholic] architectural schools of Saint-Luc.'

From that time, Art Nouveau became associated with Freemasonry and its liberal politics. However Horta never involved himself in political fighting. He agreed with the masonic moral and ethical issues, but his particular style of Art Nouveau was unique and apolitical.

THE GRAND PLACE

In 1899 he designed a masonic plaque, executed by the sculptor Victor Rousseau, in commemoration of Charles Buls, a former Master of 'Les Amis Philanthropes' who had played an important part in the development of Belgian Freemasonry. As he was also largely responsible for preserving the beautiful historic Grand Place, it is placed there under the arcade of La Maison de l'Etoile. On the plaque a girl holding a compass and scroll represents homage to Master Architects, while a boy holding a lighted oil lamp represents the beginning of the quest for esoteric knowledge, enlightenment and immortality. Around them are acacia branches symbolising rebirth and by which the Master Masons identified the tomb of the murdered Hiram, architect of Solomon's Temple.

As Horta's career progressed, he was commissioned to design many public buildings, among which, in 1896, was La Maison du Peuple for the Workers Party. The inaugural speech in 1899 congratulated and thanked him for his 'sensitive understanding of our needs and our aspirations. Horta has symbolised these and the work of the party in his glorious edifice.' He was also responsible for the Gare Centrale, the Palais des Beaux Arts and several prestigious shops, and even found time to build his own house in 1898, now Musée Horta, and give lectures at the Academies of Brussels and Antwerp.

In the First World War when he was over 50 and a famous architect he left war torn Belgium and came with other masons to London. Here, together with Count Eugène Goblet d'Alviella and others, he founded the 'Albert de Belgique' Lodge, under the Grand Orient of Belgium, but meeting in London. They met at the Waldorf Astoria Hotel in Aldwych where, on 29 May 1915, Horta himself gave a lecture entitled 'The Reorganisation of the Brussels Art School'. Horta also came to London in the Second World War, by which time King Albert had conferred on him the title of Baron for services to Architecture.

He died in September 1947 at the age of 86 and is buried in the cemetery of Ixelles, a suburb of Brussels. His grave is simple; he is only fourth on the list of the interred, and his achievements hardly mentioned. La Maison du Peuple was later demolished.

He lived for his work, which cost him his marriage and most of his friends, but he was completely true and loyal to art and its ethics. If the cost of building his design exceeded his quotation for example, he would waive his fee. It could be said that he reflected masonic ideals within his work all his life.

With acknowledgments to the following for their help: Frank Langenaken; Michel Brodsky; Mme Aubry; Antonella Roberti.

The stairway in Magasins Wolfers, Brussels, built in 1906 as a workshop and premises of the goldsmith Philippe Wolfers.

photo: akg images

ROBBIE BURNS' MAUL, AND ALL...

YASHA BERESINER VISITS THE MUSEUM OF THE GRAND LODGE OF SCOTLAND

The face of a Scottish made and decorated long case clock, about 1840.

Edinburgh is a beautiful City and Grand Lodge is situated in its heart. The bus I took to get to the George Street address let me down at the stop named *Freemasons' Hall*; festive decorations around the Street had one of the Christmas trees highlighted *Grand Lodge of Scotland*. This overt approach to freemasonry symbolised the distinct differences between our Grand Lodges.

The Grand Lodge building on four floors has the ground floor dedicated to the Grand Temple. On the third floor are the Museum and Library and Robert Cooper's impressive office. Robert, curator and effective librarian (a Grand Librarian as a Grand Lodge Officer is appointed annually), is an affable and jovial man, with vast knowledge and who takes great pride in the Masonic heritage of Scotland. He was at pains to explain his view of the striking difference between Scottish and English Freemasonry: stone masons (inadequately, according to Robert, referred to as *operatives*) met in their lodges, after a hard days work, to relax and enjoy the festive board in the comfort of informal surroundings. To these convivial evenings non-masons or Freemasons (inadequately, *speculative*) were welcomed and joined the stonemasons in their Lodges. Thus in Scotland available evidence points to a natural progression of stone mason to Freemason whereas in England the Freemason, Robert emphasises, was probably an 'invented' concept.

Whilst the Grand Lodge of Scotland was consecrated in 1736, Freemasonry was in evidence in the country a century before. The very title of the ruler of the Craft, *Grand Master Mason* was a direct manifestation of the link to stone masons and the impressive collection of mauls a further reminder.

Unlike England, the gavel is a non-existent implement in Scottish Lodges who use the maul, the working mason's tool, exclusively. On display is the large decorative symbolic maul especially made for use at the consecration of the Grand Lodge in 1736. It was also used by King George VI, Grand Master Mason, at the 200th anniversary celebrations in 1936.

Amongst the dozen or more mauls in

Painting by Stewart Watson in 1787 depicting Robert Burns' inauguration as Poet Laureate of Canongate Kilwinning Lodge, No. 2, the same year.

the collection, one is of wood from a ship of the Spanish Armada; another is that used by Robert Burns. It belonged to the St Andrews Lodge, No. 179, Dumfries, where Burns was Senior Warden at the time of his death in 1796. His signature approving the bylaws of the Lodge appears in the Lodge minute book. The mauls are also replicated in an impressive collection of whisky flasks made of pottery with elaborate Masonic designs embedded into the surface.

Robert Burns, rightly honoured as a great poet and

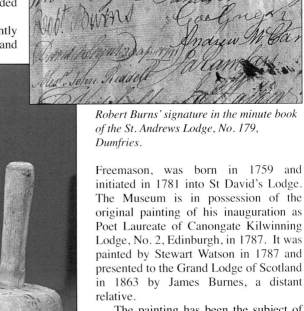

Robert Burns' signature in the minute book of the St. Andrews Lodge, No. 179, Dumfries.

Freemason, was born in 1759 and initiated in 1781 into St David's Lodge. The Museum is in possession of the original painting of his inauguration as Poet Laureate of Canongate Kilwinning Lodge, No. 2, Edinburgh, in 1787. It was painted by Stewart Watson in 1787 and presented to the Grand Lodge of Scotland in 1863 by James Burnes, a distant relative.

The painting has been the subject of controversy on two counts: firstly it is dated as an event that took place on 1st March, whereas the minutes of Canongate Kilwinning Lodge do not show Burns to have been present in the Lodge on that date. Secondly many of the individuals depicted in the painting, all of whom have been definitely identified, were already dead by 1787. Both these apparent errors are attributed to artistic licence.

Master's mauls used in Scottish Lodges: left, that used by Robert Burns, right, an operative maul used in a lodge. Centre, large maul made in 1736 for use by the Grand Master.

At the end of the spacious *Long Gallery* are two Scottish long case clocks. The first of these is made by G & W MacGill in Paisley and is decorated to order, as was the custom. Clocks were sold with blank faces and the customer's designs were then drawn onto the façade. In this instance two masons in regalia stand arm in arm under a Royal Archway representing brotherly love and the four corners below depict Scotland with the thistle and St Andrew, England with the Union Jack, Ireland with a harp and Wales with a goat and leek. Several other masonic emblems are dispersed in the design. This beautifully restored clock dates to c.1840.

On the other side is an earlier clock of c.1820 by the Scottish makers Thomas Brydon of Brechin. The design includes, appropriately, a stone mason at work. Unusually the face has a half-minute panel. The third clock in the Hall was made in Linlithgo by Alex Nimmo and has an intricate brass and silver plate face. A more unusual and slightly smaller clock in the annex room completes the impressive collection. These were presented to Grand Lodge by private masons in whose homes the clocks would have seen practical use over the centuries.

Many of the differences between Scotland and England are to be found in the furnishings and dress of the Lodge and its members. There are several Scottish Lodge Officers not identifiable in England. A good instance is the Lodge Treasurer who was substituted by a *Box Master* in charge of a large and heavy wooden box in which the Lodge funds and other treasures were kept. An outstanding example dated 1737 on display belonged to the Haughfoot Lodge

Former chain and jewel of the Grand Master Mason of Scotland, worn until 1936.

(independent of Grand Lodge and so unnumbered) and the three keyholes indicate that no single member of the Lodge could have access to the contents.

Another office is that of Substitute Master of the Lodge. He will substitute for any absent Lodge office-bearer. The jewel by which this office is identified is identical to that of the Master but for the symbol of the sun in the centre of the Master's jewel. Excellent examples of this and many other officers' collar jewels dating back to the start of the eighteenth century are on display in the *Long Gallery*. The sun symbol in the centre of the various Master's jewels is often made of a range of precious stones and radiate in the sunlight that comes through the large windows. All the jewels have Scottish hallmarks. There is evidence of a square used as a Master's jewel in a stonemasons' lodge in 1707.

The same display case has a range of Prisoner of War jewels handcrafted and mounted in watchcases dating to the Seven-Year War of 1756 and the later Napoleonic Wars. The Museum also boasts one of the most comprehensive collections of Scottish Mark Masons' Tokens - in excess of four thousand different examples ranging from the early nineteenth century.

To the side are two contrasting collars, one is an elaborate heavy silver

THE FREE GARDENERS

Regalia of the *Free Gardeners*: a velvet apron with four letters representing the four rivers that flow through the Garden of Eden: *Pison, Gihon, Hiddekel* and *Euphrates*. The symbols and letters of the password of the order are also embroidered within an interlaced triangle referring to Adam, Solomon, Noah and the Olive symbol in the centre. The All Seeing Eye radiates from the rounded flap. Very recently documentation has come to light showing that the Free Gardeners practised Orders beyond their simple Craft degrees, similar in essence to the Royal Arch and other Orders within Freemasonry.

Velvet apron of the Free Gardeners who practiced Orders beyond their simple Craft degrees.

chain collar, hand decorated on each of the plates, which was worn by the Grand Master Mason until 1936. The present collar, first worn by King George VI at the 200th anniversary of the Grand Lodge of Scotland, replaced it. The other is a simple green cloth collar with a gold border and central emblem which was last worn in 1839

The panel above the jewels displays Masonic glass. It includes decanters, a peace glass made in 1918, all kind of drinking vessels ranging from long fluted 18th century pieces to a good collection of the heavy based firing glasses (which, incidentally, are rarely used in Scotland). The majority of these are not of Scottish manufacture. One set of sherry glasses is of Scottish make: a complete set of

Jewels of the Master - with the symbol of the sun in the centre - and the Deputy Master of a Scottish lodge.

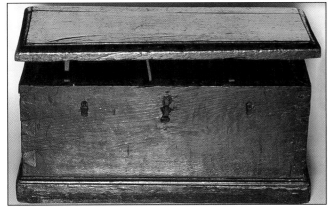

Treasurer's box needing three keys to gain access. Used by the Haughfoot Lodge, founded 1702, as a fully speculative lodge

twelve glasses was presented by Grand Lodge to Edward, Prince of Wales (later King Edward VIII) in December 1924. He, in turn, gave six of the glasses to Baron Kilmarnock who had hosted him during his visit and these were later presented to the Museum.

A single day's visit was not sufficient to cover the Museum's treasures. We will cover further aspects in the next article in this series.

The Museum at 96 George Street is open to the general public on weekdays from 9.00 am to 5.00 pm; on Saturday by special arrangement. Contact Robert Cooper through the Grand Lodge offices at 0131 225 5304.

All photographs courtesy of The Museum of The Grand Lodge of Scotland.

WORKING MEN'S ORDERS

Four aprons of Friendly Societies: the Freewrights, Freepotters, Freeshipwrights and Mechanics.

Displayed next to each other are the aprons of four Working-Men's Orders, not exclusively Scottish in origin, from the first half of the nineteenth century. The first is of *The Order of Freewrights*, the Carpenters, with a white background and gold montage of the square overlapping the compasses. The apron of *The Freepotters* depicts what appear to be either kilns or brick works and have added masonic symbols. The third is of *The Freeshipwrights*, depicting an anchor and the all Seeing Eye with two squares in a mirror image. The last, *The Independent United Order of Mechanics*, is most overtly Scottish depicting St Andrew with tartan colours and a Pascal lamb on the left of the ark of covenant. That of *The Hammermen* shows a large hand holding a hammer above an anvil. These several societies arose in imitation of Freemasonry, as the social and mutual aid clubs of actual working trade organisations.

Apron of the Hammermen.

STONE POEMS

BY MARTIN STEAD

The Land-mark

The service of *Commination or Denouncing of God's Anger and Judgements Against Sinners* is to be found in the *Book of Common Prayer*. Nowadays, it is seldom heard.

Now walk more warily in these dangerous
   days,
Upon the tablets read the precepts ten,
And keep your feet from broad and crooked
   ways,
And to each sentence, cry, "Amen! Amen!"
Now kneel and pray:
For cursed is he that slayeth innocence,
And cursed who leads the blind out of their
   way,
And cursed who taketh man for his defence.
The sons of Adam and the heirs of sin,
Must listen to the godly discipline.
But one thing yet remains – be still, and
   hark:
Cursed is he who removeth his neighbour's
   land-mark.

For when the land-marks fail, who can sow
And know that where he sows there shall he
   reap?
The widow and the fatherless neglected go,
Our children curse their parents, and our
   women weep
And wring their hands.
The land lies fallow round the roofless town,
Within the sanctuary the carven image
   stands.
Upon ourselves we bring the judgement
   down.
An eye will cost an eye, a tooth a tooth –
Why can we never see this blinding truth?
Across the wasted nation falls the dark.
Cursed is he who removeth his neighbour's
   land-mark.

A Time to Gather Stones Together

The wall has fallen, and the vine
Lies withered under wind-blown dust.
Dry shards lie in the empty press.
Stones lie scattered, and in fields untilled
Between the blasted ears stalk starving kine.
It is time to gather stones, and build,
And time to seek redress,
So gather in the conclave of the just,
That the law might be fulfilled.

Gather outside the city gate,
And hear the preaching of the Pharisee.
Stand close beside your neighbour,
But do not look into his eyes.
Who knows what he might see?
Here the young man from Tarsus stands,
So strip for holy labour,
And lay your cloaks about his feet.
A naked man kneels on the sand
Before the judgement seat,
And turns his face towards the sky.
Take up the stone, and feel the heavy weight,
Lying ready in your waiting hand.

The Gavel

The Gavel

"How long, O Lord, how long? I feel the
    pain,
The smashing blows that split along the
    grain.
Break me in pieces if thou wilt, do not
    prolong
This fearful punishment. For what have I
    done wrong?"

The Craftsman.

The Craftsman answered, "I do not work in
    haste,
But still take comfort. What's struck off is
    worthless waste.
From your uneven shape, alone I can
Carve out the perfect stone, to fit the greater
    plan.
Those that need cutting most, I do not love
    the less,
On them I spend my greatest pains and
    carefulness.
You feel the smarting blows, but you must
    understand
Behind the smiting gavel lies the guiding
    hand."

Two sonnets.

Samson

I saw my people lost and overthrown.
I trusted in my strength, and saw it fail.
Blinded and mocked, on every aching bone
I feel the blows, as from a thresher's flail.
In this false temple, how can I atone?
I smell the blood and incense, rank and stale,
My fingers touch the rough, ill-carven stone,
I hear the chanting of the priests of Baal.
Yet, as I pray, I feel the mighty stones
Crack apart; the unholy pillars spread –
Above, the massive lintel grates and groans –
The roar of masonry sounds overhead –
Buttress and column, arch, vault, turret – all
The impious temple crashes down in hideous
    fall!

Solomon

Over the chosen people called to reign,
I sent for brass, and cunning men of Tyre;
I cast the pillars and the golden chain,
And purified the silver in the fire.
Upon the threshing floor of Mount Moriah
The temple stands – but is all in vain?
How can a mortal man hope to aspire
To build for One the heavens cannot
    contain?
And yet, beneath the roof of cedar balks,
The people stand devout and dutiful,
About the pavement where the Levite walks,
Within the pillared gate called "Beautiful".
Peace lies within her walls, and all is still
Within the holy temple, on the holy hill.

A Time to Cast Away Stones
(Ecclesiastes, 3, 5)

Did you set out to build a mighty tower?
How fair the drawing of your great design!
And yet the task was far beyond your power;
What you cannot complete, you must resign.
Leave this abandoned shell,
And build an humbler house in which to
　　dwell…
But vanity, vanity –
Why is it that we burden ourselves so?
The worthless stones – the weary, heavy
　　stones,
Cast them aside, pass on, and let them go.

Did you sit down to carve in wrathful mood
And find your chisel mar, and botch, and
　　slip?
Work done in anger rarely comes to good
Or ever leads to honest craftsmanship.
But do not brood:
The broken stone can never be renewed…
But vanity, vanity –
Why do we carry them when use has gone?
The ugly stones – the spoiled, misshapen
　　stones,
Let them go, cast them aside, pass on.

Or did you feel the very worst of all?
For did you dwell in peace with those you
　　trust?
Then the foundations shifted. Down fell roof
　　and wall,
Leaving you stunned and aching in the dust.
It's in the past.
Rubble can make foundations firmer than
　　the last…
But vanity, vanity –
Why do we cling to things when hope has
　　died?
The painful stones – the cruel, jagged stones,
Pass on, and let them go. Cast them aside.

From Labour to Refreshment

The Master calls the labourers
To take a little ease,
To lay aside their burdens,
And to rest beneath the trees;
No man can always labour,
Throughout the heat of day,
So we obey the Master's law
All mortal things obey.

For when the Great Creator
Created holy light,
He also made the darkness,
For our peaceful rest at night;
For six days did he labour,
Upon his sacred plan,
Then turned he to refreshment,
And decreed the same for man.

And as unskilled apprentices,
We work with blunted tools,
And hack the stone, and rarely heed
Our Master's simple rules;
Yet soon our labour's ended,
And we'll hear the final call
From labour to refreshment,
In the grandest lodge of all.

Yet as we cannot always toil,
We cannot always rest,
For work and ease are both alike
In equal measure blessed;
So we'll beg our worthy Master,
To give us work to do:
To gird our loins for labour,
And to learn the craft anew!

THE HUMBLE BUILDERS

THREE POEMS BY MARTIN STEAD

The Plumb Rule

When the first sun-baked bricks of mud and straw
Dried on the sand,
Men found out one unalterable law:
Walls will not stand
If courses are not square, and true, and good,
And corners straight;
So men devised the simple frame of wood,
And line and weight.

And so they made the rule,
Pointing to the sky.
The plumb rule - infallible,
That cannot lie.

When the first stones were cut, and squared, and dressed,
Great works they did.
But all were subject to one simple test:
Pylon and pyramid
Were measured out, foundations were laid flat
In Babylon.
The rule that squared the ancient ziggurat,
Set out the Parthenon.

For they all knew the rule,
One must apply.
The true vertical - infallible,
That will not lie.

Before you come to carve and decorate,
Look to the wall.
If courses are not truly square and straight,
The stones will fall.
Although the gilding may flash brave and fine,
Does all stand true?
Apply the test, that simple bob and line,
Those craftsmen knew.

You must obey the rule.
Trust not your eye.
That age-old tool - infallible,
Can never lie.

Note: the Parthenon is not actually built to true squares, it looks square due to optical illusion - but the masons must still have needed to measure the true lines.

This Man Began to Build, and Was Not Able to Finish *(Luke 14: 28-30)*.

The workmen gather, wanting pay,
Then see my empty purse.
At last, unpaid, they drift away
With muttered curse.
The worthless stones and timbers lie,
Abandoned at my feet,
Around stand walls, scarce shoulder-high,
I can't complete.

Then over the deserted site,
And useless, broken tools,
Come leering through the falling night
The mocking fools.
They come to fling their stale jeers,
And hiss their searing scorns,
Their laughter crackles in my ears
Like burning thorns.

The work they could not understand,
They come now to condemn.
Can they not see that when I planned
I dreamed for them?
But then a voice within my heart,
Buried deep down inside,
Whispers that from the very start,
I dreamed for pride.

Around me hollow darkness falls,
They leave me here alone,
Huddled beneath the half-built walls
Of rough-hewn stone,
Gazing into the arching skies
Where glowing stars unfold,
Watching a mighty temple rise,
Roofed all in gold.

The Hope of Reward

The weary day draws to
its close,
The hour groweth late;
Yet ere ye go to seek
repose,
Forgather at the gate;
And come ye not from
fear of pain,
As doth the timid slave,
But in the just desire for
gain
For work ye freely gave.

We are not pressed, but
free-born men,
And free-born men entire,
And well we know the
labourer,
Is worthy of his hire.

So come, collect your wages!
The corn, and wine, and oil,
The promise of reward it is
That sweetens daily toil.
Fair recompense is all we ask,
Yet search your heart and say,
Did ye complete your ordered task,
Is truly earned your pay pay?

Our father Adam dug the earth,
Our mother Eve she span,
In pain she brought her sons to birth,
To work the life of man;
The sweat upon your brow's the lot
Of man of woman born -
But muzzle not the patient ox
That treadeth out the corn!

So hang not back, stand forth, receive,
And joyfully retire.
We are not pressed, but free-born men,
And worthy of our hire.

Martin Stead was initiated into Apollo University Lodge, No. 357, in Oxford, and is a Past Master of William Rogers Lodge, No. 2823. He teaches English at Harrow.

BROTHER LIGHTFOOTE

THE RECOLLECTIONS OF AN EIGHTEENTH-CENTURY GENTLEMAN OF THE CRAFT

Samuel Pommard Millhouse Lightfoote was born at Hammersmith, on June 21st, 1732. His father, Septimus, a successful wine merchant, died when he was seven and his mother, Penelope, née Nixon, fearing that the want of a father's hand might feminise him, sent him to Belters School (For the Sons of Gentlefolk). The name Samuel was that of his paternal grandfather, who had started the wine business in the late seventeenth century; Pommard was the name of his father's favourite vineyard, and Millhouse was a family name from his mother's side. Penelope's younger brother, Robert, 'Uncle Bob' Nixon, emigrated to America in 1760 and was an active participant in the rebellion of 1776. His signature would have appeared on the Declaration of Independence had he been sufficiently sober to hold a pen at the time. Samuel's maternal grandmother, Isobel, was one of the eleven wives of Tarquin Millhouse, the notoriously bigamous bishop of Sodor and Man.

On coming into his inheritance in 1753, Lightfoote sold the wine business, together with its very considerable stock, to Messrs. Yardy & Reed in St. James's, with the stipulation that his personal wants should be supplied by them, free of charge, for life. He purchased a house in Percy Street in London and settled down to the life of a gentleman of leisure. He married Hermione Lampwick Lipton, only child of a wealthy tea importer, in 1762, and their son, Horatio Perignon Tetley, was born the following year.

Lightfoote was initiated into his father's lodge, Stonic, in September 1755, at the Yorick Tavern in Drury Lane. It is interesting to note that the Master who presided over the ceremony was Bro. Charles Spooner, great-grandfather of the Reverend William Archibald Spooner, the renowned Oxford divine. The minutes of the meeting record that, following the obligation, the Master issued the memorable instruction, 'Rise, newly oglibated mother among basins.' Lightfoote was installed Master of the Stonic lodge in 1770 and began his celebrated journal, of which, sadly, only fragments now remain.

Apart from his masonic activities, Lightfoote's published works include 'A

Dissertation on the Effects of Divers Wines and Spirits on Speech Coherence and Balance,' and 'Alexander Pope was a Pompous Poltroon: Essays in Literary Criticism.' On his deathbed in 1812, following victory in a yard-of-gin competition, his last words are reported to have been 'Hell's teeth, I'm as full as a lawyer's wallet!'

The name Lightfoote is thought to be Viking in origin. Early Icelandic sagas record that Einar Lightfoot sailed with Erik Halfshaft and Sigur Ros in an abortive attempt to reach 'The Land Beyond The Western Sea' which ended in their boat being beached at Skegness.

BROTHER LIGHTFOOTE'S JOURNAL

The Recollections of an Eighteenth-Century Gentleman of the Craft

Saint Andrew, as I've said before, is a great favourite of mine; I named a son after him, so I did. It is recorded that he was Our Lord's first disciple, a fisherman by trade, who, when summoned, didn't simply abandon all and follow, but ran and told his brethren. By his actions, the saint demonstrated two of the traits that Lightfoote most admires in a man: he failed to do as he was told and succeeded in spreading joy, for when offered a great gift – the greatest gift of all – his first thought was to share it. I bless his name whenever there's fish on the table and I never get gut rot!

Note: the best accompaniments to fish, I find, are the white wines of Burgundy, but if these are not available, ale will suffice. Raw fillets of herring, flamed in gin, is a quite spectacular appetiser, but perhaps not for those of a delicate constitution.

A candidate for initiation has been proposed in the Stonic Lodge and this has caused great consternation. His name is Andrews, Nathaniel Andrews, and he is a rat catcher by trade. When his curriculum vitae was read out by his proposer, a fishmonger, there was a distinct and uncomfortable stirring in the ranks. A brother who considers himself a gentleman, but is, in fact, a lawyer, raised objection on the grounds that having a rat catcher in the lodge might lower the tone of our proceedings. Nathaniel's seconder, a wheelwright, countered that, though rat catching was unquestionably a dirty job, someone had to do it. The lawyer, with all the insolence of his office, observed that no-one had to be a rat catcher. Had this fellow, he enquired, been dragooned into service? Did there exist a verminous equivalent of the press gang – the rat pack, perhaps? No, Master Andrews had elected to be a rat catcher; he could have been a fishmonger, or a wheelwright, or a butcher or a baker or a candlestick maker, but rat catching was his chosen profession, and thus it was acceptable to choose to despise him for it. Laughter ensued. Lightfoote rose.

I enquired of the fishmonger as to whether Nathaniel was a family man. I was informed that he had a wife and two strapping sons, all three of whom he kept in warmth and comfort and always fed with fish on Fridays. Next, I asked the wheelwright if he knew what the rat catcher did on Sundays and was informed that he and his family, all impeccably dressed, drove to church in a dog cart (perfect in all its parts, esp. the wheels) where they furnished the choir with a

November 30th 1781
Saint Andrew's Day
Weather: Unseasonably mild
Outlook: Excellent

I will make you fishers of men

soprano, and alto, a tenor and a bass. I observed that this gentleman – and I laid stress on the word – seemed to me to exemplify domestic harmony, and got a laugh livelier than the lawyer's!

The wheelwright saw fit to add that his friend was also an accomplished player on the bassoon. I was constrained to concede that none of us is perfect. This reduced the brethren to incontinent mirth.

Lightfoote came to the point: rats.

Rats are a plague on this city. Rats, some say, brought the Great Plague to The

Great Wen, and this was only purged in the Great Fire. He who toils to rid us of such a pestilence must therefore be considered a Great Man, who does a greater service to the populace than most lawyers (on reflection, 'most' is superfluous).

Consider this: as we are not all operative masons, but rather free and accepted, or speculative, might we not ponder the possibility of free and accepted rat catchers and, indeed, speculative rats? Intolerance, injustice, intemperance and insolence are spread, like the foulest canker, from the middens of mean minds to infect humanity at large? Who resists? Who remains steadfast in the faith? Who cuts off the tales of those that tell tales and holds tight to the truth? We do, brethren. Thus are we rat catchers all, are we not?

There was silence in the House of judgement.

Nathaniel Andrew has been accepted as a candidate for initiation and I am confident that he will be an ornament to

the lodge and a handy fellow to know if one has an infestation – and who among us doesn't, from time to time?

I've done a ditty:

In his rat catcher's breeches and rat catcher's hat;
Behold now our brother: the rat catcher, Nat.
Not one of life's loafers but one of its doers;

He toils in the gutters, he delves in the sewers.
In the damp and the darkness he fights the good fight,
To arise, from the mire, in triumph, to light

And so to the herrings, flamed in gin, and good night's sleep, if the two be not mutually exclusive.

BROTHER LIGHTFOOTE'S JOURNAL

THE RECOLLECTIONS OF AN EIGHTEENTH-CENTURY GENTLEMAN OF THE CRAFT

June 7th 1795
Feast Day of St. Robert of Newminster

Weather: changeable

From the heath covered mountains of Scotia I come…

S t. Robert of Newminster, I read, was accused of "excessive familiarity with a pious woman." A perfect example of ecclesiastical hypocrisy if ever there was one: either he wasn't that familiar or she wasn't that pious but one simply cannot, as the actress said to the bishop, have it both ways.

I regret the recent lacuna in the hitherto uninterrupted flow of this journal. It is due to my taking a tour of the north country from which I am newly returned. Scotland proved to be most stimulating, perhaps a little too stimulating, and I refer not only to the effect of the local produce. It was however, a night of debauchery that led

to a day of discovery. As to whether what I witnessed is historical fact or hysterical fantasy I confess I am still unclear; perhaps setting the facts down in writing will help.

I was enjoying a fine dinner at a fine inn in the fine city of Edinburgh in the company of a fine gentleman by the name of MacDonald, a local burgher who raised what he claimed to be the best beef in the land. "Mark well my words, Lightfoote," quoth he, "One day MacDonald's will known throughout the world!" I drank his health and told him that I hoped it would be, and he drank my health and assured me that it would and we drank each other's health to settle the matter and then sat wondering what next

we might drink to. Imagine my surprise when he raised his glass to "The craft and vocation of Massonerie." I downed my goblet of Glen Hoddle and offered him my hand and found, to my delight, that I was in the company of a master of the mystic art – and the long night wore on. At some stage I assume that I must have agreed to accompany him on some sort of expedition on the following day but my memory at this point becomes, like the highland landscape, shrouded in mist.

I was informed, subsequently, by a number of witnesses, that I was helped up the stairs pledging undying loyalty to the Jacobite cause. Whatever the cause, I spent a most uncomfortable night, haunted by strange and terrible dreams, full of dreadful images culled from the penalties of my obligations and awoke, fully believing that I had suffered that of first at least, to a furious knocking, as though a regiment of tylers were practising their art. I rose from my bed, then rose from the floor, twice, before crawling to the door to be confronted by a pair of naked knees.

These belonged, I was informed, in an accent that would have been incomprehensible had I not been awash with whisky, to Willie, who was a ghillie, and had come to take me to Rossilly.

I am informed that the journey is but a few miles; perhaps we went via Penzance, using only the old, green roads, for in the ancient tumbrel that MacDonald had provided, it seemed to take days. The laird himself, Willie told me, was unable to be present due to some pressing emergency with the bullocks, at least I think that's what he said.

Rossilly, when we got there, was a ruin, as indeed was I, though my guide informed me that it had been extensively restored some forty years previously. It is an ancient chapel wrought in the most hubristic style, like a gothic cathedral shrunk in the wash. Willie recited a lengthy history of the place, painfully committed to memory and delivered in the style of a drunken deacon dictating the doings at the wardens' pedestals. I missed much of it as I was busy puking into the sparkling burn that flows merrily beside the road, but from what I could gather it is believed that a descendant of Joseph of Arimathea had brought Excalibur here after the battle of Bannockburn and that this was the basis of Freemasonry: something along those lines, anyway.

I was in no condition to argue and weakly agreed to overlook the premises according to his master's wishes, fully expecting Willie to give me a guided tour. He, however, was unwilling to go within fifty paces of the place, muttering something about the curse of the pharaohs. He handed me a pistol and said he'd await my return, but not beyond sunset.

Anxious to complete my penance, and in the certain knowledge that MacDonald was laughing his tartan socks off at the thought, I stumbled towards the forbidding pile. I had to put my shoulder to the door to gain admission and fell through it to find myself on my arse, on a damp floor, staring at a rotting roof that threatened to join me at any moment. The place was encrusted with crude carvings, decayed to the point at which their content could be construed as anything that an over-fertile imagination might conceive. I stumbled about in the gloom, searching for meaning and busting for a piss. At the far end of the place were three pillars; I relieved myself, copiously, against what must have been wisdom as I had no strength and there was little beauty involved in the act. As I concluded my libation, I received such a fright that, had I not just emptied my bladder, I'd have wet myself. A dark shape swooped down at me: was it a bat?, was it a ball?, was it a heavy maul? I will never know, but I tumbled backwards, a cocked piece in both hands. Inevitably, one of them went off.

The report was tremendous, the noise echoing around the vaulted chamber. The

ball rebounded off the stonework and flew back past my head: I'd damn' near shot myself in the sacristy. Shards of shattered statuary showered down on me. At this point I must have lost my presence of mind.

I came to in the carriage, with a petrified Willie looming over me. I told him that there was something unspeakable in that place, a veritable pool of horror. The man's eyes widened, a myth was materialising. The rest, as they say, is history… Or is it?

BROTHER LIGHTFOOTE'S JOURNAL

The Recollections of an Eighteenth-Century Gentlemen of the Craft

Homobonus is the patron saint of tailors. Sadly, my tailor passed away earlier this year. Like Homobonus, he was a good man, and he is sorely missed by all who knew him. Homobonus is also, by the by, the patron saint of the city of Cremona, where the violins come from, but no-one was ever fiddled by Bilgorri; let light perpetual shine upon him.

Mrs. Lightfoote has been most disagreeable of late, I know not why, I find myself easy enough to agree with. She, on the other hand, finds nought but fault in me: if I stand, I should go, if I go I should stand. On Wednesday evening last I could stand no more of it and went – to an extraordinary meeting of the Stonic Lodge. When I say that this was an extraordinary meeting, I don't mean that in the ordinary sense, for all our meetings are extraordinary: extraordinarily agreeable, unlike my spouse aforementioned. What I mean to say is that this was an extra meeting, summoned for a date upon which we do not, ordinarily, meet, which is once a month, on the ides, except when we don't, as in March. Under ordinary circumstances I would be happy to attend a meeting weekly; with my wife disposed towards me as she is currently, nightly! I was, therefore, the first one down to the Yorick Tavern and had downed a quart before the Tyler arrived to prepare the upper room.

The official visit

Anyway, the reason for us meeting again, happily, a mere fortnight after parting, equally so, previously, was an Official Visit from an Officer of the Grand Lodge: a new experience for all of us, and one that I looked forward to with interest. The taproom gradually filled up with brethren and I, relishing release from the petticoated persecutor, the trumpet-tongued tormentor, to wit, the wife, gradually filled up with beer. I confess that, by the time we were called to order I was as full as a bull's bundle and in the

first stage of inebriation: Jocose.

All went well to begin with, according to due form: we sang our opening air:

Gathered again are we, brethren of Stonic;
Firm and upstanding like columns Ionic;
Tuscan, Corinthian, Composite, Doric;
*Strongly established on tenets hi*storic.

The lodge was opened in due form and with antient ceremony at about ten past six precisely. The minutes of our last meeting were read, confirmed and approved and then there was a report and we were informed that our honoured (though uninvited) guest was without and demanded(!) admission. Lightfoote's suspicion was aroused.

Proud as a peacock

In he marches, proud as a peacock and done up like a dandy, followed by a waddling retinue of jingling johnnies, straight up to the Master's pedestal where he's offered the gavel, which, happily, he declines. They all take their seats, he on the Master's right hand, and we're invited to salute him, repeatedly. He greets us well, as well he might, and we proceed to pass Brother Catchpole to the Second Degree, in the course of which I give my celebrated rendering of the explanation of the tracing board.

We proceed, seamlessly, to the risings, the closing and the festive board: a magnificent haunch of beef accompanied by good ale and some excellent

November 13th 1795

Feast of St. Homobonus

Weather: unseasonably mild

Mrs Lightfoote has been disagreeable of late…

Burgundy, both of which Lightfoote partakes of liberally, wishing to prolong the pleasure of the present and blot out the dismal prospect of futurity, viz, return to Mrs. Lightfoote. The mixture of the grape and the grain advanced me, like Catchpole, to the second degree: Bellicose.

We keep our speeches brief at Stonic: `talk short, drink deep' is the motto, and so it was until our honoured guest got up on his hind legs. He proceeded to lecture us on our several failings, claiming that our demeanour was, in general, irreverent and our ritual, in particular, irregular. He made special mention of my contribution, claiming that my witty paraphrase of the tale of Jephtha and Ephraimites constituted an innovation in the ritual and suggested that I, and everyone else, might care to attend a Lodge of Instruction. At this point, Lightfoote, already feeling clamorous and turbulent, broke out into full-blown fury. I rose to respond, noting that the Worshipful Master looked a little pale. I reminded the Grand One that he was a guest and it wasn't a guest's place to tell his host how to behave; if he didn't like us, he would have to lump us. Further, I reminded him of the address made to the brethren on installation night, which points out, quite unequivocally,

that our end and aim is primarily to please ourselves, not the Grand Lodge, the Emperor of China, my wife, the landlord's dog or anyone else!

Like a cup of last night's claret, it didn't go down well. The Master's face was by now white as a sheet and our Honoured Guest's black with fury, symbolising, it occurred to me, the joys and sorrows of our chequered existence; I was moving, inexorably, from the bellicose to the morose: drunkenness in the third degree.

Off went the Grand Officer, with his flashy flunkies in tow, leaving the world to darkness and to me. I begged the Master's forgiveness, realising that I had severely damaged his chances of promotion. He, to my surprise and delight, refused to accept my apologies and called for a flagon of Rhenish. To general applause he reminded us that we were not all operative masons but rather free and accepted and that that surely meant that we were free to accept who and what we wanted. My sorrows were drowned! I passed, softly and silently, to the supreme degree: Comatose.

I awoke in my own bed with the rays

of that glorious luminary pouring in on me as the golden wine had poured the night before.

Remarkably, I felt supremely well, fortune, apparently favouring the brave, but the best was yet to come: enter Mrs. Lightfoote. I fear the very worst, but all wifely concern she is, bearing bacon and eggs and a flagon of ale, stroking my hair, mopping my brow…

It seems that the brethren who bore me home had informed her, in hushed tones of wonder and admiration, of how I had, single-handedly, fought off a band of brigands who were molesting a dear old lady. Was it so, she asked, was Lightfoote truly a hero? It was true, I confessed, simply, for women have no understanding of allegory.

BROTHER LIGHTFOOTE'S JOURNAL

THE RECOLLECTIONS OF AN EIGHTEENTH-CENTURY GENTLEMAN OF THE CRAFT

January 1st 1781
Feast of Saint Sylvester
Weather: Deep, crisp, even,
etcetera
Outlook: Improving, hopefully

Ring out the old;
Ring in the new!
Or vice versa…

S ylvester, as every schoolboy knows, was made bishop of Rome in the year 314 and is credited with having baptised the emperor Constantine. Other than this highly improbable feat, almost nothing is known about him but that has not deterred a lodge of Freemasons naming themselves after him on the grounds that their inaugural meeting was held on his feast day.

It seems odd to me that a lodge should meet on New Year's Eve, but if one insisted on so doing, one might have expected them to call themselves the Auld Acquaintance or the Neo Annum or something of that sort, but the facts remain that Sylvester does and that they didn't, so there. Further it might be supposed, quite reasonably, that a lodge that does meet on the evening of the last night of the year might order its affairs in such a way that their business would be concluded in good time for the brethren to disperse to see in the new with their families and friends… No. Sylvester holds its installation meeting on December 31st, the lodge being tyled at eleven o'clock in the evening precisely. By tradition, the duly elected, humble representative of King Solomon must be placed in his chair on the stroke of midnight in order that the minutes (no pun intended) may show that the lodge was, with the turning of the year, reborn and formed anew. Appealing, if gently eccentric, thought Lightfoote when he first heard of it; greatly eccentric, thinks Lightfoote now.

How did Lightfoote hear of the strange and singular Lodge of Sylvester? He'd invited a young fellow called Stacey to join him for supper at The Antlers Club and the boy had failed to arrive. It turned out that Master Stacey had allowed himself to be gulled into viewing some engraved prints of an highly questionable nature in some dungeon in Duke Street, plied with strong drink and induced to purchase a series entitled *Beyond the Pail or The Dairymaid Undone*, but I digress. As I loitered in the lobby, I noticed that another lurked likewise. I didn't recognise him and, on making polite enquiry, discovered that he was a guest who's inviter had failed to make the rendezvous. We shook hands and, in so doing, revealed that each of us was brother to the other. Lightfoote's course was clear, particularly as the supply of jugged hare might at any moment be exhausted: Sir Victor Mortimer became my dining partner.

If one could choose at birth whose snout might sit next to one's own in the trough of life, it would be Mortimer's, for a more amenable tablemate a man could scarce imagine.

The Perfect Guest

He ate hardly a mouthful of meat,
sweet, or bread,
But he paid close attention to all
that I said;
Of the wine and the brandy he took
scarce two sips,
But he chuckled at every one of my quips.

I must gather these verses together at some point; men have made fortunes from lines nowhere near as neat as this: Spenser, for one. Where was I?

Mortimer… By the end of the meal I had gladly accepted his invitation to attend his lodge's installation meeting. The following morning I informed Mrs. Lightfoote, who chuckled not. I was informed that elaborate arrangements were already in place for a lavish, new year celebration. I countered that, with six weeks to go, her plans could hardly be far advanced. I shall not attempt to employ this gambit again.

I was still limping slightly when the cab dropped me off in an alleyway down below The Strand at half past ten on

December the thirty-first. There was a sound of revelry that night, as one might imagine, but the silence that enveloped me as I stood before the door of Sylvester's sanctum was positively sepulchral. I raised my hand to knock but the door swung open, groaning, to reveal Sir Victor, smiling and bidding me enter. Within, the brethren were gathered and ready. I could not help but observe that the lodge appeared to be in need of an injection of new blood; not one of them was under seventy and many were considerably over! Their manners were courtly but they were all, like Mortimer, pale and wan, even their regalia was worn and threadbare, like those beeswing banners one sees, sad-hanging in cathedral churches.

The lodge was opened in due form and the minutes were read; I wondered when they might last have had an initiate; I wondered, come to that, when last they'd entertained a guest. The current master was absent, on business overseas, apparently, and so a (very) senior past master was to conduct the proceedings. The ancient, doddering candidate for the master's chair was presented and the ceremony of his installation proceeded accordingly, leading inevitably and inexorably to the crowning moment when he was placed in the Master's chair, at which point a sudden, violent draught extinguished the candles and the room was plunged into utter and profound darkness. In the silent, breathless moment that followed I heard all the bells of London strike the hour: a new year was born.

Flints were struck and wicks relit and my surroundings gradually became visible again. The aged brethren around me smiled indulgently, all was well, and then my gaze fell upon the new master. Seated in Solomon's chair was a boy who looked no older than the aforementioned absentee Stacey. I blinked and rubbed my eyes but it was no apparition, the face that grinned back at me, and winked, was as smooth and unblemished as that of a Dresden figurine.

As the ceremony proceeded I was struck cold, during the address to the master, by the suggestion that the inferior brethren of the lodge were of too generous a disposition to envy his preferment - or were they merely biding their time.

At the conclusion of the meeting, Mortimer informed me that he was looking forward to his second term as master, in just a few years time. It seems that masters of Sylvester are in the habit of disappearing, following their installation, often going abroad for extended periods, but, my host assured me, they always return, eventually, just as he had.

I have been invited to join this lodge but I am reluctant so to do; the prospect worries me strangely. Perhaps my eyes were playing tricks; perhaps I'm getting old…. If so, so be it.

BROTHER LIGHTFOOTE'S JOURNAL

THE RECOLLECTIONS OF AN EIGHTEENTH-CENTURY GENTLEMAN OF THE CRAFT

January 19th 1781
Saint Agnes' Eve
Weather: Bitter cold
Outlook: Occluded

*Not so much a wolf in
sheep's clothing
as Mutton, dressed as Lamb*

pallium is the term given to the soft, fleshy, outer covering of things such as snails and oysters, whence they secrete their shells. I recall one of my infant witticisms:

*Why wouldn't the cockles lend the crab
half a crown?
Because they were shellfish!*

Lightfoote allows himself a wry smile and senses a verse coming on - but first...I have read recently that certain dignitaries of the Church have called into question the validity, nay, the propriety, of Freemasonry, and have made it known that divines who decide, on occasion, to exchange the alb for the apron risk, by so doing, any ecclesiastical advancement. We are accused of secrecy, self-advancement and sympathy for the devil. *Credite posteri!*

It need hardly be pointed out that, were Freemasonry secret, the Anglican inquisition would be unable to identify its members, and, conversely, if they know which of their number are masons, it's hardly a secret, is it? As for the charge of mutual back-scratching, one must assume that this alludes to favouritism rather than

S aint Agnes, blessings be upon her, laid down her life rather than give up her purity and that one must admire. She refused marriage at the age of thirteen as she had dedicated her life to Our Lord and for this she was placed in a brothel. A man who gazed upon her nakedness was instantly struck blind, which served him right! The similarity of her name to the Latin *agnus* has given rise to the association of the lamb with which her and lambs are still blessed, on her feast day, in Rome. I read

also, in Hutton's Curiosities of Christendom, that the wool from these creatures is woven into the pallia of archbishops by the nuns of Saint Agnes' convent. Unsure of precisely what a pallium was, but anxious to be enlightened, I got down my Latin dictionary, upon which is inscribed, in a childish hand, *Lightfoot*(sic) *is a Lobcock*, dating it precisely to 1736, when I was in the same form at school as one Samuel Withers who, I sincerely hope, still walks with a limp. Therein I discovered that a

the freely admitted and unashamed Masonic practice of helping each other along - which extends to all. It is commonly conceived that Masons regularly favour each other in business dealings and matters of professional preferment.

Were this true, Masons wouldn't be in business for long. Faced with choice of employing, in whatever capacity - for a poor plumber may cause as much grief as a bad barber - a cack-handed companion in masonry or a master craftsman who's a cowan, which would you prefer?

Doubtless much business has been transacted over a few fraternal ales following a lodge meeting, but no more, I warrant, than is done in the average Covent Garden Coffee House or any of the new, so called "Gentlemen's" clubs that are currently springing up like grass and will, in all probability, whither as fast, in the area adjacent to that hotbed of indolence: St. James's Palace. Birds of a feather, as the saying goes, flock together, thus a man feels at ease with persons he knew at school - Withers most especially excepted - and with those with whom he has some common interest, be it fishing,

fencing, ferreting or Freemasonry. One might assume that the Church would disapprove of each of these activities therefore, except that...

Fishermen, fencers (either kind) and ferret fanciers are not, generally, held to be in league with Beelzebub. I say unto you: if the Freemasons - who trace their lineage from the journeymen who constructed the great cathedrals (yea, even the Temple of Solomon!) and whose primary guiding light is the sacred writings - are supposed to be servants of Satan, they are obviously diabolically unsuitable for the task and long overdue for dismissal!

One is tempted to write to one's bishop, in green ink, but Lightfoote stays his hand. To rise to such risible bait can only encourage more of the same to be cast. Remember the words of the Senior Warden on the occasion of one's initiatory investment, with that badge that is "more ancient than the golden fleece or Roman eagle..." and consider well their import.

I said that I sensed a staza stirring, didn't I? Not for the first time, I think it was the shellfish that brought it on, combined with St. Agnes' lamb:

The Bishop of Bath and of Wells
Wears a pallium embroidered with shells,
But under his knickers,
Like all priests and vicars,
He's no better than anyone else.

BROTHER LIGHTFOOTE'S JOURNAL

THE RECOLLECTIONS OF AN EIGHTEENTH-CENTURY GENTLEMAN OF THE CRAFT

May 28th. 1781
Feast of Saint Lanfranc
Weather: May is in her prime
Outlook: Sumer is icumen in

Where'ere I fall, I stand.

William of Normandy, known as William the Bastard but promoted, following his victory at Hastings in 1066, to William the Conqueror, appointed Lanfranc Archbishop of Canterbury in 1070. Lanfranc was consecrated in the roofless wreck of the recently incinerated cathedral and subsequently supervised its rebuilding, so there was a bit of masonry in him!

Today is also the anniversary of the Fall of Acre in 1291, when the great tower of the Templars finally collapsed under the weight of the onslaught of the Mamelukes, crushing defender and assailant together in the ultimate ruin of the Crusades, so there was a lot of masonry on them!

Masonry, fallen masonry indeed, has played as leading role in Lightfoote's life of late, having caused him to be dispersed over land and water and wishing a speedy return to his native land in no uncertain terms. I write these words from a dark and desolate domain, set in a stormy sea, where I have journeyed, at great personal risk, in search of a distressed mason. Worshipful Brother Christopher Courts was a founding member of the Stonic Lodge; he was, in fact, our sole surviving founder. I, in common with the rest of the current membership, knew his name - it's on our warrant - but had never seen his face. He had ceased to show it many years ago, having retired to the distant region of his birth and infant nurture. W.Bro. Courts had continued to pay his subscription and send his apologies, in an increasingly unsteady hand, for over a quarter of a century since his last recorded attendance. The announcement that

apologies had been received from W.Bro. Courts had become as much a part of the established ritual of the Stonic Lodge as the brass button in the alms dish and so the degree of surprise shewn by the members at learning (via his vicar) of our brother's recent decline and imminent decease might seem surprising, were not in the nature of our institution.

It was decided that one of us must go immediately to see that could be done, either for W.Bro. Courts or for his dependents. Lightfoote, being able to spare the time and bear the cost, was the obvious choice. Mrs. Lightfoote was at first unsympathetic, as she so often is, making the case that the matter could be conducted and concluded via correspondence with Courts's caring clergyman. To risk life and limb on bad roads and worse seas (and Liverpool!) seemed to her nought but folly. I told her that she was quite wrong. She was quite right.

The trip was hell. Like the poor candidate in a state of darkness, Lighfoote risked death by divers dreadful means,

finally coming to light on the shore of that ragged, rugged and remote rock that is known as the Isle of Man. I found lodging at an inn in the town of Douglas: a smugglers' haunt, named not as a memorial to someone called Douglas, but derived from the two rivers that there converge, the *Dhoo* and the *Glass*, meaning darkness and light. From here I sent word to the worthy divine, and whilst awaiting his reply, acquainted myself with some of the exquisite and unexpected delights that the island has to offer: scallops, gull's eggs, the finest smoked herrings that I've ever tasted - and quite passable ale. Lightfoote's composure was almost restored when it was shattered anew by the arrival of a breathless messenger who could barely gasp out the awful words, 'Mister Courts, he dead....'

The dishevelled creature who bore this terrible news bad me follow him directly, though the light was fading fast. We set off down the valley of the Dhoo, into the gathering gloom. By the time we arrived at I know not where, the moon was up and, I noted, very full. In a grove surrounded by gnarled oaks stood a solitary dwelling, much decayed, whence shone a single light. It was by that glimmering ray that, minutes later, I beheld the ravaged countenance of Courts. The good priest was at the bedside and had given him absolution, believing that Courts had breathed his last, but no sooner had the boy been dispatched to fetch me than he breathed again. It was as though, the cleric whispered, he had crossed over... and returned. A sigh escaped the pale lips, the rheumy eyes flickered. I leaned close to glean whatever terrible intelligence it was that had caused Brother Chris to delay his departure for Death's domain. It came to me in a whisper, as if from far, far away, 'The Harbour... The Harbour....,' and with that, he was gone.

I stayed that night in the house with him and the boy and the priest, wondering what his last words might mean. Had he seen that distant shore? Had he, truly, crossed over Jordan? Had Courts traversed the Stygian flow and brought me news of the far bank?

The morning dawned fair and bright and it was only then that I discovered

that Courts had one leg. I enquired as to whether this might have been due to some seafaring catastrophe but was informed that it was due a fall from a horse when he was but a boy. He had requested that the island's symbol, the Three Legs of Man, should be engraved on his headstone, so that, having spent most of his life as a monopod he might end it as a quadruped. His house and chattels were to be sold and the proceeds distributed among the island's poor - a fitting bequest for a mason. Apart from that, and the cryptic message he had whispered in my ear... nothing. The funeral was conducted

with proper decorum and attended, it appeared, by the entire population. Lightfoote's duty had been done; he readied himself for his return.

Breakfasting superbly, I espied from the window an approaching vessel, riding very low in the water, flying the French flag. Minutes later the ragged boy appeared, breathless, again, to inform me that my ship had come in. 'Come, come,' quoth he, 'The Harbour... The Harbour...,' Kippers is not a dish that should be rushed, and so it was with both consternation and indigestion that I found myself being hurried up the gangplank to meet the master of *La Belle Helene*. He greeted me with a well-known grip. I responded in kind and words were exchanged. He asked me my mother's age, and I told him.

He was amused, in that strange, Gallic way, that a man called Lightfoote had come to collect the cargo of a man who was a foot light...

Worshipful Brother Courts had left to his lodge the balance of his estate in the shape of three hundred barrels of fine Cognac. Lightfoote sails for Tilbury on the next tide. *Requiescat in Pace, Frater.*

BROTHER LIGHTFOOTE'S JOURNAL

THE RECOLLECTIONS OF AN EIGHTEENTH-CENTURY GENTLEMAN OF THE CRAFT

November 22nd 1783
Feast of Saint Cecilia
Weather: Cold and damp
Outlook: Occluded

Hail! Bright Cecilia, Hail to Thee!
Great Patroness of Us and Harmony

I once danced with a girl who'd danced with a boy who'd danced with the Prince of Wales. Strange days indeed, but none stranger than a recent one, at the close of which, by candle light, Lightfoote encountered Dark Forces...

The Festive Season is upon us, seeming to begin earlier every year. The holly and the ivy are put out almost before the harvest is gathered in these days – and what have the holly and ivy got to do with Christmas, one asks. Nothing, one replies, they are but the echoes, or more appropriately the embers of savage, pagan rites that marked the winter solstice. The birth of the Son has neatly superseded the birth of the sun but, in the firelight, strange shapes still flicker on a winter's night and who knows what phantoms in the shadows lurk? Lightfoote knows.

I was invited to attend, as a guest, a new-founded Lodge that meets in some picturesque ruin over in Islington. I rarely travel out of town for meetings nowadays. Mrs. Lightfoote deeply resents my coming home very late and very drunk and so I restrict myself to returning fairly late and very drunk. Could a man be more reasonable? I think not!

I set forth on a cold and blustery evening, the chill wind driving the rain in sheets, and it took me full two hours to reach my destination: a crumbling tower, so overgrown with ivy that it appeared more vegetable than mineral. Within, by the light of guttering candles, and with wind and rain flaying the windows, the brethren performed a solemn ritual of initiation that seemed to include many a noble phrase and gentle gesture long forgotten, or abandoned, by the Craft at large. At the conclusion of the proceedings we proceeded to make our way to local hostelry to dine. As we walked I had that strange feeling – we've all experienced it – of having passed that way before, even though I knew perfectly well that I hadn't.

There aren't many inns in Islington, but the brethren had found a fine one, owned by a most elegant, elderly lady, Mrs. Frederick. She had doubtless been a great beauty in her youth but now leaned heavily on a stick and walked with difficulty. She had arranged for us a feast fit for a fieldmarshal, meet, indeed, for a marquess! I confess that, having partaken of both spiritual and intellectual sustenance in large measure – drunk deep of the Pierian spring, as it were, in the temple - I was more than ready to set about satisfying the appetite corporeal and laid in to the victuals with a will.

Was it the lampreys? the lamb's liver? the pig's trotters? The partridge? Not the pigeon pie, surely? Could it have been something to do with the combination of the wines? They were individually excellent, all seven of them.

Our hostess, as if by precognition, had provided my preferred port: Yardy's '59! I drank about a bottle and a half which would normally settle the stomach just nicely, but, whatever the cause, around midnight I suddenly found myself feeling rather faint. Not like Lightfoote! Not like Lightfoote at all! I haven't flunked a feed since I was a college boy and managed to somersault down a spiral staircase at All Souls after three second-helpings of beef with oysters. Even so, I now felt distinctly dizzy and so excused myself and made my way, carefully, down a creaking wooden staircase in search of fresh air. Instead, I found a fresh face.

I seemed to have been descending for an age when I emerged into an empty

ballroom, furnished in antique style and occupied by a pretty little girl of perhaps ten years old. As I stumbled into the room her back was to me but she immediately turned, skipped across the floor and took my hand. 'There you are!' she cried, 'I've been waiting for you! Come along!' She led me to the centre of the floor and suddenly my head was clear, my eye was

clear, all was clear. 'You lead,' said she, 'Step off with the left foot,' and so I did, and music filled the air, and we danced and we danced and we danced. My feet were fleet. I was as nimble as a boy.

I was shaken awake by Mrs. Frederick who informed me, smiling, that my host was waiting to see me to his carriage. As we rumbled home through the rain, my Brother related the old maid's story sad. As a girl of ten she had attended a ball with her little beau, in a house that formerly stood on the site of the inn where we had dined. They had danced the night away, to the delight of all present, but the party had ended in catastrophe. Fire had engulfed the house, the little girl had been pulled free but her legs had been terribly burned; her unfortunate friend was utterly consumed. She had never married, never loved again, as though she thought that, one day, her pretty dancing partner might return.

'A tragic tale,' I murmured, feeling most uncomfortable, 'When was this?' 'Fifty years ago this very night,' my host explained, 'About the year that you were born, Lightfoote, was it not?'

It was… ∎

BROTHER LIGHTFOOTE'S JOURNAL

THE RECOLLECTIONS OF AN EIGHTEENTH-CENTURY GENTLEMAN OF THE CRAFT

July 4th 1781
Feast of Saint Elizabeth of Portugal
Weather: Hot
Outlook: Getting hotter

Upon this day in 1187, a Crusader force, commanded (badly) by King Guy of Jerusalem, was utterly destroyed by a Saracen army, led (brilliantly) by Saladin, at the Horns of Hattin. This decisive battle led, ultimately, to the return of the Holy Land to the people who lived there.

The Fourth of July is also, as every schoolboy knows, the date upon which the rebellious American colonists declared themselves independent of the British Motherland. One must be careful saying it these days, but I rather admire Brother Washington's initiative in securing the government of that great territory for its citizens. Nobody likes being ruled by outsiders, as both the Arab and the American have proved.

I have recently completed a pilgrimage, far out of the city, to Kingston upon Thames, to visit an ancient Freemason. Worshipful Brother Gore is an excellent example of the Craft's ability to smooth and polish the rude matter of which man is made. There can have been few ashlars rougher than Bro. Gore's - one who, to the untutored eye, might seem to consist solely of superfluous knobs and excrescences – and though he may never be perfect (which of us will?) he is greatly improved. He lives now, with his memories, in quiet seclusion in the Portsmouth Road, rarely leaving his Tameside Tomi except to snare wildfowl or to frighten children - but he keeps a most excellent and extensive cellar!

It was due to the extent and excellence of that cellar that my return to town was delayed far beyond the time that I had intended. By the time my carriage was summoned the dawn chorus seemed deafening. My host, scarce able to stand, bad me fond, fraternal farewell and then tottered off, cackling, into the mist that the ascending sun was drawing up from the river. The last thing I heard, as the carriage clattered away, was a terrible splashing and squawking, indicating that, once again, Gore had got himself a goose.

The noise put me in mind of the reception I would doubtless receive on arriving home, when further feathers were bound to fly, but that was still some way off and so I settled down to fortify myself with a few hours sleep.

It is said that, with practice, a man may refresh himself with but a minute's slumber, though I prefer about eight hours. E'en so, we couldn't have gone above a mile when my eyes suddenly snapped open to see another pair staring fixedly into them. We had stopped by the market square where a wagon was unloading. A ragged, hooded individual, bearing a number of bulging bundles, had approached, unseen by the coachee, and was peering in at me. As I woke, he spoke, 'Good morning, Brother!' 'Good morning,' I replied, perplexed. 'You'll be going by Percy Street, I take it,' he continued, smiling amiably. 'That I will,' said I, for it was the truth. 'Then we can go together,' quoth he, clambered in, closed the door, and at that the coach moved on.

Having divested himself of his various burdens he extended his hand to me. Despite his wild appearance his speech and manners seemed impeccable and so I accepted his greeting and, to my astonishment, was rewarded with the grip of a Master Mason. 'Good Lord!' I exclaimed. 'Call me Nick,' he replied, with a twinkle in his eye. I introduced myself but he knew my name already, and my address, and my Lodge, though I couldn't recall ever seeing the man before in my life. I loathe and detest those who, when faced with such a situation, attempt to bluff their way out of their embarrassment by fishing for clues as to their interlocutor's identity. Lightfoote is made of sterner stuff! 'Forgive me...' I began, but got no further. 'Be not embarrassed, my Brother,' said my new travelling companion, 'I didn't expect you to recognise me!' 'Have we met before?' I asked. 'Our paths have crossed,' he replied, smiling. 'I'm sorry I woke you. I'll sit quiet now and you go back to sleep – and don't let what's waiting at the end of your journey disturb you, let me worry about that...'

I must have dozed off again almost immediately and the next I knew I was being shaken awake by the coachman, at my own front door and quite alone. 'What became of Old Nick?' I cried. The fellow claimed not to know who I was talking about and before I could press the matter my good lady wife appeared and I was forced to steel myself for the dread onslaught. Advancing, grin-faced, she threw her arms about my neck, but not to throttle - to caress! She kissed and hugged me for all she was worth, tears brimming in her eyes.

The reason for this unexpectedly

warm welcome was, I soon discovered, the fact that news had reached London the previous night of a terrible accident at Kingston. Some poor fellow had been run over by a wagon and crushed to death. It was generally assumed that he had been drunk and so my wife had assumed it was me. Can you believe that? Anyway, Brother Nick seemed to know that all would be well in the end, whoever he was.

BROTHER LIGHTFOOTE'S JOURNAL

THE RECOLLECTIONS OF AN EIGHTEENTH-CENTURY GENTLEMAN OF THE CRAFT

DATE: August 28th 1782
Feast of St. Augustine of Hippo
WEATHER: Stormy
OUTLOOK: Stormier

*H*e who is tired of London is tired of life. So says Doctor Samuel 'See what a Big Dictionary I've got' Johnson. If one might suggest the first addition to the second edition, let it be:

LAXATOGRAPHY
n. s. Purging - words of meaning; speech of colour; language of poetry, etcetera.
c.f. Procrasturbation.

According to Johnson, Lightfoote is suicidal, yet it is not myself that I am desirous of doing away with, rather the legion of louts and low life who currently make living in the metropolis unbearable. Until recently, our capital city was a capital place to be. Now, suddenly, London is full to bursting with a plethora of pultrons, pantaloons, pimps and pigwidgeons, every one of them beating a path to Lightfoote's door. They all come here. How do they find me?

This very morning I was awoken at eight o'clock by stones being thrown at my bedroom window. I rose, for the first time, to ascertain the cause. A man was standing in the street below, smiling up at me. 'Good morning, Sir,' said he, 'I trust that I haven't disturbed you.' 'In whom do you put your trust?' I enquired. 'In the Metropolitan Insurance Company,' he replied, quick as lightning, 'and so should you!' Now I knew what he was - and what he wasn't – and what to do about it. 'Against what should I be insured, do you think?' I asked. He stepped closer. 'Fire and flood, loss and damage, personal

injury, robbery, acts of God...' I emptied the chamber pot over him and shut the window.

I decided to bathe and drank a pot of coffee whilst a bath was drawn for me and Mrs. Lightfoote sketched my shortcomings. They are legion. Madame withdrew, taking the maid with her, and left the world to bathos and to me...

Wash me throughly from my wickedness;
And forgive me all my sin...

I was just getting into my soapy, psalmy stride when there was a report. Someone was knocking at the door. I rose, dripping, for the second time, to enquire who sought admission. It was the postboy, with the post. I arrived at the front door

wrapped in a towel. The grubby urchin grinned at me. 'Having a bath, were you?' he enquired. I answered with an indulgent chuckle, a toss of the head and a knee to the groin.

There were no less than seven communications: three bills; an offer of insurance; an invitation to subscribe to a monthly magazine devoted to popular ballads - including sheet music - entitled *The Minstrel's Cycle;* a note addressed to a Mr. Litefart, informing that person, who lives somewhere in my house, apparently, that he had, possibly, won the State Lottery of Alsace, and, finally, a summons to attend the Installation Meeting of the Stonic Lodge followed by a bumper supper at DeBoulay's. The latter brightened my mood considerably. I dried myself, dressed, and then addressed the frugal fare that had been provided for me: cold guinea fowl, quails' eggs, Cheshire cheese, York Ham, veal pie, some coarse bread, a few grapes and a flagon of porter beer – hardly a meal.

Nonetheless I was glad to be able to sit down undisturbed – and then the bell rang; I ignored it. It rang again, more insistently; I ignored it, more determinedly. It rang again, continuously, accompanied by loud hammering upon the door. I drained the flagon and rose, for the third time, to see what the blasted matter was. It was a woman.

She wore blue, I wore grey. 'Good morning. Are you Mister Lightfoote?' she enquired. 'Indeed,' I replied, through gritted teeth, 'and good morning to you, my dear. What may I do for you, or indeed to you?' 'Oh nothing,' she laughed, 'This is a courtesy call!' 'On the contrary Miss,' I corrected her – as the image of correcting her with a riding crop formed, pleasingly, in my mind – 'This is a nuisance call!' 'Oh no, please don't think that, kind sir. We are in your area

and I was wondering if you would care to install a conservatory.' 'Just a moment,' I retorted, 'wait there...' I raced upstairs and grabbed my copy of *Johnson's Dictionary*. By the time I got back to the door I'd found the place.

CONSERVATORY.

n. s. A place where anything is kept in a manner proper to its peculiar nature. *Bacon*.

When I read this to her, she appeared perplexed but I reassured her rapidly. 'We

already have a place to keep bacon, but we call it the pantry; books, we keep in the library; linen in the linen cupboard; wine in the cellar; clothes in the wardrobe... I doubt we have room for another conservatory.' 'But where do you go when you want to be quiet, to contemplate, to be undisturbed?' she pleaded. 'Why, the privy, of course!' I cried. 'Goodbye!'

I closed the door, returned Johnson to the shelf and retired to the closet aforementioned with a copy of *The Gazette*. I had just noted that someone is asking three pounds for a house in Fulham when there came three distinct knocks at the door. It was Mrs. Lightfoote, newly returned. 'How long are you going to be in there.' she demanded to know. 'I'm desperate.'

Minutes later I was on my way out, heading for DeBoulay's – a place where I might be kept in a manner proper to my peculiar nature. My Lady's voice floated down to me as I strode into the street. 'Where are you going?' quoth she. 'To the conservatory, my dear,' I called back – and was gone.

BROTHER LIGHTFOOTE'S JOURNAL

THE RECOLLECTIONS OF AN EIGHTEENTH-CENTURY GENTLEMAN OF THE CRAFT

DATE: *December 6th 1783*
       Feast of Saint Nicholas
WEATHER: *Mild*
OUTLOOK: *Bitter*

And there shall come a great profit
throughout the land....

Saint Nicholas was a Turkish Bishop. He is reputed to have saved three orphaned sisters from prostitution by filling their stockings, hung out to dry, with gold coins. This pleasant practice is recalled in the tradition of children hanging their stockings up on Christmas Eve in the hope of similar reward. He is, understandably, the patron saint of unmarried girls. He is also the patron of pawnbrokers, apothecaries, perfumers, sailors and schoolboys. Some contend that the three gold balls hung up outside pawnbrokers' shops allude to his generosity to the three sisters but I suspect that they are a reference to the coat of arms of the Medici. As far as the perfumers go, it is reputed that his tomb, at Bare, issued forth sweetness in the form of myrrh. The link between schoolboys – in particular choirboys – and sailors, other than a fondness for foul language, is that he resurrected parties of both from untimely and unjust death. An all-round good fellow then, whom one would be happy to welcome into one's lodge.

The goodly bishop is known to most folk through his association with the Christmas Season and the giving of presents. As with so many practices, we have made this imperfect. As I look about me at this time of year I fear that the saint must be spinning in his scented sepulchre. Do none but I understand the difference between a present and a gift, between charity and indulgence? Gifts are given by God: the gift of beauty, the gift of music, the gift of good health! Presents are given by us, to each other, when they ought to be given to the poor! It makes me cross...

Just yesterday I was walking down Jermyn Street, thinking to buy Mrs. Lightfoote some perfume, when my ears were assaulted by what I at first took to be the cries of persons in panic and in pain. I hurried forward, ready to give what aid I could, assuming that a carriage must have overturned or some such similar catastrophe occurred –but it was carol singers! It was impossible to tell what carol they were singing, even assuming that they were all singing the same one, but whatever it was it came to a ragged conclusion as I came up. A young ruffian in a ruff rattled a box at me and demanded that I spare him a copper. 'What for?' I enquired. 'Christmas, of course,' the filthy urchin replied, bold as brass. I clarified my question. 'For whom are you collecting, boy? Widows? Orphans? The poor and distressed?' 'No!' he barked, 'It's for us, innit.' The only thing this chubby little extortioner appeared to me to be in need of was a good hiding, but thrashing choristers in

public, *esp*. during the Festive Season, might easily be interpreted as anti-social behaviour and one has to be so careful about that kind of thing nowadays.

I advanced, pursued by a torrent of obscenities that would have made a naval surgeon blush, to the doors of my grocer's shop. The place was heaving with humanity of every hue and it was only after some delay that I managed to collar a clerk and confirm the contents of the Lightfoote hamper: a ripe Stilton cheese, ditto Cheshire, a side of Hereford beef, three York hams, pork pies, rabbit pies, pigeon pies, game pies; hen's eggs, quail's eggs, duck's eggs, plover's eggs; French brandy, Scotch whisky, Plymouth gin and half-a-dozen cases of Yardy's *Wolfshead* port

to give away – I'm not wasting the '59 on trades people! Five geese, four colley birds, three French hens – the usual stuff. It suddenly occurred to me that there were people in this world – in this city – who would not have enough to eat on Christmas Day or indeed on any other day and I suddenly felt quite

guilty. I thought of cancelling my order but the thought soon passed; instead, I ordered that it should be doubled so that half may be given to those in need.

Everything that I have this Christmas, someone else will have too and my resolution for the new year is to place in the alms dish what I pay for my dinner. Buoyed up with feelings of comfort and joy I sallied forth, back into Jermyn Street in search of scent. The Carollers were still at it but I could now discern the words that they were singing.

*Ye who now shall bless the poor,
Shall yourselves find blessing!*

And a merry Christmas to you all, brethren!

BROTHER LIGHTFOOTE'S JOURNAL

THE RECOLLECTIONS OF AN EIGHTEENTH-CENTURY GENTLEMAN OF THE CRAFT

DATE: *May 4th 1780*
WEATHER: *Hot*
OUTLOOK: *Sticky*

A horse! a horse! my kingdom for a horse!
W. Shakespeare
Richard III; Act V, Scene IV

I've never had that much love for horses, though some, I note, are quite infatuated with the silly, smelly creatures. Whilst I am content to be drawn by them in a carriage, I generally avoid sitting astride them as the act demeans both parties and tempts providence. The best way to avoid falling off an 'oss is not to get on it in the first place, just as the most efficient way to avoid being eaten by sharks is not to swim where they are. I have little sympathy, therefore, for those who complain about having fallen off horses or having been eaten by sharks; their misfortune is their own fault entirely.

I have applied this simple rule to many things from my youth up and have found it infallible – until today - one version of it having been that the way to avoid losing money on a wager is not to wager, or, to put it another way: if you don't play, you can't lose.

It being the closed season, masonically speaking, and Mrs. L. being away visiting friends in Wales, I find myself at a loose end in the evenings, so last night made my way to the Yorick Tavern in search of conviviality, and found it. No less than eight other brethren of the Stonic Lodge were present, all, like me, bored. The weather being warm I decided to down a few tankards of cool, cleansing ale and immediately felt the beneficial effect of same. One of the parties – the Lodge Treasurer, no less - suggested a sweepstake. A horse race was to be run on the Down at Epsom the following day, named for Lord Derby but arranged by somebody called Bunbury who, I am reliably informed, exerts much influence in these matters. There were to be nine runners, there were nine of us, we could all draw the name of an 'oss from an 'at and he who drew the winner would take all. I proposed that, alternatively, the winner might take half and the other half be donated to the Lodge's charity fund. Brother Treasurer seconded and the proposition was carried unanimously by the brethren. I immediately felt better, for, in the (inevitable) event of my drawing a blind, three-legged donkey, I could at least console myself with the thought that fifty per cent of my folly would at least benefit some needy soul....

The admirable Master Field, a young gentleman of the university and our newest member, was delegated to copy out the names of the runners whilst further refreshment was procured. Yorick ale is truly excellent. My spirits rose.

I asked what the wager might be, assuming that a shilling would be more than sufficient, especially as Field was but a poor scholar - in every sense... To my horror, Brother Treasurer announced that it be a guinea!

My spirits fell. I reminded my worthy brother of the fact that, whereas the Lodge has many members of rank and opulence, we also have some who, for whatever reason - and mentioning no names - are reduced to the lowest ebb of poverty and distress. I jerked my head meaningfully in the direction of the scribbling Brother Field, hoping that Brother Treasurer would take the hint. I hoped in vain.

The names were put into the Master's hat, held high, and drawn in order of seniority, Brother Treasurer collecting the stake money as the process progressed. Poor Field, having scrabbled for the last lot, had to take up his pen once more to write a promissory note for the cost of it. I gave Brother Treasurer a meaningful look, which he ignored, and then unfolded my own, crumpled slip to discover, written in a spidery little hand, the Earl of Derby's

own horse! As we left, I clapped the lad on the shoulder and told him, with a wink, that I would see him right. 'Thank you, Sir, says he.' 'Don't mention it, Brother,' says I.

Next morning, I lay abed late, the ale having caused me to rise three times before dawn, when I heard three distinct knocks at the door. I went to the window and looked down, to see Brother Field, in a very fine coat, looking up and

doffing a very fine hat to me. Over lunch at the Yorick he confided to me that he had drawn Bunbury's horse, Diomed, the hot favourite who had romped home the winner! "There!" said I, and, quoting the Bard of Avon once more, 'All's well that ends well!' Field looked about the room conspiratorially, and then said 'Can you keep a secret, Brother?' 'Naturally!' I replied. 'Well,' quoth Field, 'Diomed's name was never in the hat, it was in my hand...' I was shocked. 'You have been very naughty,' I hissed. 'I know,' he whispered. 'But,' I continued, 'I shall not tell. Audi, Vide, Tace, and all that.' Field looked greatly relieved. 'I knew that I could rely on you, so here's your guinea back, and lunch is on me.' I am not easily bought, but a guinea's a guinea. I was carried home. I don't recall the hour.

Note: No Saint's feast is celebrated today. This may be due to the fact that the new Pope, Pius VI, hasn't got round to creating any new ones yet.

BROTHER LIGHTFOOTE'S JOURNAL

THE RECOLLECTIONS OF AN EIGHTEENTH-CENTURY GENTLEMAN OF THE CRAFT

DATE: **October 18th 1784**
Feast of Saint Luke
WEATHER: **Miserable**
OUTLOOK: **Dim**

Physician, heal thyself…

Saint Luke wrote the third gospel and the Acts of the Apostles, and was, it is said, an accomplished painter being credited with an icon of the Virgin. His writings are filled with compassion and his paraphrases of the parables of the Good Samaritan and the Prodigal Son still have the power to move. Thus far, he appears to be a Saint among Saints, but no man is perfect and Luke was a doctor.

The medical profession, like the teaching profession and the legal profession, is largely, if not wholly, fraudulent. Surgeons, schoolmasters and solicitors rely on their patients, pupils and plaintiffs (collectively 'victims'), helpless and vulnerable as in every case they are, having no choice but to accept 'expert' opinion. It is exactly the same as when a carpenter is called for to fix a broken chair leg, or a chimney sweep comes to unblock one's flue. They suck their teeth and tut and tell you that it's not as easy as it looks and will cost you dear to do. They're all tradesmen: a surgeon's nothing but a butcher without the sausage-making skills.

In all cases of difficulty and danger, in whom do you put your trust? Did you ever hear anyone answer, 'A medical

practitioner,' or 'My Latin master,' or – God forbid! – 'The Law?' Hardly.

I have recently been suffering from an acute, stabbing pain in the great toe of my left foot. So agonising had it become that I was constrained to go about sinisterly slipshod and needed to exercise considerable caution in stepping off with it. Mrs. Lightfoote, ever ready with the healing balm of consolation, suggested that I seek medical advice as it sounded as though my condition might well worsen by degrees. How droll is that?

There's a doctor in the Stonic Lodge. There are a couple of 'em, actually, but one specializes in an area which could scarce be less relevant and so it was to the 'general practitioner' that I turned, hobbling with the aid of a stick to the door of his spacious consulting rooms (in

truth, that should read 'specious insulting rooms') in Wimpole Street. I was supplied with a glass of sherry that tasted suitably medicinal: mustard poultice and syrup-of-figs on the tongue, with a long, smooth, cod-liver-oil finish. I described my symptoms, briefly and concisely. He nodded sagely. There was a long silence.

He sat back in his chair, steepled his fingers and stared at me in a most disconcerting manner. It was all part of the charade, of course, calculated to put me at my disease, as it were. Then he made a series of ineffably irrelevant enquiries. Did I smoke? How much did I drink? Did I take regular exercise? Patiently – I was the patient, after all – I explained to him that, were I given to holding a pipe between my toes, soaking my feet in his sherry and dancing on broken glass, these questions might be pertinent. As matters stood I could hardly stand and they seemed profoundly impertinent. 'It's my foot, you arse!' I exclaimed, succinctly.

He laughed - a patronising little physician's laugh – and then proceeded to expound, at length, on the possible causes of my crippling condition. He rambled on about melancholic pseudopodia, wrenched arches, club foot, hammer toes, Achilles' heels, lighterman's curse, French flaking, digital morbidity, militant tendons, More's Utopia, Jacob's creak, Philoctitis, Stanford's Revenge and Hampson's chorea. He didn't think, however, that any of these was likely. It was either, he concluded, an ingrown toenail or gout. I asked if he'd like to see the foot. He asked if I'd like to foot the bill. I uttered an oath which was not the Hippocratic one and took my leave.

The journey back to Percy Street was purgatory. About half way I simply had to

pause and decided to rest and recuperate briefly at a rough-looking inn with an amusing sign called The Laughing Turk. Here, beside the fire, I restored myself with pint of porter and a large measure of Old Ben Brokeback – 'from the gay glens of Galloway.' Slowly but surely, as the drink began to flow, the pain began to ebb. A fellow came and sat opposite, clutching a rummer of brandy. I thought he seemed vaguely familiar. He took off his hat and revealed himself to be none

other than young Brother Butterworth, a steward of the Stonic Lodge! As befitted his station and my condition, he went to get the glasses refilled. It transpired that he often called in there at lunchtime as he worked in a knacker's yard close by. I told him of the chain of events that had brought me there. He nodded, then smiled, then laughed! 'Well, Brother,' quoth he, 'better a Lightfoote than a foot light! If you wish it, however, you can come back with me and we'll have that hoof off in a trice!' 'My my,' said I, 'You are yet more comical than my wife.'

She was waiting for me, all sympathy, when I finally staggered through the door, thoroughly anaesthetised. I was informed that Nicholas, the boot boy, had impaled his finger on a nail that was protruding from the sole of my left shoe when he attempted to clean it. He had been sent home with sixpence and had dropped the shoe off for repair on his way. 'So you see,' she concluded, 'Your problem wasn't Doctor's concern at all, it was Cobbler's...'

BROTHER LIGHTFOOTE'S JOURNAL

THE RECOLLECTIONS OF AN EIGHTEENTH-CENTURY GENTLEMAN OF THE CRAFT

DATE: *October 21st 1784*
Feast of Saint Ursula
WEATHER: *Wet*
OUTLOOK: *Wetter*

They that go down to the sea in ships and
*   occupy their business in great waters;*
These men see the works of the
*   Lord and his wonders in the deep.*

And they're welcome to them so far as Lightfoote's concerned. If man's Creator had intended him to live a life aquatic He would surely have equipped him with gills and fins. At the very least He would have made him palmipedous but, except in some odd cases He did not. I have heard it put forward, usually by one who has imbibed enough to float a battleship, that man is somehow descended from creatures of the deep that have, over eons, crawled up on to the land, learned to walk upright and gone on to write sonnets and open bank accounts. Frankly I find this fanciful.

Easier to accept is the story of Saint Ursula, the daughter of a Christian king, who, having been betrothed to a pagan prince, was allowed a three-year stay of matrimony on the grounds that she wished to preserve her virginity. She decided to spend this time on a cruise – hardly a wise choice in Lightfoote's opinion, but who am I to argue with a Saint? – accompanied by ten noble ladies, each in their own vessel with a thousand companions. Now: if one woman on a ship is deemed unlucky, how surprising is it that Ursula's fleet of females was blown off course and that the enterprise ended in disaster? The lives of the Saints are meant to be exemplary. I should have learned from Ursula's experience, but...

Mrs. Lightfoote wished to visit friends at Teddington. Having admired the view from the top of the hill at Richmond (from which Richmond, Virginia is named), we descended, via the water meadows at Petersham, to the banks of the Thames and there boarded a skiff in order to cross to the other side. The tow path at Richmond is hardly the edge of a mighty ocean but on this occasion it proved a greater challenge than confronted Columbus. We were not twenty feet out from the bank when I realised that we were in serious trouble. I had assumed that the waterman's lusty singing was part of the service, as is the case with Venetian Gondolieri, but it now became apparent that he was in an advanced state of intoxication. The tide was ebbing and in an attempt to hold his course he had turned upstream and was rowing directly against it. We were going nowhere, slowly.

Reaching down for his jug he let go one of the oars which immediately left its rowlock and floated away. Seeing this, the fellow threw himself into the water and swam off in pursuit, followed closely by the other oar.

We were left drifting downstream at an alarming rate. Mrs. Lightfoote suggested, in an agitated tone, that I do something. I cried for help but no help came, and so I cried for help again, and again, and again. I was still crying for help when we passed beneath Richmond Bridge, from which a trio of urchins dived like kingfishers and swam, I assumed, to our aid. A length of rope was attached to the boat's prow and I offered the boys this cable with which to take us in tow (hence the expression) but

instead of so doing they simply bobbed about us like otters until the most determined of the ruffians demanded what we might pay to be rescued. I was tempted to remonstrate, but his companions, taking hold of the side, rocked the vessel in a manner so alarming that I decided to offer them sixpence. We settled on a guinea, each, in advance, on payment of which we were propelled forcefully into the stinking mud just below the site of the

old Richmond Palace. Having been deprived of all material wealth, I lost a shoe whilst carrying my wife ashore. There are parallels in all this but at the time I was in no mood for symbolism.

If anyone ever proposes a scheme whereby those in peril on the sea, or indeed, the Thames may be rescued by a trained, volunteer force, funded by public subscription, I shall approve heartily having already subscribed...

I feel that a verse may be imminent;

I'm not going down to the sea again,
To the stream or the pond or the pool;
For one never ought to travel by water,
Unless one's a fish or a fool.

SECRETS? WHAT SECRETS?

CANON RICHARD TYDEMAN SPEAKS OF WORTHY MEN AND TRUST

Every Freemason has solemnly sworn never to reveal any of the secrets or mysteries of masonry – but what exactly do we mean by that?

There is no doubt that in medieval times the secrets of the operative masons were very practical indeed. They included the methods of proving uprights and horizontals, the knowledge of tools and their uses, and – perhaps the most important – the ability to make an angle of ninety degrees to ensure that a stone was square. These secrets took a considerable time to learn and involved a long apprenticeship followed by years as a Craftsman before eventually perhaps becoming a Master of the Art.

Only in that way could the true Mystery – or Mastery – of an operative mason be preserved and passed on to future generations. But, of course, then, as now, there were unscrupulous cowboy builders – they called them Cowans in those days – who would offer to build or repair a structure without possessing the genuine knowledge. Such men would sometimes endeavour to infiltrate lodges of operative masons and try to obtain the secrets the easy way, without being worthily recommended and properly prepared. It was to prevent such conduct that passwords and tokens were entrusted to genuine masons so that they could identify themselves if, for instance, they moved to another town and sought work there.

These words and tokens were not, in themselves, the "secrets" of masonry, rather, they acted as guards to those secrets.

However, we are not all operative, but free and accepted or speculative masons. So what are the secrets that we pledge ourselves to keep inviolate? Words, signs, and tokens? Yes, of course, but these are a mere detail; they are only the guards to our privileges. The true secret of modern Freemasonry cannot be defined in such simple terms. In fact, the real secret of Freemasonry cannot be described at all; it is something that can only be learnt by experience, by humility and patience.

Well now, our critics would say, if that is true, what is the point of going on talking about secrecy? Now that the words and signs, in fact the whole ritual, can be studied in practically any public library or bookshop, what is there left to keep secret about?

There is no easy answer to this, but I would say it can be summed up under the one word "Trust". Masons trust each other because they share the same obligation. I was once approached by a newspaper reporter – a lady journalist – who wanted to ask me some questions: "Is it true", she enquired, "that masons do such-and-such? And do they really say this-and-that?", and so on. I thought a minute and then said, "Well, before I go on, if I now tell you something in strict confidence, would you be prepared to keep it to yourself and not publish it?" "Oh, of course", said the lady, "if it's in confidence".

"Now, you really mean that?" I persisted. "You believe that if one gives one's word, one should keep it?" "Oh yes", she replied. "Well", I said, "if you can understand that then you will understand why I can't tell you anything".

It is really as a test of trustworthiness that we obligate our candidates to secrecy. If they keep this promise about little things, then we know we can have confidence in them about greater things. To quote from the Bible: "He that is faithful in that which is least, is faithful also in much".

When I was made a Boy Scout – many years ago – we went through a bit of ritual that I remember to this day:

Question: Do you know what your Honour means?

Answer: Yes, it means that I can be trusted.

This was followed by the obligation: "On my Honour I promise to do my best to do my duty to God and the King (that was George V of course) to help other people at all times and to obey the Scout Law".

It seems to me that there is very little difference between that and the promise of a Freemason; it is just another way of putting the need for confidence and trust. A man who is prepared to give away what he has promised to "conceal and never reveal" is not fit to be called a mason or a member of any society of men who prize honour and virtue. Books have been written – usually by non-masons – quoting so-called "confidential material" which they claim to have learnt from former members of masonic lodges. To rely on such information would be like judging the British Constitution on evidence supplied by Burgess and Maclean. It is only traitors and perjurers who will break their vow of silence, and such men are not to be trusted.

The privilege of being accepted as a member of a masonic lodge is offered to worthy men – and, we trust, to worthy men alone; only in this way the trust we place in each other can be intensified and enlarged.